ODDBALLS AND ECCENTRICS

ODDBALLS
AND
ECCENTRICS

Karl Shaw

CASTLE BOOK**S**

Originally published as *The Mammoth Book of Oddballs and Eccentrics*

This edition published in 2004 by
CASTLE BOOKS ®
A division of Book Sales Inc.
114 Northfield Avenue
Edison, NJ 08837

This edition published by arrangement with and permission of
Carroll & Graf Publishers, Inc.
161 William Street
New York, New York 10038

First published in the UK by Robinson Publishing 2000

First Carroll & Graf edition 2000

ISBN 0-7858-1839-1

Printed in the United States of America

Contents

Introduction

King Ludwig II of Bavaria organized pan-European robberies, nearly bankrupted his country by building fairytale castles, invited his horse to dinner so he wouldn't feel lonely then watched as it trashed his dining room, beat his servants up if they sneezed or coughed in his presence and complained if the water in his grotto wasn't a certain shade of blue. His brother Otto meanwhile spent his days pulling silly faces, barking like a dog, shouting abuse and occasionally taking pot shots at his gardener with a rifle through his bedroom window. The Habsburg Emperor Ferdinand I's idea of a good time was to wedge his backside in a waste-paper basket and roll around on the floor and the only known coherent remark he ever made on any subject was "I am the Emperor, and I want dumplings". George III had conversations with long-dead friends and indecently exposed himself to his servants. Queen Christina of

Sweden had a fully working miniature four-inch cannon built so she could fire tiny cannonballs at the fleas in her bedroom. Sadly none of these people appear in this book because they were all certifiably insane and had the paperwork to prove it. This book is not about madmen, it is about eccentrics.

So, where do we draw the line between between an eccentric and a madman? Firstly, we have to decide what eccentricity is. Not an easy one, this. As human behaviour ranges from rigid conformity at one end of the scale to utterly bizarre nonconformity at the other, how do we know whether someone is eccentric, quietly neurotic or completely barking mad? Does eccentricity exist at all, or is it just a stepping stone to madness? Consider the author Jonathan Swift, for example. Throughout his life he could be considered by any reasonable definition to have been "different". He was highly opinionated, rude, unpredictable, odd in appearance, suffered from an obsessive-compulsive disorder, liked to shock his public – in other words, most people would accept that Swift qualified as an eccentric. Towards the end of his life his behaviour became even more erratic. Poor Swift realized with horror that he was slowly succumbing to progressive senile dementia, until his servant began showing him off in public for a fee. Somewhere in between Swift made the transition from eccentricity to mental illness. But where exactly? At what point are we supposed to stop admiring his uniqueness and start to pity the great man for his terrible illness?

Maybe it would help if we defined "madness". Unfortunately whenever we talk about "mad" people we again run into a brick wall. Madness is not an exact medical term, it is a general description applied by the likes of you and me to any condition which results in profoundly odd or irrational behaviour. Mental disorders have a variety of causes, including physical damage or disease. Until the eighteenth century madness was believed to caused by demonic possession. The in-vogue text on the subject of madness, a book called *Anatomy of Melancholy* by Robert Burton, had been published back in 1621. Burton taught that madness was caused by the retention of bodily excretions: the best cure was to tie patients to a wall and literally beat the crap out of them. Burton's work was soon to be usurped by the crack French physician Jean Esquirol. Mental illness, explained Monsieur Esquirol, was caused by a variety of conditions, including living in a new home, squeezing a pimple, old age, childbirth, the menstrual cycle, a blow on the head, constipation, shrinkage of haemorrhoids, misuse of mercury, disappointment in love, political upheavals, shock, thwarted ambition, excessive study, masturbation, prostitution, religion and bloodletting. The last item in particular was very confusing to a medical profession which had been brought up to believe that bloodletting was the best cure for everything, including insanity.

The situation gets even more confusing when you consider royalty. By definition royalty is an eccentric institution in which odd behaviour occurs naturally, making the line between insanity and "normal" royal behaviour almost invisible. When King George III first showed signs of madness, his aides rallied around him with an astonishing display of loyalty by pretending to be mad themselves. The strange behaviour of a few of the king's offspring hinted at a more widespread family problem. In the places of Europe it was widely believed that the British royals were all mad. The second US President John Adams was briefly determined to marry his son to one of George III's daughters, but in the end he too was scared off by the alleged family taint.

Quite recently there has been some serious research into eccentricity. According to psychologist David Weeks, who wrote a book based on a decade of work on the subject, eccentrics are more cheerful than normal people. This expert contends that it is easy to distinguish between eccentrics and the mentally ill; the eccentrics are happy. This is a difficult theory to support, given that there are a lot of happy schizophrenics and happy manics. Equally, there are lots of miserably eccentric misers and misanthropes. It is perhaps also worth pointing out that Weeks's methods and conclusions were pretty eccentric in themselves; his discovery that eccentricity is 30 per cent higher in St Paul, Minnesota than in the rest of the United States, for example. Weeks doesn't help by developing a definition of eccentricity. Instead, he settles for fifteen classifiable symptoms, which he says include nonconformism, creativity, curiosity, idealism, obsessive hobbies and a tendency to be the eldest or only child.

Britain has a great reputation throughout the world of being the home of eccentricity. A German psychologist who independently studied "oddball" behaviour concluded that the British, with a higher percentage of eccentrics than mainland Europe, lead healthier and happier lives. Dame Edith Sitwell, who wrote a book about English eccentrics, was writing from some considerable experience. She always dressed in black and wore a number of vast topaz and aquamarine rings on both hands. The rings, she would explain as she constantly fingered them, became "worried" if she didn't give them enough attention. Although massively overdrawn at the bank, she gave two parties a day at her favourite restaurant. She once wrote a highly acclaimed book on Queen Victoria, but thereafter always referred to the Queen as "that old bore".

Certainly, eccentricity requires a reasonably tolerant society in which to flourish. This is probably why there are reportedly more male eccentrics than female: society has always been more tolerant of aberrant behaviour in men than in women. A look into admissions to lunatic asylums in the 19th century might reveal the fate of many of the missing female eccentrics.

Like almost everything else, eccentricity has its fashions and behaviour that in one age seems bizarre might go almost unnoticed in another. Although the eccentricities of the vegetarian health freak Lord Rokeby seemed outrageous in his own time, today he would have fitted quite comfortably into the environmental movement. The eighteenth-century Prussian King Frederick William I was considered by his contemporaries to have been eccentric, not because he was a demented, vicious psychopath who would fly into uncontrollable rages and thrash the living daylights out of anyone who crossed him and once had to be restrained from murdering his own son, but because he washed his hands regularly. The prudish Queen Maria Cristina of Naples was thought to be quite potty in a Neapolitan court steeped in centuries of adultery because of her blameless private life, a source of amazement to everyone around her.

True eccentrics, like the American soprano Florence Foster Jenkins, are never troubled by self-doubt. Each year she would give stunningly inept renditions of standard opera arias and songs at the Ritz-Carlton Hotel. She believed she was the "goddess of song", although it was obvious to all that she had absolutely no singing talent whatsoever. As a wealthy New York socialite she had the money and the confidence to act as a world class diva. The cross-dressing film maker Ed Wood was serenely unaffected by critics who condemned his work as "among the most compelling fiascos ever committed to celluloid". Wood is now generally regarded as the worst film director of all time, but what he lacked in talent or even basic business sense he more than made up for in genuine enthusiasm. Alfred Austin, the most inappropriate person ever to have held the post of Poet Laureate, blithely interpreted the frequent scathing attacks on his pathetic efforts as professional jealousy. When it was pointed out to him that his poems were full of basic grammatical errors, Austin replied, "I dare not alter these things. They come to me from above." The worst ever American poetess Julia A. Moore, who liked to call herself "The Sweet Singer of Michigan", misread the damning reviews that accompanied her work so naively that she took to reprinting them in her promotional material. The legendary Scottish poet William McGonagall was similarly impervious to embarrassment or even the nastiest of personal attacks. When McGonagall received a letter from Queen Victoria's private secretary politely requesting that he desist from harassing the Queen with unremittingly dire verse, McGonagall was so delighted he restyled himself "Poet To Her Majesty". The unintentionally hilarious stage performances of Robert "Romeo" Coates were so remarkable that people travelled for miles to see for themselves whether he really was as bad as his reviews, but not even the sound of his audience rocking with laughter during his death scenes could dent his unwavering belief that he was the greatest tragedian of his age. The dire playwright Colley Cibber, accused of "murdering the English language with a goose quill", stuck to his guns and set out to "improve" Shakespeare by rewriting the ending to *Richard III* in the teeth of unprecedented mockery. Throughout his entire career the indomitable farting Frenchman Joseph Pujol ignored the derisive comments that accompanied his every performance, confident in his art and what he considered to be his God-given gift.

Maybe the true eccentrics are those people who are unaware of how out of step with the rest of mankind their behaviour is, unlike Salvador Dali, who took his pet ocelot for walks to the café, or Sarah Bernhardt, who slept and made love in a rosewood coffin, both of whom worked hard at maintaining their reputations for eccentricity and a carefully cultivated aura of myth. This book is not only about the lives of eccentrics, it is also about random acts of eccentricity. It includes people not generally considered to be eccentrics who were nevertheless capable of eccentricity. Charles Babbage, for example; quite normal for most of the time, invented a calculating machine now acknowledged as the forerunner of computers, but then dedicated most of his spare time to working out the statistical probability of the Biblical miracles (he calculated that the chances of a man rising from the dead were one in 10^{12}). Sir Humphrey Davy, inventor of the miner's Davy lamp; not at all eccentric until it came to dressing up for fishin' and shootin'. And then there is Alexander Graham Bell, not especially regarded as a loony, who tried to teach his dog to talk. Not all of these people are necessarily famous. A single act of eccentricity changed the life of an obscure Bolivian waitress when she lost her cool after a customer complained that he had observed her sneezing into his soup and she forced him to eat it at gunpoint. Then there was the respectable businessman in a Bangkok karaoke bar, who got so carried away singing "Candle in the Wind" for three hours that when another customer tried to take the microphone away from him he shot him dead. Or the Chinese teacher who lost it in the face of a rebellious classroom and forced his students to eat cow dung. And how about the Dutchman who went on the rampage causing £30,000 worth of damage to a barbershop, upset because the barber had exceeded his idea of "a slight trim"?

All of these people have their place in this book, alongside the incredible gluttons, the magnificent misers, the dysfunctional rulers, the mad embalmers, the strange scientists, the peculiar performers, the brilliant iconoclasts, the unhinged politicians, the ritual compulsives, the crackpot visionaries, the barmy builders, the bizarre adventurers and the touchingly deluded. The only common thread is that they can all make us laugh.

Chapter One

Aristocratic Eccentrics

"Those comfortable padded lunatic asylums which are known, euphemistically, as the stately homes of England"
Virginia Woolf (1882–1941)

"Poverty and eccentricity are very bad bedfellows"
Henry James Byron (1834–84)

The baronet Sir Hugh Rankin had controversial political views for a member of the patrician order, describing himself as "a blood-red militant Communist in every possible way". He also had one of the most entertaining entries in *Who's Who*, listing his hobbies thus: "golf (holds an amateur record of golfers of Gt

Britain in having played on 382 separate courses of UK and Eire), shooting, coarse fishing, hunting, motoring, cycling on mountain tracks to tops of British mountains (Pres. Rough Stuff Cycling Assoc. 1956), the study of ancient track ways; bowls, tennis, archaeology (wife and himself are the only persons who have crawled under dwarf fir forest for last half mile of most northerly known section of any Roman road in Europe, terminating opposite end of Kirriemuir Golf Course) . . ."

Rankin travelled widely in the Middle East, briefly became a Muslim and assumed the forename Omar. In 1935 he became president of the British Muslim Society, but resigned after a few weeks because "they were very rude". In 1944 he ceased to be a Muslim and became a Buddhist. In 1959 after a trip to the Himalayas he asserted that the existence of the Abominable Snowman was "no news . . . it is part of our known belief that five Bodhisattvas ('perfected men') control the destiny of this world. They meet together once a year in a cave in the Himalayas to make their decisions. One of them lives permanently in the Scottish Cairngorms." He added that he and his wife Robina had spotted the latter yeti in the Larig Ghru Pass.

Henry Cyril Paget, fifth Marquis of Anglesey, was one of the wealthiest men in Victorian England, and wanted everyone to know it. He was particularly fond of using his beautiful young wife Lilian to showcase his vast collection of jewellery, often the whole collection simultaneously. On their honeymoon Paget observed his new wife windowshopping in the jewellers Van Cleef and Arpels, so he purchased the entire display and made her wear all of it to the races. Marital relations were further strained when he took to waking her in the night, ordering her to strip naked, then covering her with gems. She subsequently sued for divorce on the grounds of non-consummation.

Sir Ewen Cameron of Lochiel (1629–1719) enjoyed his reputation as a tough Scot. One winter's day he was out camping in the Highlands with his grandson, Donald. The weather took a turn for the worse and as night fell they elected to set up camp in the open. Sir Ewan noticed that his young companion had rolled a large snowball to make a pillow for his head and quickly kicked it away, growling, "I'll have no effeminacy here, boy."

Charles Radclyffe, fifth Earl of Derwentwater, was a gamomaniac – an obsessive whose disorder is characterized by persistent proposals of marriage. He proposed on fifteen occasions to the reluctant Countess of Newburgh who became so annoyed by the constant harassment that she bolted herself into her home and gave her servants instructions to throw him off the property on sight. The Earl finally found a way into her house by climbing on to her roof and lowering himself down the chimney into her drawing room where, black from soot, he made his sixteenth marriage proposal. This time his persistence paid off and she agreed to marry him.

David Bertram Ogilvy Freeman-Mitford, second Baron Redesdale, was the head of the Mitford family, considered to be one of the oddest households in England during the early twentieth century. Known to his six daughters and one son as "the old sub-human", Lord Redesdale was a brave army officer who fought with distinction in the Boer War. His career took a courageous sideways move when he became editor of *The Lady* – unexpected as he was an avowed chauvinist, had no talent for writing and had hardly ever read a book. Lord Redesdale was also highly xenophobic; the family home at Swinbrook in Oxfordshire was built as a fortress, according to his daughter Jessica, to keep out "Huns, Frogs, Americans, blacks and all other foreigners". Lord Redesdale made no distinction between races. When one of his nephews married an Argentinian of pure Spanish stock, he commented, "I hear that Robin's married a black." When he died in 1958 *The Times* noted with delicate understatement that he "adhered to somewhat old-fashioned views with tenacity and boisterousness".

The Marquis of Waterford was regarded as one of the great pranksters of the nineteenth century, known to all as "the mad marquis". He inherited a vast fortune in the early part of the century but squandered most of it paying for the damage he caused by his more destructive practical jokes. Waterford once decided, on a whim, to distribute strong alcohol among London's poor. He went into a famous tavern in Haymarket and ordered the landlord to furnish him with several large casks of gin, which he took outside and served to passers-by in half-pint mugs. Within an hour he was besieged by every tramp in London and a drunken riot ensued. The police were only able to extricate Waterford from the fracas by arresting him.

He was once summoned to appear before Marlborough Street magistrates on a charge of reckless driving after apparently driving his horse and carriage through a crowded street at high speed. Waterford arrived at his hearing mounted on his horse and demanded to be let in on horseback. He explained that as his mount was a star witness for the defence it should be cross-examined, for "only he knows how fast he was going". The judge, who knew a top-drawer fruitcake when he saw one, elected to wash his hands of the case as quickly as possible and acquitted him.

On another occasion Waterford hired eight cabs and a whole troupe of musicians to sit on the cab roofs, playing while they were driven round the streets at high speed. Waterford himself took the reins of the leading cab and drove so recklessly he was almost killed. He survived this and many other dangerous pranks, but broke his neck and died in a hunting accident in 1859.

During World War II the third Lord Leconfield was once out hunting when his pack of hounds led him across a local village football game. Leconfield, stopped, stood up in his stirrups and bawled, "Haven't you people got better things to do in wartime than play football?"

The libidinous eighteenth-century Irishman Frederick Calvert, sixth Lord Baltimore, spent so little time in his native Ireland that he considered himself an "English gentleman". He once visited Turkey and was so impressed by the local customs that he decided to adopt a few for himself. With the aid of two procuresses named Mrs Harvey and Madam Griffenburg he recruited a harem of ladies and took them with him whenever he travelled. This flamboyant lifestyle occasionally presented difficulties. When he arrived in Vienna accompanied by two

eunuchs and eight women, the local head of police asked him
to indicate which one was his wife. Lord Calvert replied that as
an Englishman he was not in the habit of discussing his
personal arrangements and offered to settle the matter with
his fists.

In 1767 Calvert was staying in London when he became
entranced by a young woman named Sarah Woodcock. When
she declined to join the obese aristocrat's harem, he simply had
her kidnapped. Her family were outraged and took him to
court. Lord Baltimore conducted his own defence and, no
doubt swaying the jury with his impeccable pedigree, convinced them that the girl had been willingly abducted and that
she had been "happy, cheerful and playful" throughout her
ordeal.

Lord Berners (1883–1950), composer, novelist and dilettante,
inherited his title in 1918 along with his fortune and his estate,
Faringdon House in Oxfordshire which brought him an average annual income of £7,000 – by today's standards about
£234,000. The young Berners, prematurely balding and wearing a monocle, was already well established as a composer of
light, divertimento-style music. He was also a wit and practical
joker. It was Berners who described T. E. Lawrence as "always
backing into the limelight" and it was also he who coined the
nickname for Vita Sackville-West, "Wry Vita". He once staged
the whole of Wagner's Ring cycle inside a doll's house. Once,
during a weekend house party, he locked all the lavatories and
tossed the keys into a pond. During the Battle of Britain, he
sent a spoof invitation to Sybil Colefax, a famously shameless
social climber: "I wonder if by any chance you are free to dine
tomorrow night? It is only a tiny party for Winston and GBS. I

think it important they should get together at this moment. There will be nobody else except for Toscanini and myself." Cruelly, both the address and the signature were illegible.

Lord Berners had a number of idiosyncrasies, not least of which was his preference for dyeing the doves at his home in various pastel shades and dressing his whippets with diamond collars. The pigeons when released, wrote Nancy Mitford, resembled "a cloud of confetti in the sky". He painted pictures of his horses as they posed for him in the drawing room of his home and had a harpsichord fitted into the rear compartment of his Rolls Royce. In 1935 he built the Faringdon Folly, a 140-foot tower, explaining, "The great point of the tower is that it will be entirely useless." He then put up a notice which read: "Members of the public committing suicide from this tower do so at their own risk."

Robert Heber-Percy (1911–1987) was adopted as the protégé of Lord Berners and became squire of Faringdon when the latter died. Heber-Percy, known as "the mad boy", was almost as eccentric as his mentor. He had a brief career in the cavalry, owned an undertaker's business, acted as an extra in Hollywood and worked as a waiter. He had a famous long-running feud with the photographer Cecil Beaton, which reached a climax in 1974 when he laid Beaton out with a punch to the jaw on the doorstep of a birthday party in Chelsea. He enhanced the already exotic Faringdon estate with a few additional touches of his own, including a remarkable swimming pool overlooked by giant gryphons and a changing room floor inlaid with pennies.

The English society hostess Lady Diana Cooper (1892–1986) always wore a large hat during the day, concealing a set of

rollers underneath, and in old age she carried with her everywhere a small dog in a basket. If she went somewhere where
dogs were not allowed, she smuggled it in, concealed inside a
large muff. Her driving skills were legendary. She regularly ran
red lights and parked wherever she liked, assisted by a message
she left in her windscreen which read: "Please have pity on a
poor blind lame old lady."

Lady Cork, wife of the seventh Earl of Cork, was a hugely
popular Regency hostess, entertaining some of the most famous
people of her day, including Lord Byron, Sir Walter Scott,
Sheridan and even the Prince of Wales. The diarist Fanny
Burney, who left vivid accounts of many eighteenth-century
contemporaries, described her as "very short, very fat but
handsome, splendidly and fantastically dressed, rouged not
unbecomingly yet evidently and palpably desirous of gaining
notice and admiration". She continued to entertain in style at
her dinners and receptions until she was well into her nineties.
She was extremely proud of her extraordinary memory and when
she was in her eighties she could recite entire chapters of her
favourite books. When this faculty began to fail she kept a young
companion by her side, to whom she referred as "my memory".
   Lady Cork was also an aristocratic kleptomaniac. Her unfortunate habit of stealing things was so well known that
whenever she went out to dinner her hosts would preface
her visit by carefully hiding their best silver and pewter. When
she went shopping, London tradesmen would not allow their
goods to be taken outside to her carriage for approval, although
this was normal practice for valued customers. Shopkeepers
were always careful when she visited their stores to detail an
assistant to follow her around. When she died aged ninety-four

a society wit was moved to quip that heaven would be rather boring for Lady Cork as there would be nothing there for her to steal.

Benjamin O'Neill Stratford, sixth Earl of Aldborough, dedicated his life and his considerable fortune to building the world's biggest hot air balloon. Lord Aldborough, the last of a long line of eccentrics, was reclusive and seldom seen outside his family estate, Stratford Lodge. His workshop in the grounds was a vast hangar made from chiselled Wicklow granite where, in absolute secrecy, he worked for twenty years on his fantasy giant dirigible. Once finished he planned to pilot it himself on a grand inaugural flight across the Channel to France. In anticipation he purchased an acre of land on the banks of the Seine where he confidently expected to be greeted by swarms of admiring Frenchmen. One Sunday morning in 1856, however, tragedy struck when Stratford Lodge went up in flames. Lord Aldborough, apparently much less interested in the fate of his historic family home than in saving his precious brainchild, ran around the blazing estate urging onlookers, "Save the balloon house." Although hundreds of buckets of water were flung over the great hangar, the airship went up in a sheet of flame. Lord Aldborough was a broken man, having spent half his life and all of the family fortune on his great experiment. He moved to Spain where he made a living by breeding dogs and selling patent medicine. He became more reclusive than ever, ordering meals to be sent up to his room, but refusing to allow anyone to remove the used dishes. He died filthy and neglected in a hotel room littered with dirty cutlery and old crockery.

George Robert Fitzgerald, a descendant of the great Irish Desmond family, was one of the most reckless duellists who ever lived. He engaged in his first meeting at the tender age of sixteen; a man dared to insult the young Fitzgerald for a bet and approached him in a coffee house muttering "I smell an Irishman". Fitzgerald quickly whipped out his knife and sliced off the man's nose, observing, "Then you shall never smell another." An early duel against a fellow army officer almost cost Fitzgerald his life when he was shot in the head. As the surgeon worked to remove the bullet lodged in his skull, Fitzgerald, in agony and streaming with blood, begged him not to damage his wig. Bad tempers were hereditary in the Fitzgerald family; when George's father was informed that his son lay dying, he was so upset that he ran his sword through the first man who offered his condolences.

Although badly scarred for life the son survived, but became more unpredictable than ever, probably a legacy of his horrific head injury. He grew adept at picking quarrels and provoking duels on the flimsiest of pretexts. When he fancied an argument he would lash out at complete strangers on the street or snatch their rings or watches. Once, in Dublin, he shot off a man's wig. If he failed to pick a fight in a bar or a theatre he would stand in the middle of a narrow street waiting for someone to jostle him. Outside a Paris coffee house he drew his rapier and skewered a man who had accidentally stepped on Fitzgerald's dog. On this occasion, however, an enraged mob of Frenchmen followed him back to his lodgings, trashed his carriage and killed his valet.

By the age of twenty-seven he had fought twenty-seven duels. He was an expert marksman – he boasted that he could hit a target on any part of the human body to within one twelfth of an inch. In 1786 Fitzgerald became involved in another deadly dispute with a neighbour, Colonel McDonell.

By this time the authorities in County Mayo had finally tired of the 38-year-old psychopath and after years of using his family connections to flout the law he was tried and hanged for murder. Fitzgerald left a young daughter, who survived her father by eight years before dying suddenly and unexpectedly. It was said that she died of shock after reading an account of her father's execution in the *Gentleman's Magazine*.

The oddball Matthew Robinson, later ennobled as Lord Rokeby, believed so fervently in the spiritual power of water he spent a large part of his life in the bath. Rokeby was born in 1712, and in his early twenties paid a visit to Aix-la-Chapelle, a city famous for its baths. The visit appears to have left an indelible mark on him because from then onwards he became such a compulsive bather that he was hardly ever out of water, and became known as the "amphibious lord".

Robinson spent the first four decades or so of his adult life as a wealthy country gentleman and served as Member of Parliament for the city of Canterbury. Then, frustrated and bored with politics, Robinson told his disappointed constituents that he could no longer represent them. He retired to his home at Monks Norton in Kent and gave up public life for an existence of harmless eccentricity. From the day he inherited the family estate at Mount Morris in the same county, Rokeby stopped cutting his hair or shaving. His hair became wild and matted and he grew a remarkably luxuriant beard. As the latter lengthened, finally reaching almost to his waist, his lands too became unkempt and overgrown, with animals grazing freely. At a time when landed gentlemen were supposed to ride in carriages, Robinson insisted on travelling everywhere on foot; if he took his carriage along, it was usually for the convenience of his servants. His diet aroused much amusement: he believed that people should live on local produce, and banished such commodities as tea, coffee, and sugar from his table. He lived mostly on beef tea, but his great love was water. He had spring water in his neighbourhood collected in basins for the benefit of passing travellers, and erected little bathing huts on the sands at Hythe, about three miles from his home. He adopted the unusual habit of walking to the beach each day and immersing himself in the sea. He was always followed on these expeditions by a carriage and a servant dressed in full livery and would often remain in the water until, almost freezing to death, he passed out and had to be rescued by his waiting servant. Such behaviour attracted onlookers and eventually Robinson had to preserve his privacy by taking the plunge at home. He built a bath in a greenhouse where sunlight could warm the water and he spent his days soaking. Sometimes he stayed neck-deep in water while he ate his meals, once complaining bitterly when he was obliged to leave his bath in order to receive Prince William of Gloucester, who had been invited to dinner.

Rokeby was none the less renowned as an excellent host and he received many visitors who were curious about the bearded gentleman with the aquatic bent. The only thing that put his guests off was his passion for reading aloud very long, boring poems whenever he had a captive audience. On very rare occasions he was persuaded to get out of his bath, put some clothes on and present himself at court. His sister was frequently embarrassed, living in constant terror that her strange brother might "exhibit his amphibious and carnivorous habits at Bath". After one appearance she wrote to her husband, "I am glad he has gone back to the country. He has made a most astonishing appearance at court. I wish the beefeaters had not let him past the door."

To the end of his life Rokeby had a deep mistrust of doctors, maintaining that fresh air was the best tonic. He once ordered a nephew not to bring a physician to him, warning that if the doctor failed to kill him he would use his last strength to cut the young man from his will. At eighty-four, Rokeby was so mentally alert that he was able to publish a pamphlet on the war in France, a work praised for its clarity of thought and expression. When Lord Rokeby died at eighty-seven, he had outlived most of his critics.

By the age of twenty-two, George Hanger, later Baron Coleraine, had fought three duels, reached the rank of colonel, been wounded in the American War of Independence and married a gypsy, after which he decided to settle down to a life of mostly reckless gambling. Colonel Hanger is remembered for a very eccentric wager. He staged a race between twenty geese and twenty turkeys over a ten-mile course. Oddly, he put £500 on the turkeys, who unlike geese have never been known for their stamina, only to see them drop out of the race after three miles. He eventually wagered away his inheritance and found himself in a debtor's prison.

Sir George Sitwell (1860–1943), head of that endemically eccentric family, had seven rooms he used as studies at his family mansion in Derbyshire where he occupied himself in writing such masterpieces as *The History of the Fork* – none of them ever finished. His chief interest however was landscape gardening. He employed 4,000 men at one time to dig him an artificial lake in the grounds, with wooden towers sticking out of the water from where he could survey his various projects. To improve the view from his study window, he had Chinese willow patterns painted on to his herd of white cows. And a sign on his front door read: "I must ask anyone entering the house never to contradict me in any way, as it interferes with the functioning of my gastric juices and prevents me sleeping at night."

Lady Hester Stanhope was a member of an aristocratic family and niece to William Pitt ("the Younger"), but spent twenty-five years of her life in a Lebanese monastery waiting to be crowned Queen of the Jews. At the age of thirty-three Lady Hester, apparently inspired by a prophecy made by an inmate of Bedlam insane asylum that she was destined to be "Queen of the East", left England on the frigate *Jason* and never returned. Her ship sailed as far as Constantinople where it sank in a storm. She was rescued and landed at Rhodes, although all of her luggage was lost. From that day on she adopted the attire of a male Turk, complete with robe and turban, and never wore European clothing again. She embarked on a series of remarkable journeys through the Middle East, riding on a magnificently ornamented Egyptian saddle, wearing a lavishly embroidered costume covered with a white hooded cloak. At the risk of offending the local Muslims she rode veil-less, attracting a huge amount of attention wherever she went. Fortunately the locals were amused by her bravado and she was fêted everywhere she went. Even in Damascus, the most fundamental of Muslim cities, she rode side-saddle and refused to cover her face. Many took her to be an English princess of fabulous wealth. When the locals jokingly began to call her Queen Hester she took it as a serious sign that her destiny was to be fulfilled.

Her loyal English retinue dwindled as the cost of her travelling increased, but the greatest journey was yet to come. Lady Hester was determined to visit the ruins of the great city of Palmyra in the Arabian Desert, which had hitherto only been reached by three Englishmen. The route across the sands was infested with tribes of warlike Bedouin who were renowned for robbing and killing without mercy. Dressed as a Bedouin, Lady Hester set out with a fantastic caravan comprising twenty-one camels and mountains of luggage. Her tent was guarded by night by a black slave armed with an axe. Her reputation grew. People came from all parts of the desert to see this extraordinary woman "with the courage of a lion and the eyes of an eagle". When she reached Palmyra she was received like a queen of the desert and crowned in a mock celebratory pageant. To Lady Hester, it seemed that the prophecies were coming true. By 1814 she had had enough of wandering and found the disused monastery of Mar Elias on a hilltop overlooking the sea near Sidon in Lebanon. She created a beautiful garden and conducted her household strictly in the Turkish manner. From Mar Elias she wielded considerable influence over her Arab neighbours, refusing to be cowed by local rulers and offering sanctuary whenever there were religious wars, sheltering hundreds of refugees over the years. When Mar Elias became too small to house her refugees she moved to Djouni, another even more remote ruined monastery. From there she corresponded with some of the most famous people of her day and continued to be lavishly generous, partly because she had no money sense whatsoever. In misplaced confidence that the British government would foot the bill, she mounted an extravagant expedition to search for buried treasure in the ancient city of Ascalon. The expedition was a flop and the British government turned a blind eye.

Lady Hester spent the rest of her life waiting for the call to tell her that she had been acclaimed as Queen of the East puffing on her Turkish chibouk. She became something of a legend. Curious travellers from Europe often called on her to pay their respects. Few could believe that the strange, reclusive woman dressed in voluminous Turkish trousers, her head shaved and covered by a turban, was the niece of one of England's greatest Prime Ministers and had once been a lady of fashion. As the years progressed she became markedly more eccentric, refusing to receive visitors until after dark. The roof of her home leaked and her servants stole all her valuables. She eventually sealed up all the entrances to the monastery, leaving only one through which cattle could pass. The call never came and she died in poverty aged sixty-three. When the British consul arrived at the monastery to wind up her affairs he found that thirty-five rooms had been permanently sealed to avoid robbery. He had them opened expecting to find great treasures, but discovered only rubbish and empty medicine bottles. At her funeral, in accordance with her last wishes, the midnight procession was lit by candles stuffed in the eye sockets of her deceased ex-lover's skull.

Sir Tatton Sykes was the second of that name to live at Sledmere Hall in Yorkshire. His father had been an eccentric country squire who continued to wear eighteenth-century clothing well into the Victorian era when his son was born. His ideas of parenting were however solidly Victorian: children had to be thrashed into shape. Once, the elder Sir Tatton was observed chasing his young heir barefoot and screaming with a whip. When the boy finally inherited his father's title at the age of thirty-seven, he set about wiping out the traces of a disturbed and miserable childhood. He sold most of his father's prize livestock and destroyed Sledmere Hall's carefully cultivated orangery, hothouses and flower beds. His obsessive hatred for flowers stayed with him for the rest of his life. He forbade any of his tenants to grow the "nasty, untidy things", informing them: "If you wish to grow flowers, grow cauliflowers." He would wander through the village, walking stick in hand, ready to slash down any stray blooms he came across. He ordered all the front doors in the village to be boarded up, perhaps, some said, because he hated the sight of children enjoying themselves.

Sir Tatton was an enthusiastic traveller. He roamed extensively in America, Russia and China, but because he maintained that he had a very delicate stomach he took his cook everywhere to keep him supplied with his favourite milk pudding. He was also very keen that his body maintained a constant temperature. Whenever he went for a walk he would start out wearing several overcoats, then along the way he would shed them one by one as he got warmer. The discarded coats lay on the ground until they were retrieved by the local children who inevitably followed in his wake when word got round that Sir Tatton paid a shilling for every coat returned.

Misfortune overtook Sir Tatton when Sledmere was severely damaged by fire. When he was first informed, Sir Tatton refused to allow the crisis to disturb his digestion; "first I must finish my pudding". Following the death of his estranged wife, he became obsessed with the idea that he himself was going to die at precisely 11:30 a.m. – a time when he normally went out riding. Frequently he would wave the horse away, muttering, "No, no, can't ride, can't ride, going to die." Death came for him in 1913, inconveniently, in a London hotel. The hotel manager was so anxious not to upset the other guests by letting on that there was a corpse on the premises that he attempted to smuggle him out inside a hollow settee. The plan was evidently abandoned when Sir Tatton's son found out about it. "However my father leaves this hotel," he fumed, "he shall leave it like a gentleman."

Thomas Pitt, the last Lord Camelford, was known for his vast collection of weaponry, especially duelling pistols, and his willingness to pick an argument at the drop of a hat. When he was an officer in the Navy the pugnacious peer once shot dead a lieutenant who refused to accept an order from him. At his court martial however he escaped with an acquittal, on the grounds that he was actually putting down a mutiny. Once at Drury Lane Theatre he was politely asked by an elderly man if he would move away from a window he was obstructing; the hot-tempered Camelford thrashed the old man and almost blinded him in one eye. For this violent assault Camelford was fined £500. He continued to get himself involved in various fights and disputes until 1814, when at the age of twenty-nine he forced a fight on a friend, Captain Best. As Best was known to be an expert pistol shot, Camelford challenged him to prove it in a duel to the death. Camelford came out second best and died from his wound three days later.

Sir Ashton Lever, the eighteenth-century Lancashire squire, had a mania for collecting. He began with a vast assembly of almost 5,000 birds which he exhibited at his home at Alkrington, near Manchester. His collection became such a local curiosity that he had to make a public announcement that he would refuse admission to anyone who came on foot. According to the European Magazine, "He frequently rode from London to Alkrington with cages full of birds, which he brought safe by holding them with a full-stretched arm, and galloping till the arm was tired, and then stopping to change hands." According to the report Lever also had a tame bullfinch that he taught to sing on command, and a pet goose that waited at table with a napkin under its wing. In the early 1760s he acquired a boatload of "curious foreign shells" from France and thus began a new love, fossil collecting. The passion for bird collecting was ruthlessly abandoned. Live birds he had carefully collected and looked after for years were stuffed and nailed to perches in his museum or simply given away. In 1774 he moved his entire collection to Leicester Square in London, where he charged the public five shillings and threepence to enter. In spite of slashing the entrance fee by half when he discovered that the paying London public were indifferent to his collection, the move south was a financial disaster for Lever. After one year the Leverian Museum was closed down and all 26,000 items in the collection were sold off via a desperately undersubscribed public lottery. The winner, a Mr Parkinson, who had bought two tickets from the 36,000 on sale, found himself the proud owner of the following, as recorded by the nineteenth-century historian Tom Taylor:

1. Weapons of war of different nations, horns, bones, teeth and heads of animals. 2. Native fossils, birds (5,000 in number). 3. Extraneous fossils and birds. 4. Shells and birds. 5. Birds, beasts and marbles. 6. Beasts, including hippopotamus, rhinoceros, and great ant-eater, with cases of insects. 7. Antiquities. 8. Birds, including the great bustard, penguin, birds of paradise. 9. Birds of China and India. 10. Reptiles. 11. Fishes and corals. 12. Monkeys. 13. Ostriches and miscellanea. 14. Dresses of various nations. 15. Warlike weapons of savage tribes. 16. An elephant and zebra, which when alive belonged to Her Majesty.

The collection was moved south of the Thames to a site near Blackfriars bridge until finally in 1806 every single item was sold off at an auction which lasted sixty-five days.

Charles Seymour, sixth Duke of Somerset (1662–1748), was such a snob that he refused even to converse with his servants, communicating with them only by sign language. He also had a number of houses built along the route from his country estate to London, so that whenever he travelled he would not have to mingle with the lower classes in public inns.

The Hertfordshire squire George Edward Dering of Lockleys lived a curious double life. For years the servants at his mansion near Welwyn hardly ever saw him, except on Christmas Eve when he would suddenly appear, read his mail, then vanish again on Christmas morning. He nevertheless always maintained a full staff of seven, who had instructions to have a mutton chop handy at all times in case he turned up unexpectedly.

When Dering was in permanent residence at Lockleys he spent much of the time reading and inventing obscure electrical devices. He took out seventeen patents over a period of thirty-one years. When he was at work he demanded absolute silence. When a flock of sheep grazed in the park near his home, he had all the new born lambs removed so he couldn't hear them bleating. He spent £20,000 to have a nearby road diverted to another route because he found it too noisy.

Dering had an unexpected hobby for an English squire – he was a high wire enthusiast and a personal friend of Blondin, the famous tightrope walker. He and Blondin often practised together on a rope stretched across the river Mimram on his estate.

Dering eventually returned to Lockleys permanently in 1907 and became reclusive, occupying only one room of his mansion, never allowing anyone in to clean it. When he died his home was found to be full of archaeological treasures, which were later given to the British Museum by his daughter.

The eleventh Duke of Norfolk was Regency London's most epic inebriate. The "dirty duke" had such an astonishing capacity for alcohol that, it was said, he could drink five or six times more than any other man – even his good friend the Prince Regent, who was no slouch himself when it came to knocking back the odd pailful of cherry brandy. He and the Prince were often seen staggering around the streets of London together blind drunk. One day the Prince and his brothers decided to have some fun at the old Duke's expense by inviting him to a party, then spiking his tumblers of wine with neat brandy, so that his alcohol intake was about ten times more than he had intended. When the Duke finally decided he'd had enough, the Prince and his cronies watched as the Duke's coachman, as instructed, drove him round in circles for an hour.

The Duke was also a dedicated glutton and in old age became so obese that he couldn't get through a standard door frame. He acquired his nickname because he never washed: he complained one day to a friend, Dudley North, that he suffered from rheumatism, and had tried everything to relieve the pain without effect. "Pray, my Lord," replied North, "did you ever try a clean shirt?"

The Duke of Orleans, regent to the boy-king Louis XV, was one of France's all-time heavyweight debauchees. He held orgies at his home most evenings, had naked prostitutes served up nightly to his dinner guests on silver salvers and at one time kept a hundred mistresses, every one of them renowned for their ugliness: when his mother commented on his choice of women he simply replied, "Mother, all cats are grey in the dark." The Duke allegedly had an incestuous relationship with his eldest and favourite daughter, the smelly Duchess de Berry, a lady who regularly drank herself senseless until she rolled in her own vomit on the carpet and eventually, according to her death certificate, ate herself to death. The Duke was chiefly infamous however for his drinking binges. He was already a senile and purple-faced old man in his early forties, thanks to his capacity of seven bottles of wine a night, but his friends marvelled that he was alive at all. When he visited London bets were taken that he would be dead within three months.

In 1723, against the advice of his doctors, he took a new mistress who was nearly thirty years younger than him. He was sitting by the fireplace of his drawing room at Versailles one day when he had a massive stroke. When a doctor tried to bleed him, a lady courtier shouted, "No! You'll kill him . . . he has just lain with a whore." Two hours later the Duke was dead, aged forty-nine. Although everyone knew that the drink and wild living had killed him, royal etiquette required that there should be an official post mortem: unfortunately while it was being carried out the Duke's favourite dog snatched his master's heart and ate it.

The gentlemen of White's club in London were once famous for their willingness to bet on anything that moved and, now and then, even things that didn't. One evening a poor man fell motionless on the club doorstep and by the time he had been carried in bets had already been taken on whether or not he was dead.

The friends of a wealthy Victorian aristocrat chided him that he was so out of touch with ordinary people that he had probably never even ridden on an omnibus. The gentlemen confessed that, indeed, he had not, and made amends by boarding the first one that came along. When the conductor asked, "Where to, guv?" he replied, "A hundred and thirty-seven, Eton Square."

The Irish peer Arthur Frederick Daubeney Eveleigh de Moleyns, the seventh Lord Ventry, was an indefatigable champion of hot air ballooning and airships. Lord Ventry – who preferred to be called Olav but was generally known as Bunny – began work in 1949 on a sausage-shaped dirigible, the *Bournemouth*, the first airship to be built in Britain for nearly two decades after the famous R101 crash in 1930. The 108-foot long airship was scheduled to make its maiden flight in July 1951. Designed to hold five people, it failed however to rise and the seventeen-stone Irish peer was forced to give up his place to a lighter man. This time the *Bournemouth* rose, but subsequently became stuck on the roof of a gymnasium at RAF Cardington. Undaunted, Lord Ventry tirelessly campaigned for the revival of airships on the basis that they were "in fact more reliable than present-day aircraft and of course vastly more comfortable", also pointing out that an airship would be an ideal vehicle for "monster hunting" over Loch Ness. In 1981 he wrote to the Royal Navy with his suggestion for a new British airship, *Skyship 500*.

The bachelor peer combined his role as editor of *The Airship* and *Aero History* and chairman of the Airship Club with a devotion to scouting. He once wrote, "I can look back on some of the happiest years of my long life with the Scouts, not only of this country but also of Norway. In my view Baden-Powell did more for the youth of the world than all the politicians put together."

———————

Eighteenth-century English nobility when faced with new-fangled ideas about disease and personal hygiene clung to the belief that washing was strictly for the working classes. A duchess at a society dinner once sat down to eat with noticeably filthy hands. When the grubbiness of her fingers was remarked upon, she replied, "Madam, you should see my feet." When Queen Victoria inherited Buckingham Palace in 1837 it didn't even have a bathroom. Her predecessors the Georgian royals believed it was "sweat, damn it, that kept a man clean".

———————

In 1995 Lord Erskine of Rerrick bequeathed his testicles to the Bank of Scotland which had declared him bankrupt, because it had "no balls".

———————

The aristocrat Christopher Sykes, a close friend of King Edward VII, blew his entire personal fortune by throwing parties at the king's request. Sykes would allow Edward to pour brandy over his head and stub cigar butts out on his hand to see if smoke came out of his ears. When the business of keeping his expensive friend amused made Sykes bankrupt, Edward attached himself to another wealthy socialite Lord "Sporting Joe" Aylesford, whose idea of fun was to stand on the roof of his moving carriage and throw bags of flour at London pedestrians.

Viscount Colville always kept a spare glass eye in a little gold case suspended from his watch chain.

Lord William Russell was a bad-tempered, suspicious and parsimonious employer who believed that all his servants were thieves. He even considered having the cutlery in the servants' quarters stamped with the words "Stolen from Lord Russell". He eventually drove his valet, a man called Courvoisier, to murder him. One night Courvoiser stripped himself naked to avoid blood stains on his clothes and slit his master's throat as he slept. Forty thousand people turned up to see Courvoisier hanged outside Newgate prison two months later.

Sir Thomas Barrett-Lennard, squire of Belhus in Essex from 1857 to 1918, couldn't bring himself to ill treat any animal, even a rat. He instructed his estate workers to put out a fresh bowl of water daily for them in the corn rick. He also forbade his employees to harm any that entered his house. In time the house was completely overrun by very large rats – a daily trial for the Belhus domestic staff, as Mrs Duligal, a housemaid, observed: "The worst trouble was the rats. They were so big – they were as big as cats and as tame as tame could be. Sir Thomas wouldn't let them be killed, so everything had to be put under cover or they were all eaten up. The noise they made was like people running up and down the corridor. Sometimes you could could hear chairs moving – they must have been everywhere".

Sir Thomas was equally protective of rooks, which most farmers regarded as vermin, and of his estate deer, which he refused to kill for venison. One day Sir Thomas came across a butcher who was mistreating a pony. The butcher was astonished when the elderly squire whipped off his coat and gave him a good beating. When he thought that conditions were too tiring for the horse he would run alongside his carriage to lighten the load.

Sir Thomas was an extremely shabby dresser. He liked to tell the tale against himself about how he had once opened up the gates to his estate for a visitor, and was given a shilling tip. While walking home one day from a mental hospital where he was committee chairman, he encountered a policeman who took him to be an escaped inmate, and marched him back.

He was particularly sentimental when it came to his pet dogs. Whenever one them died he would give it a full scale funeral in his private canine cemetery – Sir Thomas would personally lead the procession wearing a long white robe and read prayers as the doggy coffin was lowered into the grave.

Sir Francis Henry Egerton, the eighth and last Earl of Bridgewater, is remembered for the important manuscript he left to the British Museum. He was also a miserable loner who preferred the company of his beloved dogs to that of people. The Egerton dogs lived like aristocrats in his family mansion, Ashridge House in Hertfordshire. He entertained them to dinner and dressed them in the latest fashions, including little handmade leather shoes. Each dog wore a linen napkin and had a footman stationed behind it. The Earl however demanded perfect table manners from his dogs. Any dog that did not behave like a gentleman "with decency and decorum" was banished from the table and forced to eat in the kitchen for a week.

The Earl spent much of his time in Paris where his estimated annual income of £20,000 allowed him to indulge his foibles in grand style. He attracted a wide circle of French artists and literary figures, although, it was noted, no Englishman ever visited him. It led many to believe that Egerton had left England because of some terrible transgression at home. Egerton became a familiar figure in the streets of Paris, especially for his large "sugar loaf" hat and his carriage, full of dogs seated on silk cushions. He would often walk down the Bois de Boulogne with umbrellas protecting his dogs from the rain. Sir Francis enjoyed Paris, but missed the English hunting season and would stage miniature hunts in his Paris garden. Dressed in sporting pink he would ride behind imported English hounds and chase an imported English fox. He also installed pigeons and partridges with clipped wings in his garden so he could shoot them easily.

Sir Francis had a peculiar obsession concerning his footwear, which he used, in effect, as a diary. He had a different pair of shoes for each day of the year. Every night he would remove his shoes and place them next to the pair he had worn the day before, until he had rows and rows of shoes removed in chronological order. The shoes were never cleaned, but left exactly as they were. Thus he could work out what the date was and what the weather had been like on a particular day by observing the state of the shoes. He died unmarried in 1829.

Lady Cardigan outraged Victorian society, not least the Queen herself, by smoking cigars and openly living "in sin" with Lord Cardigan for a year before they were eventually married. Her ladyship was also known for her unconventional dress sense. She went cycling in red military trousers and a leopard skin cape. In her eighties she would dress in full Spanish national costume, or stroll through Hyde Park wearing a Louis XVI coat and three-cornered hat over a curly blonde wig. She was a keen hunter, and when she was too elderly to ride she still turned up to the meets dressed in full hunting gear and would follow the hunt in her carriage. For several years before her death she kept a coffin in her home so that she could lie in it now and then to test it for comfort.

The Countess of Desmond, according to seventeenth-century records, was remarkable for her longevity. Apparently she died at the age of one hundred and forty-three as a result of climbing and falling from an apple tree.

Chapter Two

Religious Eccentrics

"Madam, I have been looking for a person who disliked gravy all my life. Let us swear eternal friendship"
The Rev. Sydney Smith (1771–1845)

Dr William Archibald Spooner gave his name to the mangling of consonants that produces "spoonerisms" – first recorded in 1900 and defined in the Oxford English Dictionary as "an accidental transposition of the initial sounds, or other parts, of two or more words". Spooner was born in 1844 in London and became an Anglican priest and a scholar. During a sixty-year association with Oxford University he lectured in history, philosophy, and divinity. From 1876 to 1889, he served as a dean and from 1903 to 1924 as warden and president. Spooner was an albino, very small, with very poor eyesight and a head too large for his body. His reputation was that of a kindly and hospitable man, but he was extremely absent-minded. He once invited a faculty member to tea "to welcome our new archaeology Fellow". "But, sir," the man replied, "I am our new archaeology Fellow." "Never mind," Spooner said, "come all the same." After a Sunday service he turned back to the pulpit and informed his student audience: "In the sermon I have just preached, whenever I said Aristotle, I meant St Paul." He once asked an undergraduate he came across in the quad, "Now let me see. Was it you or your brother who was killed in the war?"

Spooner did not acquire the confusing speech mannerism that made him famous until he was well into middle age. According to legend, he stood up one day in the college chapel to announce a hymn, "Kinkering Congs Their Titles Take . . ." and it sort of took off from there. Spooner's tendency to get words mixed up could happen at any time, but it occurred more often when he was upset. He reprimanded one student for "fighting a liar in the quadrangle" and another who "hissed my mystery lecture". To the latter he allegedly added in disgust, "You have tasted two worms." During World War I he reassured his students, "When our boys come home from France, we will have the hags flung out," and he praised Britain's farmers as "noble tons of soil". His chapel mistakes were legendary. "Our Lord is a shoving leopard," he allegedly once announced. He quoted I Corinthians 13:12 as "For now we see through a dark, glassly . . ." At a wedding, he prompted a hesitant bridegroom, "Son, it is now kisstomary to cuss the bride." To a stranger seated in the wrong place: "I believe you're occupying my pie. May I sew you to another sheet?" At a naval review Spooner wondered at "this vast display of cattle ships and bruisers". To a school official's secretary: "Is the bean dizzy?" Visiting a friend's country cottage, he noted, "You have a nosey little crook here." Perhaps most famously of all, he once referred to Queen Victoria as "the queer old Dean". As many alleged spoonerisms are now known to be apocryphal, perhaps the final word on the subject should rest with the great man himself. A couple of years before his death in 1930 at age eighty-six, Spooner told an interviewer that he could authenticate only one of his famous gaffes – the very first one attributed him while announcing the hymn "Kinkering Congs".

Although the Reverend Harold "Jumbo" Davidson, rector of the parish of Stiffkey in Norfolk, was descended from a long line of Protestant churchmen, he had once been a stand-up comedian. The career never took off, but he developed a taste for London's theatreland that never really left him. When he eventually entered the church as rector of the tiny Norfolk fishing village he scandalized his parishioners by skipping off back to London whenever he could. A dapper little man with a high-pitched voice, the Rev. Davidson's mission in life was to "save" young girls, especially pretty ones. He regularly accosted young women with the line, "Are you not Miss ———, the famous actress?" and as inevitably they were not, he followed up by introducing his bogus theatrical connections and promising them a job on the stage. Davidson's approach to his work was too unorthodox for the church hierarchy and in 1932 they moved to defrock him. Even on the day of his hearing he could not resist rising to the occasion with a dig at the establishment. He arrived an hour late and instead of following the bishop to the high altar as decorum required he marched on ahead of him. Davidson put up a spirited defence: had not

Prime Minister Gladstone often talked to prostitutes to lead them to salvation? The Church was unmoved and his stipend of £800 was cut off.

Davidson spent the rest of life protesting his innocence. He was a consummate publicity seeker and, fired by a burning sense of injustice as well as a need to feed his wife and large family, took to preaching as a circus side-show attraction. He sat in a booth lined with his press cuttings and harangued passers-by, and once preached from the mouth of a stuffed whale. He even went on hunger strike, sitting inside a barrel and refusing to eat until the Church reinstated him. His campaign earned a great deal of sympathy until people noticed that he did not appear to be losing weight. It turned out that he had a stash of food hidden away which he would visit every time he took a toilet break. As attempted suicide by starvation was technically a criminal offence, Davidson was arrested. In 1937 he appeared at Skegness, protesting his innocence from inside a cage which he shared with a large lion. Unfortunately the publicity stunt went awry when the lion turned on Davidson and mauled him to death. On the day of the funeral extra police were called in to control the huge gathering of mourners. His widow meanwhile caused a sensation by turning up dressed all in white. When someone asked her why she had not chosen a more traditional colour of mourning, she smiled and pointed to her black shoe laces.

Rabbis in the township of B'nei B'rak, Israel, banned hot pizza in fast food stores in 1991 because it could lead to improper contact between the sexes. The religious authorities explained that boys and girls might have to wait in line at stores for their pizzas to heat, and "might look at each other, which is an offence against modesty, or, God forbid, even touch each other". Cold pizza is however still legal.

When the Rev. Robert Stephen Hawker was appointed Vicar of Morwenstow in 1835 he dispensed with the traditional cassock, preferring to wear either a fisherman's jersey and sea-boots or a yellow blanket with a hole cut out for his head, maintaining that this was what all of the early Cornish saints wore. The truth was that, incoveniently for a man of the cloth, he hated to wear black, and even when his first wife died he had to be persuaded to tie a piece of black ribbon round his plum-coloured, brimless hat for the funeral.

He took Holy Orders and was ordained to a curacy in North Tamerton when he was fifteen. The parish had never had a curate like him; he rode his pony bareback and was always accompanied by a black pig called Gyp. It ran beside him when he went for walks and even followed him into drawing rooms. If told to stay, it did so with great dignity, "being an intelligent and obedient creature".

Morwenstow had been without a resident vicar for a hundred years before Hawker went there in 1835. He found he had taken on a parish in ruins, the church neglected and overgrown. Hawker was such an immensely powerful personality however that eventually smugglers and wreckers alike treated him with respect. There were many shipwrecks on that treacherous coastline and he was a brave rescuer. No sooner had the call gone out that another ship was on the rocks than Hawker was on his way, risking life and limb in the raging sea. Those he rescued were taken back to his vicarage, nursed, fed and clothed. On cold winter nights he would take bottles of brandy from his cellar and meat from his larder and tour the parish to see if anyone was in need. He wore his clothes until they were threadbare, and spent hours alone in a hut which clung precariously to the cliff face writing poetry.

Hawker often toured the parish on a mule, accompanied by his pet pig. He had other pets which he also took into church with him, including a small dog and several cats. When one of his cats caught a mouse and ate it on a Sunday, he excommunicated it. Hawker's church was littered with personal bric-a-brac, including bits of driftwood, candle-ends, pieces of poetry and torn-out pages from prayer books. Near the pulpit he kept a grotesque carving representing a castle attacked by a two-headed dragon. He always conducted his services wearing red gloves and at wedding ceremonies he would toss the ring into the air and catch it before handing it to the groom. At baptisms he would stride up and down the aisle holding the baby in the air, booming, "We receive this child into the congregation of Christ's flock." Parents would travel miles for a Hawker baptism.

Hawker is remembered for an elaborate practical joke he played on the superstitious people of Cornwall. In July 1815, he rowed out to sea and every night for a week he sat down on a rock just off the Bude coast, stark naked apart from a wig made of seaweed and an oilskin wrapped around his legs, wailing at the moon. A large crowd gathered and word spread that a mermaid with a fish's tail was sitting on a rock, combing her hair and singing. At the end of each performance, "she" dived off a rock and disappeared. This went on for several nights, the crowds growing bigger and more incredulous. In time Hawker grew suspiciously hoarse. He finished his performance by singing the National Anthem, and as the bemused crowd on the shoreline watched the mermaid slid into the sea, never to be seen again.

The ever-confident Rev. Homer A. Tomlinson was born in Indiana in 1892, the son of the leader of the Church of God, a little known Pentecostal sect commonly referred to as the Holy Rollers. Tomlinson moved to New York where he formed an advertising agency in 1916. After a few years he entered the ministry of his father's church, then went off to form a splinter group of his own when he failed to succeed to the leadership. He claimed a following of somewhere between 50 and 100 million people, although a more realistic estimate would have put the number at under 3,000. In 1952, claiming to have been "hailed almost as a new Messiah" during extensive travels abroad, Tomlinson ran for US president as the candidate of the Theocratic Party. He advocated the union of church and state, the abolition of taxes, the return of tithing and the creation of two new cabinet posts: secretary of righteousness and secretary of the Holy Bible. Tomlinson was to run for the presidency again, but after two failed campaigns he topped his political efforts by suddenly declaring himself to be King of the World. The Bible anticipated the appearance of a global sovereign, he said, and he was sure that the scriptures referred to him. He travelled extensively, although probably not the million air miles he claimed, to spread the news of his monarchy, briefly visiting 101 countries for a series of coronation ceremonies, mostly performed at the local airport. During these coronations Tomlinson would put on blue silk robes, hold an inflatable plastic globe as a symbol of his authority, and while seated on a folding chair would have a gold-painted iron crown placed on his head.

Tomlinson made extensive claims for the benefits to mankind of his reign as King of the World. He had fended off revolutions, averted a war between Israel and the Arabs, ended droughts and launched a period of world peace and harmony. His 1958 coronation in Moscow's Red Square, for example, had "melted the iron curtain". The Soviet press, however, unimpressed by the fact that a king had appeared in their midst and wrought instant international peace, simply referred to Tomlinson as "an American actor".

John Roeleveld, born in 1920 in Erbeck, Holland, was instructed by God to collect, stuff and mount two of every species in preparation for Armageddon. When police raided his home in 1992 in response to complaints by neighbours they found a warren of concrete bunkers crammed with thousands of stuffed animals going back forty years. Many of the specimens were antiques, but most had been stuffed by Roeleveld himself. There were also thousands of eggshells, bones and insects preserved in formaldehyde. God had promised him that his collection would rise up and live again after judgment day. God also told him that the vast collection of junk littering his garden, including thousands of items of scrap metal and broken furniture, would be made new.

The midget Pope Gregory VII (1013–85) crusaded against corruption within the Church, including clerical marriages and the keeping of mistresses by priests. His commendable campaign against moral abuse and heresy took an unexpected turn however when he declared it a bad thing for people read the Bible. It might provoke thought, explained Pope Gregory, and free thought led to heresy.

The Shrine of the Weeping Shirley MacLaine is situated in the Beta Israel Temple in Los Angeles. Consecrated by Dr Ernesto A. Moshe Montgomery, it was inspired by a vision he had while travelling in the actress's private jet. Montgomery said that a large photograph of him with MacLaine had been seen shedding tears and had inspired testimony of miraculous healings.

The Reverend Samuel Andrew Peters, who lived from 1735–1826, was the rector of Hebron, Connecticut during the American revolutionary war. Peters sympathized with the Tories, for which he was tarred and feathered. This punishment however merely provoked the rector into seeking revenge, which he did with an extraordinary bent. He returned to England to work on a *General History of Connecticut*, a vehicle for him to tell outrageous lies about his former home. His best known whopper was the tale of the Connecticut River caterpillar invasion. According to Peters, huge caterpillars with prickles and red throats marched in an army three miles wide and two miles long, devouring every shred of greenery for one hundred miles. The book became a bestseller and he returned to the United States in 1805 to live comfortably on his royalties.

To the early Christians, self-denial was one of the most certain routes to the kingdom of God, but few carried asceticism to the extremes of the eccentric Syrian, St Simeon Stylites. Born in AD 390, Simeon specialized in the very hardest paths to virtue. He once twisted a rope so tightly around his waist that it dug into his flesh, causing terrible skin ulcers that nearly killed him. After being kicked out of the local monastery where his pious suffering was considered a tad too extreme for the sensibilities of the local abbot, St Simeon retired to a hermitage near the city of Antioch, where he nearly killed himself again by completely abstaining from food and water during the forty days of Lent. The holy man apparently also enjoyed the taste of his own putrefying flesh. He once stood on one leg until the leg became ulcerous, then he ate the ulcers; his motto was "Eat what God has given you". He then moved to a nearby mountain top where he lived alone, dressed only in animal skins. As if this was not enough, he had his right leg shackled to a rock for good measure. Word of the extraordinary St Simeon got around and people came to the mountain to hear him speak and receive his blessing. It was at this point that his career took a move upwards – quite literally, for he was to spend the rest of his life on top of pillars. He began by perching at a modest height of six feet, but spent his last thirty-seven years on a platform almost seventy feet above ground level. Thus he became known as Simeon Stylites, from *stylos*, the Greek word for pillar.

The Rev. John Fitzgerald was born into a highly eccentric Suffolk family. His brother, translator of the Rubaiyat, spent his days wandering around Woodbridge wearing a grey shawl and a very tall hat which was tied to his head with a handkerchief, and in summer he walked around barefoot with his boots slung on a stick. The Reverend John himself was flamboyant in the pulpit. He liked to remove his footwear and his socks during sermons because he claimed it gave him more freedom while he was preaching. He was also prone to shedding other items of clothing, and to standing on one leg for long periods. To emphasize a point he would wave a lighted candle at his congregation, splattering wax on the occupants of the front row. His sermons were not known for their brevity. In fact his tirades against drink, slavery and Roman Catholics would often go on for two or three hours. He also had a slight speech impediment which made him hiss and whistle while he was talking. Unfortunately, the hissing, whistling and removing of clothes would also occur while other people were preaching. In spite of the length of his sermons Fitzgerald was undoubtedly high on entertainment value for he drew large crowds to his chapel at Boulge Hall.

Kaiser Wilhelm II's wife, Auguste Viktoria of Schleswig-Holstein-Sonderburg-Augustenburg, was a deeply religious woman of the fiercely evangelical variety – her hand-picked ladies-in-waiting were known as the Hallelujah Aunts. The Empress was a drab, unfashionable woman who defied the best efforts of the finest dressmakers in Germany to make her look regal or intelligent, for "Dona" as the Kaiser called her was particularly famous for a vacant, glassy-eyed expression which never left her. In 1889 the Kaiser and his wife paid a state visit to Constantinople, where they found the Sultan eager to treat them on a lavish scale. When the Empress visited the harem, she was introduced to the chief eunuch, the Kislar Aga. It was patiently explained to the Empress that the Kislar Aga's position made him one of the most important people in Turkey. The Empress nodded intently, then asked him if his father had also been a eunuch.

The Irish writer the Rev. Charles Robert Maturin came from a line of French Huguenots – one of his ancestors arrived in Ireland after spending sixteen years in the Bastille. He graduated from Trinity College, Dublin in 1800 and chose the Church as a career but soon found that a curate's stipend did not allow for his exotic tastes, especially his love of dancing. To make ends meet he began to write romances, followed by a succession of lurid Gothic novels. Soon Maturin was famous for his horror stories, of which *Melmoth the Wanderer* was the most famous. His play *Bertram* which was produced in Drury Lane in 1816 made him a literary celebrity in London and in Dublin. The profits enabled Maturin to buy a house in York Street, Dublin, where he painted the ceiling with clouds and eagles and the walls with scenes from some of his books.

Maturin had no idea how to manage money and constantly teetered on the edge of poverty. People could tell from the way he dressed how life was treating him; his wardrobe changed from flashy and fashionable to plain shabbiness, according to the state of his bank balance. However, he always insisted that his wife, Henrietta, must be at all times beautifully groomed and dressed to the nines. He spent his royalties on keeping her in the height of fashion, even if there was no food on the table.

Maturin was also incredibly absent-minded. He was often seen wearing a boot on one foot and a shoe on the other and was known to visit people wearing his dressing gown and slippers. It was not uncommon for him to turn up for parties a day or two late. After he had finished writing *Melmoth the Wanderer* he sent it to his publishers in several different parcels and without any page numbers. He had an unusual habit while writing; whenever he felt the muse upon him, he would paste a wafer to his forehead as a warning to his family that he was not to be disturbed or interrupted in any way. He was only forty-one when he died in 1814. His death was hastened by absent-mindedly taking the wrong medicine.

The theologian John Allegro (1923–1988) was known for controversial theories which led him to be known as "the Liberace of Biblical scholarship". Allegro was a brilliant undergraduate. After a period studying Hebrew dialects at Magdalen College, Oxford he was invited in 1953 to join an international body of distinguished scholars working on the Dead Sea Scrolls in Jerusalem. He authored a series of bestselling books on the subject, combining his writing career with his role as a widely respected lecturer in Comparative Semitics and Old Testament studies at Manchester University. In the 1960s his work took off in an unexpected direction when he declared Christianity to be "a phallic, drug-taking mystery cult we none of us would want anything to do with. They had visions. They went on a trip." It was around this time that he began to refer to the Bible as "these tales of this rabbi, Jesus, and his mum and dad". Allegro's academic reputation was not further enhanced when he became obsessed with "magic" mushrooms. In 1970 he published *The Sacred Mushroom and the Cross*, in which he sought to establish that most of the leading characters in the Bible, including Moses and Jesus, were in fact walking mushrooms, and that Christ's final utterance on the Cross was "a paean of praise to the god of the mushroom". This book, wrote a critic, "gave mushrooms a bad name". Allegro effectively ended his academic career with the follow-up, the similarly mushroom-influenced and prophetically titled *The End of the Road*, then in 1971 *The Chosen People*, which asserted that Moses and his followers were all high on hallucinogenic fungi, and *Lost Gods*, which asserted that the God of the Old

Testament was "a mighty penis in the heavens", who "in the thunderous climax of the storm, ejaculated semen upon the furrows of Mother Earth". The latter book prompted the *Sunday Telegraph* to note that it had "all the freshness and coherence of the conversation of a very tired man in a crowded pub rather late at night". When asked, Allegro maintained that he never consumed mushrooms himself, adding, "I wouldn't be so bloody stupid."

The Rev. Dr George Harvest, parish priest of Thames Ditton in Surrey for more than thirty years until his death in 1789 aged sixty-one, was incredibly absent-minded. Whenever he travelled he always had to borrow a horse because he always mislaid his own. People soon stopped lending him their mounts, however, since he invariably lost the horses he borrowed as well. Whenever he dined at the homes of friends, Harvest would take his leave by going upstairs, or else get lost on his way home. He was often discovered by neighbours in the wrong house sleeping in the wrong bed. He was so forgetful that he left not one but two women standing at the altar. On what should have been his first wedding day he went fishing and only remembered when he returned home at nightfall that he should have been in church. Later in his life he had a second marriage proposal accepted, but again completely forgot to turn up.

Dr Karl N. Edwards is theologian of the world's first Presleytarian Church of Elvis the Divine. The church doctrine revolves around studies of the king's movies and music and so far has attracted around a hundred followers. They face Las Vegas every day, sing Elvis's songs and even have a strict Elvis diet to follow. The First Church of The Doors meanwhile is possibly the world's most marginal religious cult as they worship Jim Morrison, lead singer of The Doors until he died a bloated heroin addict in his bath, as a god. In 1990 two members of the cult were caught attempting to rob his grave.

The Rev. John "Mad Jack" Alington (1795–1863) of Letchworth Hall in Hertfordshire inherited a fortune from his grandfather, including a manor house and forty-three farms. He also took over from his father as patron of the local parish church, where his incoherent, rambling sermons, apparently based on some of the more risqué passages from the Song of Solomon, extolling the pleasures of free love, became something of a feature. The local bishop quickly suspended Alington from office, presumably expecting an end to the matter. "Mad Jack" however was not a man to give up easily. He merely set up a pulpit in Letchworth Hall from where he continued to preach on his theme of free love. As most of the people in the village worked for him and lived in his cottages the rebel vicar had little difficulty in poaching most of the regular churchgoers, especially as he also took to handing out free beer and brandy. Occasionally his services got so out of hand that he had to threaten a few people with his shotgun.

Alington developed several unorthodox methods by which he could grab the undivided attendance of his congregation. He would begin his services by playing on an old piano and a couple of musical boxes. When the congregation was assembled he would ride up and down the aisle on a hobby-horse, propelled along by his servants. Dressed in a leopard skin he would begin reading the sermon – usually a love story. He would then disappear behind a screen and reappear in another part of of the hall through a trapdoor. To signal the end of the service he removed his wig and tossed it into the congregation.

In his spare time Alington liked to be carried around his garden in an open coffin; he explained that he was practising for the real thing. He considered it his duty to educate his farm workers, and went to extraordinary lengths to do the job properly. He turned his pond into a scale model of the world's oceans, and rowed his workers around floating model "continents" while lecturing them on geography.

Londoner Stanley Green, who died in 1992 aged seventy-eight, spent a large part of his life warning his fellow men against the dangers of protein and lust. He was also against sitting, which was perhaps as well as he spent the best part of thirty years walking up and down London's Oxford Street with a large placard which read: LESS PASSION FROM LESS PROTEIN: MEAT FISH BIRD; EGG CHEESE; PEAS incl.lentils BEANS; NUTS AND SITTING PROTEIN WISDOM.

Green worked for the civil service before he began his campaign in the 1930s. His own diet comprised porridge, fruit, steamed vegetables, lentils, home-baked bread and barley water mixed with milk powder.

He sold thousands of hand-printed leaflets entitled "Eight Passion Proteins" at 12p each, which he produced on a noisy press in his small flat, regularly annoying his neighbours on printing days. Until he qualified for his pensioner's travel pass he cycled the fifteen miles from his home in Northolt to London's West End with his placard on his back. A favourite tactic of his was to accost queues of cinema goers with the opening line, "You cannot deceive your groom that you are a virgin on your wedding night." Motorists sounded their horns and waved as they passed and whole coachloads stood up and cheered him. Not everyone was quite as appreciative. Green was twice arrested for obstruction and he wore green overalls as protection against spit. He said he never held grudges, however, as he believed that people only attacked him because they mistook him for "a religious nut".

On the occasion of her birthday, Pope Pius IX sent Queen Isabel II of Spain a gift of the embalmed body of Saint Felix. She had it permanently displayed in a glass coffin in the Spanish royal chapel.

In his day the nineteenth-century Protestant Archbishop of Dublin, Richard Whateley, was a social disaster without equal. He was born in London and became an Oxford don, where his unconventional appearance, including his large white hat, white coat and large white dog, earned him the nickname the White Bear. Whateley had been blessed with a brilliant mind and was the author of more than two dozen books on a number of serious academic subjects ranging from theology to the British Constitution. Unfortunately he was also extremely arrogant and went out of his way to belittle anyone he considered his intellectual inferior, which included just about everyone he ever met. He once announced that he considered his dogs more intelligent than most of his university students, and would often dismiss the opinions of others by remarking, "I went through that when I was twelve."

Whateley went out of his way to be boorish in company. If a conversation bored him, he would take out his scissors and trim his fingernails. People who invited him into their homes could expect to see him stretch his legs on their mantelpiece, or spin in his seat until the chair broke. His friend Lord Anglesey had six chairs broken by the Archbishop. He disliked armchairs because they restricted his arms, which he liked to wave around in an animated fashion, especially when he was talking. Once when he attended an evening's entertainment, a contemporary noted, "We were all surprised at the strange way he had of raising his right leg and foot, doubling it back over the thigh of the left one, and grasping his instep with both hands as though he were strangling some ugly animal. He did this repeatedly during the evening, especially while telling some good stories to which he did ample justice, and during the process the foot thus raised, or rather strangled, was almost on the lap of the Provost Lloyd on whose right side the Archbishop sat. I can never forget the Chesterfield suavity of the Provost's face, while his fine black small clothing was thus subjected to the treatment of a footmat." The Chief Justice Doherty was once seated next to Whateley at a Privy Council meeting. He put his his hand into his pocket for his handkerchief and was surprised to find the Archbishop's foot already there.

Whateley could be seen regularly hanging around the gates outside his palace in St Stephen's Green smoking his long clay pipe. When he felt he needed exercise he would climb a nearby tree and swing from the branches. He was also a firm believer in phrenology – the once fashionable science of studying a person's character by the shape of their head. He advised a phrenological test of his own: "Take a handful of peas, drop them on the head of a patient; the degree of the man's dishonesty will depend on the number which remain there. If a large number remain, tell the butler to lock up the plate."

The Indian mystic Baghwan Rajneesh was famous for meditation, his fleet of Rolls-Royces, interesting theories on sex, personal greed and tax evasion. Baghwan (the name means "master of the vagina") studied and taught philosophy at the University of Jabalpur, India. In 1974 he opened an ashram in Poona, but in 1981 moved to a 126-square-mile site in Oregon where he acquired a reputation for mysticism, extravagance and dubious sexual practices, although not necessarily in that order. His spiritual needs included the use of a private swimming pool with computer controlled heating, a private plane, and anything up to ninety-six Rolls-Royces. He died in 1990, possibly of AIDS, by which time his movement was renamed "Osho". The cult has now been taken over by financial opportunists, who have turned it more or less into a holiday resort for stressed Western executives.

The Rev. Francis Waring, vicar of Heybridge near Maldon, was known for his distinctive high velocity delivery and his irreverent approach to authority. He sped through his services at a terrific pace, allowed no time for the traditional responses, and edited his sermons to a couple of quick sentences. He would then run down the aisle, jump on his horse and gallop off to perform a couple of similar services in his two other churches. Waring also liked to take fashion risks and designed his own vestments. He once surprised a formal gathering of clergy by turning up in scarlet breeches and white stockings. When his bishop remonstrated with him about his dress code he offered him a visiting card and replied, "My lord, that you should condescend to notice my breeches is an honour I did not expect. Do let me recommend my tailor to you." Waring's unconventional sense of style extended to his home life. The

Heybridge vicarage had logs to sit on instead of chairs and his children were required to eat from a trough. He and his wife slept in a cradle which swung from the ceiling. He also devised a different bird call for each family member so that instead of calling them by name he could just whistle.

In 1994 a Seventh Day Adventist minister persuaded nine people sharing a canoe with him to follow Jesus Christ's example and walk with him across the water into the middle of Lake Victoria, Tanzania. They all drowned.

The Hervey family were so famous for their riotous lifestyles that according to a contemporary saying, mankind was divided into three categories – men, women and Herveys. The eighteenth-century English nobleman Frederick Hervey became Bishop of Cloyne and later Bishop of Derry, although the odds were against him as he was neither Irish nor possibly even Christian; his grasp of theology was vague and he had an aversion to the sound of church bells. Once while he was travelling on the Continent he stopped for a meal in Siena. While he was dining the procession of the Host passed under the window of his hotel. The Bishop leaned out of the window and dumped a plate of spaghetti over it. He learned of his promotion while playing leapfrog with fellow clergymen in the grounds of his palace. He shouted to his companions, "Gentlemen, I will jump no more. I have surpassed you all! I have jumped from Cloyne to Derry!" Hervey spent less than half his thirty-six years as Bishop of Derry in Ireland. For the last thirteen years of his life he lived abroad and never set foot in his diocese.

He kept his family in poverty in order to pay for his mania for building and collecting. He built himself three homes, one of which he never actually lived in, although he paid an army of workmen £80,000 to spend sixteen years working on it. The construction of his family mansion at Ickworth in Surrey, built under his distant direction while he travelled all over Europe, became an obsession through the last years of his life. He died before he saw his masterpiece completed.

An eleventh-century group of monks called the Cathars frowned upon procreation. They did however approve and practise frequent and savage flagellation with steel-tipped whips and sodomy, which they did not consider sinful as it did not involve the risk of conception. The Cathars were semi-vegetarians on the grounds that animals were produced by sexual intercourse, and that their flesh was therefore sinful. Instead, they ate lots of fish in the mistaken belief that fish do not copulate.

Father Denham, the bad-tempered vicar of Warleggan in Cornwall until his death in 1953, was a notorious misanthrope. He surrounded his vicarage with barbed wire and demanded that anyone who wanted to visit him should make an appointment – late comers were simply refused entrance. He was also extremely miserly – his home contained no furniture and he lived on a diet of nettles and porridge. Eventually, when his parishioners gave up his sermons completely, he filled his pews with cardboard effigies.

Francesca Nortyuega believed that all of God's creatures possessed souls. Accordingly she left the bulk of her considerable fortune to her niece on one condition; that she provide the only other beneficiary of the estate, her pet goldfish, with a pair of pants.

The fundamentalist community of Zion City, Illinois was built in the late 1890s by about 5,000 followers of a Scot, John Alexander Dowie (1848–1907), religious fanatic, faith healer and founder of the Apostolic Church. In 1888 Dowie emigrated from his native Edinburgh to America and purchased ten square miles of land, fifty-four miles north of Chicago on the shores of Lake Michigan, where he built a township for his disciples. It was an entirely self-supporting community with new factories built for the manufacture of lace, confectionery and furniture. Life in Zion City was dull however as there were no theatres, cinemas or dance halls. Dowie was the absolute ruler of his people, and from his church pulpit he dispensed the law, elaborated on his cranky religious theories and railed against his pet earthly sins, namely sex, oysters and life assurance, citing little known Old Testament injunctions against shellfish and randy insurance salesmen.

Dowie was an ambitious evangelist however and he embarked on an expensive and ultimately ruinous campaign to spread the word of the Apostolic Church to the rest of America. He suffered a crippling stroke and with his health and financial problems mounting he turned to a close friend and disciple Glenn Wilbur Voliva, who had made a fortune of $10 million from the manufacture of chocolate biscuits. Voliva studied Dowie's accounts and found a discrepancy of about $2 million. He denounced his old friend as a fraudulent polygamist, banished him from the community and established himself as the new leader; Dowie died insane two years later.

The new ruler of Zion City was a flat-earther. He believed that the earth was saucer-shaped, that the north pole was positioned at the centre, and the south pole was a crust of ice surrounding the outer rim. The rest of the universe, the sun, the stars and the moon were fastened to the sky, and were much closer than the astronomers – "poor, ignorant conceited fools", according to Voliva – had always claimed. "The idea of a sun millions of miles in diameter and ninety-one million miles away is silly," he confidently explained. "The sun is only thirty-two miles across and is not more than three thousand miles from the earth. It stands to reason that it must be so. God made the sun to light the earth and therefore must have placed it close to the task it was designed to do." The sun's apparent cycle of rising and setting, he continued, was merely an optical illusion.

Voliva's grasp of astrophysics was one thing, his theories on how to run a community were quite another. The 16,000 inhabitants of Zion City quickly discovered that their new chief administrator made his predecessor look like a lily-livered liberal. Voliva banned lipstick, immodest clothes including swimming costumes and high heels, cigarettes and alcohol. He kicked out all of the city's butchers, doctors and chemists, and established a ten p.m. curfew. No one was allowed to whistle, sing or drive a vehicle in excess of five miles per hour; humming was also strictly prohibited. Voliva's laws were policed by his Praetorian Guard, who wore special uniforms with the word PATIENCE written on their helmets and miniature Bibles on their belts instead of truncheons. Some offenders were summarily fined on the spot; the unlucky ones were delivered to Voliva himself and given an hour-long lecture on their sins.

Voliva's luck began to run out in 1923; this was the year he predicted the world would end and nothing much happened. He had ruled his little kingdom for almost thirty years by the time of his death, aged seventy-two.

An exclusive group of villagers in the New Hebrides islands in the Pacific Ocean believe that the Duke of Edinburgh is the true messiah and that he will one day cure all known diseases and grant them eternal youth. Prince Philip's 200 followers expect that on his return he will restore paradise on earth and assume his rightful place among them, wearing of course the traditional penis gourd. They also believe that Philip secretly runs the Commonwealth and has been able thus far to get away with the tricky business of concealing his true identity from the Queen.

George King, a former Shropshire taxi driver, was visited by aliens as long ago as 1954 when they informed him that Jesus was alive and well and living on the planet Venus, and that furthermore he had been selected by the Hidden Masters to become the "Voice of the Interplanetary Parliament". King's mission on earth is to represent spirituality in its battle with materialism. In his quest he is assisted by the Hidden Masters, who occasionally lend support by visiting humanity in their flying saucers. King has now changed his name to Sir George King, OSP,PhD,ThD, DD, Metropolitan Archbishop of the Aetherius Churches, Prince Grand Master of the Mystical Order of St Peter, HRH Prince De George King De Santori, and Founder President of the Aetherius Society. He lives in Los

Angeles with his wife, Lady Monique King, Bishop of the American Division.

In Hong Kong 32-year-old self-proclaimed "knight of God" Syed Atta Muhammad was committed to a secure unit after he assaulted a young female tour guide. He explained that her breasts were too big to serve God because they made her look like a prostitute.

In October 1980 an Indian religious mystic Khadeshwari Baba attempted to show off his incredible powers of meditation by remaining buried alive in a ten foot deep pit for ten days. In a carnival-like atmosphere a crowd of over 1,000 people including several local officials from the town of Gorakhpur watched as Baba was ceremoniously lowered into the pit, and the hole was filled in behind him. Ten days later the pit was reopened. From the accompanying stench it was estimated the mystic had been dead for at least a week.

Chapter Three

Eccentric Genius

"No great genius was ever without some tincture of madness"
Aristotle (422–384BC)

"The central fact of our epoch is that knowledge has grown; man's brain has not"
Geoffrey Pyke (1894–1948)

"I do not think you can name many great inventions that have been made by married men"
Nikola Tesla (1856–1943)

"I declare that the earth is hollow and habitable within. I pledge my life in support of this truth and am ready to explore the hollow if the world will support and aid me in the undertaking"
John Cleeves Symmes (1780–1829)

The extraordinary Sir Francis Galton (1822–1911), a first cousin of Charles Darwin, had one of the most prolific scientific minds of the Victorian age; mathematician, meteorologist, experimental psychologist, explorer, anthropologist, inventor, geneticist and the father of modern forensic science, Galton's brilliance dazzled in every field he applied himself to. He was a Fellow of the Royal Society, was awarded the Royal Geographical Society's gold medal and was elected to that body's ruling council. He was author of over 300 publications, of which *Hereditary Genius*, the pioneering study of genetics, earned him lasting fame. He was the first man to use the words "anticyclone" and "eugenics". He invented fingerprinting, pioneered the science of behavioural genetics, was knighted for his work in applied statistics and wrote seminal papers on blood transfusions, twins, criminality and exploration. Galton's obsession with statistics however went some way beyond the natural curiosity of an enquiring mind. He was compelled to write down, log, cross-reference and quantify anything and everything he came across, whether it be the number of brush strokes on a painting (the results of which he reported in his article "Number of Strokes of the Brush in a Picture" in the scientific journal *Nature*, 1905) or the curves on a woman's body. While working in a hospital laboratory, Galton decided to work his way through the pharmaceutical A–Z by testing every drug on himself in alphabetical order. His curiosity was sated at the letter C, when castor oil did its predictable best. In 1897 he published a paper in *Nature* on the precise length of rope required by a hangman to break a criminal's neck without decapitation, in which he triumphantly revealed an error in previously used calculations that did not take into account the bigger neck muscles in fat men. Inevitably, he even developed a complex formula for determining the best way to make a cup of tea.

Galton worked so hard to obtain his degree in mathematics at Trinity College, Cambridge that he swore the effort had given him a "sprained brain". In 1850 he became the first European to explore Damaraland in south-west Africa. To assist him on his journey he employed Damara guides, but was slightly frustrated by the inability of his guides to tell him how long it would take to get anywhere, as the Damarans never used numerals greater than three – despite, Galton noted with some irritation, having more than one thousand words to describe the markings on cattle. After encountering the Hottentot people he turned his analytical mind to the measurement of black African ladies' bottoms. What the natives made of Galton as he whipped out his sextant and measuring tape we will never know because, as the scientist confessed in his full account of the expedition, "I did not know a word of Hottentot, and could never therefore have explained to the lady what the object of my footrule could be, and I really dared not ask my worthy missionary host to interpret for me." Galton pressed on to Lake Omanbode, where a misunderstanding with an Ovampe king resulted in the scientist being temporarily married to the king's daughter, the princess Chipanga. Galton wrote of his "honeymoon": "I found her installed in my tent in Negress finery, riddled with reed ochre and butter, and as capable of leaving a mark on anything she touched as a well-inked printer's roller. I was dressed in my one well-preserved suit of white linen, so I had her ejected with scant ceremony."

Galton's sexuality was inscrutable. In 1853 he married Louisa Butler, daughter of the Dean of Peterborough, but his interest in his wife was neither romantic nor sexual. His biographer D. W. Forrest noted, "There is no trace of heterosexual interest after 1846, apart from his marriage in 1853, and for the remainder of his life his attitude to women is one of polite indifference." Mrs Galton was a committed hypochondriac;

she prepared for her impending death so regularly that the phrase "Aunt Louisa's dying again" became a commonplace saying in family circles. Galton's 1855 book *The Art of Travel* offered this advice:

> It is the nature of women to be fond of carrying weights. You may see them in omnibuses and carriages, always preferring to hold their baskets or their babies on their knees to setting them down on the seats by their sides. A woman whose modern dress includes, I know not how many cubic feet of space, has hardly ever pockets of sufficient size to carry small articles, for she prefers to load her hands with a bag or other weighty object.

This, incidentally, was written by a man who regularly carried around with him a brick wrapped in brown paper and tied to a length of rope so he could stand on it to see over people's heads in a crowd.

Galton was far from socially gifted and quite incapable of interacting with other people. He believed he could get around this by instructing his wife Louisa in a complex system of secret hand signals which she used to let him know if he was boring people, or talking too loudly, or too quickly. At dinner parties, he placed pressure sensors under his dining room chairs, apparently to record the body movements of his guests. He theorized that if the party was going well, the guests would incline their chairs towards one other. He installed a warning signal in his dining room to let his guests know when the lavatory was engaged. He explained, "It saves a futile climb upstairs, and the occupant is not subjected to the embarrassment of having the door handle rattled."

Although born into a family of Birmingham Quakers he became vehemently atheist. Typically, he wrote a thesis demonstrating that prayer was a complete waste of time, citing statistical proof that public prayer for kings, queens and other heads of state was obviously ineffective because the average age of royals at death was lower than that of the rest of us. Galton startled his colleagues with a series of inventions, warming to his "sprained brain" theory by creating a ventilating top hat which would allow an overheated cranium to cool. The hat had a hinged lid that could be raised and lowered by squeezing a rubber bulb, thus allowing fresh air to circulate about his head. He defended this invention by asserting that it was "better than falling into a fit upon the floor". He invented spectacles to allow him to read a newspaper underwater. He wrote: "I amused myself very frequently with this new hobby, and being most interested in the act of reading, constantly forgot that I was nearly suffocating myself, and was recalled to the fact not by any gasping desire for breath, but purely by a sense of illness, that alarmed me." He threw his energies into compiling a "beauty map" of the British Isles to show where the best-looking women lived. This map was compiled from a statistical assessment of females he encountered on the street, and which he recorded on his latest invention, a strategically concealed pocket calculator, classifying the girls he passed as "attractive", "indifferent" or "repellent". He thus sought to demonstrate that Britain's ugliest women lived in Aberdeen.

After the beauty "league table", Galton produced a boredom chart, based upon the average number of fidgets at a play or a concert. From his lengthy observations of audiences he knew that the heads of very bored people tended to sway back and forth to a degree by which their degree of boredom could be measured, whereas the heads of attentive audiences maintained a steady distance between them. He set out to assess the proportion of optimists to pessimists, by randomly stopping strangers on the street and asking them how they liked the weather. He made a similar survey of people he encountered with fair hair and blue eyes. He studied court cases in various countries to work out which race was the most honest. He concluded that the British could be relied upon more than any other race to tell the truth, while "the centre of gravity for lying" was Greece.

At the International Health Exhibition held at South Kensington in 1884 he set up his "anthropometric laboratory". He set out to collate a vast database of physical information by measuring people – their weight, height, width, reaction times, eyesight, the size of their heads, the length of stride and, crucially, their thumb prints. It was after studying 2,500 sets of such prints that he realized they were all different. He moved his experiments to a permanent site in the South Kensington Museum and by 1893 had amassed enough material to publish a 200-page essay, simply titled "Fingerprints".

His experiments included a test for human and animal sensitivity to high notes. He invented the Galton whistle, a device which could produce extremely high-pitched notes above the human threshold. He had his device fixed into a hollow walking stick, and operated it by squeezing a rubber bulb on the handle. He would go out on to the street with his stick until he found some unsuspecting person about their own business, point his stick at them and emit a high-pitched note. If he got a reaction, he knew they had heard it.

A select bibliography some of his more esoteric works might include "Arithmetic by Smell" (*Psychological Review*, 1884), "Intelligible Signals between Neighbouring Stars" (*Fortnightly Review*, 1896), "Gregariousness in Cattle and in Men" (*Macmillan's Magazine*, 1861), and "Statistical Enquiries into the Efficacy of Prayer" (*Fortnightly Review*, 1872), not forgetting his seminal "Cutting a Round Cake on Scientific Principles" (*Nature*, 1906). He did in fact produce one bestseller which ran to four reprints. His survival manual *The Art of Travel* became almost standard reading for the British Army. It was packed with tips, some of them useful, some less so. His suggestion for avoiding blisters, for example, was to break a raw egg into each boot and fill one's socks with soapsuds. To get rid of lice, he advised making beads from mercury, old tea leaves and saliva and wearing them in a necklace. To keep one's clothes dry in a rainstorm you should remove them and sit upon them.

At the age of eighty-nine, after a harsh winter, Galton fell ill with severe asthma and was given oxygen as he lay on his deathbed. Although barely able to breathe or speak, he died struggling to explain to his doctor that he had once done experiments with oxygen.

Charles Babbage, the nineteenth-century mathematician, designed a calculating machine which is now acknowledged as the forerunner of computers. He devoted much of his spare time however to working out the statistical probability of the Biblical miracles. Babbage calculated that the chances of a man rising from the dead were one in 10^{12}.

If the cliché "mad scientist" had not existed already they would have had to invent it to describe Geoffrey Nathaniel Pyke. He was already a household name in England long before his finest hour as civilian adviser to Combined Operations, a special unit headed by Lord Mountbatten during the Second World War. During World War I Pyke went to Berlin to send back dispatches to the *Daily Chronicle*, but was soon spotted by the German authorities and was almost shot as a spy. Pyke was sent to an internment camp, from where he managed to escape with another English inmate. His exploits made him a public hero, and he wrote a book about his adventure and gave lectures. After the war he made a small fortune from stocks and shares and spent the money on founding his own school. It had long been Pyke's dream to create an educational environment that was to be the antithesis of his own miserable schooling. Pupils in Pyke's school were never punished or reprimanded or forced to learn any particular subjects; they were encouraged to find things out for themselves. It worked for a while, but the school lost so much money that it was forced to close.

In 1939 the British boffin hatched the first of a series of truly eccentric plans that were to earn him the name "Professor Brainstorm". He devised a cunning plan to avert World War II by simply presenting the results of an opinion poll to Hitler showing that the majority of Germans wanted peace. Hitler would see the results, become discouraged and call the whole thing off. As Pyke had correctly assumed that the fascist dictator was probably dead against opinion polls per se, he planned to flood Germany with students, disguised as golfers, carrying clipboards in one hand and golf clubs in the other. Germany was not at that time known to be a nation of golf enthusiasts. He in fact did persuade a few students to dress up as golfers and travel to Germany. Unfortunately Hitler had other ideas and invaded Poland anyway. Fortunately the students were able to flee before the Gestapo spotted them.

When war with Germany was declared Pyke was quickly co-opted as civilian adviser to Combined Operations by his friend, Lord Mountbatten. His brief was to come up with new and original ideas for defeating the enemy. Pyke alarmed the army top brass with his straggly beards, his shabby suits and his habit of never wearing socks; he once famously introduced himself to the Canadian Prime Minister Mackenzie King with his flies open. He often worked from his bed so as not to waste time by getting up and dressing, and he would summon military chiefs to bedside conferences in his Hampstead flat among piles of papers, bottles and other debris. His ideas for defeating the enemy however flew thick and fast. His suggestions were always a constant source of amazement and amusement to the army top brass. Some of Pyke's zanier suggestions prompted Lord Zuckerman to speculate that he was in fact "not a scientist, but a man of vivid and uncontrollable imagination and a totally uninhibited tongue". Pyke was asked, for example, to come up with a plan for the destruction of Romania's oil fields. He suggested sending in St Bernard dogs carrying brandy, so that the Romanian guards would get drunk before the British attacked. He later improved on this plan by recommending that women carry the brandy – even more distracting! When neither idea found much favour with the military he came up with a new ploy: start a few small fires, then the British commandos could simply drive about the oilfields dressed as Romanian firemen in replica fire engines. Instead of putting out the fires, the "firemen" would stoke them up by spraying them with water mixed with fused incendiary bombs.

Pyke also invented a motorized sledge to aid travel in occupied Norway. It was to be controlled by a man walking behind holding reins, so that if the sledge fell into a crevasse, the driver did not, unless he forgot to let go. Unfortunately as this also left the driver completely exposed to gunfire, most preferred to ride inside and take their chances with crevasses. A refinement to this was Pyke's "torpedo sledge". The sledge was to be driven slowly up a slope to tempt the Germans into giving chase. Halfway up the slope the torpedo was to be released to roll down on to the Germans and blow them up. To prevent the Germans from tampering with any equipment they came across it was to be marked with a sign in German warning them to keep clear as it was a secret Gestapo death ray, or "Officers' Latrine for Colonels only". The Germans, Pyke explained to his incredulous employees, were a very obedient race.

Pyke's most spectacular invention was the ship *Habbakuk*, a huge aircraft-carrier, half a mile long, made entirely of ice, reinforced with wood shavings – a material he modestly dubbed "Pykrete". The ship would be fitted with self-refrigerating apparatus, to keep it from melting. As the hull was thirty foot thick it would be virtually unsinkable. Pyke theorized that huge ice ships, clad in timber or cork and looking like ordinary ships but much larger, could serve as transport and aircraft-carriers, while smaller ships could be adapted to attack enemy ports. The plan was for them to sail into the port and capture enemy warships by spraying them with super-cooled water, encasing them in ice and forcing them to surrender. Blocks of Pykrete would then be used to build a barrier round the port, making an impregnable fortress. From there special teams would spread out into the countryside, spraying railway tunnels with super-cooled water to seal them up and paralyse transport.

Mountbatten thought it was a fantastic idea. He liked Pyke's plan so much, it was said, that he rushed into Churchill's bathroom with a lump of Pykrete and dropped it into his hot bath to prove it would not melt. Churchill in turn demonstrated the strength of Pykrete in front of a group of generals by drawing his revolver and firing at it – the bullet ricocheted off the solid lump and narrowly missed one of the generals. Although a prototype *Habbakuk* was actually built on a Canadian lake and it lasted through the summer without melting, the Allied invasion of Europe was already too advanced for it to be put to practical use. In fact very few projects inspired by Pyke ever got off the ground and he ended his war an embittered and disillusioned man.

After the war Pyke spent a couple of years helping the fledgling National Health Service solve staffing problems and published articles and broadcasts, hoping to introduce his ideas to influential people. Years of frustration and mockery however had made him deeply depressed. In 1948, aged fifty-four, he shaved off his beard and took his own life by swallowing a bottle of sleeping pills.

Alexander Graham Bell (1847–1922) tried to teach his dog to talk. He also kept his windows permanently covered to keep out the "harmful rays" of the full moon.

During the 1930s and 1940s Charles Kay Ogden was considered one of Britain's most brilliant linguists, editor of several distinguished journals and co-author of a bestselling book on words, and the famous creator of a radically simplified form of English. Born in 1889 the son of a schoolmaster, Ogden was afflicted with rheumatic fever at the age of sixteen and had to be kept in a darkened room for two years. By the time he attended Cambridge University, Og, as his friends knew him, was a fully blown agoraphobic. He was also an obsessive collector of everything from music boxes to shoes. He was especially fond of his large collection of masks. Later, during interviews, he would put on a mask and invite his interviewer to do the same. This, he explained, would help keep the conversation focused on logic, unhindered by personalities. He was also an insomniac, and would tramp the streets of London and Cambridge at night, knocking on the door of any friend who stayed up late. Towards the end of his life, he kept his coffin permanently on display in his front hallway. He was a great admirer of the philosopher Jeremy Bentham. For Bentham's centennial, Ogden organized a change of underwear for Bentham's remains, on display at University College in London.

Ogden's inspiration for his life's greatest work was his belief that most people other than himself were basically stupid. Basic English, stripped of all but eighteen verbs and pared down to 850 simple words, was a language the whole world could learn and understand. With the personal support of Prime Minister Winston Churchill, the British government began to underwrite Ogden's work and in 1943 he opened the Orthological Institute in London to train Basic English teachers. At first it appeared that Basic English was a runaway success and would sweep the world, thus transforming Ogden into a wealthy man. The eccentric linguist however insisted upon making himself a laughing stock among British journalists by running in and out of the room during interviews, each time sporting a new mask. After a series of false starts, the government paid Ogden £23,000 to cover his losses and took over the Basic English business. By the early 1950s, Ogden had abandoned his creation, and Basic English slid into obscurity. Its inventor died of cancer in 1957.

Zeno was the Greek founder of Stoicism, a school of philosophy characterized by impassivity and an indifference to pleasure or pain. He hanged himself at the age of ninety-eight after falling down and wrenching his finger.

The American theoretical physicist Richard Feynman (1918–88) was the most brilliant figure in his field in the post-World War II era. Born in New York, Feynman was descended from Russian and Polish Jews. The expectation of his parents had a profound impact on young Richard; his father announced even before the boy was born that his son would be a famous scientist. When he was still a baby his father placed various tiles in front of his eyes to get him accustomed to looking for patterns. As an infant he devoured books, even the *Encyclopaedia Britannica*. It was said that he and his friends traded mathematical formulae like baseball cards. At high school he was nicknamed "the mad genius". As a student Feynman suffered a nervous breakdown and when he recovered learned a technique called dream control which enabled him to dream the same dream again and again, with variations, at will.

During World War II, Feynman worked on the atomic bomb project at Princeton University and Los Alamos, New Mexico. He contributed to the key equation for the efficiency of nuclear explosion and organized the world's first large-scale computing system, which comprised electro-mechanical calculators and teams of women passing colour-coded cards. He was co-awarded the Nobel prize for physics in 1965 for his work on light, radio, electricity, and magnetism, and for almost twenty years he taught a course known as "Physics X" in which undergraduates would gather to pose any scientific question they wished, and he would improvise.

Feynman's achievements might have been even greater had he not suffered from an obsessive-compulsive disorder which compelled him to explore every aspect of life he came across no matter how trivial the subject. He learned umpteen foreign languages including Chinese, as well as how to play the bongos expertly, give massages, keep very accurate track of time in his head, crack safes, train dogs, make columns of ants march to his bidding, and pick up women in bars and persuade them to take their clothes off.

The British inventor Percy Shaw made millions from his "cat's eyes" – small reflectors sunk in road surfaces and used today in virtually every country in the world. The sentimental Yorkshireman however refused to let his success change his lifestyle. He continued to live in the same house all his life. His house had no curtains because they obscured the view, and he never owned a carpet because they attracted tobacco ash. He did, though, allow himself a few small luxuries. He owned three television sets which were switched on at all times, tuned to three different channels, and his greatest extravagance was his custom built Rolls-Royce, fitted with electrically operated petrol cap and reclining seats, cocktail cabinet and reading lamps at the front and rear. However, Shaw rarely travelled in it as he always maintained that Yorkshire already had everything he wanted.

Sir Joseph Banks, President of the Royal Society until his death in 1820, was described by the diarist John Byng as "a wild and eccentric character". It was however his daughter Sarah, herself a respected natural historian, who was generally regarded as the oddest member of the Banks household. Although she had been a fashionable young girl, over the years she became increasingly eccentric especially when it came to her clothes. Her dress sense was so bizarre that it drew the attention of some of London's top caricaturists of the day. The writer J.T. Scrub noted that "she was looked after by the eye of astonishment everywhere she went".

She inherited her father's obsession with only ever wearing wool. She owned three woollen riding habits which she wore on all occasions, even at dinner parties. Her best outfit she called Hightum, the second best was Tightum and the worst Scrub.

The obsessive Wilson "Snowflake" Bentley (1865–1931) was the first person in the world to photograph individual snow crystals through a microscope, and discovered a way to measure raindrops. Bentley grew up a loner on a remote farm in Jericho, Vermont and became so engrossed with the unique characteristics of snowflakes that he had acquired his nickname before his twentieth birthday. By the time he died he had pursued his unusual passion for forty-five years, amassing a collection of more than five thousand glass plates, some of which were sold to Tiffany for jewellery designs.

Herbert Spencer, the famous nineteenth-century philosopher, first coined the phrase "survival of the fittest". Spencer was a fussy traveller. Whenever he had to go somewhere by train he always took with him his own chair, a large supply of rugs and cushions and a hammock. He also carried with him his manuscripts wrapped in brown paper and tied to his waist with a piece of string. Spencer also had an irresistible urge to keep checking his pulse. It was something he had to do even in the most inappropriate situations, as one of Spencer's biographers recorded: "The carriage was at once brought to a standstill no matter where he might be, whether in a quiet place or in the middle of the busiest traffic in Regent Street. Silence reigned therein for some few seconds in order that he might feel his pulse. If it was regular the driver continued. If not, and he feared injurious consequences, the order was given to return home."

Although not quite as famous as his contemporaries Thomas Edison and Guglielmo Marconi, the Serbian scientist Nicola Tesla (1856–1943) is recognized as one of the greats in the history of electricity. He invented the induction motor and alternating current power transmission and was responsible for the first commercial use of AC motors and generators. Even as a small child Tesla loved to experiment. Once he perched on the roof of the barn, clutching the family umbrella, convinced he could fly. He plunged to earth and lay unconscious for a while until he was carried off to bed by his mother. Another childhood experiment, his sixteen-bug-power motor, was made of splinters forming a windmill, with a spindle and pulley attached to live June bugs. When the glued insects beat their wings the bug-power engine prepared to take off. This line of research was abandoned when a young friend dropped by who fancied the taste of June bugs. Noticing a jarful standing near, he began cramming them into his mouth. The young Tesla watched in horror then threw up. As a student, Tesla's obsessive behaviour revealed itself in his extraordinary powers of concentration and self-discipline. Once, on a whim, he decided to read the complete works of Voltaire. He had no idea at this point that the works of Voltaire spanned one hundred volumes of small, dense print. Although it almost resulted in a mental breakdown, Tesla refused to quit until he had finished reading the lot. In the 1880s he claimed that his hearing had become hypersensitive. He claimed that he could hear a clock ticking three rooms away, the whistle of a steam engine twenty miles away, and the landing of a fly on a nearby table as a loud thump.

Tesla emigrated to the United States in 1884 and became a US citizen in 1891. At one time he worked for Thomas Edison at the Edison Machine Works, but after a year he resigned over a financial dispute and the two men became bitter rivals. As Edison was a champion of direct current (DC) power the two men became embroiled in an acrimonious and often petty public dispute over the relative merits of AC and DC power which lasted for many years. In the 1890s Tesla was famous for his showmanship, especially his striking public demonstrations of electrical power. At the Chicago World Fair in 1893 he ran 200,000 volts through his own body. Newspaper reports said that his clothing and body continued to glow for some time after the current was switched off. Tesla informed his audience that a similar surge of power could keep a naked man warm at the north pole. He also advocated electrical power as an anaesthetic, recommended that lethargic schoolchildren should be wired to their desks and given shock treatment, and suggested that actors could be "stimulated" by running electrical surges through their bodies before performances.

Tesla suffered from a combination of compulsive-obsessive disorders that turned his daily life into a series of bizarre rituals. He spent most of his adult life in expensive New York hotels where his irrational behaviour became a daily trial of the hotel staff's patience. He suffered from various numerical obsessions, especially one with the number three. He always insisted that his sheets, towels and napkins were provided in numbers divisible by three. Before entering his hotel he was compelled to walk around the block three times, always counting his steps to make sure the total number was divisible by three. He chose room numbers that were divisible by three. He also had a fear of germs and insisted on doing his own dusting and cleaning, and washed his hands obsessively. Before meal times he always phoned the hotel in advance with detailed instructions for preparations for his meals. He demanded precisely eighteen clean napkins and towels each day. He would sit down and inspect each napkin in turn, then discard them in a pile in the middle of the table. Before eating he would then move on to counting every item of crockery and cutlery on the table.

Also in the 1890s Tesla began experimenting with X-rays, a recent discovery by Wilhelm von Roentgen. At first he was blissfully unaware of the dangers and took part in horrific experiments on both himself and his laboratory assistants. He repeatedly exposed his head to X-rays "to stimulate the brain". He wrote, "An outline of the skull is easily obtained with an exposure of 30 to 40 minutes. In one instance an exposure of 40 minutes gave clearly not only the outline but the cavity of the eye, the lower jaw and connections to the upper one, the vertebral column and connections to the skull, the flesh and even the hair." He noted later, however, "In a severe case the skin gets deeply coloured and blackened in places and ugly, ill-foreboding blisters form; thick layers come off, exposing the raw flesh. Burning pain, feverishness and such symptoms are natural accompaniments. One single injury of this kind in the abdominal region of a dear and zealous assistant – the only accident that ever happened to anyone but myself in all my laboratory experience – I had the misfortune to witness."

Tesla was a prolific inventor of projects that never really took off. One Tesla invention was the trans-Atlantic mail tube. To post a letter, the sender would insert it in a water-tight container at one end and a huge pump would force water through the tube, shooting the letter from Europe to America. Another of his discoveries was a vibrating platform that had a strong laxative effect. His good friend Mark Twain, claimed Tesla, once stayed on the platform too long and had to run for the toilet. Tesla built a powerful radio receiver in his lab, and in 1900 announced to the world that he was receiving messages from Mars. The British physicist Lord Kelvin was the first to congratulate Tesla on his remarkable discovery. Kelvin went on to explain that Mars was indeed sending messages to America and not, say, England, because New York was "the most marvellous lighted city in the world" and the only place visible from Mars. The majority of the scientific community were more disposed to ridicule Tesla's claim and demanded proof of his "discovery" – proof that Tesla declined to offer.

Tesla never married and was celibate all his life, apparently believing that sex was a drain on creativity. He told a reporter who asked why he had never married, "I do not think you can name many great inventions that have been made by married men." He also had a couple of phobias however that made dating difficult, especially his revulsion for women's jewellery, especially earrings and pearls in any form and the fact that he could never bring himself to touch anyone else's hair, except, he once admitted, "perhaps at the point of a revolver".

Tesla had trouble forming relationships with people but he was obsessed with pigeons. He spent the last years of his life, like "the bird man of Alcatraz", holed up in the Waldorf Astoria completely surrounded by pigeons, living exclusively on a diet of warm milk and Nabisco crackers. He was a regular but moderate drinker and believed that alcohol was an elixir. He also had a long-standing prediction that he would live to the age of 140. When the US Constitution embraced Prohibition in 1919 he withdrew his prediction because he thought his health would suffer. He died of a heart attack aged eighty-six. A maid who had not heard from him for several days ignored the "Do Not Disturb" sign on his New York hotel door and discovered the emaciated corpse of the scientist on his bed.

Girolamo Cardano, the Italian mathematician and astrologer, was renowned as a sixteenth-century Russell Grant, and was so famous that he drew up horoscopes for the crowned heads of Europe, including England's young King Edward VI. Success gave Cardano an inflated view of his own self-importance. He predicted his own death, down to the very hour. When the time arrived and Cardano found himself in robust good health, he topped himself rather than be proved wrong.

The Irish scientist Richard Kirwan (1744–1812) was internationally famous for his studies in minerology, geology and meteorology. His pioneering work included systems for forecasting the weather, many of which are in use to this day. Kirwan suffered from a rare throat disorder called dysphagia, which made it difficult for him to swallow. He was sorely embarrassed by his problem and was terrified by the prospect of other people seeing him eat. His entire diet comprised ham and milk – the ham was always cooked on Sunday and reheated every day for the rest of the week. Although he always ate alone, Kirwan was a renowned conversationalist and his home became a regular meeting place for famous scientists. Every Thursday and Friday he invited guests for music and conversation. These soirées always began promptly at six p.m. and ended at nine p.m. He had a subtle system to ensure that no one arrived or left late. He removed the door knocker after the party had begun and any guests remaining at nine p.m. would be escorted to the door by their host in his pyjamas.

Kirwan was also a hypochondriac and went to extreme lengths to avoid catching colds. His living room had a huge fire blazing all year round and he took to wearing a hat indoors lest his body heat should escape through his head. Kirwan believed that the body could store heat, rather like a large Thermos flask. He occasionally braved the elements to walk his several large dogs, and to exercise his tamed eagle, which always sat on his shoulder; he had trained the bird to be loyal by starving it. Before venturing outside he would sit for an hour in front of his huge fire to absorb the heat. Once outside he would walk very briskly, with his mouth tightly shut so that no body heat would escape. Naturally, he refused to talk to anyone while he was walking. Kirwan's servant, a man named Pope, was required to sleep in the scientist's bedroom. Pope had instructions to wake Kirwan every couple of hours and pour hot tea down his throat. The point of this nocturnal tea drinking was to maintain Kirwan's body temperature through the night. Ironically, Kirwan caught a chill and died aged seventy-nine.

The great British philosopher Jeremy Bentham (1748–1832) was so cripplingly shy that he shunned social interaction of any kind. He could never bring himself to tolerate more than one visitor at a time and the thought of meeting a stranger for the first time filled him with dread. He even found contact with people by post difficult. He frequently wrote letters to fellow philosophers only to lose his nerve and not send them. Bentham substituted animals for human companionship, especially his numerous pet rats, which he allowed to nibble on and ruin his writings. After his death Bentham's friends and students had to piece together and rewrite some of his most important works from the tattered remains of his rat-ravaged manuscripts.

Bentham also had a strange habit of giving names to inanimate objects, including ordinary household articles. He had a favourite walking stick called "Dapple". His rare visitors were bemused to hear him address his teapot as "Dick". Bentham hardly ever stopped writing. When ideas came to him he would jot them down, pin them to the walls or the curtains or just leave them lying on the floor. Ideas came so thick and fast to him that he worked at times literally knee deep in pieces of paper. He frequently lost track of what he had written. One day he came across his important paper on parliamentary reform. He wrote on the cover, "What can this be? Surely this was never my opinion?" When Bentham wasn't writing copious reams of notes he dreamed up inventions. He thought up "conversation tubes" which were to be laid between houses, like water pipes. He also designed a "frigidarium", a type of igloo-shaped cold house for storing meat, including his "bullock hearts, calves' hearts and liver, rabbits and chickens, sprats and smelts, oysters and salmon". He also drew up plans for a "panopticon" – a radically new type of prison, based on a huge wheel shape, with an inspector at the hub able to see everything going on inside via a series of reflectors.

Thomas A. Edison, Jr was born in 1876 to the first wife of the famous inventor of the same name. Like many fathers of the Victorian era Edison had little involvement in the upbringing of his children, a situation aggravated by his impossibly long work hours. Young Tom Edison spent his childhood away from his parents living in boarding schools, where he was a poor student with few friends. Motherless at an early age, he grew increasingly bitter and hostile towards his remote famous dad. His name also burdened him with unusually high expectations. Unfortunately Edison Junior did not have the same temperament or talent as his father. He was a strange, sickly and sensitive young man who tried to mask his insecurities with very heavy drinking. In 1899 he married an alcoholic actress named Mary Touhey who took advantage of his name before running off with his best friend a year later. She was the first of many to capitalize on the Edison family name. Tom Junior was to become the figurehead for many outlandish enterprises. In the late 1890s he fronted such companies as the Thomas A. Edison, Jr Chemical Co., makers of "Wizard Ink" tablets and the "Magno-Electric Vitalizer", a patent cure-all for everything from rheumatism to deafness; the Edison Jr Electric Light and Power Company, and the Thomas A. Edison, Jr Improved Incandescent Lamp Co. These products were sold with some outrageously misleading advertising material under headings including "The Brain Of Edison Has Achieved Another Triumph" and "The Latest Edison Discovery". The Magno-Electric Vitalizer had a sixty-page sales brochure including a form to return to Tom Junior, detailing the patient's specific problems, which Tom Junior supposedly "personally" reviewed in order to give specific instructions on how to use the machine. The US government shut down the company for fraud in 1904. In an affidavit entered in the court by the senior Thomas Edison, he stated that "his son has never shown any ability as an inventor or electrical expert, and that deponent believes his said son is incapable of making any invention or discovery of merit". The *New York Times* reported, "Accompanying the papers is a statement from young Mr Edison saying he did not work out the vitalizer, but that others designed it and he merely signed the application for the patent that was sought by the promoter of the scheme. He denies that he gave any attention to the business of the concern, but admits that he drew a salary of $35 a week from it."

He began to concoct a series of wild business ideas of his own, none of which came to fruition. His father noted with disgust, "His head is now so swelled that I can do nothing with him, he is being used by some sharp people for their own ends. I could never get him to go to school or work in the laboratory, he is therefore absolutely illiterate scientifically or otherwise." By the turn of the century Tom Junior was passing bad cheques, drinking even more heavily and was under investigation for mail fraud. The Edison name continued to be used for all sorts of shady enterprises. Edison Senior finally went to court and obtained an injunction to forbid his son from using his name in commercial enterprises and legally disowned him. In 1903 however the family lawyer negotiated a peace treaty between the estranged father and son, by which Edison agreed to give Tom Junior an allowance of $35 a week in return for which his son was to stop exploiting the Edison name.

Until the 1920s Tom Junior lived under a pseudonym, calling himself Burton Willard or Thomas Willard. Edison set his son up on a mushroom farm in New Jersey, where he lived with his second wife Beatrice, sinking deeper into alcoholism. In the 1920s his stepbrother Charles managed to get him a menial job in the Edison laboratory, but he continued to fight a losing battle with the bottle and on 25 August 1935 Thomas A. Edison, Jr died under an assumed name in a hotel in Springfield, Massachusetts. His death, as his life, was a tragic mystery. Some Edison biographers believe that he committed suicide, others claim that he died of heart disease.

The physicist and chemist Henry Cavendish (1731–1810) has been acclaimed as probably the greatest of all eighteenth-century scientists. Although his brilliant research spanned many fields his contribution to science was never fully acclaimed in his lifetime because he was too pathologically shy to accept public acclaim. Many of his most important discoveries were wrongly attributed to other scientists. His agonizing fear of any social interaction kept him from publishing most of his experimental findings, so that the real breadth of his contribution remained a secret until well after his death.

In an era of first-rate experimenters, Cavendish was the best. He was the first to identify the element hydrogen and to discover that water was not, as was then believed, an element in itself, but a compound of hydrogen and oxygen. He did pioneering work with condensers and discovered the rules of electrical resistance more than half a century before they were quantified by German scientist Ohm. At sixty-seven, he calculated the mean density of the planet. He outlined the molecular basis of heat long before the theory was publicized by a rival. However, these groundbreaking achievements lay hidden in notebooks read by no one but Cavendish during his lifetime.

The reclusive genius was born into one of England's wealthiest and most distinguished families. Henry's father, Lord Charles Cavendish, was brother to the third duke of Devonshire and a distinguished scientist in his own right. Although Henry was probably the richest man of science who ever lived, he was extremely shabby in appearance. He wore clothes that were fifty years behind the style, topped with a tricorne hat. As he refused to sit for portraits the only likeness of him ever done from life was a watercolour sketch, secretly composed from a distance. There was one subject however that Cavendish absolutely refused to discuss, and it was money; he was entirely uninterested in it. When his banker asked him what he should do with the fortune left to Cavendish by his father, the scientist rebuked him for bothering him with so trifling a matter. Whenever Cavendish was asked for charitable contributions, he would simply look up the largest previous donation and match it.

Cavendish was an obsessively private individual to a degree that went way beyond any ordinary shyness or social phobia. Lord Brougham once said of him, "Cavendish uttered fewer words in the course of his life than any man who ever lived to fourscore years, not at all excepting Trappist monks." He was a prominent member of the Royal Society but he hardly ever spoke at meetings, and then only on technical matters. The only people who ever got to talk with him were fellow scientists and even they were only able to squeeze a few stammered words out of him. When he was once recognized and praised by a foreign visitor to the Society, Cavendish fled in mortified silence. New members were advised to talk to the great scientist without looking at him. When someone broke the rule, Cavendish ran ashen-faced from the building. He was especially shy of women. He kept in touch with his female household staff by leaving notes for them with instructions for his meals; as he only ever ate mutton, the notes were usually brief. His staff were given orders to keep completely out of his sight at all times – if he saw one of them, even by accident, they were dismissed. Eventually he had a second staircase built for his servants' use so he could avoid them more easily.

Cavendish couldn't even bear human company on his deathbed. As he lay dying he told his servants that he had "something to think about" and didn't want to be disturbed. They left the room and he died alone, aged seventy-eight. Cavendish left his estate to his closest relative, Lord George Cavendish. During his lifetime, this nephew was only ever granted an annual audience of half an hour and could have had no idea how much his inheritance was worth. In fact the will revealed Cavendish to be the largest holder of bank shares in

Britain. Caring nothing about money, he had let his neglected fortune grow, unattended, to a value of some £1,750,000.

The eminent Victorian mathematical physicist Oliver Heaviside (1850–1925) established the foundation of modern electric circuit design and his work made possible, amongst many other things, long distance telephone. Heaviside was born in a London slum and had no formal education after the age of sixteen but became regarded by his peers as the greatest scientific mind of the age. In 1870 Heaviside became a telegraph operator in Denmark – it was to be the only paid job he ever had. In 1874, at the age of twenty-four, he "retired" and decided to spend the rest of his life in private study in a darkened, tightly shuttered room. His friends and family were appalled by his decision to give up work but did their best to support him, often by anonymously leaving trays of food outside the door of his room. Heaviside's choice of diet was eccentric, as he would occasionally go for days living on bowls of milk, like a cat. Heaviside suffered from an inferiority complex, often signing his correspondence "WORM". He also suffered from a morbid fear of dying from hypothermia. Around the house he wrapped himself in several layers of blankets and wore a tea cosy on his head. He required increasing quantities of fuel to keep his house at an unusually high temperature and spent his last years in a running battle with the gas board over unpaid bills. He narrowly escaped with his life when he once opened up a mains gas pipe and ignited it, causing a huge jet of flame to singe his hair and clothing.

Heaviside kept his housekeeper, Mary Way, a virtual prisoner. He forbade her to leave the house without his permission, prevented her from seeing her friends and got her to sign a series of contracts which effectively controlled her movements until she was to all intents and purposes a slave, cut off completely from the outside world. She remained thus for seven or eight years until she was rescued by a member of her family. A niece arrived in a car one day without warning, and finding her aunt in a near catatonic state whisked her away, leaving behind most of her belongings. Heaviside, when asked to explain her disappearance, asserted that she "had become mad and had to be put away".

For the last seventeen years of his life he lived as a hermit in a small seaside cottage in Devonshire. He replaced all his furniture with granite blocks and painted his nails a brilliant cherry pink. His neighbours, mostly unaware of the great scientific achievements, shunned him as a lunatic. He died of complications after falling from the top of a ladder.

Dr Paul Erdös was one of the most gifted mathematicians of all time with more than 1500 published papers to his credit. Erdös was born into a Hungarian-Jewish family in 1913. He founded the field of discrete mathematics, the basis of computer science. He lived as a homeless derelict, shunning material possessions, because "property is nuisance", and travelling from lecture to lecture with a tatty suitcase containing all his meagre belongings. He had no interest in anything but numbers. He died aged eighty-three while attending a maths lecture in Warsaw. Erdös was repulsed by human contact, even the accidental touch of another person, and was appalled by the idea of sexual intercourse.

The physical and mental well-being of Charles Robert Darwin (1809–82), the naturalist whose discovery of the theory of evolution by natural selection revolutionized biology, has always been something of a mystery. When Darwin returned from his famous voyage he immediately began drawing up lists of the benefits and drawbacks of marriage. He may have been the first person to elucidate on the dangers of inbreeding, but he wasn't quite bright enough to avoid marrying his own first cousin Emma – a poor idea as there were signs of eccentricity on both sides of a family which was already dangerously inbred. His grandmother and great-grandfather were unstable drunks, his uncle Erasmus was insane and committed suicide, and his brother Erasmus was a chronic and neurotic invalid. His grandfather, yet another Erasmus, had a terrible stammer, was considered a leading expert on the treatment of the mentally ill, and had whirling beds and gyrating chairs fitted into most of the country's lunatic asylums so that patients could be rotated until blood poured out of their ears, eyes and noses. Charles Darwin himself was also a stammerer and a morose hypochondriac: he suffered from fainting fits and would take to his bed for months on end.

Charles and Emma Darwin had ten children; two died in infancy and a third died aged ten. The surviving five sons went away to boarding school; three became distinguished scientists, and one, a major in the army, was also an engineer and eugenicist. Darwin was devoted to his wife and daughters but treated them like children. His wife had to ask him for the keys to all the drawers, cupboards and other locked depositories in the house.

Within a year of his voyage Darwin retreated to the countryside and became a virtual recluse. He was worried about alienating and offending people with his theory of evolution. Darwin was inherently conservative and his fear of ostracism was one reason he waited before publishing it. Darwin felt particularly bad about the pain his views would inflict on his close Christian friends and especially his wife Emma. Some believe that Darwin's anxiety about this caused him to have a mental breakdown. The once carefree and adventurous young naturalist became a semi-invalid and a hermit before his fortieth year. Over the years doctors have continued to puzzle over Darwin's condition and have suggested diagnoses such as parasitic disease, arsenic poisoning, depression, epilepsy and inner ear disorder.

The Oxford don Richard Porson, a friend and contemporary of literary giants Lord Byron and Samuel Rogers, was famous for his Keith Richards-like capacity for alcohol and late night drinking sprees. Porson was a huge man and immensely strong – he once carried a young woman around his Temple chambers by his teeth for a bet. The ravages of alcoholism took their toll most obviously upon his nose, which he often disguised by covering it with a cone made from a scrap of brown paper. He was usually to be seen shuffling around in a large black coat covered with cobwebs. His epic stamina had the Fellows at Trinity in awe. Porson, it was said, could "drink all night and talk all day". He once downed a whole bottle of embrocation, and on another occasion drank spirits from a lamp, mistaking it for gin. On one of his academic visits to Germany, the learned Greek scholar Professor Porson wrote:

> I went to Frankfurt, and got drunck
> With that most learned Professor Brunck;
> I went to Würtz, and got more druncken
> With that more learned Professor Runcken.

Porson was once invited to dine with Horne Tooke, who knew about his guest's reputation but reasonably assumed that as Porson had not slept for the previous seventy-two hours he could be assured of an early night. Tooke had miscalculated; Porson kept his host awake, drinking all night. In the morning the flagging Tooke, desperate to be rid of his guest, pretended that he had to meet someone in a local coffee house. The plan misfired when Porson offered to go with him. When they were a safe distance from the house Tooke slipped away and ran home, instructing his servants not to answer the door if Porson followed him.

Albert Einstein (1879–1955) once said that the following was about the most characteristic anecdote that could be told of him. Einstein and an assistant, having finished an important paper, searched the office for a paper clip. He finally found one, but it was too badly bent for use. He looked for an implement to straighten it, and after opening many more drawers came upon a whole box of clips. Einstein at once shaped one into a tool to straighten the bent clip. His assistant, puzzled, asked why he was doing this when there was a whole boxful of usable clips. "Once I am set on a goal it becomes difficult to deflect me," said Einstein. The journal *Scientific American* once ran a competition for the best exposition of relativity in three thousand words. A prize of several thousand dollars was at stake. "I'm the only one in my entire circle of friends who is not entering," remarked Einstein ruefully. "I don't believe I could do it."

John Burden Sanderson "JBS" Haldane was one of the best known British scientists of the twentieth century, thanks largely to a series of hugely popular science articles he wrote in the national press which helped make him a household name. Haldane was a brilliant academic, especially in the fields of mathematics and genetics. In 1914 he left Oxford with a double first at the age of twenty-two. He went straight into the army and was posted to France where he served with enthusiasm until he was almost blown up by a shell and had to be taken away in a field ambulance driven by the Prince of Wales, the future King Edward VIII. At one point Haldane neglected to remove his boots for three weeks, which caused General Haig to observe that he was "the bravest and the dirtiest soldier in the army". After the war Haldane became interested in politics; he started out as a Liberal, later became a socialist and ended up communist. Haldane was larger than life in every sense. He was a formidable presence at around seventeen stone, and for a while volunteered as a bouncer at Labour Party rallies. His habit of removing hecklers by sticking a finger up each nostril them hauling them backwards up the aisle "like hooked trout" alarmed his fellow party workers sufficiently to get him sacked.

In his quest for scientific knowledge JBS subjected his own body to a bizarre and horrific series of experiments. To test one theory he drank a bottle of hydrochloric acid then cycled home to see what effect it would have. To test another he swallowed a near-fatal dose of calcium chloride, which resulted in violent diarrhoea followed by painful constipation. To probe his lung capacity, he swallowed one and a half ounces of bicarbonate of soda then ran up and down a 150-foot flight of stairs twenty times. JBS was also prepared to experiment on others without necessarily giving them any warning. At a public meeting on the dangers of gas in trench warfare, his unwitting audience watched as JBS vaporized a spoonful of pepper over a spirit lamp, causing the hall to fill with pungent smoke. As people fled for the exits with their eyes streaming and gasping for air, he shouted after them, "If that upsets you, how would you like a deluge of poison gas from an air fleet in real war?"

JBS was merely maintaining a family tradition of academic eccentricity. His father "Uffa" was years ahead of his time when he announced his dislike of performing scientific experiments on animals, often preferring to carry them out on himself. His kindness to animals however did not extend to rats. He once filled a ship's hold full of them, then pumped the sealed area full of sulphur dioxide to test its effectiveness as a rat poison. He ran around the ship amid the noxious vapours, holding his breath, to see how many dead rats he could remove before he passed out. On this occasion, as on many others the young JBS accompanied his father. In one of the more bizarre experiments, father and son crawled for miles along a narrow coal seam until they found a pocket of methane gas. The young JBS was instructed to stand up and recite a passage from Shakespeare, which he attempted to do before passing out. JBS recovered consciousness to hear his father inform him, "You have just learned that gas, being lighter than air, always rises."

William Buckland, Professor of Geology at Oxford, was responsible for the world's first description of a recognized dinosaur fossil when, in 1824, he published "Notice on the Megalosaurus or Great Fossil Lizard of Stonesfield". He was a deeply religious man who devoted his life to using geology to support scripture, although his eccentric methods were often criticized by theologians and scientists alike. During a public lecture he once strutted about the room imitating the gait of giant birds he believed left their footprints in ancient deposits, causing one of his colleagues to scoff, "The grossness of the Buffoonery acted on me like an emetic." Buckland hit the headlines briefly in 1875 with his dramatic discovery of dinosaur dung in Lyme Regis, until his "find" was denounced as a fraud by the Royal Geographical Society.

Buckland earned more notoriety as an eccentric epicure; he enjoyed a reputation for having an extraordinarily well developed sense of taste. One dark winter's night he was travelling to London by horse with a friend when they became lost. Buckland dismounted, picked up a handful of earth, and tasted it. "Uxbridge!" he announced triumphantly, then set off on his way. He devoted his spare time to travelling the world indulging in bizarre gastronomic experiences. At times his breath variously smelled of crocodile, hedgehog, mole, roast joint of bear and puppy. Buckland was prepared to eat anything that moved, although he admitted that he wasn't too wild about horse and said the foulest thing he ever ate was stewed mole and bluebottle. Buckland's most unusual claim was to have eaten the heart of King Louis XIV, which had been plundered from its grave during the French revolution and had found its way into the possession of Buckland's friend the Archbishop of York.

For the long-suffering Mrs Buckland there were even more trying times ahead. Their son Francis not only inherited but pushed to new limits his father's indiscriminate eating habits. After experimenting on his fellow students at Oxford by cooking them mice on toast, Buckland Junior went on to form the Society for the Acclimatization of Animals in the United Kingdom, ostensibly to teach the British public how they could ease food shortages by eating new types of meat, but mainly as an excuse for Buckland and his strange pals to munch their way through boiled and fried slices of porpoise head, boiled elephant trunk, grilled panther, garden snails, slug soup and earwigs. Visitors to the surgeon and naturalist's Euston home had to put up with many surprises. Friends arrived one day and found him making a rhinoceros pie, which he later said tasted not unlike very old beef. He served his visitors alligator or mice on buttered toast. The famous anatomist Richard Owen and his wife were served roast ostrich. His home was a menagerie. In his living room resided his beloved monkeys, which did terrible damage and bit everyone in the house. He plied these favourites with beer every night, and a drop of port on Sundays. A mongoose and several pet rats also had the run of the house. Apart from the living creatures, the house was crammed with stuffed specimens, including snakes and green frogs kept in cases in his dining room. At a formal Society dinner in 1862 Francis and his friends enjoyed a blowout of steamed and boiled kangaroo, wild boar, roasted parrot and leperine. Buckland's piece de resistance was stewed Japanese sea slug. Buckland wrote, "They are said to be the most succulent and pleasant food, not unlike the green fat of turtle," although he later admitted that they actually tasted more like the contents of a glue pot.

In 1861 Buckland discovered a new love that was to occupy him for the rest of his life – fish farming. He joked that he had hatched 30,000 salmon in his kitchen in Albany Street, and as that fish always returned to its birthplace he anticipated that he was going to need a bigger house. Much of Buckland's money was spent setting up a museum of fish culture in South Kensington. Queen Victoria went to see it and was so impressed she invited him to visit her at Frogmore. In 1867 Buckland was appointed Inspector of HM Salmon Fisheries. This job required him to travel the country, making sure that salmon could negotiate weirs and other man-made obstacles on their way to the sea. At one particularly difficult spot he left the salmon a notice: "No road at present over this weir. Go downstream, take the first turn to the right and you will find good travelling water upstream and no jumping required – F.T.B."

Buckland cared little for personal comfort or his appearance. He became a well known figure on the railways, but because he so often stank of fish he was usually given a carriage to himself. In winter he would rub himself all over with hair oil and wear a waterproof suit, which often froze solid and clung to him like armour. As a result of asthma and inflammation of the lungs however he had to abandon his outdoor work. When his surgeons wanted to operate on him he refused chloroform because he wanted to watch them work. He died in December 1880. In his will he had written: "God is so good, so very good to little fishes. I do not believe he would let their inspector suffer shipwreck at last. I am going on a long journey where I think I shall see a great many curious animals . . . this journey I must go alone."

The great sixteenth-century Danish astronomer Tycho Brahe wore an artificial nose made from silver and gold.

Sir Isaac Newton (1642–1727) spent a large amount of his time trying to change base metals into gold. His laboratory assistant Humphrey Newton (no relation) noted that the great scientist was obsessed with alchemy and spent many sleepless nights poring over mystical texts. Sir Isaac also had a few other unconventional ideas; he claimed that the mathematical formulae in his *Principia*, which contained some of the cornerstones of modern science, were first revealed by God to a group of mystics at the dawn of civilization, a tradition to which Newton was chosen as heir. He may even have experienced a period of insanity because of his experiments with mercury: he fell ill immediately after boiling several pounds of it.

Newton was extremely absent-minded. One day he invited a friend to dinner, then forgot all about it. When the guest arrived he found his host in a trance-like state, so lost in thought that he forgot to eat his dinner even when it was brought up and laid out on the table before him. Eventually the guest decided, at the risk of being rude, to eat his meal. Newton subsequently snapped out of his trance and became aware of his guest and the empty dishes before him. "Well, really," exclaimed the scientist. "If it weren't for the proof before my eyes, I could have sworn that I had not yet eaten."

The great nineteenth-century naturalist and explorer Charles Waterton became famous after the publication in 1826 of his book *Wandering in South America*, the result of many years spent in an unknown jungle often entirely alone. During his research in the rainforests Waterton spent six months sleeping with his foot dangling out of his hammock in the hope that he would be bitten by a vampire bat. He confessed to being "bitterly disappointed" when "the provoking brutes" failed to take the bait. In Guiana he watched as his native guides struggled to capture a large boa constrictor. Waterton simply ordered them to stand aside, then he removed his braces and tied them around the snake's jaws. He once also captured a crocodile by jumping on its back, hanging on to the front legs. He observed afterwards that it had been no more difficult than riding with his local hunt. Waterton was extremely scruffy, his clothes so shabby that he was often mistaken for a vagrant. They were also smelly and very stiff, the result of his insistence upon habitually dipping them in biochloride of mercury, a substance he used to preserve his natural history specimens from decay.

When he retired to Walton Hall in West Yorkshire in the 1820s he created a large animal sanctuary on his estate. At the time this in itself was considered highly eccentric. It was what he did with them when they died however that was truly odd. He found orthodox taxidermy too boring and kept himself amused by grafting stuffed parts of different animals on to each other in grotesque combinations. One such creation – he called it the Nondescript – looked much like the head of a bearded man, but was made from the skin of a howler monkey. He created a bird he called Noctifer by combining parts of a bittern with a barn owl. Waterton also enjoyed imitating animals. He liked to surprise visitors by hiding in the hallway, crouched on all fours, then biting their legs as they hung up their coats. On one occasion he disconcerted his dinner guests by displaying the partially dissected corpse of a gorilla on his dining table. When he wasn't shocking them with his gruesome collection of dead animals, Waterton might demonstrate to his guests the benefits of being double-jointed by spending the entire meal with his foot wedged behind his ear.

After the premature death of his wife he refused to sleep in a bed. For the remaining thirty-five years of his life he spent every night lying on the floor wrapped in a cloak with a block of wood for a pillow. He was a remarkably fit man, thanks to his spartan lifestyle. He rose at 3:30 a.m., spent an hour at prayer, then breakfasted on dry toast and watercress and weak tea. He was still climbing trees at the age of eighty-three; his death in 1865 was caused by a fall from one.

The distinguished scientist Sir Humphry Davy (1778–1829), inventor of the coalminer's Davy lamp, was an enthusiastic angler. When he fished he always disguised himself as a form of natural greenery – he wore a green coat, green trousers and a green hat. According to a fellow angler, "Davy flattered himself he resembled vegetable life as closely as it was possible to do." When he went shooting however Davy did exactly the opposite. As he didn't trust the marksmanship of his fellow sportsmen he made himself as conspicuous as possible to avoid being shot by mistake by wearing brightly coloured clothing and a huge wide-rimmed bright red hat.

John Cleves Symmes, US Army veteran, shopkeeper and self-taught scientist, was born in Sussex County, New Jersey in 1780. Symmes, an avid bookworm, was one day hit by the blinding revelation that Sir Isaac Newton had got it all completely wrong and that gravity was the result of an atmosphere "filled with microscopically invisible hollow spheres of ether". There was more; the Earth was hollow, with room inside for five other planets. Furthermore there were gaping holes at both the north and south poles, and it was possible to sail into them to discover what was going on inside. Inside the hollow Earth, he conjectured with some excitement, we would no doubt discover another race of human beings, animal and life and lush vegetation. Symmes searched through science books to look for supporting evidence for his conclusions and uncovered some more interesting theories. The Babylonians, for example, thought that the world was a hollow mountain, supported and surrounded by the sea. Inside the mountain lay the world of the dead. Symmes also came across the writings of a Professor Burnet, who taught that the Earth had been a small core covered with oil, to which the fluid of the atmosphere had stuck, thus forming the Earth's crust. Another eminent professor thought the Earth comprised separate strata, similar to onion rings. Yet another believed that the Earth was a large egg, with a shell, albumen and yolk. Symmes was particularly excited however by the teachings of a German mathematician who propounded that inside the Earth was another planet, complete with a flourishing civilization. He was finally convinced when he read that Halley, the great seventeenth-century astronomer, had speculated about other planets beneath the Earth's crust.

In 1818 Symmes set out to raise money to finance a great expedition that would prove his theory once and for all. From his Missouri shop he mailed 500 pamphlets to the wealthy and influential, thoughtfully including a medical certificate stating that he was sane. His mailing produced few takers, so he moved his family to Newport, Kentucky, where he believed he would meet more people with money and power. He embarked on a lecture tour, drawing large crowds of incredulous Americans. His audiences sat in open-mouthed astonishment as he told them about the fantastic underworld that lay beneath the Earth's crust. Symmes was at his most persuasive when there were few people prepared to ask probing questions. He flew into a dreadful temper at the slightest sign of ridicule or cynicism. On those who were prepared to take his words at face value, however, including US congressman Richard M. Johnson, Symmes made a terrific impression. The gullible Johnson, who went on to become Vice-President, was so taken by Symmes's theories that he actually asked Congress to fit out two ships for the proposed expedition to the centre of the Earth. After brief discussion, Congress passed over Johnson's project as "unsound". Symmes was undeterred by this setback and renewed his arguments. By 1823 he had raised a petition bearing the names of hundreds of people who were prepared to support him, including some very distinguished Americans. He pointed out that his expedition not only would rewrite the science books, but was also full of exciting commercial possibilities. Johnson was thus persuaded to put Symmes's case a second time. A vote was taken in the House of Representatives; this time a minority of twenty-five congressmen indicated their readiness to send him to Siberia with as many reindeer, sleighs and "brave comrades" as he needed. Symmes continued with his strenuous lecture tours, but his expedition never came to pass. Halfway through an arduous lecture tour of Canada in 1829 he was taken ill and died, aged forty-nine.

Symmes's story had a happy ending, of sorts. His son, Americus Vespucius Symmes, gathered together all his late father's writings and had them published in a book, *Symmes' Theory of Concentric Spheres and Polar Voids*. Symmes Junior was a firm believer in his father's theories and had one or two of his own, including his conviction that the ten lost tribes of Israel would one day be discovered deep beneath the Earth's crust. The writer Jules Verne came across the Symmes book and used it as the basis for his novel *Journey to the Centre of the Earth*.

Chapter Four

Political Eccentrics

"Personally I am a great believer in bed, in constantly keeping horizontal. The heart and everything go slower and the whole system is refreshed"
>Sir Henry Campbell-Bannerman (1836–1908),
>British Prime Minister

"If you have a mother-in-law with only one eye and she has it in the centre of her forehead, you don't keep her in the living room"
>Lyndon Baines Johnson (1908–73), US President,
>when asked about his policy on Vietnam

"Driving alternately at high and low rates of speed; stopping at every filling station on the highway, walking around the car, always looking, then going on; entering a dark street in a residential area at night, making a sharp U-turn, pulling into a side alley and extinguishing the car's lights; entering a heavily travelled intersection on a yellow light, hoping to lose any followers or cause an accident"

> J. Edgar Hoover (1895–1972), transvestite head
> of the FBI, explaining the give-away traits
> of a Communist

"We are a grandmother"

> Margaret Hilda Thatcher (b.1925),
> British Prime Minister

Peter Bowen was an unsuccessful candidate for governor of Missouri in 1998. During his campaign Bowen, a disciple of the American right-winger Lyndon Larouche, told an audience of students that rock music "stimulated sexual frenzy", lambasted sheep for spreading AIDS by coughing, attacked Buckingham Palace for holding "homosexual parties upstairs", and accused the FBI of framing Larouche followers with credit card fraud. He added that the birthmark on former Soviet leader Mikhail Gorbachev's forehead was the Satanic mark of the Beast, citing as conclusive proof the fact that Gorbachev hardly ever agreed to be photographed without his hat.

Thirty-six-year-old David Griffiths was expelled from the Twickenham branch of the Conservative Association in 1995 because his views were considered too right wing. Griffiths told a meeting in August of that year that he favoured the death penalty for all crimes, that homosexuals should be encouraged to commit suicide and that people who claim social security should gun each other down on the street. Griffiths returned to politics a year later when he ran for the Twickenham seat in the 1996 General Election as the Antichrist. He said that he had been aware that he was the Antichrist for some time, but had kept quiet about it in case it damaged his career in the Conservative Party.

British Prime Minister Lord Salisbury was so scruffy that he was once arrested by a farmer who thought he was a poacher. While Prime Minister in 1866 he was actually refused admission to the Casino at Monte Carlo because he was taken for a tramp. Salisbury often attended church wearing a skull cap to protect his head from draughts. Later however he took to wearing a grey woollen glove on top of his head instead. He was a keen but less than gifted amateur scientist and he loved to dabble in his little private laboratory, built in his basement and connected to his study by a spiral staircase. He once emerged from an explosion in his lab, covered in blood, explaining that he had been "experimenting with sodium in an insufficiently dried retort". He also experimented with electric lights in his home at Hatfield, an alarming experience for his dinner guests. Above the dining room table there were often "miniature storms of lightning ending in complete collapse". Occasionally members of his family would interrupt their conversation to throw cushions when the wires sparked. Salisbury was notoriously vague about remembering names and faces. He was once standing behind the throne at a court ceremony when he saw a young man smiling at him. He asked a colleague, "Who is

my young friend?" The reply was, "He's your eldest son."
Queen Victoria was well aware of what she called Salisbury's
"peculiarities" but she was said to be extremely fond of him; it is
said that he was the only man she ever asked to sit down.

Colonel Charles de Laet Waldo Sibthorp, Conservative Member of Parliament for Lincoln from 1826 until his death in 1855,
according to his biographer "set a standard of reaction, na-
tionalism and xenophobia unrivalled in parliamentary history". Sibthorp was opposed to any sort of change to the
English way of life, especially railways, which according to the
MP "are run by public frauds and private robbers whose
nefarious schemes will collapse, and the old and happy mode
of travelling the turnpike roads, in chaises, carriages and stages,
will be restored". Sibthorp enjoyed just one triumph when, to
the dismay of Lincoln's businessmen, he stopped the Great
Northern Railway from running through his constituency.
Most of all, Sibthorp loathed foreigners, claiming, "It would
take ninety-nine foreigners to make one thorough good Englishman." He opposed the 1851 Great Exhibition on the
grounds that it would attract foreign spies and voted to have
the allowance of Queen Victoria's consort Prince Albert cut by
half, because he was German. The Queen vowed never again to
visit Lincoln while Sibthorp was MP.

When the eccentric Irish aristocrat Viscount Mountmorres had
finished preparing a speech he intended to deliver to the Irish
House of Lords he was so pleased with his efforts that he
handed an advance copy of it to the press. He was so confident

that it would be a success that he had written at strategic points in the margin the words "clapping", "cheering" and "wild applause". Unfortunately the debate was postponed and the speech was never delivered. Lord Mountmorres shot himself in 1797, apparently unhinged by a disappointment in love some twenty years earlier. He had proposed to and been rejected by a young lady. One morning he learned that she was staying at a nearby inn, so he burst in on her while she was in the middle of breakfast and attempted to abduct her. She cried for help and a number of her friends and servants gave him such a savage beating that he never fully recovered.

Martin Van Buren, US President from 1836 to 1840, had a reputation for exuberant clothing. A local journalist described his appearance at a church service in New York State one Sunday morning:

His complexion was a bright blond and he dressed accordingly. On this occasion he wore an elegant snuff-coloured broadcloth coat with velvet collar to match; his cravat was orange-tinted silk with modest lace tips; his vest was of pearl hue; his trousers were white duck; his silk hose corresponded to his vest, his shoes were Morocco; his nicely fitted gloves were yellow kid; his hat, a long-furred beaver, with broad brim, was of Quaker colour.

Van Buren was also known for his extensive use of lace, his bright green dress coats, his white-topped boots, and for being vain enough to have his portrait painted twice while he was merely Secretary of State. President Van Buren omitted to mention his wife in his autobiography on the grounds that a gentleman would not bandy a lady's name in public.

Robert, Lord Clive "of India" twice failed to shoot himself in 1744. After the second attempt he declared, "It appears I am destined for something. I will live."

The fourth Earl Russell, John Conrad Russell (1921–87), styled Viscount Amberley, was the eldest son of the philosopher Bertrand Russell. Unlike his father however he was a less than gifted free thinker. He was chiefly renowned for his rambling and often spectacularly confused speeches in the House of Lords. In 1978, during a debate on aid for victims of crime, he demanded the total abolition of law and order, lengthily advising that police should desist from raping young people in their cells. He startled the slumbering peers by announcing, "There should be universal leisure for all, and a standing wage sufficient to provide life without working ought to be supplied . . . so that everybody becomes a leisured aristocrat . . . aristocrats are Marxists." He went on, "In a completely reorganized modern society, women's lib would be realized by girls' being given a house of their own by the age of twelve and three-quarters of the wealth of the State being given to the girls so that marriage would be abolished and the girl could have as many husbands as she liked." He finally advised that "Mr Brezhnev and Mr Carter are really the same person", before suddenly exiting the Chamber without further comment. When the full text of his speech was published it became a collector's item. The playwright and anarchist

Healthcote Williams declared Russell to be "the first man since Guy Fawkes to enter the House of Parliament with an honest intention".

The American financier George Francis Train mixed business genius with a bizarre compulsion for attention seeking. Born in 1829, Train founded a hugely successful shipping business and by his mid-twenties was already extremely rich. In the 1860s he decided to run for the US presidency. He created a completely new political party and to demonstrate his vigour announced that he was to leave the country for a trip around the world that took eighty days. This feat later inspired the French novelist Jules Verne to create Phileas Fogg, hero of *Around the World in Eighty Days*.

George Train was forty-one when "psychic forces" first persuaded him to circle the globe. His journey around the world was an extraordinary feat. He set out from New York, travelling through dangerous native country to reach San Francisco by the shortest possible route. From there he sailed for the Orient, arriving in Japan twenty-five days later, astounding the Japanese by leaping into a public bath in the nude. On he went to Hong Kong, Saigon and Singapore, through the newly opened Suez Canal and from there to Marseilles. Train had a weakness for revolutionary causes and his reputation went before him. When he arrived in France a number of locals begged him to forget his journey and become leader of their commune. He declined, but lost precious time at Lyons when he was mistaken for a revolutionary and thrown into jail. It was only through the intervention of his friend Alexandre Dumas and the US President that he was eventually bailed out and expelled after just under two weeks in prison. He hired a private train and sped across France to the Channel. Once in England, he headed for Liverpool, caught a boat in the nick of time and arrived in New York eighty days after setting out.

Unfortunately Train's unique attempt at absentee campaigning failed abysmally; he did not in fact register a single vote. A reporter covering the election noted, "The Train of ideas sometimes lacks the coupling chains." Train's political ambitions however remained firmly on track. He completed two more global circumnavigations, each time bettering his old eighty-day record, then announced that he would run again for office, not this time as President, but as Dictator of the United States. The only item on his manifesto was a new calendar based on his birth date.

Train made a habit of landing himself in prison. After innocently publishing a column of quotations from the Bible relating to sexual intercourse in order to prove some obscure point, he was arrested on obscenity charges and thrown in Tombs jail. While there he gave interviews to the press, dressed in a sealskin coat. He also became friends with a murderer known as "the famous Sharkey". Sharkey was so impressed with Train that he had him elected President of Murderers' Row. Everyone knew that the obscenity charge was unlikely to stick and Train behind bars was a huge embarrassment to the establishment. The authorities did their best to get rid of him by offering him deals and even leaving his cell door open, but he refused to budge, insisting upon a fair trial. When the judge brought in a verdict of "guilty but insane", Train was furious and after that began to call himself "the great American crank", playing up to the part with great relish. As Train became older, his natural eccentricity flourished. He gave up talking to people, preferring to communicate only in writing "to save up my psychic powers". He greeted people by shaking his own hand. On one of the few occasions people did hear him speak, he urged the invasion of Canada. The once brilliant entrepreneur spent his final years sitting on his favourite New York park bench feeding pigeons and playing with small children.

Calvin Coolidge (US President from 1923 to 1929) allegedly loved to eat breakfast in bed while having his head rubbed with Vaseline.

John Fransham (1830–1910) fought his parliamentary campaign promising to prohibit people from making their beds more than once a week. He believed that daily bed making was "the height of effeminacy".

The bibliomaniac MP Richard Heber (1774–1833) rarely bothered to attend Parliament, as his almost unlimited wealth had given him a head start in his book-buying obsession. He had already acquired a large collection by the age of eight and once bought an entire library comprising 30,000 volumes in Paris. Heber attempted to buy multiple copies of every book ever published. He said that every gentleman should own at least three copies of a book: one for himself, one to lend to friends and one copy for his country house. When Heber died his house was completely chocked with books, the rooms and corridors crammed to the ceilings. The executors of the will later discovered that not only were his three houses in England similarly crammed with books, but he also owned secret ware-houses full of books scattered around Europe, including An-twerp, Ghent, Paris and Brussels.

The third Duke of Portland, William Henry Cavendish-Ben-tinck, who served in the reign of King George III, was known to posterity as the laziest and most ineffectual British Prime Minister of all. During his second ministry he never spoke in Parliament, rarely attended Treasury meetings and was so infrequent in attending planned Cabinet meetings that his colleagues got into the habit of neglecting to even tell him about them.

Charles Watson-Wentworth, second Marquis of Rockingham, served as Prime Minister during the reign of King George III. He was a compulsive and eccentric gambler and would bet on anything. He once ran a race from Norwich to London between five geese and five turkeys.

Emil Matalik put himself forward as a candidate to become US President in 1975, claiming there was an "excess of animals and plant life, especially trees". He advocated a maximum of one animal and one tree per family. Matalik's bid for the US Presidency was apparently merely a stepping stone towards his long term plan to become President of the World. "The problems of the world are building up to an explosive point," he explained. "The only solution is a world president." His choice of world capital? Bennett, Wisconsin.

William Lamb, Lord Melbourne, was perhaps the most idiosyncratic British Prime Minister of all. He had a unique record among first ministers of being accused of adultery in two court actions, and a lifelong interest in flagellation. Over the years his handwriting grew so poor that it became completely illegible and he once admitted to Queen Victoria that it had got to the stage where even he could no longer read his own writing. He had a tendency to doze at inopportune moments and even fell asleep three times during an audience with the Queen. He was also in the habit of talking loudly to himself. At Queen Victoria's coronation he appeared to be alarmingly dishevelled, according to Disraeli: ". . . his coronet cocked over his nose, his robes under his feet, and holding the great sword of state like a butcher." It later transpired that the day before the coronation Melbourne had violent diarrhoea, which he had tried to suppress with huge amounts of laudanum and brandy. Afterwards Melbourne failed to attend Cabinet meetings for a whole week.

The British Prime Minister William Pitt the Elder (1708–78), like his brother Thomas and four of his five sisters, was mentally unstable. Pitt's favourite hobby was landscape gardening, an activity he threw himself into with an almost manic intensity. He spent a huge amount of time and money planting, taking up and then replanting trees at both Hayes and Burton Pynsent. He often planted trees by torchlight, and once ordered 150 trees to be sent by sea from Halifax to Burton Pynsent. They arrived at Plymouth and had to be sent by cart across the whole of Devon and Somerset.

William Pitt the Younger, British Prime Minister from 1783–1801 and 1804 to 1806 was advised as a young man to drink a bottle of port a day for his health. He took the advice to heart and peaked at a daily intake of around six bottles of port, two bottles of madeira and one and a half bottles of claret. Pitt was often drunk when he was making speeches in the House of Commons and was sometimes seen to duck behind the Speaker's Chair to throw up. He finally drank himself to death aged forty-six.

US President Andrew Jackson's wife, Rachel, was not the only First Lady known to smoke a pipe. President Zachary Taylor's First Lady, Margaret, refused to attend any formal social functions during her time in the White House, and spent most of her time in her room smoking a corn-cob pipe. Her 22-year-old daughter Betty acted as host to visiting dignitaries while Margaret remained upstairs, only ever venturing out to go to church. When her husband died in office in 1850 she left Washington immediately after the funeral and never mentioned the White House again.

Queen Victoria's Liberal Prime Minister William Ewart Gladstone could survive on very little sleep. He regularly took a stone hot water bottle to bed with him, filled with tea. As Gladstone seldom slept for more than four hours, the tea was still warm enough for him to drink when he awoke. He believed that the only way to achieve a long and healthy life was to chew every mouthful of food precisely thirty-two times. Gladstone suffered from a variety of nervous tics which animated his conversations. He was also a legendary bore on just about any subject – a constant source of irritation to his colleagues, who once found themselves being lectured by the great man for half an hour on the relative benefits of soft and hard boiled eggs. One day they decided to get their own back. After days of careful research they sat down to a meal with Gladstone and began in-depth discussion on ancient Chinese music – a subject they were sure was too obscure even for him. Gladstone listened quietly for a while, then said, "You have evidently read an article I wrote some ten years ago" . . . and proceeded to monopolize the conversation.

Gladstone had a great love of walking, especially when it involved walking the streets looking for "fallen" women. He spent his evenings prowling London's brothels "rescuing" prostitutes and used to flog himself afterwards with a whip. He admitted he was a pushover for a pretty face and probably succumbed to temptation more than once. His "rescue work" was not always understood or appreciated. Many people thought that chatting up prostitutes on the streets of Soho was an unhealthy pastime for a prominent member of Her Majesty's government. His Private Secretary once asked him with amazement, "What will your wife say if you bring this woman home with you?" Gladstone replied innocently, "It is to my wife that I am bringing her." The girls were not always grateful for his help either. Back at his home, Gladstone's wife would give them a meal, lots of sound advice and a bed for the night. The next day they would be secured a place in one of the temporary shelters, such as the House of St Barnabas. Conditions in the shelters were so grim and depressing that the girls thought they were better off on the streets. A prostitute wrote to Gladstone after running away from the shelter, "I did not fancy being shut up in such a place as that for perhaps twelve months. I should have committed suicide."

In 1853 Gladstone's work found him on the receiving end of a bizarre blackmail demand. While walking through the West End of London he was approached by a woman and after talking to her for some time he went with her back to her lodgings in King Street, Soho. When they arrived at the house a young man named William Wilson stepped out of the shadows. He told Gladstone that unless he secured him a job with the Inland Revenue, he would tell the world that he had picked up a prostitute. Wilson was subsequently charged with attempted blackmail and sentenced to one year's hard labour, reduced to six months after a personal appeal by Gladstone to the Home Secretary.

Britain's first Prime Minister Sir Robert Walpole was renowned for his dirty clothes, foul language and his habit of staying awake during debates in the House of Commons by eating apples. Walpole swallowed about 180 lbs of soap in the last few years before his death in 1745 in an attempt to get rid of a stone in his bladder.

Thomas Jefferson is credited with several inventions, including the swivel chair, a pedometer, a machine to make fibre from hemp, a letter-copying machine, and the "lazy Susan". However he wrote his own epitaph without mentioning that he served as President of the United States from 1801 to 1809.

Margaret-Ann Tyrell (1870–1939) attempted to combine her public duty as the wife of a British diplomat with a lifelong obsession, which was to write a complete history of the world from 2000 BC to the twentieth century. The research for this ambitious work involved simultaneously tracing, cross-referencing and indexing all events in all parts of the world, a vast and nigh impossible task which so completely consumed Lady Tyrell that she was prone to absent-mindedness and the odd social gaffe – like the time she took the future King George VI to be her husband's private secretary. When Lord Tyrell was posted to the British embassy in Paris she avoided official functions completely by sitting in a tree in the embassy gardens, working on her book.

Stanley Baldwin was afflicted by an array of nervous habits, including a variety of facial tics which caused him to make odd, darting head movements. He also had a habit of sniffing his notes and licking the edges of the paper. In old age however Baldwin became so comatose that someone remarked to Winston Churchill that he might even be dead. "No, not dead," replied Churchill, "but the candle in that great turnip has gone out."

Joaquin Balaguer, known to foreign diplomats as the "Wizard of Id", became President of the Dominican Republic in 1966 with the help of US marines who feared another Cuba, and remained in power for the next thirty years thanks to ballot box fraud. Balaguer liked to travel the countryside in a "pope-mobile" type vehicle with a glass tower, from which he handed out gifts to the local populace, ranging from sweets and bicycles to money and plots of land. He marked the 500th anniversary of Columbus's visit by spending a ruinous amount of money on a gigantic white lighthouse in the shape of a crucifix. When the lighthouse was first switched on it caused a massive and disastrous drain on the national grid – unnoticed however by the 60 per cent of his people who still do not have electricity. Although blind, deaf and eighty-nine years old, in 1996 he challenged a civil servant suspected of fraud to a duel, but changed his mind at the last minute and settled for a speech in Parliament instead.

George Washington, noted for not smiling very much for his portraits, had at least four sets of false teeth which he soaked in port overnight to make them taste better. He probably lost his own as the result of his habit of cracking Brazil nuts in his mouth. By the time he became President in 1789, he had only one tooth left and a set of dentures fashioned from cow's teeth. Washington later contacted a leading dentist in Philadelphia, who produced a state-of-the-art set carved, not from wood, but from hippopotamus tusk. The new dentures were thoughtfully drilled with a hole to fit over his one remaining tooth: unfortunately they were a very bad fit and were the cause of constant pain, which the President tried to ease by taking laudanum. Washington also had a morbid fear of premature burial. He left instructions that after he died he was to be laid out for three days just to be on the safe side. He had a fiery temper that, as Thomas Jefferson put it, "was naturally irritable", and when "it broke its bonds, he was most tremendous in his wrath". On one occasion, Washington scolded Alexander Hamilton for keeping him waiting for ten minutes. Hamilton, who said it was only two minutes, promptly resigned from Washington's staff. Washington enjoyed dirty jokes and often told obscene anecdotes. While he and his wife Martha destroyed most of his letters a few did survive. In the late 1920s, multi-millionaire J. P. Morgan bought some, but he burned them saying they were "smutty". Washington believed that shaking hands was beneath a president, and so he always bowed to his White House visitors. He also owned six white horses which had their teeth brushed every morning on his personal instructions.

Thanks to the French revolutionary Maximilian Robespierre the guillotine near his Paris home in the Place de la Revolution was in almost continuous use. Ironically Robespierre himself suffered from haematophobia – a fear of blood. He was so squeamish that he couldn't bring himself even to look at the blood stains on the street cobbles.

President Zachary Taylor habitually chewed tobacco and was known as a "sureshot spitter". As a military officer he hated wearing uniforms. "He looks more like an old farmer going to market with eggs to sell than anything I can . . . think of," one fellow officer said, while another man described him as wearing "a dusty green coat, a frightful pair of trousers and on horseback he looks like a toad". The dandified 21st President Chester A. Arthur meanwhile is remembered only for his nickname "Elegant Arthur". He owned eighty pairs of trousers and changed clothes several times a day.

The Romanian dictator Nicolae Ceausescu suffered from an irrational fear of germs. When he and his wife staged a "walk-about" for publicity purposes which required them to shake a few hands and kiss small children, his secret police selected volunteers beforehand and had them locked up for weeks and regularly disinfected in readiness for the big day.

Benjamin Franklin was a practising eighteenth-century nudist. He took his "air baths" by sitting naked in front of an open window. President Adams too regularly swam nude in the Potomac River. Anne Royall, a journalist, heard of Adams's early morning skinny dips, and after being refused interviews with the President several times she went to the river, gathered his clothes and sat on them until he agreed to speak to her. Before this, no woman journalist had ever interviewed a president.

The eighteenth-century Tory Party leader Viscount Boling-broke was jointly renowned for his debauchery and his oratory. He once described a perfect day: "Got drunk, harangued the Queen, and at night was put to bed by a beautiful lady, and was tuck'd up by two of the prettiest young Peers in England Lord Jersey and Bathurst."

Mackenzie King, Prime Minister of Canada from 1921 to 1943, famously liked to amuse himself by building architectural follies on his 220-acre estate near Kingsmere Lake in Ontario. One hobby he preferred to keep quiet about however was his practice of communicating with the dead. King was a frequent participant in seances. It began when he became convinced of an association between his deceased mother and his beloved dogs, especially an Irish terrier named Pat. King wrote in his diary, "Dear little soul, he is almost human. I sometimes think he is a comforter dear mother has sent to me, he is filled with her spirit of patience, and tenderness and love." When the dog died, King wrote, "I kissed the little fellow as he lay there, told him of his having been faithful and true, told him of his having saved my soul, and being like God – thought of how I felt as I knelt at dear mother's side in her last illness." King went on to note that the Irish terrier had crossed to the spirit world "bearing messages of love to take to father, mother" and several other King family members. King thought nothing of communicating with the dead from his kitchen table at Kingsmere. He sought advice from Leonardo da Vinci and Lorenzo de Medeci and chatted with Louis Pasteur. Meanwhile messages from King's dead relatives came to him in the form of voices via mediums or coded knocking on his table. One medium later revealed that King had once received advice on an important matter of state from the late Franklin Roosevelt, who apparently urged King to remain in office for as long as he could. Few Canadians knew of his mystical jaunts until the publication of his diaries after his death in 1950.

The nineteenth-century Irish politician Charles Parnell was compelled to always make a mental note of the number of paces it took him to walk between two points. Parnell could never bring himself to finish his journey if the total number included the numbers four or eight. If he was walking home and arrived at his front door at a figure containing either numeral he would keep walking around in circles until he hit upon a more favourable total. Parnell however thought that seven was a good number, and "nine is a real symbol of good luck and I can go in rejoicing".

———————

Louis Abalofia ran for US President in 1975. His sole piece of campaign literature featured a photo of him in the nude, above the slogan "I have nothing to hide".

———————

American Civil War General Ulysses Grant was very thin as he was a sparse and faddy eater. He abhorred red meat of any kind and the sight of blood made him nauseous. Consequently, he insisted on his meat being cooked until it was on the verge of being charred. He refused to eat any kind of fowl but was fond of pork and beans, fruit, and buckwheat cakes. Grant's un-flappability, if not his diet, was a constant source of amazement to all around him. He could write dispatches while shells burst around him and in the heat of battle, while his staff officers panicked, Grant calmly sucked on his cigar. He was intolerant of any kind of profanity and rude stories were banned in his presence. He was also tone deaf and could not recognize any of the popular tunes of the day. It was said that he especially hated military music.

———————

In 1996 New Zealand parliamentary candidate Hamish Nixon ran with the slogan "Nixon – The Name You Can Trust". The failed candidate reflected later, "I can't understand why people laugh when I talk about the need for trust and integrity in politics. It's as if they know something I don't."

———————

President William McKinley's First Lady, Ida, was both hypochondriac and unusually possessive towards her husband, forbidding him to leave her side. In 1873 shortly after the birth of their second daughter she fell ill with phlebitis and suffered epileptic seizures. The baby died and a short time afterwards their elder daughter died also. Ida became convinced that she and the President were being punished by God. Thereafter her health was permanently "delicate" – she always appeared as though she was at death's door, a state she existed in for the next thirty-four years. McKinley had to organize his entire career around his invalid wife, who was carried along wherever he went in a small rocking chair. He had to leave important business whenever she summoned him, which was often. When she was in the White House she always received guests sitting in a blue velvet chair, holding a small bouquet so that she didn't have to shake hands with anyone. She ignored protocol and insisted on always being seated next to her husband at formal dinners. Occasionally she would have "seizures"; whenever the President saw one coming on he would throw a napkin over her head until it passed.

———————

Joseph Biggar was the nineteenth-century Tory who invented "obstruction" and brought about the Commons guillotine.

Biggar had a hunchback, a grating voice, a speech impediment, a "face like a gargoyle", bony hands and abnormally large feet. He also took to wearing in the Commons a bizarre foul-smelling waistcoat fashioned from an unknown species of animal skin. When Biggar rose to make his maiden speech, a startled Benjamin Disraeli turned to a colleague and said, "What's that?"

Victoria Woodhull (1838–1927) the first woman ever to run for President, was once considered the most shockingly eccentric woman in America. Woodhull was born on 23 September 1838 in the frontier town of Homer, Ohio. Her mother told fortunes and practised hypnotherapy on her children. Victoria started talking to spirits when she was three years old; she said later that her only friends in childhood were angels. One summer night the local mill burned down in suspicious circumstances and Victoria's father, suspected of arson, was asked to leave town. For several years the family wandered, selling patent medicines concocted from vegetable juices. When Victoria's youngest sister, Tennessee, announced that she could also hear spirit voices, their father hit upon a money-making scheme and set both his attractive young daughters to work holding seances. Before she was sixteen Victoria was married to a young doctor called Canning. She bore him two children, a boy called Byron and a girl named Zulu. Throughout this time Victoria and her sister continued to give noisy seances at a dollar a head. When they added fortune telling and magnetic healing to their routine the customers piled in, especially men. Eventually her doctor husband could no longer stand having his wife's entire family around and abandoned her for a life of drink and womanizing. Victoria took to claiming that Demosthenes, the ancient Greek orator, was guiding her life. She looked to Demosthenes for her next move and he pointed her in the direction of St Louis, where she fell in love with a handsome customer, Colonel James Harvey Blood, who called to seek her advice as a spiritualist. As soon as she saw his side whiskers she was besotted. Her entrapment method was unique. She went into a trance, crying out that their destinies were linked and they were to be joined in marriage. Unfortunately both Blood and she were already married, but Woodhull told him they had been betrothed "by the powers of the air". Blood promptly left his wife and children to live with her and their home became a meeting place for bohemians and radicals.

After a brief period of relative domestic stability Victoria's muse Demosthenes led her to Cornelius Vanderbilt, the richest man in America. Vanderbilt was a sick and desperate man, having lost faith in orthodox medicine. When Victoria and her sister were introduced to him as miracle healers, he decided to give the two beautiful women a chance. Soon, Tennessee and Vanderbilt were lovers. Occasionally Vanderbilt asked Victoria for spirit world guidance on stock market issues, but he soon found that his own instincts were better than that of a long dead Greek orator. In 1870 Victoria and her sister however opened a brokerage office, the first to be run by women in the history of Wall Street. Business flourished and the sisters became wealthy. They rented a mansion and filled it expensive furniture including gold chairs and gilt mirrors and hired servants.

Three months after the sisters' appearance on Wall Street, Victoria astonished the whole of New York by announcing her candidacy for US President. As she had proved herself in business to be the equal of men she could now act for unfranchised American women. She campaigned all over the country and launched a newspaper in which she wrote articles supporting free love, abortion, birth control, legalized prostitution, vegetarianism, magnetic healing and easier divorce laws. The newspaper was a sensation. Meanwhile the Woodhull household arrangements were as bohemian as ever. She obtained a divorce and married Colonel Blood only to see her first husband turn up on her doorstep, his health wrecked by drink and morphine. She took pity on him and let him move in. Her hysterical mother, who detested Blood, told police that her son-in-law had assaulted her, revealing to the world that her daughter now had two lovers under one roof. Predictably the press revelled in an orgy of speculation about the sex life of the presidential candidate.

Things became a little more complicated when her "friend" Stephen Pearl Andrews appeared on the scene. He was an intellectual who could speak thirty languages and had written a book in Chinese. Victoria was more candid about her sleeping arrangements with another boyfriend who joined the household, Theodore Tilton. The latter was already involved in a major scandal. His wife had been seduced by the Rev. Henry Ward Beecher, the most famous preacher in America. Victoria was incensed by Beecher's hypocrisy. She tried to expose him as an adulterer and later, bizarrely, even tried to sleep with him. When she tried to blackmail Beecher he burst into tears and begged her to let him off the hook. Victoria Woodhull's famous "Free Love" speech at the Steinway Hall, ostensibly to expose Beecher as a hypocrite, proved too much for the shocked American public. She was thrown out of the mansion she rented and spent a night on the pavement before she could persuade a boarding house keeper to take her family in. Her brokerage business suffered and Vanderbilt withdrew his backing. The suffragette movement alone stood by her. Victoria decided it was time the whole of America knew the truth about the Beecher–Tilton scandal. She and her sister Tennessee issued

a special edition of their newspaper in November 1872, reve
the whole sensational story. They were both arrested for havii
circulated "an obscene and indecent publication" and thrown
into jail, spending six months behind bars before gaining a
verdict of not guilty. The Beecher scandal however dragged on
for many years and his reputation never recovered. The scandal
also effectively killed Victoria's bid for the presidency.

In 1877 Vanderbilt died and Victoria made it known that
the old man owed her $100,000. His heir paid up with the
proviso that both Victoria and Tennessee left America until
the business of the will was settled. In England, Victoria met
the highly respectable banker, John Biddulph Martin. He was a
partner in Martin's Bank, the family firm, and thirty-six years
old; she was forty-five. Martin's family were appalled by his
association with Victoria, so she set about reinventing herself
as a noble and innocent martyr. Six years later she became Mrs
John Biddulph Martin and settled down to play the role of wife
to respectable banker in Hyde Park Gate, London. She was
never quite able to live down her eccentric past however and
spent the rest of her life denying the outrageous things she was
supposed to have said and done. When she came across two
documents on the shelves of the British Museum Library
detailing the part she had played in the Beecher–Tilton scandal
she persuaded her husband to sue the trustees of the Museum
for libel. The unprecedented trial lasted for five days, Victoria
utterly convincing in her role as much-wronged woman. The
jury recorded a frankly bizarre verdict that libel had been
committed but without attempt to injure, and awarded her £1
damages.

When John Biddulph Martin died of pneumonia in 1879,
Victoria sold the Hyde Park Gate house and moved into her
husband's country manor, there to live the life of a respected
dowager. At the age of sixty-three however she became bored

gave part of her estate to an organiza-
...g women to farm, opened a school
...ucation, and again took up spiritualism.
...he refused to sleep in a bed because she thought
...uld cheat death that way. On the morning of 9 June
1927 she was found dead after drifting off to sleep in her
chair.

In 1980 the Philippine President's wife Imelda Marcos had a "mystical vision" which led to her blow $100 million in an attempt to create a Filipino version of the Cannes film festival. Most of the money was spent on an extravagant new film theatre. The builders and everyone else associated with the Marcos family were so corrupt that no one was particularly surprised when in 1982, two months before the official opening, half of the building collapsed killing at least thirty workers. To avoid delaying construction she had concrete poured over the dead men and had the theatre exorcized to appease the superstitious. The grand opening went ahead almost exactly as Imelda had planned, with one alteration to the schedule: she had invited the Pope, but had to settle for Brooke Shields. Imelda's second International Film Festival in 1983 was even more farcical: in order to recoup the huge losses incurred by her first effort she showed pornographic movies.

As well as attempting to corner the world market in shoes (the Philippine government confiscated 1200 pairs of them when they arrested her) Imelda Marcos became in the late 1970s the world's single biggest private buyer of jewellery. She had stores opened by night for private showings and had her bodyguards pay for her gems with thousand dollar bills stashed in paper bags. As she always insisted on a discount, shop owners put their prices up by 25 per cent as soon as they knew she was coming then offered her 15 per cent off.

Thomas Pelham-Holmes, the Duke of Newcastle, served as Prime Minister during the reign of King George II. Newcastle was considered one of the most comical figures in eighteenth-century politics and is known to posterity for his innate lack of any qualities of leadership and an uncanny knack for doing the wrong thing. He was known by several nicknames, especially "Hubble Bubble" because of his talent for buffoonery, and "Permis" because every time he spoke to the King he prefaced everything he said with "Est-il permis?" When Newcastle heard of his brother's death in 1754, a diarist noted that his reaction was typically hysterical:

> Either grief for his brother's death, or joy for it had intoxicated him. He flung himself at the King's feet, sobbing and crying "God Bless your Majesty" and lay there howling and embracing the King's knees, with one foot so extended that Lord Chesterfield, who was luckily in waiting, begged the standers-by to retire, with "For God's sake, gentlemen, don't look at a great man in distress", endeavoured to shut the door, caught his grace's foot, and made him roar out with pain.

Newcastle was also a hypochondriac and was terrified of catching a cold. At the funeral of George II the Duke of Cumberland, finding that he was unable to move, looked over his shoulder to discover that Newcastle was standing on his robes to keep his feet warm. Newcastle once visited an ailing

William Pitt at his bedside to discuss important matters concerning the Seven Years War. As there was no fire in the room, Newcastle climbed, fully clothed, into a second bed. The Under Secretary entered the bedroom to find his two senior ministers shouting to each other from under the bedclothes of adjoining beds.

David "Screaming Lord Sutch", former head of the Monster Raving Loony Party, was Britain's longest serving party leader until he took his own life by hanging in June 1999. His party had been fielding candidates in British elections since 1970. The MRLP manifesto has included such proposals as towing Britain 500 miles into the Mediterranean Sea to improve the country's climate and requiring dog owners to feed their pets phosphorescent food so that pedestrians could more easily avoid stepping in their faeces.

Both US President Ronald Reagan and his wife Nancy relied heavily on the advice of astrologers before making important decisions. Their schedules were dictated by astrological charts drawn up by the likes of Jeane Dixon, Carroll Righter, Ed Helin and Joan Quigley. Ed Helin, who began doing charts for Reagan in 1949, revealed, "He called me to determine the best timing for invading Grenada, for bombing Libya, for launching the Challenger – things like that." The President's reliance on astrology was first made public by Reagan's former chief of staff, Donald Regan, and later confirmed by several other White House employees and the President's son, Ron. Speaker of the House Jim Wright commented, "I'm glad the President was consulting somebody. I was getting worried there for a while."

Few people serving in the diplomatic corps have served as conspicuously as Queen Anne's cousin Edward Hyde, Lord Cornbury, third Earl of Clarendon. Hyde, Governor of New York from 1701 to 1708, was a fully blown transvestite. He began wearing women's clothes when he was eight years old. He always employed expensive dressmakers, milliners and shoemakers and owned a vast wardrobe of gowns, wigs, fans and stockings big enough to rival that of any fashionable lady about town. Some of his outfits, it was said, were even sent to him by the Queen herself. Lord Cornbury made an unlikely woman as he was a large man with a jowly face. Far from keeping his perversion a secret he liked to show off his clothes and boast how much they cost him. He would often go out on to the streets of New York at night wearing a hooped skirt and powdered wig, or he would sit at an open window fanning himself. On one occasion he walked out of an official reception being given in his honour in order to change his dress. At the opening of the New York legislative assembly in 1702 the English aristocrat astounded guests by making his entrance in a blue silk gown, an elegant diamond studded headdress and satin shoes and carrying a fan. When diplomats complained that Lord Cornbury had made them a laughing stock he dismissed their "American stupidity", adding, "In this place and on this occasion, I represent a woman, and in all respects I ought to represent her as faithfully as I can." American businessmen took a dislike to having to conduct their affairs with a burly Englishman dressed in a frock. Besides, Cornbury was also a poor administrator and an incurable spendthrift.

When Queen Anne heard about her embarrassing cousin she quickly had him removed from office, and in December 1708 the cross-dressing governor was recalled, arrested, and kept in custody until he paid his debts. Hyde quickly rose to power again however and in 1711 was made a member of Queen Anne's Privy Council.

Chapter Five

Legal Eccentricities

"We might define an eccentric as a law unto himself, and a crank as one who, having determined what the law is, insists on laying it down to others"

Louis Kronenberger, author (b.1904)

"There's not a damn line here nowheres that makes it illegal to kill a Chinaman"

Judge Roy Bean (1823–1903)

Justice Sir Melford Stevenson (1902–1987) was renowned for his forthright opinion and judicial toughness, a style hinted at in the name of his Sussex home, "Truncheons". He once referred to bookmakers as "a bunch of crooks", and upset Mancunians when he commented during a divorce case that the husband "chose to live in Manchester, a wholly incomprehensible choice for any free man to make". He told a man acquitted of rape, "I see you come from Slough. It is a terrible place. You can go back there." During a bribery case Justice Stevenson described Birmingham as "a municipal Gomorrah". In the 1945 General Election Stevenson unsuccessfully tried to enter Parliament as Conservative MP for Maldon, Essex. He launched his campaign by announcing that he wanted a clean fight and would not therefore in any circumstances mention "the alleged homosexuality" of his opponent Tom Driberg. He later referred to the 1967 reform of the homosexual laws as "a buggers' charter", for which he was reprimanded by the Lord Chancellor. In one day in 1976 he had a record three decisions overturned by the Court of Appeal, a setback which caused him to comment later, "A lot of my colleagues are just constipated Methodists." Nevertheless Justice Stevenson took part in some notable trials, including that of Ruth Ellis, the last woman to be hanged in Britain. He also presided over the Kray twins' trial, and was later overheard to observe that the twins had only told the truth twice – first when one brother described a barrister as "a fat slob", second when the other brother complained that the judge was biased.

In Montana and Florida the only legal way for a man and a woman to have sex is in the missionary position. In North Carolina you must stay in the missionary position and have the curtains drawn; masturbation is also illegal. In Virginia you can't have sex with the lights on, or in anything other than the missionary position. Oral sex is illegal in Indiana, Missouri,

Virginia, Maryland, South Carolina and San Francisco. In North Carolina it is illegal to have sex in a churchyard. In Tremonton, Utah it is illegal to have sex in a moving ambulance. In Massachusetts taxi drivers are prohibited from making love in the front seat of their taxi during their shifts, nor may a woman ever be on top during sexual activity. In Oregon it is illegal to whisper "dirty" things in your lover's ear during sex. In Dallas it is illegal to possess a realistic dildo. In Arizona it is illegal to have more than two dildos in a house. In Lebanon, Virginia it is illegal to kick your wife out of bed. In Logan County, Colorado it is illegal for a man to kiss a woman while she is asleep. In Iowa, kisses may last for as much as, but no more than, five minutes. In Minnesota it is illegal to sleep naked.

For senior British judges a demonstration of eccentricity in matters of contemporary issues is de rigueur. In 1979, while presiding over a case involving the English Football Association, Mr Justice Cantley asked a barrister, "Kevin Keegan, does he play for England or Scotland?" In 1985 Mr Justice Harman asked, "Who is Bruce Springsteen?" Neither however could compete with the Canadian judge who was completely baffled in 1977 by the occupation of one Keith Richards, on trial for possession of heroin. He asked Richards's defence counsel, "Who are the Rolling Stones?"

In Los Angeles it is illegal for a man to beat his wife with a strap wider than two inches without her consent. In Arkansas a man can legally beat his wife, but not more than once a month. In

Jasper, Alabama it is illegal for a husband to beat his wife with a stick larger in diameter than his thumb. In South Carolina it is legal to beat your wife on the courthouse steps, but only on Sundays. In Stafford County, Virginia it is also legal to beat your wife on the courthouse steps, but only before eight p.m.

Californian District Attorney William Tingle once had three members of the jury removed from an attempted murder case because one was "grossly overweight", one had braided hair, which he considered "somewhat radical", and the third because of her "braids, obesity, size, and manner of dress".

In Tulsa it is against the law to open a soda bottle without the supervision of a licensed engineer. In Victoria, Australia only licensed electricians may change a light bulb. In Pennsylvania no man may purchase alcohol without written consent from his wife nor may he sing in the bathtub. In Texas the Encyclopaedia Britannica is banned because it contains a formula for making homebrew. In Clarendon, Texas it is illegal to dust any public building with a feather duster. In Washington it is illegal to paint polka dots on the American flag.

John Toler, later Lord Norbury (1745–1831), was Ireland's most notorious judge. Like the infamous Judge Jeffreys, he was without mercy and his sentences were usually harsh. His reputation however grew from his courtroom manner, described as "a combination of buffoonery and sadism". Norbury was noted by a contemporary to be "fat, podgy, with small grey cunning eyes, which ever sparkled with good humour and irrepressible fun, especially when he was passing sentence of death". He was sometimes known as "Puffendorf" from his habit of inflating his cheeks as he spoke. Norbury addressed his court with a mixture of drollery and vicious dry wit. He would point to a prisoner in chains and observe, "What have we here? A young man in the flower of life. Yet the flower may never come to fruit." During his twenty-seven years as a judge his courts became so notorious for rowdiness that they were more like theatre. Norbury often brought the house down. Once when defence counsel John Philpot Curran rose and opened his mouth to speak, an ass suddenly brayed outside the court window. "One at a time, please," boomed Norbury. He would send men down with long rambling speeches peppered with quotations from Milton and Shakespeare, occasionally throwing his wig in the air. He once sentenced ninety-seven men to death in a single day. He was also known for one single act of clemency, towards an alleged murderer. Although the evidence against the man was overwhelming, there was a gasp of astonishment around the courtroom when Norbury recommended the jury to bring in an acquittal. The crown prosecutor interrupted to point out that the sheer weight of evidence proved that the man's guilt was surely undisputable. Norbury replied in a stage whisper, "I know all that, my good fellow. But I hanged six men at last Tipperary assizes who were innocent, so I'll let off this poor devil now to square matters."

Towards the end of his career Norbury's performances in court became increasingly erratic and his reputation declined. He often fell asleep in court and could be heard snoring loudly through a capital trial. He would awake without any recollection of the case or even where he was. He finally retired in 1827 aged eighty-two. Four years later, on his deathbed, he received news that his near neighbour, Lord Erne, was also dying. Norbury told his manservant, "James . . . run round to Lord Erne and tell him with my compliments that it will be a dead heat between us."

In Clawson, Michigan there is a law that makes it legal for a farmer to sleep with his pigs, cows, horses, goats, and chickens. In West Virginia it is legal for a male to have sex with an animal as long as it does not exceed 40 lbs. In Oklahoma it is illegal to have the hind legs of a farm animal in your boots. Having sexual relations with a porcupine is illegal in Florida.

In 1998 Nebraska's Judicial Qualification Commission recommended that Omaha Judge Richard "Deacon" Jones be removed from public office. Charges against him included signing official court papers with names "A. Hitler" and "Snow White"; setting eccentric bail amounts, including "13 cents" and "a zillion pengos", personally and indiscreetly supervising a young male probationer's urine test and setting off a firework in the office of a judge with whom he had an argument.

In Port Arthur, Texas it is illegal to break wind in an elevator. In New York people may not greet each other by "putting one's thumb to the nose and wiggling the fingers". In Staten Island it is illegal for a father to call his son a "faggot" or "queer" in an effort to curb "girlie behaviour". In Lafayette, California it is forbidden to spit on the ground within five feet of another person. In El

Paso, Texas, churches, hotels, halls of assembly, stores, markets, banking rooms, railroad depots, and saloons are required to provide spittoons "of a kind and number to efficiently contain expectorations into them". In Burlingame, California it is illegal to spit, except on baseball diamonds. In Oklahoma you may not take a bite out of another's hamburger without permission. In Waterloo, Omaha barbers are forbidden to eat onions between seven a.m. and seven p.m. In West Virginia no children may attend school with their breath smelling of "wild onions". In Champaign, Illinois it is considered an offence to urinate in your neighbour's mouth. In Freeport it is illegal to spit from any second-storey window. In Georgia it is illegal to use profanity in front of a dead body in a funeral home or in a coroner's office. In Tombstone, Alaska it is illegal for men and women over the age of eighteen to have less than one missing tooth visible when smiling. Texan law requires criminals to give their victims twenty-four hours' notice, either orally or in writing, and to explain the nature of the crime to be committed. In Jonesboro, Georgia it is illegal to say "Oh, boy".

The Texan Judge Charles J. Hearn liked to demonstrate his Christian faith by adding a "smiley" face to his signature. Critics pointed out that this was not appropriate behaviour for a judge, especially a judge signing a death warrant. The defence lawyer for a man sentenced to death by Judge Hearn in 1993 complained, "It's like he's saying, have a nice death."

In 1623 the Profane Oaths Act made swearing illegal in England. The popular oaths of the day, the colourful Gog's malt, the suggestive cat's nouns, or the extremely naughty a turd i' your teeth could earn you a shilling fine or a good whipping. Most people took no notice and carried on swearing, and so in 1745 the law was beefed up with stiffer penalties. By this time most people were saying stap me vitals or possibly even ods niggers noggers to the Act, which curiously enough lay neglected and ignored on the statute books for over 200 years until it was repealed in 1967.

In the history of American jurisprudence Judge Roy Bean is remembered as the most colourful barrister to preside over a court of law. Bean dispensed justice in Texas for twenty years, presiding from a saloon bar the Jersey Lily in the town of Langtry. As a young man Bean followed the railroads across Texas until he found himself in the town of Vinagaroon where he was appointed "justice of the peace" by the local road-gang workers. It was Bean's first taste of how the law could be used to his own advantage. After a short stay in Vinagaroon, Bean jumped aboard a southern train until he alighted on Langtry, a desolate spot named after the popular British actress, Lillie Langtry. He received the appointment of "justice of the peace" in Langtry on 2 August 1882. He occupied the biggest shack in town and erected a number of signs including "Judge Roy Bean, Notary Public", "Justice of the Peace", "Law West of the Pecos", and "Ice Beer". Bean charged two dollars for inquests and five dollars for weddings and divorces. He had no judicial power to grant divorces, but said, "I guess I got a right to unmarry 'em if it don't take." He made most of his money by selling alcohol. He would always start off any important case by requesting everyone buy a bottle so they could liven up the proceedings. He often interrupted trials to serve drinks. Whenever he presided over a marriage ceremony he always finished with the line "May God have mercy on your soul". Bean usually bent over backwards for anyone who worked for the railroad, since the Southern Pacific made a regular stop at his small town and was the only source of supplies and business to Langtry. In 1882 he dismissed a murder charge brought against one of his regulars because "it served the deceased right for getting in front of the gun". The case against another regular drinker in the Jersey Lily was also dropped because the victim was Chinese. According to Bean's version of Texan law, there was "not a damn line here nowheres that makes it illegal to kill a Chinaman". Presiding at a funeral, he fined the corpse forty dollars for carrying a concealed weapon.

No one was allowed to bring up Lillie Langtry's name without buying a drink and toasting her picture behind the bar. When the actress toured America in 1888, the "Judge" went to San Antonio to see her, wearing his best suit and an old top hat, paying a staggering price for a front-row seat at a local theatre. He sat in awe during the entire performance, but he did not have enough courage to visit her backstage later. Roy's reign continued off and on through the turn of the century. Later in his career, his reputation became well known and many visitors travelled to see the legendary judge sitting on the front porch of his courthouse. Even Lillie Langtry finally paid a visit to the town that bore her name, but her biggest fan was already dead. Bean drank himself into a coma in San Antonio in March 1903 and was carried back to Langtry and placed in the back room of the courthouse. He died the following day.

Thanks to the Waltham Black Act, the most notorious piece of legislation on the subject of capital punishment ever, the number of offences punishable by death in England by the early nineteenth century was more severe than anywhere else in the world. Added to the already impressive list of offences for which one could be hanged were the heinous crimes of "associating with gypsies", "writing on Westminster bridge", "impersonating a pensioner of Greenwich Hospital", "writing a threatening letter", "appearing on a highway with a sooty face", "damaging a fish-pond", or "cutting down a tree". In 1800 a ten-year-old boy was hanged for "secreting notes in a post office", and in 1801 a thirteen-year-old boy was hanged for stealing a spoon.

In Massachusetts goatee beards are illegal unless you first pay a special licence fee for the privilege of wearing one in public. In Eureka, Illinois a man with a moustache may not kiss a woman. Women in Florida may be fined for falling asleep under a hair dryer, as can the salon owner. In Tylertown, Mississippi it is unlawful to shave in the centre of Main Street. In Nebraska it is illegal for a mother to give her daughter a perm without a state licence. In Omaha a man may not be seen in public with a shaved chest. In Mesquite, Texas it is illegal for children to have unusual haircuts.

In the middle of a high profile criminal trial in 1977, Judge Alan King-Hamilton turned to the jury and announced, "The Australians are four for one wicket." In 1986 Judge Michael Argyle told a jury that the lack of Test Match cricket on television was "enough to make an Orthodox Jew want to join the Nazi party".

In Seattle you may not carry a concealed weapon that is over six feet in length. In Marlboro it is illegal to buy, sell or possess a water pistol or to detonate a nuclear device in the city. In Chico, California, detonating a nuclear device within the city limits can lead to a $500 fine. In Milwaukee it is illegal to purchase or use Sparklers, but you can buy a fully disassembled automatic machine gun. A by-law in North Andover, Massachusetts prohibits the use of space guns. In Boston duels to the death are permitted on the common on Sundays provided that the Governor is present. In Kennesaw, Georgia all citizens must possess a firearm of some kind. In Kansas City minors are not allowed to purchase cap pistols, but they may buy shotguns. In Montana, seven or more Indians are considered a raiding or war party and it is legal to shoot them. In Nevada it is still legal to hang someone for shooting your dog on your property. In Tasmania, until the Port Arthur killings of 1997 it was legal to own an AK-47 but not legal to be gay.

On 8 February 1986 a judge in Philadelphia refused to convict a man for rape on the grounds that the alleged victim was "the ugliest girl I have ever seen". He went on to say that the experience had put him off rape trials for good and requested that he be excused from presiding over any more.

In Texas you are considered legally married by publicly introducing a person as your husband or wife three times. In Utah you can marry your first cousin, but only when you have reached the age of fifty.

Sir George "Bloody Jeffreys" of Wem (1648–89) was Britain's most sadistic Lord Chief Justice ever. He passed 331 death sentences and had hundreds more deported – usually a fate worse than hanging. One of his most notorious sentences was conferred on Lady Alice de Lisle, whom he ordered to be roasted alive. The Church was outraged by the sentence and demanded clemency: Lady Alice had her sentence commuted on appeal and got away with a beheading. Jeffreys never allowed a word of self-defence and always drove the prosecution through at high speed. The cause of this behaviour was his painful bladder-stone: he was compelled to urinate hourly and had to get through the trials as fast as possible to reach the lavatory.

In Wyoming a woman may not stand within five feet of a bar while drinking. In Montana, it is illegal for married women to go fishing alone on Sundays, and illegal for unmarried women to fish alone at all. In Owensboro, Kentucky it is against the law for any woman to buy a hat without her husband's approval. In Michigan a woman may not cut her own hair without her husband's permission. In New York it is illegal for a woman to be on the street wearing "body hugging clothing". In Paulding, Ohio females are forbidden to do their own hair without being licensed by the state. In Schulter, Oklahoma women may not gamble in the nude, in lingerie, or while wearing a towel. In Pennsylvania it is illegal to have over sixteen women living in a house together because that constitutes a brothel. It is however possible for up to 120 men to live together without breaking the law. In Pennsylvania housewives may not hide dirt and dust under a rug in a dwelling. In Vermont, women must obtain written permission from their husbands to wear false teeth. In Seattle women who sit on men's laps on buses or trains without placing a pillow between them face an automatic six-month jail term. In Florida the law prohibits unmarried women from parachuting on Sunday.

In 1983 a Manhattan criminal court judge was barred from office after deciding the length of a jail sentence on the toss of a coin, and asking courtroom spectators to vote on which of two conflicting witnesses was telling the truth.

In Alaska it is legal to shoot bears, but waking a sleeping bear for the purpose of taking a photograph is prohibited. In Alabama it is illegal to exploit bears by promoting, engaging in or being employed in a bear wrestling match, receiving money for the admission of another person to a place kept for bear wrestling, selling, purchasing, possessing or training a bear for wrestling, or subjecting a bear to surgical alteration in any form including, but not limited to, declawing, tooth removal, and severing tendons. In Alaska, moose may not be viewed from an airplane nor is it legal to push a live moose out of a moving airplane. In Fairbanks, Alaska it is considered an offence to feed alcoholic beverages to a moose. In Hayden, Alaska it is unlawful to bother the cottontails or bullfrogs. In California it is unlawful to shoot at any kind of game from a moving vehicle, unless the target is a whale. It is also illegal to set a mousetrap without a hunting licence. In Pacific Grove, Ontario molesting butterflies can result in a $500 fine. In North Carolina it is illegal to use elephants to plough cotton fields. In Kentucky any person who displays, handles or uses any kind of reptile in connection with any religious service or gathering shall be liable to a fine of up to one hundred dollars. In Columbus, Georgia it is illegal to cut off a chicken's head on Sunday, or to carry a chicken by its feet down Broadway. In South Bend, Indiana it is illegal to make a monkey smoke a cigarette. Kansas state law prohibits shooting rabbits from a motorboat, catching fish with your bare hands and the use of mules to hunt ducks. In Minnesota a person may not cross state lines with a duck on their head. In Ohio it is illegal to get a fish drunk. In Oklahoma you can be fined, arrested or jailed for making ugly faces at a dog. In Texas it is illegal to shoot a buffalo from the second storey of a hotel. In Detroit, alligators may not be tied to fire hydrants. In Los Angeles you may not hunt moths under a street light, nor it is legal to lick toads (the toad secretes a chemical that some people were licking to produce an effect like heroin). In Klamath Falls, Oregon it is illegal to walk down a sidewalk and knock a snake's head off with your cane. In Arizona is it illegal to hunt camels. In Tennessee it is illegal to use a lasso to catch a fish. In Utah it is against the law to fish from horseback. In Wisconsin you may not take a photo of a rabbit during the month of June. In Scotland it is illegal to be drunk in possession of a cow.

In 1972 the Los Angeles Judge Justice Title awarded $4,500 damages to the owner of an elephant called Bimbo. The judge ruled that as a result of injuries received in a road accident, Bimbo had completely lost interest in dancing and water skiing.

In Alabama it is illegal to play dominoes on Sunday or to wear a fake moustache that causes laughter in church. In Tampa Bay, Florida it is illegal to eat cottage cheese on Sunday after six p.m. In Boston it is illegal to play the fiddle or kiss in front of a church. In Detroit it is illegal for a man to scowl at his wife on Sunday. In Nebraska a parent can be arrested if his child belches during a church service. In Marion, Oregon, ministers are forbidden to eat garlic or onions before delivering a sermon. In Houston it is illegal to sell Limburger cheese on Sunday. In Vermont it is illegal to deny the existence of God. In Nicholas County, West Virginia, no member of the clergy is allowed to tell jokes or humorous stories from the pulpit during a church service. In Switzerland clothes may not be hung to dry on Sunday, nor may you wash your car or mow your lawn. It is also illegal to flush the toilet after ten p.m. if you live in an apartment. In Wawa, Canada it is illegal to show affection in public on Sunday. In Israel it is forbidden to pick your nose on Saturday as it is considered by the Jewish Faith to be "work".

Raynor Goddard was one of the most enthusiastic hangers and floggers to have held the post of Lord Chief Justice. It is claimed that he was sexually aroused by sentencing young men to death and once achieved orgasm while pronouncing the death sentence.

The state of California forbids animals from mating publicly within 1,500 feet of a tavern, school, or place of worship. In Arizona donkeys may not sleep in bathtubs. In Lompoc, California it is illegal to possess, own or raise roosters. In

Los Angeles it is a crime for dogs to mate within 500 yards of a church. In San Francisco it is illegal to pile horse manure more than six feet high on a street corner. In San Jose it is illegal to own more than two cats or dogs. In Atlanta it is against the law to tie a giraffe to a telephone pole or street lamp. Kirkland forbids bees to fly over the village or through any of its streets. In Marshalltown, Iowa, horses are forbidden to eat fire hydrants. In Baltimore it is illegal to take a lion to the movies or to sell chicks or ducklings to a minor within one week of the Easter holiday. It is illegal to let your pig run free in Detroit unless it has a ring in its nose. In McDonald, Ohio it is illegal to parade your goose down Main Street. In Memphis it is illegal for frogs to croak after eleven p.m.

In 1992 Pennsylvanian judge Charles Guyer was sacked after a hidden video camera recorded him offering a novel form of plea-bargaining; he offered convicted men lighter sentences if they allowed him to shampoo their hair.

In Alabama it is legal to drive the wrong way down a one-way street if you have a lantern attached to the front of your automobile. In Glendale, Arizona cars may not be driven in reverse. In California women may not drive in a housecoat and no vehicle without a driver may exceed sixty miles per hour. In Baldwin Park, California it is unlawful to ride a bicycle in a swimming pool. In Detroit, couples are banned from making love in an automobile unless the act takes place while the vehicle is parked on the couple's own property. In Charleston, South Carolina all carriage horses must wear diapers. In

Australia you can load as many people into a car as you want and drive away, as long as five people are using the seat belts. In Oklahoma it is illegal to read a comic book while operating a motor vehicle.

Washington State Municipal Judge Ralph H. Baldwin resigned from the bench in 1998 after inviting a lawyer and two jurors back into the jury room to finish off a twelve-pack of beer. Judge Baldwin told them, "Bet you've never met a judge like me before."

In Lee County, Alaska it is illegal to sell peanuts after sundown on Wednesday. In Connecticut, for a pickle to be officially considered a pickle, it must bounce. In Gainesville, Georgia, chicken must be eaten with the hands. In Idaho a man may not give his sweetheart a box of candy weighing less than 50 lbs. In Nebraska it is illegal for bar owners to sell beer unless they are simultaneously brewing a kettle of soup. In Lehigh, Nebraska doughnut holes may not be sold. In Newark, New Jersey it is illegal to sell ice cream after six p.m., unless the customer has a note from his doctor. In Ocean City, New Jersey people may not slurp their soup. In Trenton, New Jersey you may not throw a bad pickle in the street. In Marion, Ohio you may not eat a doughnut and walk backwards on a city street. In Ridley Park, Pennsylvania you cannot walk backwards eating peanuts in front of the Barnstormers Auditorium during a performance. In Quebec, Canada, margarine has to be a different colour from butter. In Alabama you may not carry an ice cream cone in your back pocket at any time.

In 1998 an appeals court in São Paulo, Brazil overturned an earlier ruling and agreed to pay compensation to Valdir Martins Pozza after a grindstone broke a tendon in one of his little fingers. The first judge had turned down Pozza's claim, because "the pinkie serves little use and tends to disappear with the evolution of the human species".

In Little Rock, Arkansas, flirtation between men and women on the streets can result in a thirty-day jail term and it is unlawful to walk one's cow down Main Street after one p.m. on Sunday. In Abilene, Texas it is illegal to idle or loiter anywhere within the corporate limits of the city for the purpose of flirting or mashing. In Mobile, Alaska it is unlawful to wolf-whistle at ladies inside the city limits, nor may women legally wear stiletto heels (this law was passed to prevent more lawsuits after a lady who got a heel caught in a sidewalk grating fell and injured herself). In California it is illegal to remove your clothes in a bath house. In Durango, Colorado it is illegal to go in public dressed in clothes "unbecoming" on one's sex. In Lewes, Delaware it is illegal to wear pants that are "form fitting" around the waist. In Florida men may not be seen publicly in any kind of strapless gown. In Ottumwa, Iowa it is unlawful for any male person within the corporate limits of the city to wink at any female person with whom he is unacquainted. In Carrizozo, New Mexico it is forbidden for a female to appear unshaven in public. A by-law in Nogales, Alaska prohibits the wearing of suspenders. In Ohio women are prohibited from wearing patent leather shoes in public, lest men see reflections of their underwear. In Oxford, Ohio it is illegal for a woman to strip off her clothing while standing in front of a man's picture. In Nashville, males may not be sexually aroused in public. In

Saudi Arabia it is illegal to kiss a stranger. In Thailand it is illegal to leave your house if you are not wearing underwear. In Tel-Aviv it is forbidden to walk outside your home without wearing socks. In Victoria, Australia it is illegal to wear pink hot pants after midday Sunday. In Kentucky, no female shall appear in a bathing suit on any highway unless she is escorted by at least two officers or unless she is armed with a club. The provisions of this statute however do not apply to females weighing less than 90 lbs nor exceeding 200 lbs.

The eighteenth-century earl Lord Monboddo, reputed to be "the most learned judge of his day", spent his life convinced that babies were born with tails and that there was a universal conspiracy of silence among midwives who cut them off at birth. Monboddo's faith in his tail theory remained intact even after witnessing the births of his own children. He concluded that the crafty midwives had tricked him and destroyed the evidence. Monboddo published a six-volume treatise called *The Origin and Progress of Language*, the first work to suggest that man is descended from apes, in which he asserted that the human tailbone was a vestige of our ape ancestry. His lordship became the butt of tail jokes for the rest of his life, but in the light of Darwin's theory of evolution, published about seventy years later, he was at least partly vindicated.

A practising nudist, Monboddo refused to ride in a horse-drawn carriage because he believed it was an affront to ride behind a horse instead of upon it. He was also near-sighted and hard of hearing. In 1785 he travelled from Edinburgh to visit the King's Bench in London, and during his visit part of the court roof collapsed, causing lawyers and judges to flee for their lives. Monboddo alone however sat unmoved among the debris and confusion. When asked later why he had not reacted, he replied that he thought he was observing some native court ceremony with which he was unfamiliar.

In Fort Wayne, Indiana you may not sell or broadcast the record "It's In the Book". In France between the hours of eight a.m. and eight p.m., 70 per cent of the music on the radio must be by French composers. In Israel 50 per cent of the music a government radio station plays has to be by Israeli artists. In Waterbury, Connecticut it is illegal for any beautician to hum, whistle, or sing while working on a customer. In Globe, Alaska it is illegal to play cards in the street with a Native American. In Gary, Indiana you are prohibited from attending a movie house or other theatre or from riding a public streetcar within four hours of eating garlic. In Iowa one-armed piano players must perform for free. In Maine you can be fined for having your Christmas decorations still up after 14 January. In New Hampshire you may not tap your feet, nod your head, or in any way keep time to the music in a tavern, restaurant, or café, or sell the clothes you are wearing to pay off a gambling debt, or book into a hotel under an assumed name, or pick seaweed up off the beach. In North Carolina it is against the law to sing off key. In Fargo, North Dakota you can be jailed for wearing a hat while dancing or for wearing a hat to a function where dancing is taking place. In Portland, Oregon you may not whistle underwater or wear roller skates in restrooms. In Texas it is illegal to take more than three sips of beer at a time while standing. In Monroe, Utah, daylight must be visible between partners on a dance floor. In Milwaukee it is against the law to play a flute and drums on the streets to attract attention, or to be in public during the day if you are "physically offensive looking". In

Wyoming it is illegal to wear a hat that obstructs people's view in a public theatre or place of amusement. In New Mexico it is illegal to perform 400 words of "sexually explicit material" from Shakespeare's *Romeo and Juliet*. In Glendale, California it is only legal to show horror films on Mondays, Tuesdays, or Wednesdays.

Clarence Seward Darrow (1857–1938) was a US lawyer renowned for his conduct of labour litigation and murder cases. He was notoriously dishevelled and newspaper reporters would on occasion tease the energetic and hardworking Darrow about his scruffiness. Darrow retorted, "I go to a better tailor than any of you and pay more for my clothes. The only difference is that you probably don't sleep in yours."

In Prunedale, Ontario two bathtubs may not be installed in the same house. In Los Angeles you cannot bathe two babies in the same tub at the same time. In Indiana baths may not be taken between the months of October and March. In Kentucky it is required by law that you must bathe either by shower or bath no less than once a year. In San Francisco it is illegal to wipe one's car with used underwear. In Denver, Colorado it is unlawful to lend your vacuum cleaner to your next-door neighbour, or to mistreat rats. In Acworth, Georgia all citizens must own a rake. In Pueblo, Colorado it is illegal to let a dandelion grow within the city limits.

Chicago law forbids eating in a place that is on fire, feeding whiskey to a dog, flying a kite within the city limits, spitting, drinking beer out of a bucket while sitting on the kerb and fishing while sitting on a giraffe's neck. It is however legal to protest naked in front of City Hall as long as you are under seventeen years of age and have legal permits.

In Devon, Connecticut it is unlawful to walk backwards after sunset. San Francisco prohibits elephants from strolling down Market Street unless they are on a leash. It is illegal to drive more than two thousand sheep down Hollywood Boulevard at one time. In Toronto, Canada it is illegal to drag a dead horse down Yonge Street on a Sunday. In Hartford, Connecticut you must not cross a street while walking on your hands. In San Francisco persons classified as "ugly" may not walk down any street.

James Curtis spent twenty-five years at the Old Bailey taking down verbatim reports of all the trials in the famous old court of law, not because he worked for a newspaper, but because he was obsessed with court cases. It was said that the only thing that could keep him away from a court case was the promise of a public execution. Curtis became such a courtroom fixture that he got to be on first name terms with many of the prisoners. His favourite trial was that of a man named Corder who murdered Maria Marten in the Red Barn. Curtis was even allowed to stand alongside him in the dock (eventually he also wrote a biography of the famous nineteenth-century murderer). It led to an unfortunate mistake by a provincial newspaper artist, who had been sent to draw a picture of Corder and accidentally sketched Curtis instead. Curtis could have sued when his picture appeared in the newspaper as a murderer, but in fact he was quite pleased by the mistake.

In Frankfort, Kentucky it is against the law to shoot off a policeman's tie. In New Jersey it is against the law to "frown" at a police officer. In Louisiana biting someone with your natural teeth is "simple assault", while biting someone with your false teeth is "aggravated assault". It is also illegal to gargle in public places. In New Orleans a dog is entitled to his "first bite" of a person. In Paulding, Ohio a policeman may bite a dog to quiet him.

In Memphis it is illegal to give any pie to fellow diners or to take unfinished pie home; all pie must be eaten on the premises. In Massachusetts, mourners at a wake may not eat more than three sandwiches. In Richmond, Virginia it is illegal to flip a coin in a restaurant to see who pays for coffee. In New York it is against the law to throw a ball at someone's head for fun. Putting salt on a railroad track in Alabama is punishable by death. In Arizona any misdemeanour committed while wearing a red mask is considered a felony, and the maximum prison sentence for cutting down a cactus is twenty-five years. In New York the penalty for jumping off a building is death.

In North Dakota it is illegal to lie down and fall asleep with your shoes on. In West Virginia it is illegal to snooze on a train. In South Dakota it is illegal to lie down and fall asleep in a cheese factory. In Racine it is illegal to wake a fireman when he is asleep. In Hawthahorne, Oklahoma it is unlawful to put any hypnotized person in a display window. In West Virginia doctors and dentists may not place a woman under anaesthesia unless a third person is present.

Chapter Six

Military Eccentrics

"I'm afraid the war will end very soon now, but I suppose all good things come to an end sooner or later, so we mustn't grumble"

> British Field Marshal Earl Alexander (1891–1969)
> in a letter to his aunt Margaret, 1917

"Practically everyone but myself is a pusillanimous son of a bitch"

> General George S. Patton, Jnr (1885–1945)

"My only great qualification for being in charge of the Navy is that I am very much at sea"

> Sir Edward Carson (1854–1935)

"Thank God I wasn't born a flea, a monkey or a Frenchman"
                              Colonel A. D. Wintle (1897–1966)

Digby Tatham-Warter, company commander of the 2nd Bat-
talion Parachute Regiment, won a DSO for his part in the
battle of Arnhem in 1944 after famously leading a bayonet
charge equipped with an old bowler hat and a tattered umbrella. Tatham-Warter's trademark brolly became a symbol of
defiance to the British, who stubbornly held on to the north
end of a road bridge, although outnumbered and short of
ammunition, food and water. On one occasion he was seen
nonchalantly strolling around with his brolly under heavy fire
and a fellow officer commented, "That won't do you much
good." Tatham-Warter replied, "But what if it rains?"

Pillars of the Prussian military machine had a love of uniforms
bordering on fetishism, and none more so than Queen Victoria's grandson, Kaiser Wilhelm II. He owned over four hundred
uniforms stashed away in his mahogany wardrobes, although
not one single dressing gown (his grandfather Wilhelm I had
once refused a silk robe, growling "Hohenzollerns wear no
dressing gowns"). In the first seventeen years of his reign the
Kaiser redesigned the uniforms of his German army officers
thirty-seven times. He had a squad of tailors in his palace on
permanent standby. There were uniforms for every occasion:
uniforms for attending galas, uniforms to greet every one of his
regiments, uniforms with which to greet other uniforms, uni-

forms for eating out, even "informal" uniforms for staying in. It was joked that he had an admiral's uniform which he only ever wore to see performances of *The Flying Dutchman*. When he attended military parades there was little danger of mistaking the Kaiser among all the other brightly uniformed Prussian automatons: he was the only one wearing a solid gold helmet.

The French military hero Marshall MacMahon crushed a Paris left-wing uprising in 1871 and went on to become President of France from 1873 to 1879. One day he was visiting a field hospital when he came across a soldier who lay ill with a tropical fever. "That's a nasty disease you have there," sympathized the great man. "You either die of it or go crazy. I've been through it myself."

Colonel A. D. "Mad Jack" Wintle, born the son of a British diplomat in 1897, was a fierce patriot even as a child, and went to bed every night thanking God that he was English. In fact Wintle was an old fashioned xenophobe with a particularly intense dislike for Germans and was delighted therefore to find himself at war with them in 1914. He begged his father to let him join the Royal Military Academy as a gentleman cadet and passed out in four months – an Academy record – before being sent to France with the Royal Garrison Artillery. On his first day at the front, Wintle immediately walked into a heavy German bombardment and watched as the young officer standing next to him was blown to pieces. Wintle was terrified, but forced himself to stand for attention for thirty seconds, to enable himself, he explained, "to again become an Englishman". The incident was typical both of a series of amazing Wintle escapes and his stiff upper lipped reaction to adversity. At Ypres in 1917 he was again lucky: his gun carriage wheel hit a landmine and he woke up in a field hospital minus his left eye, one kneecap and several fingers. His right eye was so damaged that he had to wear a monocle from that day on; he was nineteen years old at the time.

Wintle was sent back to England to convalesce. For him the war was over, or so it was reasonably assumed, but Wintle had other ideas. He planned his escape from the Southern General Hospital back to the front. At his first attempt he disguised himself in a sister's uniform, weirdly electing to attend a nurses only dance on the evening before his escape. His monocle however was a dead giveaway. His second attempt was more successful and he escaped back to France by train. By November 1918 he was again in the thick of the action near Jolentz, where he single-handedly took thirty-five prisoners, a feat of bravery which earned him the Military Cross. Armistice Day came and went, but Wintle's personal war with the Germans did not abate. He simply refused to believe that the Germans had been defeated; the filthy Boche had merely sued for peace in order to lull the rest of Europe into a false sense of security while they regrouped. Wintle's views did not endear him to his fellow officers, and thereafter for the best part of twenty years he was shunned as a monocled crank. He spent a brief period working in the German section of the War Office where his opinions and abrasive manner made him highly unpopular. In 1920 he was posted to Ireland as Head of Military Intelligence, Limerick Brigade.

Wintle was a keen horseman; he maintained that "time spent dismounted can never be regained". After a year he applied for a transfer to a cavalry regiment and joined the Eighteenth Royal Hussars at Secunderbad, India. For an Englishman at that time this was a world of endless privilege, polo and cocktails in the officer's mess. Wintle's Indian career however was cut short when he fell off his horse and broke a leg. In Aldershot military hospital he encountered a trumpeter with the Royal Dragoon Band named Cecil Mays. The young Mays was suffering from mastoiditis and diphtheria, and was expected to die soon. One day Wintle hobbled over to Mays on his crutches and demanded, "What's all this nonsense about dying, Mays? You know it is an offence for a Royal Dragoon to die in bed? You will stop dying at once – and when you get up, get your bloody hair cut." Forty years later Mays revealed, "After that I was too terrified to die."

Wintle's brand of *Boy's Own* caricature Englishness was often laughed at, especially when he continued to fulminate on the subject of "the bloody Boche" to anyone prepared to listen. The Germans, he said, "are like their dogs; they cannot be trusted. The wolf will out." Wintle's opinion of the British War Office was even lower, staffed as it was by "bloody traitors". It was a triumphant Wintle therefore who found himself vindicated in September 1939 when England was once again at war with Germany. Although "Mad Jack" was regarded with deep distrust in Whitehall he was sent to France on an intelligence gathering mission, to assess how long the French army could be expected to hold out against Germany. His dislike for rules and red tape quickly got him into deep trouble. Impatient to resume hostilities against the Germans since 1918, he tried without permission to commandeer an aircraft to fly to France, and was arrested and sent to the Tower of London after pulling a revolver on the British Director of Intelligence and telling him, "You and your kind ought to be shot." His captors discovered however that although Wintle was quite possibly insane, he was not a traitor and he was allowed to live in some style, with his batman, a private bathroom, access to a telephone and his daily whisky on the stroke of noon.

At Wintle's court martial, held at the Duke of York's Barracks in Chelsea, he continued to embarrass the authorities by threatening to name everyone in Whitehall he considered "ought to be shot". In order to silence him the original twelve charges were reduced to one, and Wintle was allowed to go with a reprimand. In 1941 he was back in action in France, this time as an undercover agent. His mission was to find out what sort of conditions Allied prisoners of war lived in. Wintle set off across France in native disguise, with gold coins strapped to his armpits in case of emergency. He made an unconvincing Frenchman however and was quickly arrested as a spy and thrown into prison in Toulon, denouncing his captors as "swivel-eyed sons of syphilitic slime frogs". His weight went down to seven stone and he briefly considered suicide, but he then decided to "do something positive". His warders were a bunch of scruffy, down at heel French collaborators whose appearance had fallen below what Wintle considered to be acceptable military standards. He warned them that if they didn't smarten themselves up he would starve himself to death. Unexpectedly, they gave in to his request to a man. He did eventually escape by burying himself in the contents of the prison refuse cart, and made his way home via Spain. By Wintle's standards it had been an uneventful war. Later dubbed "Colonel Bogey" by the popular press, Wintle boasted that his immaculate umbrella had only ever been unfurled on one occasion, and that was to insert a note reading, "This umbrella has been stolen from Colonel A. D. Wintle."

The US Confederate General Jackson was a strict Presbyterian known as "Deacon Jackson" before he won his new nickname "Stonewall" at the first battle of Bull Run. His deep religious convictions meant that he refused to fight on Sundays. During the thick of the battle of Mechanicsville in 1862 Jackson spent the day praying alone on a nearby hill, refusing to speak to anyone, while his troops took heavy casualties. Jackson was convinced that one side of his body weighed more than the other; whenever he walked he kept one arm raised to restore his balance. He also always stood while eating. Once, as a junior officer, he wore his thick army greatcoat throughout a long and very hot summer because he had not received an order to do otherwise. In 1863 he was mistakenly shot and wounded by his own men, and died a week later.

During the Battle of Waterloo, Lord Uxbridge had his horse shot from under him nine times. Eventually, as he was riding beside Wellington, he too was hit by French grapeshot. "By God, sir, I've lost my leg," he informed Wellington. "By God, sir," the Duke replied, "so you have."

Lieutenant Commander Geoffrey Spicer-Simpson was one of the most undistinguished British sea captains of World War I and one of the oddest. He was the oldest lieutenant commander in the British Navy when war broke out and he was mysteriously chosen to command an expedition on Lake Tanganyika in central Africa. When he was given two ships, formerly belonging to the Greek air force, he was asked by his superior Admiral Jackson to give them names, as they only hitherto had numbers. Spicer-Simpson responded by naming them *Dog* and *Cat*. The British First Sea Lord was unamused and asked Spicer-Simpson to come up with something more suitable – perhaps something slightly more warlike in the great British naval tradition. Spicer-Simpson renamed them *Mimi* and *Toutou*.

Spicer-Simpson had a talent for embarrassing his men. A large muscular man with a pointed beard, he was tattooed from head to foot with snakes, birds, insects and flowers, and given to suddenly bursting into song, or relating outrageous stories about his great achievements as a big game hunter or as captain of a destroyer. He also took to wearing skirts, which, he was careful to point out, had been made for him by his wife. Spicer-Simpson's sole victory in a naval battle – itself a complete fluke – was celebrated by cutting off the German commander's ring finger, wearing the ring and keeping the severed finger in a bottle.

During fighting in Beirut in 1983 Syrian General Mustafa Tlass instructed his men not to attack Italian peacekeeping soldiers because he had a lifelong obsession with the Italian actress Gina Lollobrigida. General Tlass told his men: "Do whatever you want with the US, British, and other forces, but I do not want a single tear falling from the eyes of Gina Lollobrigida."

The British Admiral Sir Algernon Charles Fiesché Heneage, or "Pompo" as he was known to the men under his command, was obsessive about his appearance. He wore his hair set in curls and took 240 shirts to sea with him. He sent the dirty ones home for laundering on any available ship bound for England. Even when he was rounding Cape Horn, in some of the world's most treacherous waters, the return of his dirty laundry on a passing ship was uppermost in his thoughts. Admiral Heneage was also a stickler for regulations. If any of his subordinates dared touch him, as one did when "Pompo" stumbled as he was climbing a gangplank, the Admiral became apopleptic with rage. He once had a ship's carpenter arrested for entering the captain's cabin without first being formally announced by an appropriate officer. Later, the same carpenter was arrested a second time for entering the captain's cabin to shut his portholes when seawater was leaking in and flooding it.

Orde Charles Wingate, a brilliant but unorthodox British military leader in the Second World War, in six years rose from the rank of captain to major-general and his three campaigns in Palestine, Ethiopia, and Burma established him as a military legend. According to one of his staff officers in Ethiopia, Wingate "was the most complex character I've ever met. He had a driving passion and was unnecessarily impatient. Generous yet self-promoting with enlarged claims. He had a phenomenal memory and loved holding centre stage. Some of his personal habits were a bit outré. He had great strategic vision but his tactics were poor. He was not a lovable person but he was a great leader."

Wingate was most often seen wearing a rumpled and dirty uniform with a pith helmet and sporting a beard. He also ate large quantities of raw onions in the belief they were good for his health. During his campaign in Ethiopia he took to wearing a miniature alarm clock strapped to his wrist so as to time his interviews. During conversations with visitors he would rub his naked body with a rubber brush, a grooming method he preferred to bathing. He was famously offensive to people who failed to see his point of view and his frequent rudeness made him enemies easily. Wingate was often verbally and physically abusive. On several occasions he struck Ethiopian soldiers who made mistakes and during the Burma campaign he threw violent tantrums. On one occasion, suffering from depression and taking medication, he tried to commit suicide with a knife.

The twelfth-century Holy Roman Emperor Henry VI used to motivate his troops by having nuns stripped and smeared with honey, then decorated with feathers and sent on horseback through the ranks of cheering men.

The eighteenth-century king of Prussia Frederick William I was known to posterity for his freakish army of giants, a regiment of very tall grenadiers known as the Potsdam Giant Guards. The minimum height requirement for the Potsdam regiment was six feet, although most were over seven feet and the tallest were almost nine feet tall. All of them wore special pointed headgear which sometimes reached a height of ten feet. Height was the only criterion, as many of them were mentally retarded. Frederick William was insanely proud of his Potsdam Giant Guards. Wherever he travelled his giants would march alongside his carriage holding hands over the top of it. His favourite giants were immortalized in lifesize oil paintings. When one exceptionally tall Norwegian grenadier died the king had him sculpted in marble.

The recruits were press-ganged from his own country, or were bought or kidnapped from all over the world. The Prussian king was prepared to spend any amount of money, and to go to any length, even at the risk of war, in his pursuit of tall men. His army of recruiting agents had instructions to use whatever force was necessary. A giant carpenter was once tricked into lying down in a box then found himself locked inside and shipped to Potsdam. As his captor had forgotten to drill air holes in the box however the carpenter was found to be dead on arrival. The king was furious: the agent who captured him was charged with causing the loss of a recruit and imprisoned for life. Even foreign diplomats weren't safe from King Frederick William's press-gang. An exceptionally tall Austrian diplomat was seized in Hanover, but was able to escape. An Irish giant called Kirkman was kidnapped on the streets of London and delivered to Potsdam at a cost to Frederick William of a thousand pounds. A tall priest was kidnapped from Italy in the middle of Mass, and a monk was spirited away from a monastery in Rome. They kidnapped Portuguese, Hungarians, Slavs, Russians, Englishmen, Turks, even Ethiopians and Americans. They were men of every profession, including doctors, lawyers, accountants and teachers.

The rest of Europe observed the Prussian king's hobby with amusement until his agents began to trespass on their soil. One of Frederick William's less reputable tactics was to induce tall men in the armies of foreign countries to desert. Many of his recruits however were gifts from other European courts. Whenever the king went on a state visit he would broadly hint that the sort of farewell gift he would most appreciate would be a giant or two. The Austrian and Russian courts were particularly obliging benefactors. Peter the Great, another great admirer of freaks, sent the Prussian king hundreds of Russians all over six foot four. Other European courts found that they had hit upon a novel method of bribing Frederick William. Tall men became diplomatic bargaining chips as word spread that the king of Prussia would agree to virtually anything if you gave him a few tall freaks. The British government persuaded him to sign a pact which was highly biased in their favour by slipping him a "gift" of fifteen very tall Irishmen. The Saxon foreign minister sent Frederick William a birthday present of two expensive Turkish pipes and a load of high grade tobacco. The package was delivered by a seven foot tall messenger complete with note which contained a birthday greeting: at the bottom it read PS, keep the delivery boy. The king acquired an eight foot tall Swede from Augustus the Strong of Saxony. Frederick William was delighted with his new plaything, but was frustrated when the Swede turned out to be so mentally retarded that he couldn't be drilled, despite many beatings. The king despaired and threw him out of the guards, probably the only time that anyone ever left the Potsdam Grenadiers freely. The poor childlike giant drifted into Berlin where, unable to support himself, he died a beggar on the streets.

When the procurement of conscripts by abduction became too expensive and too dangerous, the king turned to crude genetic engineering. Every tall male in Prussia was forced to marry a tall woman. When this breeding programme proved too slow and unreliable he went back to kidnapping. Eventually Frederick William acquired two thousand of his precious giants. The price in human suffering however was high. Living conditions for members of the Potsdam freakshow were pitiful and morale was dreadful. Almost all of the men who passed through the regiment were held against their will. They mutinied regularly, and several times they tried to burn down the whole of Potsdam in the hope of killing the king in the process. About two hundred and fifty giants successfully deserted each year, but violent deaths during escape attempts were commonplace and reprisals were brutal. The king dispatched bounty hunters on manhunts to track them down:

those who were recaptured had their noses and ears sliced off and were locked in Spandau prison. Many of the giants resorted to self-mutilation or suicide, or took part in mercy killings of their fellow soldiers to end their misery.

The Mexican General Antonio Lopez de Santa Anna stubbornly observed the tradition of siesta even in life-threatening situations. In 1836 Santa Anna and his troops found themselves near a wood known to be full of Texan soldiers, but nevertheless insisted on taking their usual afternoon nap. While Santa Anna and his men quietly snoozed the Texans attacked and routed the entire Mexican army in under twenty minutes. Santa Anna escaped, but two years later had a leg torn off in a skirmish with the French. He recovered the leg and when he eventually became the most powerful man in Mexico he gave it a full state funeral.

Queen Victoria's father Edward, Duke of Kent, the "Flogging Duke", was an army bully who believed that the only way to lick a soldier into shape was to flog him into submission. The added bonus for the perverted Duke was that he was sexually aroused by the sight of men being whipped, which unfortunately also made him wet his trousers. Consequently, he quickly made his mark as a brutal and tyrannical disciplinarian who would thrash his soldiers at the drop of a hat, and the number of floggings in the Duke's regiment went up roughly in line with his laundry bill. He was posted to Gibraltar as Colonel of the Royal Fusiliers, where he first earned his nickname "the beast" and his reputation as the most hated man in the British Army. From five a.m. every morning he thrashed, marched and drilled his men into the ground. The slightest mistake by any of his soldiers would turn him into a seething psychopath. Naturally, the floggings multiplied. When news filtered back to England that the Gibraltar garrison was at the point of mutiny, the darkly disturbed Duke was quietly removed and sent to Canada. He had learned nothing from his mistakes at Gibraltar and viewed his new posting as a fresh opportunity for more floggings, again driving his troops to the brink of mutiny with a regime of outrageous punishments.

Francisco Lopez, President of Paraguay from 1862 to 1870, was an extremely ugly and obese man – one of the more flattering descriptions of him was that he looked like "a tidal wave of human flesh". Lopez also had a Napoleon fixation and kept one hand tucked inside his jacket at all times. Even in the competitive field of South American dictatorship, Lopez enjoyed a reputation for whimsical ruthlessness; he had his 70-year-old mother publicly flogged then executed when she let on to him that he was a bastard. He spent most of his reign waging a hopeless war against Argentina, Brazil and Uruguay, training his men so hard and for so long that many didn't live long enough to see a battle. His misguided war effort, combined with his refusal to allow any of his men to surrender, reduced the male population of Paraguay by nine-tenths.

Lopez's incompetence guaranteed that his military position grew ever more hopeless, so he organized a spying system which encouraged every third man in his army to spy on his comrades and to shoot anyone, including officers, who showed any sign of cowardice. The resulting widespread paranoia among the ranks led to many of his men's marching into battle backwards because they feared their own side more than the enemy. When his senior commander found himself surrounded and facing certain defeat, he opted to blow his own brains out rather than face his President, but missed and only shot one eye out. When things started to go really badly Lopez organized a mass suicide pact and ordered the entire population of his nation's capital Asuncion to march off into the jungle with him. He changed his mind at the last minute and ordered the national treasure to be thrown off a cliff into a deep jungle instead. The treasure was swiftly followed over the cliff edge by all the witnesses to ensure secrecy.

In 1870 Lopez arbitrarily declared himself a Saint of the Christian Church. When the matter was put to the bishops of Paraguay, the twenty-three who admitted they were not keen on the idea were shot. 'Saint' Francisco was duly anointed and that date officially entered into the Christian calendar. His final act was to have a new medal minted which he awarded to the entire population of Paraguay, or at least what was left of it.

In the eighteenth century Czar Paul, as commander-in-chief of the Russian army, indulged a childlike obsession with his military hero Frederick the Great. He made his troops wear a uniform slavishly copied from the Prussian military handbook right down to the last detail of old-fashioned gaiters and powdered pigtails, entirely at the expense of military efficiency. The costumes were so tight fitting that breathing was difficult and fighting practically impossible. Underneath the troops wore straitjackets to make them stand erect, and on their heads they wore thick, heavy wigs with iron rods inserted in them to make the hairpiece sit straight. To make his soldiers goose-step perfectly without bending their legs, the Czar strapped steel plates to their knees. The night before a parade his men would labour until dawn to cover their wigs with grease and chalk. They all knew that even a hair out of place could mean arrest, a thrashing, or deportation. His officers grew to fear his unpredictability so much that they got into the habit of saying a final farewell to their wives and families before they went on parade. For no apparent reason he once ordered an entire regiment on a four thousand kilometre march which took two years to complete and killed hundreds of horses.

King Louis XIV's cousin, the gluttonous Duke of Vendôme, although a famously brave soldier combined his enthusiasms for sodomy and alcohol in roughly equal measure. He allegedly retired to bed blind drunk every single night for forty years, and never arose before four p.m. the following day. In spite of his wild drinking sprees, his catamites and his mistresses, Vendôme remained a great personal favourite of the king. The Duke's ruinous lifestyle had left him with a gaping hole where his nose should have been – a common side effect of syphilis. When Vendôme left the court to seek a cure for his venereal affliction the king jokingly told him to get better and return "in a state in which one might kiss with safety". When the Duke returned minus his nose, Louis instructed his courtiers to pretend not to notice.

Frederick Augustus, Duke of York (1763–1827), brother of King George IV, was immortalized in nursery rhyme as the Grand Old Duke of York, a ditty which reflected what most people thought about his military incompetence as commander-in-chief of the British Army. He was very tall, very bald, and although he had very skinny underdeveloped arms and legs he had an enormous gut, counterbalanced by a huge backside: "one was always afraid that he would tumble over backwards," noted a contemporary. Frederick became a bishop when he was seven months old – not the most normal of childhoods even for a member of the British royal family – but preferred to spend the rest of his life trying to drink himself to death.

When the Duke of York was forty he set up home with a Mrs Clarke, the daughter of a London stoneman. His mistress was to completely destroy what little was left of his reputation by selling army commissions while he was commander-in-chief. He was charged in the House of Commons with "personal corruption and connivance". They weren't able to prove however that he knew what she was up to, but the trial was highly damaging, especially when the entire House of Commons sat laughing as excerpts of his love letters to Mrs Clarke were read aloud, details which were later widely reported in the press. The Duke was in fact married to the Prussian Princess Frederica, but in thirty years of wedlock they hardly shared a single night under the same roof. His wife was a strange women, badly marked by smallpox. It was said that she rarely ever slept, and spent most nights in her smelly garden grotto where she kept forty dogs, plus several kangaroos, monkeys and parrots.

The US Civil War General S. Ewell, or 'old bald head' as he was known by his Confederate troops, was a brave but flawed military leader who harboured the delusion that he was a bird. The problem became frequently apparent whenever he cocked his head to one side, pecked at his food and made chirping noises. To complete the picture, Ewell was also known for his beaky nose.

Lord Fitzroy Somerset lost an arm when it had to be amputated on the evening after Waterloo. After it was removed he snapped at an orderly, "You, bring that arm back. There is a ring my wife gave me on the finger."

Sir William Erskine was one of Wellington's senior commanders during the Peninsular War. As Erskine had twice been confined to a lunatic asylum, Wellington received news of the appointment with stunned disbelief and wrote to the Military Secretary in London for an explanation. The Secretary replied, "No doubt he is a little mad at intervals, but in his lucid intervals he is an uncommonly clever fellow, and I trust he will have no fit during the campaign, although I must say he looked a little mad as he embarked." During one of Erskine's less lucid intervals he was found at dinner when he should have been defending a strategically important bridge. He eventually sent five men to defend it: when a fellow officer queried his decision Erskine changed his mind and determined to send a whole regiment, but pocketed the instruction and forgot all about it. Sir William's mental health wasn't his only problem. His eyesight was so poor that before a battle he had to ask someone to point him in the general direction of the battlefield. Erskine committed suicide by jumping out of a window in Lisbon. Found dying on the pavement, he asked bystanders, "Why on earth did I do that?"

Prussian Field Marshall Leberecht von Blücher, the Duke of Wellington's famous ally at Waterloo, suffered from delusions. Blücher once confided to Wellington that he was pregnant and about to give birth to an elephant, and that moreover the cad who had raped him was a French soldier. He also took to walking around the room on tiptoe because he believed the French had developed a dastardly plan to burn his feet by heating the floor.

In 1943 the American military boffin Dr Louis Feiser unveiled a new secret weapon he was confident would bring to an early conclusion to the war with Japan – the incendiary bat. Feiser's cunning plan was to collect millions of bats and keep them cold, thereby inducing a state of hibernation. The slumbering bats would then be released over Japan, each carrying a tiny incendiary device containing one ounce of napalm. As the bats fell they would warm up, settle under the eaves of buildings and set fire to them. Feiser's plan was abandoned after trials when the bats set fire to and destroyed a US army hangar and general's car.

The Greek commander General Hajianestis, who led his country's army in the war with Turkey in 1921, had a keen sense of self-preservation. Rather than rouse himself to command his troops he lay in bed pretending to be dead. Another ploy he sometimes used was to claim that he couldn't get up because his legs were made of glass and might break if he moved.

When General Kitchener was fighting the Boers in South Africa in 1900 he complained bitterly that the enemy didn't fight fairly. Apparently the bounders were always on the move or taking advantage of surrounding cover, he said, instead of standing quite still in the open while they were shot down by British rifles and machine guns.

During the Crimean War British generals found themselves with a new plaything, the electric telegraph. One day Lord Panmure cabled General Simpson, "Captain Jarvis has been bitten by a centipede. How is he now?" The General was not amused to find that he had been awoken in the middle of the night by a trooper who had been required to ride two miles under enemy fire to deliver such trivial news. Nevertheless the next morning General Simpson sent a mounted dragoon to enquire after Captain Jarvis, four miles away, only to discover to his disgust that Jarvis "has never been bitten at all, but has had a boil, from which he is fast recovering".

Simpson received a second telegraph from Lord Panmure, this time on behalf of his lordship's favourite nephew Captain Dowbiggan: "I recommend Captain Dowbiggin to your notice, should you have a vacancy, and if he is fit." Confusingly, the message was relayed by the telegraph operator as "Look after Dowb". Subsequently "Look after Dowb" became the standard catchphrase for nepotism in the army.

Chapter Seven

Medical Eccentrics

"Man will always be mad and those who think they can cure them are the maddest of all"

Voltaire (1694–1778)

"An erection is a flagstone on the grave"

Dr John Harvey Kellogg (1852–1943)

The Austrian psychotherapist Wilhelm Reich (1897–1957) was a contemporary and disciple of Sigmund Freud. Reich also believed that freedom of sexual expression was the key to stable mental health. Unlike Freud however he also held that a suppressed orgasm could lead to physical and psychological ill health. When critics pointed out that there were many neurotics at large who were not short of orgasms, Reich would airily defend his point by maintaining that some orgasms were "good" and some "bad", the latter including those achieved by homosexual or erotic fantasies, or even those which were not of the correct length. Reich had a very hands on approach. He treated his patients with a combination of psychotherapy and massage, a technique he called "vegetotherapy". His methods were, at best, confrontational. He also conducted a number of highly questionable experiments to prove the existence of "sexual electricity" which, he postulated, was discharged from various erogenous zones during orgasm.

Reich was an avowed Communist. Capitalism, he argued, repressed sexuality and caused "sadism, greediness, envy and perversion of all kinds". World War I was caused by the unsatisfactory sex lives of the Kaiser and the German ruling classes. From 1928 to 1930 he set up half a dozen "socialist sex clinics" in Vienna, hoping to unleash a communist revolution by freeing men from their sexual inhibitions. The Austrian Communist Party was not entirely on the same wavelength and it moved to have his clinics shut down. Reich moved to Berlin, joined the German Communist Party and opened more clinics, eventually enlisting 40,000 members of his German Association for Proletarian Sex Politics. The German Communist Party was similarly unmoved; it kicked him out of its ranks and banned his books. Reich became a social pariah, at one point upsetting Sigmund Freud by pointing out that the great man had "poor psychic health" because of his unsatisfactory marriage. He made even more enemies when he suggested that the entire Nazi movement was the result of sexual repression. He narrowly escaped with his life, disguised as a tourist, to Denmark. The Danes, he hoped, would be more tolerant towards his ideas. When the Danish Minister of Justice heard his proposals for nude teachers and classrooms full of naked schoolchildren however he had him kicked out of the country as an undesirable alien.

Reich went to the US, where in 1940 he built his first "Orgone Accumulator". This was a large wood and metal box, big enough for a patient to sit in and accumulate "cosmic orgone energy" – a process, Reich claimed, which could promote general psychic and sexual well-being and even cure cancer. He built a total of 170 Orgone Accumulators over the next seven years, renting them out for ten dollars a month. In 1954 the US Food and Drug Administration closed in on him and in a twenty-seven-page document declared him a fraud. Reich ignored an injunction banning him from selling his boxes, and he went to prison, where he died of heart failure.

The eighteenth-century anatomist and chemist Dr George Fordyce was renowned for his remarkable appetite and his unusual capacity for alcohol. The doctor's studies in comparative anatomy led him to conclude that as the lion was the king of the jungle it was wisest to eat as a lion did – once a day and then as much as possible. Fordyce followed the same regime for twenty years. Every day at four p.m. he entered Dolly's Chop House in London and demolished twenty-four ounces of rump steak and half a broiled chicken or a large plate of fish, washed down by a tankard of strong ale, a bottle of port and a quart of brandy. He then drank a glass of brandy and water at the nearby Chapter Coffee House, a second glass at the London Coffee House, and a third at the Oxford Coffee House. Thus refreshed, he returned to his lectures on chemistry. He didn't eat again until four p.m. the next day at Dolly's.

In 1936 Dr Heil Eugene Crum became sole practitioner of an obscure branch of medicine known as radionics when he obtained a United States patent on a gadget which he called Dr Crum's Co-etherator. The device comprised a small wood box with a number of holes in the front, over which various strips of thin coloured paper were pasted. On the inside of the box was an ordinary light bulb. The bulb could be moved about so that light would shine through the various paper-covered holes. The box also contained a quantity of disconnected wire and a glass tube filled with ordinary water. There was a pedal and a dial on the outside of the box, neither of which had any obvious connection with the interior. Crum's preferred method for treating ailments was to have the patient moisten a slip of paper with saliva and deposit it through a slot on the top of the box, although he also claimed that the same results could be obtained by similar use of the patient's photograph or a specimen of his handwriting. After this had been done, Dr Crum rubbed the pedal with his thumb and talked to the machine, repeating the popular names of diseases and organs of the body. Among the diseases which Crum claimed to be able to cure by this method were cancer, blindness, arthritis, nervous disorders, haemorrhoids, abscesses, kidney ailments, stomach disorders, leakage of the heart, skin ailments, ovarian trouble, varicose veins, and tumours. Crum could lengthen or shorten a patient's leg, cause amputated fingers to grow back into place and fill cavities in teeth. He even claimed that it was not necessary for patients to be present or to visit his office – he could broadcast treatments to them wherever they might be located.

Crum's gift was not limited to the telepathic treatment of human ills. He also claimed to be able to administer "financial treatments", he could fertilize fields to a distance of seventy miles; kill dandelions over any particular area; and treat golf greens as far from Indianapolis as Decatur, Illinois, so that clover would die and give the grass a chance to grow. The state of Indiana eventually revoked his medical licence after they became suspicious of Crum's qualifications. Obtained from the College of Drugless Physicians in Indianapolis, they included Doctor of Naturopathy, Doctor of Electro-Therapeutics, Doctor of Chiropractic, and Doctor of Herbal Materia Medica.

Dr Albert Abrams, a respected physician around the beginning of the twentieth century, developed a theory that diseases had unique "vibratory rates" that could be detected by tapping on the patient's abdomen or spine. Abrams refined his diagnostic techniques with invented devices such as the "dynamizer" – a box containing a mass of wires. His students were never permitted to examine the wiring in the boxes, which were rented to trained practitioners. One wire ran to an electrical source, another was attached to the forehead of the patient. A drop of blood was obtained from the patient on a piece of filter paper and placed inside the box. Abrams would then tap the abdomen of the patient who was stripped to the waist and always, for reasons never made clear, facing due west. By listening to the sounds Abrams claimed he was able to diagnose the ills of the patient. Without the patient's even being present, Abrams could determine his or her age, sex and religion. If a drop of blood from the patient was not available a lock of hair or even a handwriting sample would suffice. As patients did not have to be present for diagnosis by the devices, a thriving mail order industry was created by which people sent in blood samples and received diagnoses through the mail. On one occasion a sceptic sent blood from a rooster to Abrams, who diagnosed "malaria, cancer, diabetes, and two venereal diseases".

As well his critics Dr Abrams also had many converts, among them the author Upton Sinclair, who wrote: "Abrams has made the most revolutionary discovery of this or any other age. I venture to stake whatever reputation I ever hope to have that he has discovered the great secret of the diagnosis and cure of all major diseases. Abrams had treated over fifteen thousand people and my investigation convinces me he has cured over ninety-five per cent." Shortly before the doctor's death however a committee of scientists opened one of the magic boxes. Their report concluded that the box contained an ohmmeter, rheostat, condenser and other electrical gadgets randomly wired together for no apparent reason.

Martin van Butchell (1735–1812) was one of the most high-profile Londoners of his era, often seen riding through the city on a white pony painted with purple spots. Van Butchell prided himself on his dentistry skills, assuring the wary that "gums, sockets and palate formed, fitted, finished and fixed without drawing stumps or causing pain". He achieved fame however not through his dexterity with the pliers, but because of his unorthodox devotion to his deceased wife. Mrs van Butchell decided to repay her husband for years of marital misery with a spiteful will which decreed that her fortune was to pass to a distant relative "the moment I am dead and buried". The resourceful dentist however believed he had found a loophole in the will by simply keeping her body well above ground. Van Butchell, a skilled embalmer, fitted her out with a new pair of glass eyes, and filled her veins with oil of turpentine and camphorated spirit of wine. She was then dressed, propped

up in the drawing room and put on public display from nine
a.m. to one p.m., from Monday to Saturday. The rush to see
the corpse was so great that van Butchell was forced to restrict
viewings to private appointments only. A notice in the *St
James's Chronicle*, 21 October 1775, read:

> Van Butchell (not willing to be unpleasantly circum-
> stanced, and wishing to convince some good minds they
> have been misinformed) acquaints the Curious, no stran-
> ger can see his embalmed Wife, unless (by a Friend
> personally) introduced to himself, any day between Nine
> and One, Sundays excepted.

When he remarried his new wife took an instant dislike to the
ex-Mrs van Butchell and ordered her out of the house. The
corpse was presented to the Royal College of Surgeons, where it
remained for more than 150 years until the museum was
destroyed by Hitler's bombers.

The first-century Greek scholar Pliny worked to the best
practice available to him in his day, but his advice was
undeniably eccentric. He taught that you could prevent toothache by eating two mice a month, and recommended "perva-
sive green frogs, burnt heel of ox, toads and worms" as a cure
for halitosis.

William Hervey (1578–1657) was the great English physician
who discovered how the heart pumps blood around the body.
His patients included James I, Charles I and the philosopher

Francis Bacon. As a young man he was highly temperamental. He always carried a dagger on his hip and was likely to draw it at the least provocation. Hervey loved the dark, claiming that it helped him think more clearly, and constructed caves beneath his home in Surrey in which he could work. Hervey also had a disorder known as hypergraphia – excessive writing. He often repeated letters at the end of words for no apparent reason; for example, he spelled the word "pig" as "piggg".

Sylvester Graham (1794–1851), famous in the US as the inventor of the sugared brown crackers used in pie crust, spent a lifetime crusading against masturbation and poor eating habits. Graham believed that most health problems could be traced to sex or diet. His ideas were greatly influenced by an English clergyman William Metcalfe, a pioneer of vegetarianism and a firm believer in the future of asparagus seed as a coffee substitute. Graham was mainly concerned with the carnal passions provoked by meat-eating. He rejected established medical science, theorizing that as the stomach was the major organ of the body it was also the seat of all illness. Hunger or sexual desire was a drain on the immune system and increased the chance of disease and death. Graham's cure for virtually every human sickness was simple: exercise, to help prevent "nocturnal emissions", a proper diet to facilitate regular bowel movements, and sexual moderation – more than once a month for married couples was definitely not advisable. His "Lecture to Young Men" written in 1834 was the first of a whole genre of medical tracts on the subject of masturbation, which he preferred to call "self-pollution". According to Graham, a masturbator grows up "with a body full of disease, and with a mind in ruins, the loathsome habit still tyrannizing over him, with the inexorable imperiousness of a fiend of darkness". It was the chief cause of teenage acne: ". . . ulcerous sores, in some cases, break out upon the head, breast, back and thighs; and these sometimes enlarge into permanent fistulas, of a cancerous character, and continue, perhaps for years, to discharge great quantities of foetid, loathsome pus; and not unfrequently terminate in death." By the end of the 1830s Graham's career was over, but not without having first influenced a generation of diet experts.

On 14 November 1854 Indiana doctor Alpheus Myers patented his "Trap for Removing Tapeworms from the Stomach and Intestines". Myers's invention comprised "a trap which is baited, attached to a string, and swallowed by the patient after a fast of suitable duration to make the worm hungry. The worm seizes the bait, and its head is caught in the trap, which is then withdrawn from the patient's stomach by the string which has been left hanging from the mouth, dragging after it the whole length of the worm."

Dr John Harvey Kellogg, inventor of the cereal flake, probably performed more enemas than any human in history. He was raised in a devout Seventh-Day Adventist family and was indoctrinated from an early age with the strict tenets of vegetarianism advocated by his church. In 1876, at the age of twenty-four, Kellogg became the staff physician at the Battle Creek Sanitarium. Originally "the San" or the "Kellogg Sanitarium" as it popularly became known had been the world headquarters of the Seventh-Day Adventists. Kellogg was highly regarded in Adventist circles for his no-nonsense medical journalism and his unwavering belief in the power of roughage. The San offered hydropathy, electropathy and radium cures. For a time, Kellogg promoted "Fletcherizing" or chewing food until it slithered down the throat. Fletcherism was the brainchild of Horace Fletcher, an American billionaire who once lived solely on potatoes for 578 days. Fletcher preached that food should always be taken in very small bites then masticated thirty-two times – one chew for every tooth in the perfect adult mouth. Kellogg changed his mind about Fletcherizing when he decided that excessive chewing destroyed the fibre content of the food.

Kellogg made an issue of personally abstaining from all sexual relations to prove that sex was an impairment to good health: "an erection", he announced, "is a flagstone on the grave". The chief target for Kellogg's invective were "chronic masturbators". He imposed a ban on masturbators from the San, recommending: "A remedy which is almost always successful in small boys is circumcision . . . the operation should be performed by a surgeon without administering an anaesthetic, as the brief pain attending the operation will have a salutary effect upon the mind . . . in females, the author has found the application of pure carbolic acid to the clitoris an excellent means of allaying the abnormal excitement."

Dr Kellogg designed a variety of house specialities for his patients, included Caramel Cereal Coffee, Bulgarian yogurt and meat substitutes called Protose and Nuttose, the latter a veal substitute made entirely from nuts. This was Kellogg's "nut period": he wrote a medical paper, "Nuts May Save the Race", and also invented peanut butter. After a couple of years at the San, Kellogg had a minor break-through when he came up with a mixture of oatmeal and corn meal, baked into biscuits which he named Granula – a controversial decision, given that the only other cereal in existence at the time was also called Granula. Once sued, Kellogg unimaginatively renamed his product Granola. After more trial and error Kellogg discovered a new treat for his patients called Granose, the first flaked wheat cereal. He set up production in a barn behind the Sanitarium, and soon the whole town of Battle Creek was gripped with "flake fever" as cereal and health food manufacturers appeared overnight.

Dr Kellogg's brother William had no interest in crusading against masturbation or bad eating habits, but he had some business sense and saw a potential fortune in the doctor's invention. William eventually persuaded his eccentric brother that they should form a new company to manufacture corn flakes, and the Battle Creek Toasted Corn Flake Company was born in 1906. Dr Kellogg was the majority shareholder, but he distributed part of his stock among the Sanitarium doctors. Later, while Dr Kellogg was away, William quietly bought up the shares until he personally owned a majority, and became the new president.

Kellogg's greatest obsession however was the rectum. Ninety per cent of all illness, he asserted, originated in the stomach and bowel. "The putrefactive changes which recur in the undigested residues of flesh foods" were to blame, he explained. Patients who arrived at 'the San' soon learned that their bowel was a toxic sewer full of poisons. Kellogg made sure that the bowel of each and every patient was plied with water, from above and below. His favourite device was an enema machine ("just like one I saw in Germany") that could run fifteen gallons of water through a bowel in a matter of seconds; every water enema was followed by a pint of yogurt – half eaten, the other half administered by enema "thus planting the protective germs where they are most needed and may render most effective service".

John Harvey Kellogg died on 14 December 1943 at the age of ninety-one, still active as a physician. The doctor was famous for his fifteen-hour days, and for keeping two secretaries busy with his dictation. At his death, Kellogg held more than thirty patents for food products and processes as well as exercise, diagnostic and therapeutic machines. He is also credited with developing such diverse products as a menthol nasal inhaler and the electric blanket.

In 1999, 56-year-old Edward Bodkin of Huntington, Indiana was arrested and charged with performing unlicensed surgery. Bodkin allegedly removed the testicles of at least five men and was ready to castrate a sixth when the patient panicked and handed over to police a videotape Bodkin had loaned him of some of the operations. Some of the testicles were discovered in jars in Bodkin's apartment. When asked to comment on the patients' motives, state prosecutor John Branham said, "I can't sit here as a reasonable human being and give you an intelligent answer to that."

In 1998 E. Frenkel, one of Russia's growing number of psychic healers, claimed to have successfully used his mental powers to stop moving vehicles, including a streetcar. When Frenkel decided he was ready for something bigger he stepped in front of a freight train. Frenkel died from his injuries in Astrakhan, on an undisclosed date.

Queen Victoria spent much of her reign in the hands of her court physician Sir James Clarke, a man described by Lord Clarendon as "not fit to attend a sick cat". In 1839 Clarke was involved in a court scandal which became known as "the Flora Hastings affair". The Queen's young unmarried lady-in-waiting Flora Hastings fell ill with a swollen stomach, convincing several people including the Queen herself that she was pregnant. To prove her innocence, Miss Hastings agreed to a humiliating internal examination by the Queen's doctor. Clarke reported that although he could not find evidence of pregnancy, he could see no other good reason for her swollen stomach. He then produced a medical statement which concluded, somewhat mysteriously, that although Flora Hastings was still a virgin this did not necessarily mean that she was not pregnant. He had come across a few cases in his time, he explained to the Queen, of pregnant virgins. The truth became evident a few months later when the girl died in agony from a tumour on her liver.

The incompetent Clarke's career should have been terminated, but the Queen retained his services. When her husband Prince Albert fell ill in November 1861, Dr Clarke was on hand again to assure both the Prime Minister Lord Palmerston and the Queen that the Prince Consort was suffering from no more than a nasty cold, and that there was absolutely no need for concern. Within six weeks Prince Albert was dead. Clarke said later that with hindsight he thought he recognized typhoid symptoms. He was wrong on this count also because the Prince Consort almost certainly died of cancer.

The eighteenth-century Scottish physician Dr James Graham was a well known dandy, often seen walking through the streets of London in one of his white linen suits, carrying a gold-headed cane in one hand and a posy of flowers in the other. He was better known however as proprietor of London's first ever sex clinic. Graham was chiefly famous for his invention the "celestial bed", which he claimed could help childless couples to conceive. Graham had left his Edinburgh clinic in the 1770s to open a more lucrative practice in London, where his Temple of Health promised wealthy customers a cure for impotence via waves of magnetism and electricity, via about 15 cwt of compound magnets attached to a bed, a bizarrely ornate piece of furniture decorated with cherubs and standing on eight brass legs. Childless couples were charged up to £500 to spend a single night in the bed. For their money they also got soft lights and soothing music, lavish furnishings and appearances by several scantily clad Greek goddesses – among them Emma Hart, later to become Lady Hamilton and mistress of Horatio Nelson.

At his Temple Graham was attended by black servants as he looked after his patients' sexual problems, sitting them on magnetic thrones and soothing them with music, massages and mud baths. Horace Walpole visited the Temple in 1780 and wrote that he had encountered a number of astonishing experiences, including an invisible woman "warbling to clarinets on the stairs". Although Graham's methods were scorned by the medical establishment his Temple did a roaring trade for several years until his techniques became unfashionable and he was obliged to return to his native Edinburgh. He continued to preach the benefits of magnetism and electricity for impotence until he was finally committed to a lunatic asylum.

––––––––––––

The messianic San Francisco dentist Dr Henry Cogswell believed that it was his duty to spread the good news of modern dentistry to a caries-ridden populace. He so fervently believed that he was the embodiment of all that was good about dentistry that he donated to the city several statues of himself offering glasses of ever-flowing water to thirsty citizens.

Lord Dawson of Penn served as royal doctor to four sovereigns: Edward VII, George V, Edward VIII and George VI. Although he was the best paid doctor in the country it didn't necessarily follow that he was the best at his job. One of the more vicious stories which circulated about his alleged incompetence was that he once treated a man for jaundice for six weeks until he realized that his patient was Chinese.

The Englishman Dr Scott was a prolific advertiser and maker of "electric hair brushes" and related products in America in the 1880s. Scott received his first US patent for a brush handle in 1872, and introduced his line of "electric brushes" in 1880. Dr Scott's brushes and other devices all contained slightly magnetized iron rods in their handles, although Scott elected to use the term "electric" rather than "magnetic" in all his advertising. Scott made many claims for the power of his electric brushes, including hair growth and relief from headaches. He discovered over a period of time however that every disease added to the advertising claims opened up a wider potential market for his brushes. Other conditions his brushes could cure soon included constipation, malarial lameness, rheumatism, diseases of the blood, and paralysis. Every hair brush box carried the following printed warning: "In no case should more than one person use the brush. If always used by the same person it retains its full curative power."

In addition to his popular hair and flesh brushes Scott marketed electric plasters, insoles, rheumatic rings, shoulder braces, throat protectors, nerve and lung invigorators, body belts, wristlets, sciatic appliances, anklets, leg appliances, office caps, and other special appliances made to order. He also sold electric curry combs for horses. His advertising literature boldly asserted, "There need not be a sick person in America (save from accidents), if our appliances become a part of the wardrobe of every lady and gentleman, as also of infants and children."

Scott's patents were always deliberately vague about the alleged curative powers of the brushes and other gadgets. In his 1881 patent, for example, he claimed a brush with embedded magnet. "The object of the invention is to secure within the interior of the brush one or more natural or artificial magnets, which, according to the belief of many persons, founded upon a theory of magneto-therapeutics which has become widely prevalent, have the effect of rendering brushes to which they are applied advantageous in use for relieving headache, preventing baldness, and other similar purposes." Several other patents granted to Scott were for the elaborate designs on the backs of his brushes to prevent others from making exact copies. They also allowed him to use the term "patented" in his ads, thus implying that the US Patent Office had approved his devices on their medical merit. Scott's final patent in 1889 was for "improvements to his electric corsets".

Dr Robert Lefever specializes in helping people who are obsessed with helping other people. The 500 patients a year who visit his London clinic include women who compulsively marry alcoholics so they can cure them and a patient who was sent to hospital with exhaustion after looking after an overweight woman and obsessively pushing her in her wheelchair to places she did not really want to go.

The only Portuguese Pope, John XXI, was also the only doctor ever to become pontiff. In the mid thirteenth century, largely on the strength of his medical treatise in which he prescribed lettuce leaves for toothache, lettuce seed to reduce sex drive and pig dung to stop nosebleeds, he was appointed physician to the Vatican. While receiving his medical advice three popes, Gregory X, Innocent V and Adrian V, died in quick succession. The doctor was duly elected pontiff, possibly in the hope that his medical skills would enable him to live longer than the previous three. Within twelve months of his election however the roof of his new palace fell in, crushing him horribly, and he died six days later.

Michael Potkul, thirty-three, won a $400,000 malpractice award against surgeon Dominic Brandy in Pittsburgh, US in 1996. Brandy had promised Potkul that he could give him a nearly full head of hair by grabbing the hairy scalp at the back of his head and stretching it over the bald bit on top. Potkul became so depressed after six unsuccessful operations that he attempted suicide.

The bizarre John Richard Brinkley, "the Milford Messiah", was the world's foremost practitioner of Goat-Gland Science, the oft-forgotten predecessor of Viagra. Brinkley was born in Tennessee in 1885, and set up a small town doctor's practice in Milford, Kansas. One day an elderly farmer entered his clinic complaining of erectile dysfunction and asked Brinkley if anything could be done. Remembering a book he had once read about endocrinology, Brinkley theorized that by transplanting the sexual glands of a goat into the male scrotum he could renew the male sex drive. Incredibly, and in spite of his severely limited experience as a surgeon, he persuaded the desperate farmer to allow him to test his theory. A year after his "transplant" the farmer's wife gave birth to a baby boy named Billy.

Flushed with success, Brinkley offered his services for a mere $750 to anyone else willing to undergo his surgery, and found plenty of eager subjects. The first few transplants, using transplanted gonads from the odourless breed of Toggenberg goats, were performed without any major hitch. The next two recipients however were fitted with testicles from the Angora breed. According to the doctor they left the operating theatre smelling like "a steamy barn in midsummer". From now on Brinkley would use only Toggenberg gonads, even allowing his patients to select their own donor goat from a pen outside the clinic.

Brinkley's goat-gland therapy came to the attention of Harry Chandler, owner of the *Los Angeles Times*. Chandler also underwent Brinkley's surgery, and highly satisfied with the results began to publicize the technique in his newspaper. The publicity made Brinkley famous, but with it also came the unwanted attentions of the California state medical authorities who quickly revoked his licence to practise and began criminal proceedings against him. Brinkley fled back to Kansas where he found his surgery in ever increasing demand, thanks to his radio station KFKB, an eccentric mixture of medical lectures and country and western music. Hundreds of males from all over the US flocked to Kansas, and at one stage about forty goats a week were being shipped to the Brinkley clinic by rail.

In the 1930s Brinkley hit upon a new scam which he thought would be even more financially rewarding than goat gonad transplants. He launched a new show on his radio station called "Dr Brinkley's Medical Question Box." Listeners were invited to write to him with their health problems and he would prescribe treatments on air. These cures invariably involved his own product line of patent medicines, which for the most part were coloured water. The Kansas authorities finally had the excuse they needed to revoke his broadcasting licence for blatantly unethical practice. Brinkley simply moved his operation to Del Rio, Texas, and set up a huge new transmitter across the Mexican border. His new station, XER, could now be heard throughout North America, and continued to bring him patients. In the late 1930s Mexican officials, pressured by the US government, shut down Brinkley's transmitter and eventually he was forced to declare bankruptcy. In 1942, as the US fraud squad moved in, he evaded trial by dying in San Antonio, Texas. His amazing career had in fact left an important legacy by prompting a complete overhaul of medical practice and telecommunications by the US government.

In 1891 the French surgeon Dr Varlot developed a method of preserving corpses by covering them with a thin layer of metal – in effect, he was electroplating the dead. Dr Varlot's innovative technique involved making the body conductive by exposing it to silver nitrate, followed by immersion in a galvanic bath of copper sulphate, producing a one millimetre thick coating of copper – "a brilliant red copper finish of exceptional strength and durability". Why Dr Varlot wanted to do this at all however is unclear.

The "production line lobotomy", performed with an ice pick under local anaesthetic, was the tour de force of the maverick Dr Walter Freeman, Professor of Neurology at the George Washington University. His first live patient was a manic depressive 63-year-old woman from Kansas, who chose surgery rather than face a lifetime in a mental institution. On the operating table however she had second thoughts when she learned that her headful of curls would have to be completely shaved off. Freeman reassured her that she could keep her precious curls, confident in the knowledge that after the operation she would no longer care.

In the 1940s and 1950s the Freeman lobotomy was performed on more than 20,000 patients as he toured across the US in his specially equipped camper van, which he called his "Lobotomobile". Nurses and hospital officials who witnessed Freeman in action, wielding his hammer and ice pick on patient after patient, quite often fainted. His most famous patient was the rebellious Hollywood starlet Frances Farmer, who was subjected to the Freeman lobotomy at the age of just thirty-four. Freeman had a photo taken of himself performing the lobotomy on her, which he would show off to friends. He performed his last lobotomy in 1967 when he was seventy-two years old.

In 1994 the licence of US neurosurgeon Dr Raymond Sattle was revoked after he left a patient alone on the operating table with his brain exposed for half an hour while he went out for his lunch break in the middle of aneurysm surgery. The North Carolina Board of Medical Examiners heard that Dr Sattle also frequently forgot the names of his surgical equipment during operations, allowed an untrained nurse to drill holes in a patient's head, and had intravenous fluids pumped into his own veins while he was operating to help him stay on his feet.

Every morning without fail Sir Astley Cooper, surgeon to George IV and the Duke of Wellington, rose between five and six a.m. and dissected two corpses before breakfast. If Sir Astley couldn't get hold of a fresh human cadaver, London Zoo would occasionally chip in with a dead elephant.

Seventy-two-year-old doctor Charles Brown-Séquard caused a medical sensation in 1889 when he announced to the French Society of Biology his discovery of the elixir of youth. The elderly doctor described how he chopped and ground up the testicles of puppies and guinea pigs then injected himself with the resulting compound. He said that he was now physically thirty years younger and boasted that he was able to "visit" his young wife every day without fail. The lecture caused a stir, albeit briefly: soon afterwards his wife left him for a younger man, and shortly after that the doctor dropped dead from a cerebral haemorrhage.

In 1916 a Viennese professor named Ludwig Steinach promoted an even more controversial theory, that the male vasectomy was in fact the much sought after elixir of youth: one snip and your ageing processes would stop, your hair would grow thicker and your sexual potency would increase. In the years that followed thousands of men underwent "Steinaching" – including his near neighbour Sigmund Freud – until the professor was forced to admit that he'd got it all badly wrong.

Florence Nightingale was a hypochondriac who lived every day to the ripe old age of ninety complaining that she was an invalid. To her death she refused to believe in the existence of bacteria and kept a miniature pet owl in her pocket which she took with her everywhere.

The extraordinary surgeon John Hunter was the unrivalled expert of eighteenth-century anatomy. Like many of his fellow anatomists, Hunter collected the corpses of executed criminals for dissection. His prize exhibit was the body of a 7 ft 8 in Irishman, Charles Byrne, which he had acquired in spite of stiff competition from a number of local anatomists who were keen to lay their hands on the Irish "giant". Byrne himself had lived with a dreadful fear that he might end up in a museum, and made special arrangements to be buried at sea in a lead coffin. When he finally died of tuberculosis, however, Hunter bribed officials to fill the coffin with rocks and gave them £500 for the corpse. Hunter was intensely proud of his latest plaything. He propped the corpse up beside him on his coach while doing his rounds, then took it home and boiled it in a large vat to separate the flesh from the bones.

Hunter was an obsessive collector of anatomical artefacts, including embalmed foetuses, corpses and human and animal skeletons. Over a period of thirty years he amassed about 65,000 items. His wife Anne is said to have only once complained about her husband's homework and that was when he arrived on the doorstep with a stuffed giraffe which was too tall to fit inside the house. Hunter shortened it by hacking the legs off below the knee and placed it in his hall.

In order to study venereal disease Hunter deliberately injected himself with pus from a gonorrhoea patient who, unknown to Hunter, also had syphilis. The experiment cost him his life.

John Hunter's brother William was also an anatomist who specialized in the collection of female corpses in various states of pregnancy. In total he dissected between 300 and 400. As pregnant women were never executed, none of his specimens could have been acquired legally.

A twentieth-century trepanation movement was founded by a Dutchman, Dr Bart Huges, who in the 1960s figured out that a person's peace of mind was related to the amount of blood swilling around in the brain. He promptly cut a hole in his own head with an electrical drill to achieve "a permanent high", then wrote a book about it called *Bore Hole*. The medical and legal authorities were so impressed by his discovery that they rewarded him with a spell in a Dutch lunatic asylum. Dr Huges did in fact manage to attract two converts to his cause, the London couple Joey Mellen and Amanda Fielding. After failing to find a member of the medical profession to do it for them, they finally managed to drill holes in their own heads with the help of an electric drill and generous quantities of LSD, after several abortive attempts with a hand-worked corkscrew and a saw.

An effective method of tooth extraction was devised in the eighteenth century by Dr Monsey, Resident Physician to the Chelsea Royal Hospital, home of the Chelsea Pensioners. He took a strong piece of catgut, wound one end around the patient's tooth, then threaded the other through a specially prepared bullet with a hole drilled through it. The bullet was loaded into his revolver and fired.

One of the most painfully misguided medical fads of the twentieth century was the fashion for surgically removing human colons. The king of the British colon movement was the Irishman Sir William Arbuthnot Lane, a surgeon at Guy's Hospital, London. Lane recommended oiling the colon daily with a pint of cream and sleeping flat on the belly, and failed to understand why the medical world was less than impressed with his astonishing discovery that red-haired women were naturally immune to constipation. His greatest contribution to medical science however was yet to come: in 1903 he became convinced that the colon was surplus to the requirements of the human body – it was merely a useless tube of tissue and muscle, full of foul smells. With a missionary zeal Lane set about ridding the world of colons. Soon, surgeons all over the country were agreeing with him, and the humble colon took the rap for a whole range of diseases including cancer and tuberculosis. No colon was safe from Lane: patients who came to see him for minor ailments would have their colons removed and tossed into the incinerator as a matter of routine: a nagging wife who nearly drove her husband to suicide had hers whipped out to make her more docile. This ruthless rectal campaign raged for about ten years until fellow doctors, noting that none of Lane's colon-less patients ever benefited from their loss, took a more studied look at his theory and began to detect a strong whiff of bullshit. Lane died, discredited, aged eighty-six.

Muhammed Saeed was a bogus Bradford doctor who was granted a licence after arriving from Pakistan and allowed to work for the National Health Service for thirty years before he was finally outed as a fraud. "Dr" Saeed was jailed for five years in 1992 after variously prescribing to his 3,000 patients shampoo to be taken internally, creosote for a tooth complaint, sleeping pills to be taken three times a day, cough mixture to be rubbed into the skin, and suppositories to be taken orally.

Czar Peter the Great was a keen amateur surgeon and anatomist. During a trip to Holland, just after a heavy meal, the Czar watched with fascination the anatomical dissection of a human cadaver. When two of his nauseous attendants made it clear that they didn't share his enthusiasm for human intestines, Peter forced them to bite into the flesh of the corpse. Although the Czar was an incompetent surgeon no one ever dared to disappoint him when he volunteered to wield the knife. When the Czarina Martha Apraxina, widow of his half-brother Theodore III, died, Peter personally opened up her corpse to find out if the rumour that she was still a virgin at the age of forty-nine was true. He once removed 20 lbs of water from the dropsical wife of a rich Russian merchant named Borst. The Czar was extremely proud of his handiwork, but was furious when the woman selfishly died shortly afterwards. He ordered an autopsy to prove that he hadn't been responsible for the death – naturally the inquest found that the Czar was entirely blameless.

Czar Peter once saw a bad tooth being pulled, and was suddenly consumed with ambition to turn his hand to amateur dentistry. Overnight the Czar's retinue of 250 courtiers became unwilling accomplices to his new hobby. He carried out spot dental checks on anyone who happened to be passing – if any tooth looked suspect he whipped it out. Unfortunately he was quite unaware of his own strength and sometimes he got carried away and accidentally removed gums also. Peter kept the teeth he'd drawn from his courtiers in a little bag. One day a courtier appealed to him for help: his wife had terrible toothache, he said, but she was so scared of having it pulled she would pretend nothing was wrong whenever a dentist approached her. The Czar obliged, and ignoring the screams and protests of the woman, pulled the tooth and popped it in his bag. Only later it did it emerge that the woman had never had toothache in the first place: her husband just wanted to teach her lesson.

The Czar built a Museum of Curiosities to satisfy his fascination for freaks of nature. His collection included a man without genitals, a child with two heads, a five-footed sheep, a deformed foetus, the organs of a hermaphrodite, "the hand of a man who died by excessive drinking with all its blood stagnated in the veins" and the corpses of Siamese twins. Each specimen was individually pickled in an alcohol-filled jar. The museum caretaker, a badly deformed dwarf, could look forward to the day when he too would be pickled. One of Peter's prize exhibits was a pickled phallus, donated by the Prussian King

Frederick William. This item had caught the Czar's eye on his trip to Berlin and the Prussian king was only too delighted to get rid of it. Peter thought it would be a good jape to persuade his wife Catherine to kiss it: she accepted his invitation, but only after he made his offer more attractive by offering to cut her head off if she declined.

In 1995 a dentist from Tennessee, Stephen Cobble, was charged with professional incompetence following the death of a patient. Cobble also faced complaints from former patients that he had given them check-ups by having his assistant rub their backs, stomachs, and arms; sedated patients by administering injections to their groins and navels; transferred scar tissue to treat a jaw disorder; made a patient stand with one foot on a stack of magazines; and prescribed a diet of beef, salt, and eggs and a quarter-pound of butter daily.

Chapter Eight

The Eccentric Muse

"Coleridge holds that a man cannot have a pure mind who refuses apple dumplings. I am not certain but he is right"

Charles Lamb (1775–1834)

"I am like an unpopular electric eel in a pond full of flatfish"

Edith Sitwell (1887–1964)

"I am reborn. I am born from the egg. It is a perfect cube"
Salvador Dali (1904–89)

"You must not mind me, madam. I say strange things, but I mean no harm"

Samuel Johnson (1709–84)

"Thrippy Pilliwinx – Inkly tinky, pobblebockle able squaks? Flosky! Beebul trimble flosky! Okul scratch abibble-bongibo, viddle squibble tog-a-tog ferry moya-sitty amsky flamsky crocklefether squiggs. Flinky wisty pomm"

Edward Lear (1812–88), letter to
Evelyn Baring, Lord Cromer, 1850

William Cornyns Beaumont, a well known Fleet Street journalist in the early part of the twentieth century, held a variety of controversial beliefs including a firmly held conviction that there was a Jewish conspiracy to overthrow the British Empire. Beaumont believed that the Holy Land was in fact Britain and part of Scandinavia. The lost world of Atlantis had also been one of the British Isles, and it was from Atlantis that a race of giant Aryans had populated the earth, colonizing it as they spread from country to country. He was convinced that Egypt, the seat of the mighty Pharaohs, had in fact been situated in Western Scotland. Moreover, London was actually Damascus, York was Babylon, Glastonbury was the garden of Eden, etc. etc. Apparently Earth had been hit by a giant meteor not far from Edinburgh, or Jerusalem as it was in those days, an event which led to Noah's flood and caused Britain to lose its sub-tropical climate and become cold and damp. Thereafter the Roman Emperor Hadrian and that well known Yorkshire-man Constantine the Great had been responsible for ex-pounding the malicious and wholly ridiculous lie that the Holy Land was not in Britain, but somewhere in the Middle East. It seems that none of these views were considered incompatible with William Cornyns Beaumont's job as a leading staff writer with the *Daily Mail*.

———————

From childhood the Victorian "nonsense poet" and artist Edward Lear suffered from what he called "the Demon" epilepsy or "the Morbids", a state of mind which he always attributed to excessive masturbation.

———————

Percy Grainger, Australia's best known composer and arranger through such classics as *Country Gardens* and *Londonderry Air*, habitually walked on high window ledges and often slept naked on top of or underneath his piano. He also commissioned several lifesize papier mâché models of his best friends.

Grainger was driven by bizarre sexual desires which included flagellation and taking photographs of his sex sessions. He was quite open about his love of being whipped – he called his scars his "blue roses". Grainger had an intense and suspect relationship with his mother Rose, which he described as "the only truly passionate affair of my life" – many believed that it was incestuous. Grainger's mum committed suicide after she was driven insane by tertiary syphilis.

In 1935 the composer founded the Grainger Museum at the University of Melbourne, where he intended to show his collection of musical souvenirs to the Australian public. His last wish was that his skeleton should also go on display in the museum. The request was quietly ignored by the trustees.

———————

The nineteenth-century German composer Robert Schumann had two imaginary friends called Florestan and Eusebius. They gave him ideas for his scores. He also had an irrational fear of metal, especially disliking keys.

Jonathan Swift, author of *Gulliver's Travels*, entered the Church at the age of thirty-three and was appointed rector of a small Irish parish, where his odd appearance and strange behaviour earned him the nickname "the mad parson". He was extremely parsimonious and lived very frugally. He also had an odd counting obsession; he would tell acquaintances that the walk from his apartment in Chelsea to the centre of London was five thousand seven hundred and forty-eight paces. Swift had a reputation for being extremely rude to strangers. His irritability may have been partly attributable to a health problem – he suffered from a condition which caused gritty matter to accumulate in his bowels. One day he was sitting in a coffee house when he was approached by Dr Arbuthnot, who had no idea who Swift was. Arbuthnot had just finished writing a letter and the ink was still wet. He enquired as to whether Swift had any sand about his person. "No, sir," Swift replied, "but I have the gravel and if you will give me your letter I will piss upon it."

Swift hated mankind, especially Scots, women and children. Women, he once wrote, "were a sort of species hardly a degree above a monkey". Swift was an inconsistent ladies' man. He once declared that no woman was really worth giving up the middle of your bed for. In his satirical essay "A Modest Proposal", he recommended, straight-faced, that the Irish solve their over-population problem by eating babies. Towards the end of his writing career he became obsessed with bodily functions. He wrote a treatise on excrement in 1733 called "Human Ordure" under the pen-name "Dr Shit", which caused many of his admirers, including William Eddy, to shudder at "a scatalogical ugliness that is nauseating to the most hardened cynic". Swift dreaded old age and foresaw the prolonged illness and the terrible consequences of dementia. He once told a friend, "I shall die like a tree; I shall die first at the top." This was prophetic. He lost his mind and became obsessed with exercise and dieting, even took to eating his meals while walking round the room. Before he died prematurely senile at seventy-eight his manservant showed him off to members of the public for a fee.

Apart from Swift, Aristophanes, Chaucer, Rabelais, Ben Franklin and Mark Twain have all written about farting. Erasmus once wrote a treatise about flatulence and belching, and warned that a stifled fart was a health hazard.

H. G. Wells (1866–1946), on leaving a Cambridge party, accidentally picked up a hat that did not belong to him. Discovering his mistake, he decided not to return the headgear to its rightful owner, although his name was inside the brim. The hat fitted Wells comfortably and furthermore he had grown to like it. He wrote to the former owner: "I stole your hat; I like your hat; I shall keep your hat. Whenever I look inside it I shall think of you and your excellent sherry and of the town of Cambridge. I take off your hat to you."

The operatic composer Giacomo Meyerbeer (1791–1864) lived with a constant fear of premature burial. He arranged to have bells tied to his extremities so that any movement in his coffin would attract attention.

James Agate (1877–1947) was one of the most flamboyant theatre critics ever, his extravagance legendary. According to his biographer he would hire a taxi just to cross the road to his gentlemen's club and then keep it waiting with the meter running into the early hours of the morning while he played bridge.

Hans Christian Andersen (1805–75), Danish author of children's fairy tale classics including *The Steadfast Tin Soldier* and *The Ugly Duckling*, was hypochondriac, dyslexic and highly effeminate. He was also phobic about arriving late, which caused him to turn up at railway stations hours early. He always carried a coil of rope with him for fear of being caught in a hotel room fire, and compulsively returned to a room he had left twice to check that the candles were out. He never ate pork for fear of catching tapeworm.

Gustav Mahler (1860–1911), famous for his funeral marches, had a morbid fixation about death. He wrote his first funeral march when he was six.

For more than 2,000 years writers have been intrigued by lipograms, i.e. literary works in which one or more letters of the alphabet are excluded. The Greek poet Lasus of Hermione may have been the world's first lipogrammatist. His sixth-century-BC hymn to Demeter was written entirely without the letter S because, according to one scholar, Lasus hated its "unpleasant hissing".

The American author Ernest Vincent Wright was perhaps the most ambitious man ever to tackle such a compositional challenge, when he wrote a 267-page novel to prove the point that the letter E, used most frequently in the English language, was not indispensable. In his book *Gadsby*, the author completely avoided the fifth letter of the alphabet and somehow maintained grammatical correctness. Wright composed his lipogram while living in a California home for war veterans, and used string to tie down his typewriter's E key to make sure that it was never used during the five and a half months that he spent composing his opus. Wright noted in the introduction to the book: "At first a whole army of little Es gathered around my desk, all eagerly expecting to be called upon. But gradually as they saw me writing on and on, without even noticing them, they grew uneasy; and, with excited whisperings amongst themselves, began hopping up and riding on my pen, looking down constantly for a chance to drop off into some word." Despite the magnitude of his bizarre achievement, Wright's prose suffered as a consequence. One biographer noted that it was "as if it had been written by a wooden-eared alien". By the time *Gadsby* was typeset, the author was seriously ill and he died on its October 1939 publication date. Although *Gadsby* was not a bestseller, rare copies are now highly collectible.

Niccolo Paganini (1782–1840) was a pathological show-off. He deliberately played on frayed violin strings in the hope that one would break so it would give him an opportunity to impress by playing expertly on the remaining strings.

Hilaire Belloc (1832–1953), the English writer of French and British descent, wrote novels, biographies, travelogues, books of light verse and literary criticism, and is one of the most versatile and most prolific of modern English writers. Belloc turned out book after book, not always up to his highest standard, merely in order to make ends meet. During the 1930s in a railway carriage Belloc noticed a man in front of him reading a volume of his *History of England*. He leaned forward, asked him how much he had paid for it, was informed of the price, took a corresponding sum out of his pocket, gave it to the man, snatched the book from his hand, and tossed it out of the window.

James Joyce (1882–1941), whose most famous novel *Ulysses* was considered so lewd that the full version was banned from publication in Britain and the US for nearly twenty years, was an underwear fetishist. He kept a tiny pair of doll's knickers in his pocket: his party trick in public bars was to slip them over his fingers and "walk" them across the table top.

John Christie, founder of the Glyndebourne Festival Opera, had a passion for tapioca pudding, possibly as a result of spending sixteen years as a schoolmaster at Eton. He once ate seven helpings at one sitting. By the outbreak of war in 1914 Christie had lost an eye in a sporting accident and acquired a permanent limp from a riding mishap. He was an unflappable leader in the trenches. When a soldier was blown to pieces by a shell only a few feet away from Christie and his men, he produced a copy of Edmund Spenser's poem *The Faerie Queene* from his pocket and read it aloud to restore calm.

Christie threw lavish parties at his Glyndebourne home, spending a fortune on champagne, yet allowed his guests to freeze as he always refused to switch on the heating. He was so fearful of wasting electricity that he employed a man just to turn the lights off around his house. He was often seen around London with a large hot water bottle sticking out of the back of his trousers. Christie generally favoured an old pair of tennis shoes, even in formal evening dress, although he also went through a "lederhosen period" in the 1930s, when all of his visitors were required to follow his lead and wear leather shorts for dinner. He was also known to hand out knitting needles and balls of wool to his lady guests to give them something to do while the men talked.

Christie was a bulk buyer. He once acquired 2,000 pairs of cheap plastic dancing pumps, because he thought that one day they might come in useful. His most ambitious bulk purchase was in America when he acquired a ton of sugar and rice and went home with it on the *Queen Mary*. As this was shortly after the Second World War and rationing was still in place it was illegal for one person to bring such a large quantity of sugar and rice into the country. Christie got around the problem by persuading his fellow passengers to take small portions through Customs with them in their hand luggage, then once safely ashore he retrieved it all and stored it under the floors at Glyndebourne. A friend once was driving him along Bayswater

Road in London when Christie suddenly opened his briefcase, took out several old collars and socks, and threw them into the gutter, noting, "It's the easiest way to get rid of them." One evening Christie was sitting next to the Queen at a dinner party. He removed his glass eye, polished it with his handkerchief, popped it back in, turned to Her Majesty and enquired, "In straight, ma'am?"

Gioacchino Rossini (1792–1868) suffered from alopecia which made him completely bald. The composer took to wearing a wig; in exceptionally cold weather, however, he wore two or three wigs simultaneously.

Marcel Proust (1871–1922), who wrote most of his novels lying in bed in a room lined with cork, had various bizarre and unpleasant habits, including a sexual fixation with butchers. He had his manservant Alfred procure a young butcher's apprentice. During sexual activity with Proust the lad was required to answer questions about butchery: e.g. "How do you kill a calf?" and "Did it bleed much?" Whenever Proust visited male brothels he also had an unusual routine involving photos of his relatives. The young males he procured were instructed to leaf through the photos, more often than not of his mother, and make derogatory remarks along the lines of "Who is this little tart?" Proust also had his chauffeur bring him live rats, which he would pierce with hat pins until they bled to death.

The nineteenth-century German composer Richard Wagner always worked in a stiflingly hot room perfumed with roses while wearing a silk dressing gown, which belied the fact that he was also a notorious womanizer. Wagner was touchy about critics: he often invited friends around, treated them to a sneak preview of his work, then asked them for a frank opinion. Anyone who didn't offer a glowing review would be threatened with physical violence.

The American composer Charles Ives (1874–1954) spent much of his time and money advocating an amendment to the US Constitution that would prevent any American citizen from earning more than $20,000 a year.

G. K. Chesterton (1874–1936) was a British essayist, novelist, critic and poet. He was so preoccupied with writing that he became extremely absent-minded and frequently forgot to keep appointments. He relied on his wife in all practical matters. Once, on a lecture tour he sent her the following telegram: "Am in Birmingham. Where ought I to be?" She wired back: "Home."

Lady Mary Wortley Montagu, (1689–1762) wit, poet and letter writer, was one of the most colourful English women of her era and a member of one of England's most eccentric families. Her letters from Turkey published after her journey there in 1716 revealed her as an extraordinary personality, a woman of boundless and fearless curiosity. Although beautiful, head-strong and aristocratic, in 1712 she eloped and married, against her family's wishes, the incredibly boring Edward Wortley Montagu, or, as she was to know him, her "Prince Sombre". A good example of Montagu's dullness can be found in the notes he made to himself in the margins of political speeches he planned to deliver; "pause for a minute"; "cough"; "look round"; etc. Lady Mary later emerged as a star at the court of George I; it was she who famously noted that the king was "an honest blockhead". She competed with the young Alexander Pope for the role of the wittiest poet of the day, until smallpox nearly killed her and left her without eyelashes and condemned to a lifetime of painful eye problems. A famous quarrel between the two resulted in probably the most astonishing exchange of poetic insults in history. She especially enjoyed showing off to guests a lavatory bowl decorated with the heads of both Swift and Pope. The thought of defecating on them daily, a visitor noted, gave Lady Mary considerable satisfaction.

Her husband's position as the new Turkish ambassador took them abroad in 1716, a trip that made Lady Mary famous in the role of intrepid and eccentric upper-class lady on her travels. She later introduced into England the practice of inoculation against smallpox, a procedure she had observed in Turkey. Her son Edward was said to be the illicit fruit of a passionate affair with the Sultan of Turkey. Edward himself was a famously eccentric traveller. He grew a brightly braided beard that reached down to his waist, wore a colourful Turkish headdress and flowing robes, slept on the ground and drank only water. The only occasional luxuries he allowed himself were tobacco and coffee.

Dylan Thomas (1914–53) was perpetually short of money and died prematurely of alcoholism soon after presenting in New York his play for voices, *Under Milk Wood*. On one occasion when Thomas had been drinking and talking freely for some time, he suddenly stopped. "Somebody's boring me," he said. "I think it's me."

Arguably the most unusual performance art of all belongs to the French artist Orlan who expresses her theme of human beauty via plastic surgery. For several years she regularly volunteered to face the surgeon's scalpel to recreate herself as a woman with a stereotypically beautiful face. Her later work however took a different direction when she took to experimenting with ugliness. Orlan had horn-like protrusions implanted above her eyebrows and other similar operations. Wherever possible, Orlan has a local anaesthetic in order to watch the operations which are always caught on camera and the videos sold to collectors.

Piero Manzoni was the sole exponent of the art movement *arte povera* which inspired him to exhibit cans of his own excrement.

The work of Canadian feminist sculptor Louise Bourgeois mostly features severed penises and huge testicles hanging singly or in pairs or bunches, including a piece called "No Exit" – a stairway with two huge testicles restricting egress at the bottom – and "Untitled (with Foot)", in which a baby is crushed by a large testicle.

So great was the dread of premature burial in the nineteenth century that over 200 books were written on the subject, and societies were formed to prevent it. Writers, it seems, were the biggest worriers. Harriet Martineau left her doctor £10 with instructions that he should make sure she was well and truly deceased before her burial by cutting her head off. The novelist Edmund Yates similarly left a 20 guinea fee for any surgeon kind enough to slit his jugular vein before interment. Novelist Wilkie Collins always carried a letter with him imploring anyone finding him "dead" to contact the nearest doctor for a second opinion.

Ferdinand Flocon (1800–66) made it his lifetime's ambition to render the French Civil Code more accessible by turning all 22,891 articles, statutes, amendments and annotations into a 120,000-word poem. He died in obscurity.

Louisa Ramé, better known as Ouida, was famous for her romantic novels – a mid-nineteenth-century Barbara Cartland. Her nom-de-plume came from the childhood mispronunciation of her Christian name. By 1867 at the age of twenty-eight she had written no fewer than forty-seven novels and was so successful that she was able to leave London to live in Florence, where she rented the Villa Farniola at Scandicci. Her love life was fraught with difficulties. After an infatuation with an Italian singer called Mario she fell in love with a nobleman, the Marchese della Stufa, who was unfortunately already in the throes of an affair with the married English historian Janet Ross. When she discovered the affair Ouida was deeply wounded, but was able to turn the whole thing into yet another novel, *Friendship*.

By this time Ouida had become a highly eccentric and reclusive figure whose only companions were her dogs. She created a canine cemetery in the grounds of her villa. She lived well beyond her means, eating at Doneys, the Anglo-Florentine meeting-place, and ordering all her dresses from Worth, the Parisian designer. She was eventually evicted from the Villa Farniola and began to wander around the Florentine boarding houses with her aged mother and her pack of beloved dogs. In 1895, she moved into a villa outside Lucca, where she continued to write, although her novels had long since gone out of fashion. After another six years of wandering Ouida died penniless in Viareggio in 1909 and was buried in the English cemetery in Bagni di Lucca in a tomb which shows her lying down with her feet resting on a faithful dog, paid for by the British consul in Lucca.

Richard Gibson, a Canadian sculptor, exhibits pieces made from freeze dried human body parts, especially limbs and ears. In 1986 he advertised an appeal for spare parts and was arrested and fined £500 for conduct likely to cause a breach of the peace.

James Abbott McNeill Whistler (1834–1903) lived most of his life in London after 1860. He once dyed a rice pudding green so that it wouldn't clash with the walls of his dining room. He was cantankerous and opinionated and made many enemies in the art world. A snobbish Bostonian approached Whistler at a party one evening. "And where were you born, Mr Whistler?" she asked. "Lowell, Massachusetts," replied the painter. "Whatever possessed you to be born in a place like that?" exclaimed the lady. "The explanation is quite simple," said Whistler. "I wished to be near my mother."

Captain Philip Thickesse was a highly successful travel writer in the eighteenth century. His account of the Grand Tour was a best seller, reprinted twice and translated into French and German. He completed his entire tour in a two-wheel cabriolet, accompanied by his wife and two daughters, a spaniel, a parakeet and a monkey. Captain Thickesse had a violent and unpredictable temper, partly due to the fact that he suffered from gallstones and drank huge quantities of laudanum. He also had a talent for making enemies. His brief career as an apprentice to an apothecary ended abruptly when he told all his customers that patent medicines were useless and a complete waste of money. In fact Thickesse spent most of his life quarrelling with people and suing them for slander. He also kept up a running battle with his two similarly argumentative sons. He died in 1792 just as he was about to start on a journey to Italy, leaving behind a remarkable will which began: "I leave my right hand, to be cut off after my death, to my son Lord Audley; I desire it may be sent to him, in hopes that such a sight may remind him of his duty to God, after having so long abandoned the duty he owed to a father, who once so affectionately loved him."

The Californian artist Ronnie Nicolino once created a two-mile-long sand sculpture comprising 21,000 size 34C breasts. Nicolino promised that his next project would be a giant chain of bras long enough to span the width of the Grand Canyon, adding that in no way was he obsessed with breasts.

Contemporary British artists Gilbert and George once staged a show at the South London Art Gallery comprising sixteen large glossy photos of themselves surrounded by a series of "defecation motifs", including turd circles and turd sculptures, which they called *Naked Shit Pictures*. One critic described the work as "almost biblical".

Although he was never regarded as a truly great artist, by sheer hard graft Joseph Nollekens became one of England's most prolific and most successful sculptors in the late eighteenth century. His chief claim to fame however was as an incredibly eccentric miser. Nolleken's father was also notoriously mean. The family home was besieged by an angry mob in 1745, partly because they were Catholics and partly because the rioters expected to find large amounts of money stashed away by the tightfisted Nollekens Senior.

Born in London in 1737, Joseph was apprenticed to a local sculptor and eventually travelled to Rome, where he modelled famed actor David Garrick and author Laurence Sterne. Nollekens also turned his talents to faking Roman antiquities and smuggling goods home in hollowed-out busts. Around this time he revealed his extraordinary appetite for cheap but dreadful food cooked by a housekeeper who used scrapings of gristle and fat she found on a butcher's floor. When he returned to London, Nollekens found a wife who was even more parsimonious than he. The couple would sit in the dark at home rather than use candles, and only ever lit fires for guests, quickly extinguishing them as soon as the company departed. Nollekens brought home the excess lather from a barbershop shave to use as bath soap. Marriage did not improve Nollekens's taste in cheap food, which included flour fried in rancid butter.

He managed to draw commissions from scores of the greatest luminaries of his age, including the Duke of Wellington, Samuel Johnson, William Pitt and King George III. Some of the greatest buildings of London were adorned by his plaster statues and Nollekens's monuments were displayed in several cathedrals, including Westminster Abbey. Nollekens's work however was influenced not so much by his muse as by his pathological thrift. He hated to pay for marble, so he would buy up pieces that other artists had rejected as too small. To fit his commissions to the stone, he ordered his sitters to pose with their heads cocked backwards, looking over their shoulders. A model for his Venus statues posed for eight hours at a time, naked in his freezing cold home, with nothing to eat or drink, for a fee of two shillings.

Unorthodox talent occasionally demands an unorthodox personal life, but not in the case of René Magritte (1898–1967). Although the surrealist artist produced the most hauntingly bizarre images, his private life was by contrast astoundingly dull. He refused ever to leave his native Belgium, where he stuck to a rigidly boring daily routine. Magritte always wore a suit and tie, always took a morning stroll wearing his bowler hat to the local grocery store with his dog, and every day went to the same café, at precisely the same time, for a quiet game of chess.

Catherine Gregory's 1992 exhibition in Scarborough featured a dismembered dog chopped into nine pieces and suspended from the ceiling, sixty-three squashed mice mounted in plastic and the butchered remains of three rabbits. She said she did it for the animal rights movement.

The legendary William McGonagall (1825–1902) is widely accepted to have been the worst ever poet in the English language. Although chiefly known for his dire verse, McGonagall, the son of an Irish handloom worker who settled in Scotland, also had a brief and notably unsuccessful career as an actor. His career as an amateur "Tragedian" began in 1858 when he and a few friends bribed the manager of Dundee's Theatre Royal to let him play the leading role for a remarkable two-act version of *Macbeth*. In the combat scene McGonagall, instead of dying when run through the body by the sword of Macduff, maintained his feet and flourished his weapon about the ears of his adversary with such enthusiasm that the performance almost ended in real bloodshed. The actor who was playing the part of Macduff, having repeatedly and audibly told McGonagall to die or else, became so incensed that he gave him a smart rap over the fingers with the flat of his sword. Although this had the effect of making McGonagall drop his weapon he had no intention of taking a dive and he continued to dodge round Macduff like a prize fighter. The latter eventually flung his sword away, grabbed hold of McGonagall by the neck and wrestled him to the ground.

McGonagall retired from the stage in 1877 when, according to *The Autobiography of Sir William Topaz McGonagall, Poet and Tragedian, Knight of the White Elephant Burmah*, McGonagall received a "divine inspiration":

> . . . Dame Fortune has been very kind to me by endowing me with the genius of poetry. I remember how I felt when I received the spirit of poetry. It was in the year of 1877 and in the month of June, when the flowers were in full bloom. Well, it being the holiday week in Dundee, I was sitting in my back room in Paton's Lane, Dundee, lamenting to myself because I couldn't get to the Highlands on holiday to see the beautiful scenery, when all of a sudden my body got inflamed, and instantly I was seized with a strong desire to write poetry, so strong, in fact, that in my imagination I thought I heard a voice crying in my ears – "Write! Write!"

He dedicated the next twenty-four years of his life to composing terrible verse. The first piece he wrote was "An address to the Rev. George Gilfillan" in the *Weekly News*, only giving the initials of his name, W.M.G., Dundee. His output was immense and his choice of subject matter was eclectic. In "Tribute to Dr Murison", for instance, McGonagall explains how his life was saved by a physician's advice:

> He told me at once what was ailing me;
> He said I had been writing too much poetry,
> And from writing poetry I would have to refrain,
> Because I was suffering from inflammation of the
>   brain.

He was often inspired by contemporary news events. In "The Famous Tay Whale", for example, McGonagall recounted the true story of how a "monster whale" swam up the Tay estuary and offered itself to a fleet accustomed to chasing whales in the treacherous waters off Greenland. There were also three memorable poems about the Tay Bridge. Less than two years after its completion, the bridge collapsed, killing seventy-five passengers. McGonagall celebrates the bridge's opening:

> Beautiful Railway Bridge of the silvery Tay,
> With your numerous arches and pillars in
>   so grand array,
> And your central girders which seem to the eye,
> To be almost towering to the sky.
> And a great beautification to the river Tay,
> Most beautiful to be seen
> Near by Dundee and the Magdalen Green.

His regular readings in public houses were occasionally halted by the police on the grounds that his poems constituted a breach of the peace because the locals invariably pelted him with rotten vegetables. He became a cult figure in Dundee, however, where his readings drew large audiences; he was blithely unaffected by the laughter which invariably greeted his performances. The literary critic William Power saw one of these spectacles, at which McGonagall would wear full Highland dress and wield a broadsword, to jeers and laughter from the audience. Power left the hall early, "saddened and disgusted".

McGonagall, however, was convinced of his own genius. Some of his most famous work was dedicated to Queen Victoria. Whenever she visited the Highlands he made himself available at Balmoral in the hope of giving his sovereign a recitation of his latest work, although he never succeeded in getting beyond the palace gates. One day, after regaling the Queen with reams of unremittingly dire verse, he received a letter from the Queen's private secretary, Lord Biddulph, which stated that Her Majesty was unable to receive samples of his work. This near-brush with royalty went to McGonagall's head and he quickly restyled himself "Poet To Her Majesty". Although he once managed to sell just one copy of his poems to a policeman on the gates of Balmoral for twopence, the only work that he was ever commissioned to write, and for which he received two guineas, was a rhyme to promote Sunlight Soap.

His subsequent attempts to sell more poems, including his sole attempt to crack the American market, did not bear fruit. Fifty hitherto unknown poems were discovered and published in 1962 in *More Poetic Gems*. Other volumes have followed: *Last Poetic Gems* (1968), *Further Poetic Gems* (1980), *Still More Poetic Gems* (1980) and *Yet More Poetic Gems* (1980).

In 1996 the New York artist Brigid Berlin showcased her collection of 500 photographs of penises, contributed by people she met in the early 1970s during her acquaintance with Andy Warhol. She was previously known for her Tit Prints drawings, using her nipples instead of a brushes, and Penis Pillows – photo-montages of penises, photocopied and stuffed into plastic pillows.

George Bernard Shaw suffered from coitophobia – fear of sex. He lost his virginity to an elderly widow at the age of twenty-nine. He was so shocked by the experience that he didn't bother to try it again for another fifteen years.

Julia A. Moore, by common consent the worst ever American poetess, had a penchant for writing about violent death, which caused one critic to note that she rattled off poems "like a Gatling Gun". She was born Julia A. Davis, in Plainfield, Michigan, in 1847, the eldest of four children. As her mother was an invalid, Julia had the task of bringing up the family, although she still found time to write songs which she described with some degree of understatement as "sentimental". The deaths of neighbours, stories she read in her histories and in newspapers, heroic gossip of Civil War deeds and her own childhood memories inspired her with subject matter. Her magnum opus was her first collection of poems, *The Sweet Singer of Michigan Salutes The Public*, first published in 1876. On the cover was a picture of the author. The publisher, J. F. Ryder, of Cleveland, Ohio, sent copies to reviewers, accompanied by letters.

Dear Sir –

Having been honoured by the gifted lady of Michigan, in being entrusted with the publication of her poems, I give myself the pleasure of handing you a copy of the same, with my respectful compliments. It will prove a health lift to the overtaxed brain; it may divert the despondent from suicide. It should enable the reader to forget the "stringency", and guide the thoughts into pleasanter channels . . . It must be productive of good to humanity. If you have the good of your fellow creatures at heart, and would contribute your mite towards putting them in the way to finding this little volume, the thanks of a grateful people (including authoress and publisher) would be yours. If a sufficient success should attend the sale of this work, it would be our purpose to complete the Washington monument.

Julia A. Moore had arrived. Many critics, realizing that the book was a milestone in the history of bad poetry, ironically praised the work as a masterpiece. The *Rochester Democrat* noted: "Shakespeare, could he read it, would be glad that he was dead . . . If Julia A. Moore would kindly deign to shed some of her poetry on our humble grave, we should be but too glad to go out and shoot ourselves tomorrow." The *Chicago Tribune* asserted: "Mrs Moore's fame . . . will live as it deserves in the memories of men. Joaquin Miller can hardly survive the test of competition." The *Danbury News* pointed out that "each page" of this book "is a coal of fire on the altar of poetry". "The author, said the *Connecticut Post*, had "presented a collection the like of which has never tested the strength of type before . . . well calculated to lift the broken heart, though unmercifully shattered; rare food for the lunatic. . ." The *Pittsburg Telegraph* called Mrs Moore the Great American Poet and compared her to Walt Whitman. The *Worcester Daily Press* noted the poet was one "who reaches for the sympathy of humanity as a Rhode Islander reaches for a quahaug, clutches the tendrils of the soul as a garden rake clutches a hop vine, and hauls the reader into a closer sympathy than that which exists between a man and his undershirt." Mark Twain later claimed it had kept him laughing for the best part of twenty years. She had "the touch that makes an intentionally humorous episode pathetic", Twain noted, "and an intentionally pathetic one funny". Twain satirized her in *Huckleberry Finn* as Emmeline Grangerford.

In 1878 she published her new collection of poems prefaced

with seventy-four pages of these notices blissfully convinced that "Although some of the newspapers speak against it, its sale has steadily progressed. Thanks to the Editors that has spoken in favour of my writings; may they ever be successful . . . The Editors that has spoken in a scandalous manner, have went beyond reason. . . ." The work passed through three editions, all of which sold well. *The Sweet Singer of Michigan Salutes the Public*, as it was first styled, or *The Sentimental Song Book*, as it was later known, was one of the poetic bestsellers of the day. By 1878 however a new work, called *A Few Words to the Public With New and Original Poems by Julia A. Moore*, did not fare well and she published no more poetry.

The public recitations of Mrs Moore were greeted with laughter wherever she went, but like McGonagall and Austin she was impervious to embarrassment or even the most stinging of personal attacks. It is likely that she would have even enjoyed this assessment in *The Oxford Book of American Light Verse*: "A writer so transcendentally, surpassingly, superlatively bad that she belongs in a special genre in which normal rules and habits of judgment were magically suspended." She died at her home near Manton, Michigan, in June 1920.

American artist Newton Harrison staged an exhibition at the Hayward Gallery, London called "Portable Fish Farm" at which he planned to publicly electrocute sixty live catfish. The electrocution was called off after a protest by Spike Milligan, who made his feelings known by lobbing a brick through the gallery window.

The Roman poet Virgil (70–19 BC) spent the equivalent of £50,000 on the funeral of his pet fly.

The Scottish Royalist Sir Thomas Urquhart (1611–60) was taken prisoner by Roundheads during the English Civil War and imprisoned in the Tower of London. During his imprisonment he tried to save his neck by writing a book called *Peculiar Promptuary of Time*, which set out to prove that Urquhart was directly descended from Adam (153rd on his father's side) and Eve (147th on his mother's side). Urquhart was chiefly known for his bizarre use of language – his penchant for obscure, lengthy, complex prose made him one of the most difficult writers in the English language. One of his pet projects was a proposal for a universal language – a forerunner of Esperanto. It was predictably complex: verbs had four voices, seven moods and eleven tenses; nouns and pronouns had eleven cases, four numbers and eleven genders, and "every word in this language signifieth as well backward and forward, and however you invert the letter, still shall you fall upon significant words". Urquhart died laughing when he heard about the restoration of the monarchy.

Ludwig van Beethoven had such a disregard for personal cleanliness that his friends had to take away his dirty clothes and wash them while he slept. Beethoven may have had a form of disease known as systemic lupus erythematosus, which usually begins in early adult life with a fever accompanied by mental confusion. His moods changed constantly. Friends and acquaintances were always on their guard in case an innocent chance remark might be misconstrued or anger him in some way. He often misunderstood the meaning of a facial expression and accused friends of conspiracy, and would fly into a rage at the slightest provocation.

When Beethoven was twenty-nine he began to suffer from an annoying roaring and buzzing in both ears and his hearing began to deteriorate, eventually to fail completely. Already impatient, unreasonable and intolerant, his deafness made him suspicious and paranoid. His digestion began to suffer and he began to drink heavily. The cause of Beethoven's death, liver failure due to cirrhosis, was the result of heavy drinking over a thirty-year period. According to eye-witnesses, as Beethoven lay dying a sudden flash of lightning illuminated his death-chamber followed by a violent thunderclap and the composer suddenly raised his head and stretched out his right arm "like a general giving orders to an army". Although the story of Beethoven apparently "shaking his fist at the heavens" in one final act of defiance has been dismissed as a romantic fiction, it may be accurate clinical observation. People who die of hepatic failure, as Beethoven did, often react in an exaggerated way to sudden stimuli such as bright light, due to the accumulation of toxic waste products normally excreted by the liver.

Hermann Nitsch, an Austrian artist, staged a performance in 1975 using a dead bull and eleven deceased sheep.

In July 1993 retired Texan US Air Force Major Bill Smith filed a lawsuit in Fort Worth against the estate of Elvis Presley.

Major Smith charged that Presley's estate had perpetrated a fraud by keeping up the pretence that the King had died in 1977. The Major complained that this had interfered with his attempts to sell his new book on Elvis's current whereabouts.

The novelist Sir Walter Scott liked to break the ice at parties by introducing dinner guests to his novelty salt cellar, which was made from the fourth cervical vertebra of Charles I. The relic had been stolen by a surgeon during an autopsy on the royal corpse when Charles's long lost coffin was rediscovered at Windsor Castle in 1813. Scott kept it on his dining table for thirty years until Queen Victoria got it hear about it. She was distinctly unamused and ordered that it be returned to St George's chapel.

The post of Poet Laureate has been held by a few greats, including Dryden, Wordsworth and Tennyson, many mediocre poets, and several truly bad poets. Of the latter category, Alfred Austin (1835–1913) was outstanding. Austin was a leader writer in the *Standard*, known for his hard-line right-wing politics. He had twice failed to be elected to parliament when he was mysteriously awarded the laureateship by the Prime Minister Lord Salisbury. It was a blatantly political appointment as Austin had no track record as a poet whatsoever. He was sublimely ignorant of his obvious limitations however and took his appointment as proof that he was officially, in his own words "at the head of English literature".

Austin quickly became known for his overblown epics and political insensitivity. One of his most notorious works, a poem

about the infamous Jameson raid in which Austin acclaimed
Jameson as a hero, was so controversial that it even earned a
rebuke from Queen Victoria. His efforts were universally
panned by the critics who followed his career with mounting
disbelief, but Austin struck a pose of lofty indifference, continuing to churn out rubbish and to lecture his public about the
literary deficiencies of his contemporaries and how all critics
were idiots. He interpreted the scathing attacks on his efforts as
jealousy. When it was pointed out to him that his poems were
full of basic grammatical errors, Austin replied, "I dare not alter
these things. They come to me from above."

In 1863 the author Louisa May Alcott fell ill, and described in
her journal how she suffered from terrible hallucinations, in
which she was repeatedly molested by a big Spaniard with soft
hands. She recovered and went on to write *Little Women*.

When the mistress of the nineteenth-century French novelist
"Eugene" Sue died, she willed him her skin with instructions
that he should bind a book with it. He did.

Queen Victoria had the misfortune of reigning through the
careers of two talentless but patriotic poets who were both
driven to bombard her obsessively with excruciating verse.
Joseph Gwyer, the "McGonagall of Penge", pursued his two
great obsessions, poetry and potato growing, with roughly
equal enthusiasm and often combined the two with effortless

and devastating effect, as evidenced by his 1875 volume *Sketches Of The Life Of Joseph Gwyer (Potato Salesman) With His Poems (Commended By Royalty)*. The title was optimistic, given that at no time in his career was any of Gwyer's work ever commended by anyone, let alone royalty. A good example of the genre was his "Love and Matrimony" in which he points out that the most important thing a man should look for in his choice of bride is an ability to cook and roast POTATOES (in Gwyer's work, the word "potatoes" was always underlined or written in capitals). The importance of Gwyer's potato theme in contemporary literature often baffled his public but was not lost on all of his critics. *Punch* began a review of his epic "The Alexandra Palace, Muswell Hill, Destroyed By Fire", "We consider this work no small potatoes."

Speaking to an audience at the Folger Shakespeare Library in Washington, DC, novelist Kathryn Harrison read aloud a letter she had composed to her late grandmother in which she confessed to sticking her finger into the woman's cremated ashes and licking it. According to the *New York Post*, "the crowd responded with polite applause".

The reclusive Ulster poet Amanda McKittrick Ros (1860–1939) developed a highly unusual style which she attributed to never having read any books. It showed, agreed her critics. "My chief object of writing is and always has been to write if possible a strain all of my own," she once explained, adding, "This I find is why my writings are so much sought after." Her works were in fact much sought after by connoisseurs of kitsch, for she had her very own appreciation society, established at Oxford in 1907. From her home in remote Co. Antrim she issued a torrent of mostly abusive verse on her pet subjects, which were lawyers, fashion, the Kaiser, the abandonment of moral standards, clerics and, inevitably, critics. Her two best known collections of verse were *Poems of Puncture* (1932) and *Fumes of Formation* (1933), although she was equally famous for a series of remarkably bad and quite unfathomable romantic novels. For the most part she was blissfully impervious to criticism, although she never quite recovered from what she took to be the massive snub of failing to secure a nomination for the Nobel Prize for Literature in 1930.

The Reverend Cornelius Whur (1782–1853) was a Wesleyan minister from East Anglia, easily the worst of a tradition of nineteenth-century cleric-poets. He put to verse his pious observations and homespun pontifications, mostly on the state of the Victorian poor. Whur's fame rests upon two epic collections, *Village Musings on Moral and Religious Subjects* (1837) and *Gratitude's Offering – Being Original Productions On A Variety Of Subjects* (1845). Nicholas T. Parsons, author of *The Joy of Bad Verse*, says of this literary phenomenon: "The Reverend Whur possesses the most pedestrian mind in English literature, yet he makes compulsive reading."

The nineteenth-century French poet Gérard de Nerval often took his pet lobster for a walk on the end of a length of ribbon.

The poet Henry James Pye (1745–1813) was a bookish country squire who specialized in rambling dirges on largely agricultural themes, including his extraordinary treatise *The Effect Of Music On Animals*. Unfortunately Pye was also Poet Laureate, a job handed to him by William Pitt the Younger, evidently as compensation for losing his parliamentary seat. Pye's position, blessed as he was with a chronically dull prose style and a complete lack of imagination, was made even more difficult by the fact that his patron, George III, went completely and irretrievably mad during his laureateship. Pye did his best to avoid or to manfully circumnavigate the subject, a tricky business at the best of times but especially when it came to the obligatory annual King's Birthday Ode.

By the time he died of a stroke in 1982 aged fifty, the reclusive Canadian pianist Glenn Gould had established himself as one of the strangest musicians the concert world has ever known. Gould, born and raised in Toronto, was a prodigy with a unique playing style, hunched virtually at eye level over the keys. Gould established himself as an interpretive genius with his first recording of Johann Sebastian Bach's Goldberg Variations in 1955. It took longer than usual to make thanks to his habit of humming or singing with his performances; for the rest of Gould's career it drove his recording engineers to distraction. Gould had a phobia about shaking hands and once sued Steinway after a piano salesman gripped his hand too vigorously. He dreaded flying and drove everywhere, even to the Canadian Arctic. During a concert tour of Israel in 1957, finding himself struggling to interpret Beethoven's Piano Concerto No. 2 in Tel Aviv, he suddenly jumped into his rental car and drove off into the middle of the desert.

Gould lived in morbid fear of draughts, which led him to regularly appear on stage as though dressed for an Arctic expedition, swathed in furs, scarves and mittens. Before every performance, he would soak his hands in warm water or warm them in front of a propane heater. He cared little for his diet and lived mostly on custard, milk shakes, and scrambled eggs. He was also insomniac. He never rose before noon and he did most of his recording work after midnight. He talked incessantly or sang to friends in late-night telephone calls, and often created imaginary personalities for himself on the phone, including Sir Nigel Twitt-Thornwaite, dean of British conductors. In his later years, he had a recording studio built in a Toronto hotel, where he could order dinner at four a.m.

When the Armenian artist Arshile Gorky decided to take his own life he tried out half a dozen suicide venues first where he even tested a few nooses. He finally topped himself in 1948 in a woodshed in Connecticut, having first chalked up a message on the shed wall, "Goodbye My Loveds."

The French eighteenth-century anatomist Dr Honoré Fragonard, unlike his cousin Jean-Honoré Fragonard who was famous for his paintings of landscapes and rosy-cheeked cherubs, made sculptures from actual human and animal cadavers. His pieces, carefully skinned, preserved in formaldehyde and posed, are now on public view in the Fragonard Museum, which comprises three rooms of the National Veterinary School, in the shadow of the nearby Charenton insane asylum in Maisons-Alfort, a town on the eastern outskirts of the

French capital. Fragonard set up the museum himself in 1766 at the school where he worked as a teacher. The school authorities, upset by their employee's nauseating hobby, relieved Fragonard from his duties in 1771, but decided to keep the museum. Fragonard went on to enjoy a cult status among members of the French aristocracy, who liked to keep curious objects in their homes. By the time the anatomist died in 1799, aged sixty-six, hundreds of his sculptures were being used as conversation pieces at the very best dinner parties.

The Lithuanian artist Chaim Soutine (1893–1943) was so dirty that when he complained of an earache his doctor discovered a nest of bugs in his ear. He was also highly paranoid: he was afraid to deposit any money in his bank account for fear that the security guard would creep up from behind and strangle him.

The British poet Algernon Charles Swinburne (1837–1909) was wild and brandy-sodden and spent most of his money paying prostitutes to flog him. Most of his biographers assume that his obsession with flagellation stemmed from Eton, which at that time was notorious for birchings: one headmaster was said to be more familiar with his pupils' behinds than their faces. Swinburne also claimed he had once copulated with a monkey dressed as a woman.

Arnold Bennett's novels were renowned for obsessive attention to detail. Once he was complimented on his description of the death of Darius Clayhanger in the Clayhanger series, a death scene acclaimed as the most realistic of its kind in the history of English literature. Bennett explained later how this had been possible: "All the time my father was dying I was at the bedside making copious notes." Bennett himself died of typhoid after cheerfully drinking a glass of tap water in a Paris hotel to demonstrate how completely safe it was.

Thomas De Quincey, author of *Confessions of an English Opium-eater* (1822), had an intake of opium which varied between 800 and 8,000 drops per day and five or six glasses of laudanum every night. The habit caused him to lose his teeth and his skin took on the appearance of cracked parchment. De Quincey lost his wife and two sons within a period of three years, which caused his mental state to deteriorate. Although his gift for writing never deserted him, he was incapable of coping with the practicalities of everyday life and was extremely absent-minded. While poring over his manuscripts by candlelight he frequently set fire to his hair. When his lodgings became crammed with books he would simply leave them and move elsewhere. He was incapable of dressing unaided. He was also quite hopeless with money. He once approached a friend for a loan of seven shillings and sixpence. By way of security, he offered a screwed-up ball of paper which he said was a "document". It turned out to be a £50 note.

Elizabeth, the wife of the poet and painter Rossetti, died in 1862 after accidentally overdosing on laudanum she was taking for her neuralgia. Rossetti, himself an alcoholic and morphine addict, was so grief-stricken that as a token of his love he had a pile of his unpublished manuscripts wrapped in her golden hair and buried with her in her coffin. Seven years later however he had a change of heart and decided he wanted them back. Up came Elizabeth, and the poems were dusted off and published to great critical acclaim.

Percy Bysshe Shelley loathed cats: he once tied one to a kite in a thunderstorm to see if it would be electrocuted. When Shelley drowned in 1822 he was cremated, but as an afterthought his friends saved his heart from the flames and presented it to his wife Mary. She kept it with her, wrapped in silk, everywhere she went for the rest of her life. When their son Percy died the poet's heart was buried with him.

The German poet and dramatist Friedrich von Schiller (1759–1805) couldn't work without placing his feet on a block of ice and inhaling the fumes of rotting apples.

The nineteenth-century French novelist Honoré de Balzac consumed vast quantities of black coffee, sometimes up to fifty cups a day. He always worked wearing moroccan slippers and a white cashmere monk's robe, tied with a belt made from Venetian gold, from which he hung a paperknife, scissors and a penknife. He had a mania for cleanliness and owned a vast collection of gloves. He also considered sex a drain on his creativity. After several months of abstinence he was once tempted into a Paris brothel, but complained afterwards, "I lost a novel this morning."

The nineteenth-century American poet Emily Dickinson always wore white, rarely left her room, and hid her poems in little boxes.

Samuel Johnson (1709–84), the great English essayist, scholar, poet, playwright and lexicographer, suffered from a number of physical afflictions in his early years which probably contributed to his bizarre behaviour in adulthood. In his own words he was born "almost dead" and as an infant contracted scrofula – tuberculosis of the lymphatic glands. At the age of two and half he was taken to London to receive the "royal touch" of Queen Anne, whose gold "touch piece" he kept on his person for the rest of his life. Scrofula, or any combination of the quack medical treatments available at that time, bequeathed him a badly scarred face and neck, near blindness in his left eye and a very noticeable facial tic. He grew up however into robust adulthood – he once turned on a heckler in a theatre audience and hurled the man and his seat into the stage pit.

Although he was the most entertaining of conversationalists, Johnson's unpredictability terrified people who didn't know him well. At the dinner table he would mutter, grimace and gesticulate wildly, or suddenly reach down and pluck a lady's shoe from her foot. He was a messy, often frenzied eater, even in front of royalty. His biographer James Boswell noted that Johnson ate like a wild animal, gorging himself until his veins swelled and sweat poured from his head. His behaviour displayed some of the traits of Tourette's syndrome as well as a number of obsessive-compulsive disorders. He had a morbid fear of certain streets and alleys and would make elaborate detours to avoid them. He was a hypochondriac, never stepped on the cracks in paving stones, and always touched every post along the road as he walked – if he missed a post by accident he would make his walking companions wait while he returned to touch it. Although academically brilliant, he was unable to tell the time by looking at a clock. Perhaps Johnson's most notably aberrant behaviour involved his extraordinary routine whenever he passed through a doorway. He was compelled to jump through from a precise number of steps away, as recorded by his friend Boswell:

> He had another peculiarity, of which none of his friends even ventured to ask an explanation. It appeared to me some superstitious habit, which he had contracted early, and from which he had never called upon his reason to disentangle him. This was his anxious care to go out or in at a door or passage, by a certain number of steps from a certain point, or at least so as that either his right or his left foot (I am not certain which) should consistently make the first actual movement when he came close to the door or passage.

When Johnson was twenty-six years old he fell in love with and married a woman who was twice his age, crude, very short and overweight. In order to support her, Johnson taught from home. He only found three students, however, as most were put off by his bizarre mannerisms, especially his violent facial contortions.

Although Johnson's *Dictionary of the English Language* established him as the world authority on his mother tongue it earned him a relatively small amount of money and he lived mostly in poverty. He complained that he lived "a life radically wretched", but his sense of humour was never in doubt. The *Dictionary* was full of witty and idiosyncratic entries which gave insight into Johnson's personality, for example:

> fart: Wind from behind.
> "Love is the fart
> Of every heart;
> It pains a man when 'tis kept close;
> And others doth offend, when 'tis let loose."
> to fart: To break wind from behind.
> "As when we a gun discharge,
> Although the bore be ne'er so large,
> Before the flame from muzzle burst,
> Just at the breech it flashes first;
> So from my lord his passion broke,
> He farted first, and then he spoke." – Swift.

In 1994 the Danish artist Christian Lemmerz put six dead pigs in a glass case so that visitors to the Ezbjerg gallery could watch them decompose. The artist declared it a triumph for people who value reality in art. The gallery owners said it was a triumph over their old ventilation system which was unable to cope with the stench.

Surrealist painter Salvador Dali (1904–89) was a calculated eccentric. In an attempt to make himself more attractive to his girlfriend Gala, he shaved his armpits until they bled and wore a perfume made of fish glue and cow dung. He ate large quantities of ripe Camembert cheese before retiring to bed. He believed that the cheese made him dream more often and more vividly, fuelling his imagination with images he could transfer to his paintings.

Dali's famed bristling moustache was intended mainly as an attention-seeking device. He often compared it to insect antennae, although later he abandoned his insect metaphor for something more contemporary. "My moustache is my radar," he announced. "It pulls ideas out of space. Great painters need a luxuriant moustache like mine. The points have to be just under the eyes to get the right perspective." Dali later changed his mind and said that the waxed points of his moustache were actually used to "perforate dollars".

Dali once took his pet ocelot with him to a New York restaurant and tethered it to a leg of the table while he ordered coffee. A middle-aged lady walked past and looked at the animal in horror. "What's that?" she cried. "It's only a cat," said Dali. "I've painted it over with an op-art design." The woman, embarrassed by her initial reaction, took a closer look and sighed with relief. "I can see now that's what it is," she said. "At first I thought it was a real ocelot."

Chapter Nine

Cracked Actors
& Peculiar Performers

"One is always considered mad when one perfects something that others cannot grasp"

Ed Wood, Jr (1924–78)

"Start every day off with a smile; get it over with"

W. C. Fields (1879–1946)

"If I treat my body properly, I believe I'll live to be 150"

Michael Jackson (b. 1957)

The British actor Edwin Jehosophat Odell was a formidable presence, once described as "a fearsome compound of Rasputin, Wallace Beery and the Old Man of the Sea". At the age of ninety, Odell found himself homeless and decided to take up permanent residence on a sofa in his London club, the Savage, to the astonishment of many members and the great displeasure of the club committee. In an effort to dislodge him the club withdrew his membership, so Odell simply hung around outside the building for several days until his friends mounted a campaign to reinstate him. He was given the use of a carriage outside the door to sleep in and meals were smuggled out to him from the dining room. Eventually the committee relented and he was allowed back in. They hoped that since Odell was already ninety they wouldn't have to put up with him for much longer, but he lived to be a hundred. He refused to allow anyone to use his favourite chair – even the Duke of York, later George VI, was once abruptly ordered to give it up. Old Savage members knew that it was unwise to lend Odell money. When a new member reminded Odell after six months that he owed him ten shillings, Odell barked back, "I haven't finished with it yet." When he died the members placed a brass plate on his chair with the inscription "Here Odell Sat".

The subversive avant-garde musician Frank Zappa led twenty-five rock bands up to his death aged fifty-two, but he made his name as leader of the band Mothers of Invention from 1964 to 1978. The hallmarks of a Mothers concert were the props: stuffed giraffes, gallows, boxes of rotting vegetables. During one show in New York Zappa persuaded two US Marines to dismember a doll on stage by telling them, "Pretend this is a gook baby." There was once an apocryphal story doing the rounds that Zappa had enlivened a performance by eating faeces on stage. He denied it: "I never performed this act on stage. The nearest I ever came to it anywhere was at the Holiday Inn buffet in Fayetteville, North Carolina in 1973."

Although hailed as a genius, Zappa's work, which spanned rock, jazz, blues and other forms, did not always inspire acclaim. In 1967 when he was working on a collaboration with several members of the London Philharmonic orchestra, rehearsals were temporarily halted while one of the string section wept and threw up. In the same year he became an unlikely popular bedsit poster icon when he had the idea of posing nude in a lavatory. In 1971 he was performing live in London when a drunk pulled him offstage. The singer suffered several broken bones and a crushed larynx, which caused the pitch of his voice to drop permanently. "Having a low voice is nice," Zappa said afterwards, "but I would have preferred some other way of acquiring it."

In 1975 the Royal Albert Hall abruptly cancelled a Zappa concert on the grounds that his lyrics were potentially obscene. Zappa sued, resting his case on the fact that he could have easily changed the offending lyrics if given the chance. At the Old Bailey Mr Justice Mocatta was required to listen to a number of Zappa songs, which he did with his head in his hands. In the 1980s Zappa took objection to the American practice of placing warning stickers on "offensive" records. He wrote a letter to Ronald Reagan: "Must all sexual practices in the United States be tested and approved by the moral majority? And when they test them, do we get to watch?" By the end of his life Zappa had become almost wholly nocturnal, working up to fourteen hours at a stretch in his home-made recording studio, the Utility Muffin Research Kitchen. He died in 1993 survived by four children, Moon Unit, Diva, Ahmet and Dweezil.

Sir Herbert Draper Beerbohm Tree, thespian, wit and eccentric, was one of the finest actors of the nineteenth century, although on occasions he was guilty of below par performances. One particularly inept rendition of Hamlet was drowned in a sea of catcalls and abuse from the audience. Tree walked to the footlights and held up both hands to ask for silence. "Thank you, ladies and gentlemen," he said, "I still have a few pearls to cast." Once, during a rehearsal of *Macbeth*, he found himself interrupted by a clap of thunder. Tree peered into the auditorium and said sharply, "When I require the assistance of the sound effects department, you may be sure that I shall ask for it." A voice offstage replied, "I think you will find that was real thunder, Sir Herbert." "Ah," replied Tree. "I thought it wasn't as good as ours." When asked how he was, Tree invariably replied, "Radiant! Absolutely radiant!" Once he was in a post office and he asked the girl behind the counter if she sold stamps. She said that she did. "Then show me some," said Tree. When she produced a large sheet of stamps, he studied, then pointed to one in the middle, saying, "I'll have that one." Tree had a dread of motor cars, and continued to use horse-drawn cariages to the end. Only once did he agree to travel in an automobile; he spent the entire journey, terrified, cowering on the floor of the vehicle with his hands covering his eyes.

The legendary producer Phil Spector was a perfectionist in the recording studio. Once, while working with Leonard Cohen, he held a gun to the singer's head in order to achieve the vocal performance he was looking for. Spector was once married to Ronnie Spector, singer with the 1960s US girl band the Ronettes. She revealed that her ex-husband always switched the light off when they went to bed so he could remove his toupée in private, then applied so much solvent to get rid of the glue that held it in place that he spent the rest of the night reeking of a smell that would kill a horse.

Florence Foster Jenkins (1868–1944) was a wealthy New York socialite who harboured a delusion that she was a highly gifted soprano. Technically she was incapable of holding a note or even of keeping time, yet she pursued her muse with the kind of single-minded application that only vast amounts of money allow. Her singing career was the fulfilment of a lifelong ambition. The daughter of a wealthy Pennsylvania banker, she had pleaded at age seventeen to go abroad to pursue a singing career, but her straitlaced father refused to let her go. She resurrected her stillborn career as a middle-aged woman, every year giving a private performance at the Ritz-Carlton hotel, accompanied by her pianist Cosme McMoon. She sang a variety of standard opera arias, plus a few written for her by McMoon. The audience usually howled with laughter and her singing was the subject of unparalleled critical scorn, but the indomitable Madame Jenkins attributed it all to professional jealousy. Her dress sense was almost as unusual as her vocal style. She had extravagant costumes made for her performances, usually at least three per recital. One of these outfits, which she called Angel Of Inspiration, was a fantastic creation of silk, tinsel, tulle and feathered wings. The First Lady of the Sliding Scale, as she was sometimes known, built up a fan club that included the likes of tenor Enrico Caruso, who regarded Jenkins's efforts with some affection. Among the phonograph recordings of her work, only two remain, including her incomparable rendition of the Queen of the Night's second aria from Mozart's *Magic Flute* – a famously demanding work even for the greatest voices. Jenkins sang the piece once, unrehearsed, and pronounced the result too good to be improved upon.

In 1943 she was involved in a taxi-cab accident after which she claimed that she could now sing "a higher F than ever before". Instead of suing the taxi company she sent a box of cigars to the driver. Her last performance, also her Carnegie Hall debut, was sold out weeks in advance. There had never been a Carnegie Hall performance quite like it. Touts charged an outrageous twenty dollars per ticket for an unforgettable night of opera; thousands were turned away. Reviewing Jenkins's performance at the Carnegie, one critic noted, "It would be a presumption to speak of the artist's achievements in technical terms for there can be none where freedom of expression is rampant." *Time* magazine noted, "Mrs Jenkins' night queenly swoops and hoots, her wild wallowings in descending trill, her repeated staccato notes like a cuckoo in its cups, are innocently uproarious to hear." The *Bulletin* advised, "Madame Jenkins' vocal art is something for which there is no known parallel." One month after her Carnegie Hall triumph, the voice of the incomparable Florence Foster Jenkins was finally silenced by death. She wrote her own epitaph: "Some people say I cannot sing, but no one can say I didn't sing."

Mexican entertainer Ramon Barrero played "the world's smallest harmonica" until, mid-performance in 1994, he inhaled a D-minor and accidentally choked to death.

The life of Enrico Caruso, the great Neapolitan tenor, was dominated by a series of irrational fears and superstitions.

Caruso was born in a seven-storey apartment complex in a working-class neighborhood in Naples, Italy. He was the eighteenth child out of twenty-one, and the first to live past infancy.

As a child he worried constantly that Mount Vesuvius might erupt. This phobia overcame him when he visited San Francisco, just in time for the great earthquake of 1906. He swore he would never again go back to such a city, "where disorders like that are permitted." He would never cross a large body of water without an astrologer's approval, nor would he travel at all on Tuesday or Friday, which he considered evil. He would not wear a new suit on Friday, and he changed his clothes completely every time he entered his apartment. Caruso owed everything to his voice, but it didn't prevent him from smoking fifty or sixty cigarettes a day – a habit which cost him his life aged forty-eight. Caruso tried to protect his throat with a variety of quack remedies including wearing a home-made necklace of anchovies, stringing together slivers of the fish, pickled or salted, around his throat, chewing garlic or spraying his vocal passages with caustic ether. Caruso also had an obsession for bookkeeping. He kept track of every single penny that he spent in his life, jotting it down meticulously in a little black diary. When he died in 1921, he left behind a record of his fiscal neurosis in literally hundreds of little black books.

A group of reporters once asked him what he thought of Babe Ruth. Caruso, who was unfailingly polite and amiable, replied that he didn't know because unfortunately he had never heard her sing.

The flamboyant American pianist Liberace, in the early part of his career, performed under the stage name Walter Busterkeys in an attempt to adopt a more macho image. It never really

worked, although he did manage to sue the *Daily Mirror* for
£8,000 in 1959 after taking a dislike to their journalist William
Connor, who, writing about Liberace's appearance at the
London Palladium, described him as a "scent-impregnated,
luminous, quivering, giggling, fruit-flavoured, mincing, ice-
covered heap of mother love". In fact Liberace was so devoted
to his Polish mother Frances that he and she would appear at
concerts wearing identical furs and jewellery. When she died he
exhibited many of her personal effects, including her knitting
basket, in his Liberace Museum.

His tastes in most things made Elvis's Las Vegas period look
like a model of quiet self-restraint. In 1984 he sported a
£200,000 rhinestone-studded Norwegian blue fox cape with
a sixteen-foot train and in 1986 he stepped on stage from his
Rolls-Royce, which was painted with stars and stripes, wearing
stars and stripes hotpants. The master bedroom in his home
featured an exact replica of the ceiling of the Sistine Chapel.
His swimming pool was piano-shaped and his lawn had central
heating. Bizarrely, even for Liberace, he owned a piano made
from thousands of toothpicks. He also owned a retracting toilet
that would sink and vanish into the bathroom floor at the flick
of a switch. He explained, "There is no reason why you should
walk into a bathroom and see a toilet – it is unglamorous." It
was estimated that Liberace received about 27,000 Valentine
cards and 150 marriage proposals a year.

The US film industry writer/actor/producer/director Edward
D. Wood, Jr (1924–78) was ignored throughout his spectacularly
unsuccessful career and died penniless, but he was dramatically
accorded cult status in the early 1980s when he acquired the
semi-official status of Worst Film Director Of All Time. During

his fifty-four years Ed Wood produced a string of low-budget films which one American critic called "among the most compelling fiascos ever committed to celluloid".

Although happily married to the same woman until his death, Wood was also an enthusiastic transvestite; technically speaking, in fact, Wood was a transvestite war hero. Six months after Pearl Harbor he enlisted in the Marines, where he earned several medals including the Bronze Star, the Silver Star and the Purple Heart. He took part in the invasion of Tarawa, where of over 4,000 Marines only one man in ten survived. After the battle he confessed to a fellow Marine, "I wanted to be killed, Joe . . . I didn't want to be wounded because I could never explain my pink panties and pink bra." He was injured, however, losing his front teeth to a rifle butt and taking several bullets in the leg.

By 1948 Ed Wood had reached Hollywood and had written, produced, directed and performed in his first big failure, a stage play, *The Casual Company*. The play's subject matter was close to Ed's heart; a handsome man man fell for a pretty woman wearing a fluffy angora sweater. Wood was an angora fetishist. He tried to break into the film industry, initially without success, but finally landing the chance to direct a film based on the Christine Jorgensen sex-change. The result, *Glen or Glenda*, was a semi-autobiographical tribute to Wood's fetishism, an almost unthinkable subject for an early 1950s feature. His debut film also revealed the total absence of talent that would be the hallmark of all his subsequent films. His film with Bela Lugosi, *Bride of the Monster* (1954), was no better. Wood only shot a few seconds of footage of Lugosi for his next film before the latter died. Undaunted, Wood based his follow-up *Plan 9 From Outer Space* (1958) around this material, casting it with his usual troupe of inadequate actors. *Plan 9*, now generally considered to be the worst film ever made, has a considerable cult following today.

After this, his career peak, Wood went into decline, directing soft and later hardcore pornography before his premature death. Only one of his movies, *Bride of the Monster*, made money. Sadly, Wood had already sold in excess of 100 per cent of the film to backers. What he lacked in business sense he more than made up for in genuine enthusiasm, however. According to legend, he could type faster drunk than most typists could sober. Wood died an alcoholic in 1978.

Junius Brutus Booth (1796–1852) was an Anglo-American actor, born in Britain, and father of President Lincoln's assassin John Wilkes Booth. He was regarded as one of the greatest tragedians of his day, particularly in Shakespearean roles. Booth carefully chose parts that he felt suited his relatively small, lean frame. In addition to Richard III, he often played Iago, Hamlet, Shylock, and Macbeth. Personal tragedy, including an unhappy marriage and the death of two children, led to mental instability and alcoholism, but his audiences never lost their affection for him. At the end of his career some critics insisted that he put on his best performances when he was most troubled. Booth's face was marred by a badly broken nose. "You're such a wonderful actor, Mr Booth," a female admirer gushed one day, "but to be perfectly frank with you, I can't get over your nose." "There's no wonder, madam," replied Booth. "The bridge is gone."

The actor/manager Colley Cibber, poet laureate during the reign of George II, made many enemies amongst fellow actors and writers with his high-handed manner. Most of his twenty-seven years as Poet Laureate were spent in literary feuds with writers, especially a long quarrel with Alexander Pope. Cibber was a mediocre poet and his efforts were mercilessly ridiculed by his contemporaries. Fielding accused him of "murdering the English language with a goose quill". Cibber is chiefly remembered however for his unwavering belief that he could "improve" Shakespeare. His "original" version of *Richard III* in fact was still being performed until the nineteenth century. Cibber's final stage appearance as an actor was in his own bastardized version of Shakespeare's *King John*. At the time he was seventy-four years old and had lost all his teeth.

Sir John Gielgud is famous for his gaffes, once admitting that he had "dropped enough bricks to build a new Great Wall of China". He once dined with Prime Minister Clement Attlee after a play at Stratford, and found himself seated next to Attlee's daughter. "I have a very convenient home in Westminster," Gielgud told her, "where do you live?" Miss Attlee replied curtly, "No. 10 Downing Street." On another occasion Gielgud was dining at the Garrick with a famous old playwright, when a man passed by their table. "Thank God he didn't stop", said Gielgud. "He's a bigger bore than Eddie Knoblock." His dinner companion was Eddie Knoblock.

The little known American actor Conrad Cantzen bequeathed $266,890 to the Actors' Fund with instructions that any unemployed actor who required new shoes could apply to the fund for a new pair from a well known Manhattan footwear store. His will stated, "Many times I have been on my uppers and the thinner the inner soles of my shoes were, the less courage I had to face a manager in looking for a job." Cantzen was however far from wealthy. For years he wore the same threadbare suits and died with $11.85 in his pockets – he had simply scraped the money together by years of denial. According to his Actors' Fund biography the bequest was "sum total of all the meals he had not eaten, the drinks he had denied himself, the rooms he had not occupied on the road, preferring to spend the night in railroad stations, bus terminal and parks."

The stage performances of veteran British actor A.E. Matthews (1869–1960) became increasingly eccentric with age. He could only remember his lines if he had dozens of prompts concealed around the stage and in the wings and he would often make unscripted exits to jog his memory. During one performance his memory deserted him at a particularly critical moment. On stage a telephone rang and he could not remember how he was supposed to answer it. Turning to his fellow actor he simply said, "It's for you." His performance during rehearsals of *The Manor of Northstead* was particularly erratic. "Don't worry, chaps," he reassured the worried producer and director of the play; "I promise you, even if we had to open next Monday, I'd be all right." "Matty," the director replied, "we do open on Monday."

Clark Gable (1901–60) was obsessive about personal cleanliness. He showered every two hours during the day and always shaved his chest and armpits.

A nineteenth-century American known as Oofty-Goofty became famous in post-gold rush San Francisco, wandering the streets dressed in furs and making loud animal noises. He had started out as the Wild Man of Borneo in a Barbary Coast sideshow. When people approached his cage he would growl and mutter "Oofty goofty", and the nickname stuck. He once played Romeo in a production where the lead actress proved too heavy for the balcony, so they switched positions. True to form, Oofty-Goofty ad-libbed a few monkey noises in addition to his lines. He hit upon a new sideline when he discovered that he had an extraordinarily high threshold for pain. He began to make a living by inviting passers-by to kick him for 10 cents, to cane him for 25 cents, and to club him with a baseball bat for 50 cents. His career ended when he let heavyweight boxing champion John L. Sullivan hit him across the back with a pool cue. Sullivan had his 50 cents' worth, thus dispatching Oofty-Goofty to hospital with a fractured spine and into retirement. Thereafter Oofty walked with a limp and whimpered at the slightest touch.

The lead singer of Milwaukee rock band the Toilet Rockers was convicted of disorderly conduct in 1991 after exercising what he claimed was his "constitutional right" to defecate onstage and fling his turds at the audience.

The ubiquitous TV-flinger Keith Moon, drummer for The Who from 1965 to his death in 1978, was the greatest hotel wrecker in rock music. His antics caused The Who to be banned from numerous hostelries around the world; Holiday

Inn banned the group after a rampage when Keith celebrated his twentieth birthday by spraying everything in sight with a fire extinguisher. He once dropped an explosive down the toilet in an American hotel, blowing a large hole in the bathroom floor. When a hotel manager complained about the loud music emanating from his room, Moon blew the door off. He smashed up bedroom furniture with axes and began a trend that made hurling TV sets through hotel windows obligatory. He once drove a brand new Lincoln Continental into a hotel swimming pool, just to get a reaction. Over a period of about ten years he estimated that his hotel wrecking escapades cost him about £200,000 in damages. His destructive behaviour was said to be the inspiration for Jim Henson's Muppet "Animal".

Rock singer Ozzie Osborne really did bite off the head of a dead bat, but it was not a deliberate act of rock 'n' roll machismo. He mistook the ex-mammal, flung onstage by a fan, for a rubber toy. Osborne was immediately rushed to hospital for a course of tetanus jabs which left him unable to walk for days. He said it was "like eating a Crunchie wrapped in chamois leather".

The entertainer Nicholas Wood, billed as the Great Eater of Kent, could at a single sitting consume a whole sheep, thirty dozen pigeons, or eighty-four rabbits. It was said that he once ate sixty pounds of cherries followed by a whole hog. For dessert he downed three pecks of Damson plums. According to legend, a man named John Dale once wagered that he could buy Wood more than he could eat with only two shillings. The bet was agreed upon, and Dale bought six pints of ale and twelve loaves of bread, which he soaked in the beer. Wood began to eat the meal, but the fumes caused him to fall asleep and he lost the bet.

The Eton-educated fourth Earl of Wharncliffe, Alan James Montagu-Stuart-Wortley-Mackenzie, briefly held down a job as drummer in the Johnny Lenniz band and went on a concert tour of Britain and Europe, cutting a few discs on the way, including "Shake, Rattle & Roll". He later became landlord of the Wortley Arms, a public house in Yorkshire, where he was known to the locals as "Mad Ike", as he once shot a black and white tom cat called Elvis which he had discovered in his kitchen. Although a member of the Institute of Advanced Motorists, the Earl was banned from driving on several occasions. In 1976 he earned a three-year ban for drink driving and vowed never to drink again. A few days after the ban ended the Earl was involved in a car crash near Barnsley in which a pub landlady was killed. The Earl himself spent six weeks on a life support machine, but after being announced "clinically dead" recovered to face a charge of reckless driving. While awaiting trial he fell from his crutches and broke another leg, eventually appeared in court on sticks and was sentenced to six months in prison. Months after his release his eldest daughter was killed in a car crash.

Next to sex and gluttony Elvis's favourite nocturnal pastime was visiting the Memphis morgue to look at the corpses. Presley also had a secret desire to become a law enforcement officer. For some of his final recordings he dressed himself in a full police captain's uniform, and his most prized possession, which he took with him everywhere, was a bag containing his collection of honorary police and sheriff's badges. Presley was perversely appointed as a "special" federal narcotics agent by President Richard Nixon, who was unaware that the King had been popping pills in industrial quantities for years. Elvis once had a vision of Stalin in the sky above Arizona and was convinced that he could turn the Gracelands sprinkler system on and off by the power of his thoughts. One of Elvis Presley's more eccentric eating habits was his ability to consume four bowls of Shredded Wheat at one sitting. He died on the toilet in 1977.

Former Pogues singer Shane MacGowan, in order to demonstrate the cultural inferiority of the United States, has eaten a Beach Boys album.

The camp comic Kenneth Williams, best known for his double entendres in the British Carry On films of the 1960s, was obsessively tidy. He never, ever invited anyone to visit his London flat in case they might want to use his lavatory; he confessed he just couldn't stand the thought of someone else's bottom on his loo.

The English character actress Hermione Gingold was, according to the critic Sheridan Morley, "an original, a one hundred per cent, solid gold eccentric". At the age of eighty-one while performing on Broadway she began an affair with a man aged twenty-six, commenting "the trouble with men is that there are not enough of them". Her gift for spontaneous witty repartee was legendary. When asked by a playwright what she thought of his script, she replied, "My dear boy, in future I will advise you to write nothing more ambitious than a shopping list." When a TV chat show host asked her if her husband was still living, she replied straight-faced, "It's a matter of opinion." As a guest at a Buckingham Palace garden party, she was approached by Prince Philip who asked her, "What are you doing here?" She quickly replied, "I was about to ask you the same thing." In New York she could be spotted rummaging through other people's dustbins. She was unrepentant about this, boasting that she had once found a complete set of Encyclopaedia Brittanica, and on another an antique table.

The French singer, composer, actor and film director Serge Gainsbourg achieved fame in the UK for his heavy-breathing collaboration with the English actress Jane Birkin, "Je t'aime moi non plus", which topped the charts thanks to the massive publicity generated by a BBC ban. In France however Gainsbourg was famous for his more serious contributions to fast living and a talent to shock. He trained as a painter, but by the end of the 1950s began a career as a film actor in low-budget productions. His performances drew mixed responses from the critics. He recalled that at the premiere of one of his films, set in ancient Rome, he had been obliged to flee the cinema while the audience shouted, "Die, you bastard." In 1973 he upset the French authorities with *Rock Around The Bunker*, a collection of songs about the Third Reich, including a version of "Smoke Gets In Your Eyes" which was considered by many to be in questionable taste. In 1979 he outraged his countrymen again when he recruited a group of Jamaican reggae musicians to record a highly irreverent version of "La Marseillaise", which provoked riots when his concerts were disrupted by angry French war veterans. He was finally banned from live TV after a series of very drunken appearances on chat shows which ended with him making an obscene suggestion to the US singer Whitney Houston. Although Gainsbourg grew increasingly more disgraceful as he grew older, he found the French public less easy to shock. He managed it however in 1984 with his song "Lemon Juices", an idiosyncratic reading of Chopin's Etude No. 3 in E Major, Opus 10, the video for which showed Gainsbourg in bed with his 14-year-old daughter Charlotte.

For four decades Gainsbourg consumed awesome quantities of alcohol and tobacco. He continued to smoke thirty to forty Gitanes a day after a heart attack when he was forty-five, pointing out to interviewers that he was in better health than his doctors, three of whom died long before he did as if to prove the point. Although Gainsbourg had neither a driving licence nor a chauffeur, for ten years he kept a 1928 Rolls-Royce "as an ashtray". During the time of the heart attack he actually stopped smoking for three days, but only because he believed that his Gitane would cause the oxygen cylinder to explode.

The actress Marlene Dietrich was so obsessed with germs that she was known to Hollywood insiders as "the Queen of Ajax".

Before discovering Elvis, Colonel Tom Parker's most notable success was "Colonel Parker's Dancing Chickens", an act which involved persuading chickens to perform by sticking them on an electric hotplate.

There are today an estimated 48,000 Elvis impersonators worldwide. In the Islamic state of Mogadishu in Somalia alone, however, it is illegal to impersonate Elvis without a beard.

Monsieur Dufour, a Frenchman who made his stage debut in 1783, added "comedy" to his uniquely unpalatable eating act. Ricky Jay records in his book *Learned Pigs & Fireproof Women*:

His last appearance in Paris was most remarkable. The dinner began with a soup of asps in simmering oil. On each side was a dish of vegetables, one containing thistles and burdocks, and the other fuming acid. Often side dishes of turtles, rats, bats, and moles were garnished with live coals. For the fish course he ate a dish of snakes in boiling tar and pitch. His roast was a screech owl in a sauce of glowing brimstone. The salad proved to be spiderwebs full of small explosive squibs, a plate of butterfly wings and manna worms, a dish of toads surrounded with flies, crickets, grasshoppers, church beetles, spiders, and caterpillars. He washed all this down with flaming brandy and for dessert ate the four large candles standing on the table, both of the hanging side lamps with their contents, and finally the large centre lamp, oil, wick, and all. This leaving the room in darkness, Dufour's face shone out in a mash of living flames. A dog had come in with a farmer, who was probably a confederate, and now began to bark. Since Dufour could not quiet him, he seized him, bit off his head and swallowed it, throwing the body aside. Then ensued a comic scene between Dufour and the farmer, the latter demanding that his dog be brought to life, which threw the audience into paroxysms of laughter. Then suddenly, candles reappeared and seemed to light themselves. Dufour made a series of hocus-pocus passes over the dog's body, then the head suddenly appeared in its proper place, and the dog, with a joyous yelp, ran to his master.

Dufour capped this wildly amusing stunt by "tearing the cat from limb to limb and then eating the carcass, then after suitable byplay extracting it whole again from his mouth".

William Claude Dukenfield was better known as W. C. Fields, the red-nosed comic actor. A child runaway at eleven, he lived in packing crates and stole food from back porches where watchdogs gave him a lifelong phobia of canines. His comic talents soon earned him a place in the Ziegfeld Follies and Hollywood, although his difficult early years left a mark that lasted a lifetime. The comedian had a profound mistrust of banks, especially when large sums of his money were concerned. Instead of concentrating his wealth in any one account, Fields spread it around. He was also perpetually afraid that he would be stranded somewhere without money and so he opened bank accounts everywhere he went, hundreds of them under a bewildering variety of fictitious names, many of which he couldn't remember. He tried to keep track of all his scattered accounts in notebooks, but many of the books became lost.

He had another reason for hiding money away, namely his failed marriage to Harriet Hughes. For years after their separation the estranged couple fought viciously over money and Fields bitterly resented the ruinous payments that he was forced to send his spouse. The consequences of his lifelong habit began to emerge after Fields died in 1946, at the age of sixty-six. He left a fortune of $700,000, most of it to charity. According to some estimates however the amount found was probably only about half the amount that actually existed. The rest was lost in accounts under forgotten pseudonyms all over the world.

Robert Powell, an eighteenth-century stage performer, claimed a distinguished list of patrons, including the Duke of Cumberland, the Duke of Gloucester, Sir Hans Sloane and several members of the Royal Society. Powell's act involved a number of fire-resisting stunts and ingesting quantities of resin, pitch, beeswax, sealing wax, brimstone, alum and lead with a large spoon. After a long and successful stage career he went into medicine. Alarmingly, he advertised himself available to perform amputations "so easily as scarce to be felt", and sold a medicine which allegedly cured scalds and burns, and "is necessary to be kept in all families".

Quite a few entertainers have been crucified onstage, in the case of Tommy Minnock, quite literally. Minnock was a variety artiste who plied his trade in Trenton, New Jersey in the 1890s. He would allow himself to be nailed to a wooden cross onstage and while the nails were being driven into his hands and feet, Minnock would sing "After The Ball Is Over".

Sarah Bernhardt, real name Henriette-Rosine Bernard, was born in Paris, and studied acting at the Paris Conservatory. After she became a star in the 1870s, she opened the Sarah Bernhardt Theatre in Paris, which she managed until her death. Her most popular role was in *The Lady of the Camellias*, known in America as *Camille*. Bernhardt was considered an unrivalled stage talent, but modesty was never her strong point. On her first visit to America she was told that her rapturous reception exceeded that given to Dom Pedro of Brazil. "Yes," Bernhardt replied, "but he was only an emperor." She signed letters to her grandchildren, simply, "Great". Oscar Wilde called her the Incomparable One; most others called her the Divine Sarah. Everyone apart from playwright George Bernard Shaw agreed that she was the greatest tragic actress of her age, the first international stage star. "She is not an individual," observed French critic Jules Lemaitre, "but a complex of individuals." An admirer of a young English performer was discussing her acting with Sarah Bernhardt, who was not at all convinced of the young woman's talent. "But surely," said the man, "you will at least admit that she has some wonderful moments." "Maybe, but also some terrible half-hours," countered Sarah.

Bernhardt, the illegitimate daughter of a Jewish-Dutch courtesan, carefully cultivated her reputation for eccentricity. Onstage and off, she was a consummate performer who knew how to mould her public persona as a Magnificent Lunatic. She was painfully thin, once described as "a nicely polished skeleton". She also liked to paint her face chalk-white and lie in a rosewood coffin with her eyes closed and her hands laid across her chest. The satin-lined coffin had been made for her when she was a teenager and close to death with tuberculosis. She kept it, often slept in it, even made love in it. She made sure that everyone was aware of her death obsession and of the small rosewood coffin and how she loved to be photographed in it. She dined from a human skull autographed by Victor Hugo. Her fascination with blood and gore was quite genuine. She once watched with fascination from a closed carriage while two of her lovers duelled over her. She even came close to killing one of her lovers herself when she pushed him from a second-storey window, and she horse-whipped another four times. Although a bitter public opponent of capital punishment, in private she used her influence to attend several executions. She once visited the Chicago stockyards to watch the bloodshed.

Her passion for animals, especially big cats, was also genuine and equally highly publicized. She owned pumas, cheetahs and ocelots, giving them a free run of her homes. A tame lion however had to be shown the door when the accompanying smell became impossible to live with. Bernhardt once turned a cheetah and a wolfhound loose at a garden party in London, just to see what happened next. Novelist Alexandre Dumas once paid a call on the great actress and looked on as a puma ate his straw hat. When an alligator she brought back from Louisiana ate her pet dog, she reluctantly had the reptile shot.

Bernhardt was extravagant. She habitually spent more than twice her income on houses, servants, furniture, rugs, art and bizarre pets. On an almost daily basis she threw lavish dinner parties and entertainments for her "court", a circle of friends that included a couple of genuine royals, among them the Prince of Wales, the future King Edward VII. The constant need for more money drove Bernhardt to abandon the French stage for tours of England, North and South America, and even Australia, where she insisted when possible on payment in gold coins. She carried them with her constantly, in a bag or in a metal-bound chest.

Soon after her seventieth birthday surgeons amputated her right leg, but her theatre career continued with parts specifically written for her, mostly in wheelchairs. When she was asked if the loss of a leg would end her outrageous sex life, she replied, "Only when I draw my last breath." Even with one leg Bernhardt found an occasion for extravagance, by insisting on moving around in a white and gold sedan chair with retainers to carry her where she wanted to go.

When 78-year-old Divine Sarah died in March 1925, 50,000 people walked past her funeral bier, and tens of thousands more followed the casket through Paris. Her final resting place was a plain mausoleum marked with a single word: Bernhardt.

Signora Girardelli, the nineteenth-century celebrity cook, held centre stage with an act pitched somewhere between Delia Smith and the Marquis de Sade. Staples of her cookery "act" included running a red hot poker over her limbs, frying eggs in boiling cooking oil in her cupped hands, and climbing inside a huge blazing oven to keep an eye on her baking. Signora Girardelli first arrived in England in 1814 claiming to have royal patronage, and made her debut in London billed as "The Great Phenomenon of Nature". She put boiling lead in her mouth, walked barefoot on hot irons and passed the poker over various parts of her body, then had a mouthwash of boiling oil.

Dwarfs, for anyone who could afford to keep them, were an early equivalent of TV. If you were royalty and rich you had one in every room. Czar Peter the Great was mad about dwarfs. At the birth of his second son he celebrated with a banquet. An enormous pie was placed on the men's table, the crust rose and out stepped a completely naked female dwarf. A similar pie was on the ladies' table, this time complete with a naked male dwarf. King George I had a court dwarf Christian Ulrich Jorry who entertained at his supper parties, a gift from a German nobleman. He didn't have a salary but the king bought his clothes. Queen Victoria was easily amused by dwarfs. She showed an "infantile delight" in General Tom Thumb – the dwarf Charles Stratton – and he was invited back to give several royal command performances.

Matthew Buchinger, a German who lived in the late seventeenth century, was the most extraordinary dwarf performer of all. Born in Anspach near Nuremberg in 1674, he was the youngest of nine children. As a boy he mastered a dozen musical instruments, became a fine dancer and a brilliant magician. He was also an excellent marksman, a superb bowler and an accomplished calligrapher. His chief claim to fame however he was that he was only 2 ft 4 in tall and possessed neither arms nor legs. His freakish appearance ensured that he became a star turn for royalty, especially King George I. His advertisements boasted appearances "before three emperors and most of the kings and princesses of Europe including Leopold I, Joseph I, and Karl VI." Although Buchinger supported his family comfortably for a while he later hit financial troubles when even his act was no longer considered a novelty. He constantly added to his repertoire in an increasingly desperate effort to draw new audiences; he played a Bavarian folk instrument called the heckebret, the dulcimer, trumpet, bagpipes, guitar, oboe, drum, kettledrum and flute. He shaved himself while he played, threaded a needle, ground corn into flour and carved figures in wood. Although Buchinger had neither feet, thighs nor arms, he did in fact have at least one fully functioning appendage. He married four times and sired fourteen children, including three illegitimately. A contemporary account of Buckinger titled "The Wonderful Little Man of Nuremberg" tells a story about one of Buchinger's wives:

> He got a great deal of money but his last wife was a very perverse woman who would spend all his money very prodigally and luxuriously in eating, drinking and clothes and would not permit him to eat nor drink as she did and did beat him cruelly, which he had born patiently but one day, she having beat him before company, that so provoked him, that he flew at her with such force that he threw her down and getting upon her belly and breast did so beat her in the same manner if she ever did so any more – and she became after a very dutiful and loving wife.

The American entertainer Orville Stamm had a unique act that involved lying on his back and singing with a piano on his chest: while Orville sang, the pianist would bounce up and down on Orville's thighs, belting out the tune to "Ireland Must Be Heaven Because Mother Comes From There".

Robert "Romeo" Coates (1772–1848) is generally recognized as the worst professional actor to ever set foot on the English stage. He first trod the boards in 1809, but it was his debut performance in *Romeo and Juliet* in the spa town of Bath about a year later that earned him his first serious notices. From the moment he made his first entrance in his sequin-spangled cloak, vast red pantaloons and enormous plumed hat, it became obvious to all that they were witnessing a unique talent. He went on to tour the British Isles, creating mayhem wherever he performed. He regularly fluffed his lines, ad-libbed as he went along, invented entire scenes, and generally brought the house down. If a particular scene went well with the audience, or so he thought, he would think nothing of replaying it three or four times over. His signature role was the part of Romeo, often in versions that he had modified himself. He was convinced that Shakespeare's original ending was too tame; on one occasion the audience sat open-mouthed as Romeo appeared wielding a crowbar, trying to open Juliet's tomb. Once, when it was pointed out to him that he was straying from the text, he replied, "Aye, that is the reading, I know, for I have the whole play by heart, but I think I have improved on it."

His unique style of acting was described thus by a contemporary critic: "In the school of Coates, dignity is denoted by strutting across the stage in strides two yards long, agony by the furious stamp of the foot at the end of every line." His tour de force was the Romeo death scene; no one ever died on stage quite like Coates. It was always performed in exactly the same way. He would produce a silk handkerchief from his top pocket with a mighty flourish and proceed to dust the stage with it. He then carefully laid down the handkerchief, placed his plumed hat upon it, then threw himself on the hat. One of his death scenes was received with such a great ovation that Coates jumped up, took a bow, then "died" all over again.

People were prepared to travel great distances to see for themselves if he was truly was as bad as his notices. When he played the part of Lothario in *The Fair Penitent* at London's Haymarket Theatre at least a thousand people were turned away and the crowd even stormed the stage door and stood in the wings. He was indomitable. Not even the sound of his audience exploding with laughter during a death scene would put him off his stride. At a performance in Richmond, Surrey, he caused several people to laugh so hard that they had to be carried outside and receive medical treatment.

Coates was the son of a millionaire and had inherited a fabulous collection of diamonds which he often used to dress up his stage costumes. For his Romeo role Coates wore a blue silk cloak covered with diamonds, a Stuart period wig and a top hat. For Lothario he donned a silver suit, a pink silk stole and a large hat decorated with ostrich feathers. His mode of travel was at least as eccentric as his dress sense. He travelled in two carriages, one the shape of a large cockleshell, the other resembling a huge kettledrum, decorated with serpents. Coates died in 1848, aged seventy-five, when he was struck by a hansom cab and killed instantly.

The bisexual Hollywood screen siren Tallulah Bankhead (1903–68), known for her astonishing private life and her self-deprecating wit, was obsessed with maintaining her reputation for being outrageous. She stripped naked at parties and in restaurants, and whenever she met a man for the first time would inform him, "I've slept with every man here, and now I'm going to sleep with you." At a society wedding, as the bride and groom made their way down the aisle, she announced conspicuously, "I've had both of them, darling, and neither of them is any good." She once bumped into Joan Crawford and her new husband Douglas Fairbanks, Jr on a train. She told Crawford, "Darling, you're divine. I've had your husband – you'll be next." Of her various addictions, she once said, "My father warned me about men and booze, but he never mentioned a word about women and cocaine." Of her sexuality, she noted, "I don't know what I am, darling. I've tried several varieties of sex. The conventional position makes me claustrophobic, and all the others give me either a stiff neck or lockjaw."

When King Louis XI of France, noted for his odd sense of humour and bizarre whims, once demanded to be entertained by "a consort of swine voices", opportunity knocked for the Abbot of Baigne – France's only entertainer on the novelty pig organ. The abbot laid a range of pigs out side by side, and when he struck the organ keys small spikes would prick the pigs causing them to squeal "in such an order and consonance as highly delighted the king and all his company".

The Frenchman Joseph Pujol, "Le Petomane" (roughly translated, "the manic farter"), was undoubtedly the most unusual performer of his generation thanks to an extraordinary gift. One day while swimming alone he discovered that by contracting his abdomen he could suck up as much water as he liked and eject it in a powerful stream. Soon Pujol started to practise with air instead of water and he discovered that he had the ability to produce a variety of sounds. At the time he was working in a Marseilles bakeshop, but in the evenings he entertained at local music halls by singing, doing comedy routines and playing his trombone. In private however he amused his friends with his other "act", and after some coaxing he agreed to turn this parlour trick into a full-fledged routine for public audiences.

Pujol rented a space in Marseilles to perform in. His friends promoted the show heavily themselves through posters and handouts. Word-of-mouth spread reports of the uniqueness of Pujol's shockingly funny new show, and soon people from all over Marseilles came to see him. The first performance had a mixed reception, but once the audience had overcome their initial shock he became a huge success. Pujol's friends urged him to take the act to Paris and 1892 he was brave enough to audition for the Moulin Rouge before the formidable theatre manager Monsieur Oller. When Oller asked him to explain his act he replied straight-faced, "You see, sir, my anus is of such elasticity that I can open and shut it at will . . . I can absorb any quantity of liquid I may be given . . . [and] I can expel an almost infinite quantity of odourless gas." He gave Oller a quick demonstration and the latter booked Pujol to perform that very night.

Pujol dressed formally for his act, wearing a coat, red breeches, white stockings, gloves and patent leather shoes. He introduced himself and explained that he was about to demonstrate the art of "petomanie". He explained that he could break wind at will, but assured his audience not to worry as his parents had "ruined themselves" in perfuming his rectum. Then Le Petomane began his act. He imitated the farts of a little girl, a mother-in-law, a bride on her wedding night, the same bride the day after and a builder. He imitated thunder, cannons and the sound of a dressmaker tearing two yards of calico. After the imitations, Le Petomane placed one end of a yard-long rubber tube into his anus and smoked a cigarette at the other, after which he used it to play a couple of tunes on a flute. For his finale he removed the tube, blew out some of the gas-jet footlights from a safe distance away, and then led the audience in a rousing sing-along. Oller immediately offered Pujol a contract.

The act was the talk of Paris. One newspaper critic noted that Pujol "ended with an attempt to run though the gamut of sounds. In reality he produced only four notes, the do, mi, sol, and do of the octave. I cannot guarantee that each of these notes was tonally true." To allay any rumours that his performance was faked, Pujol occasionally gave private performances clad in a bathing suit with a large hole in the backside to prove that his act was performed without mechanical assistance. Doctors examined him and published an article in *La Semaine Médicale* that described his health but offered no new explanation for his ability. It did however record that he could rectally project a jet of water four to five yards. One Sunday the Moulin Rouge took in 20,000 francs for a Le Petomane performance – more than double the receipts grossed by Sarah Bernhardt at the peak of her career there.

Eventually Pujol had a row with the manager of the Moulin Rouge and left the theatre, for which he was subsequently sued by Monsieur Oller for breach of contract. Oller retaliated by hiring a female "Petomane", Angele Thiébeau. When it was later discovered that Madame Thiébeau was a fraud (she hid a bellows-like contraption under her skirt) Pujol issued a counter writ against the Moulin Rouge.

Pujol created his own new Theatre Pompadour, including mime and magic and other acts performed by Pujol's family and friends. He changed his own act into a woodland tale punctuated at the end of each couplet by Le Petomane sound effects and imitations of the animal and bird characters. Pujol's fart theatre prospered for many years and continued to be an enormous draw until around 1900, when the interest of the show-going public began to wane. Throughout his entire career Pujol had been serenely unaffected by the mockery and derisive comments that accompanied his performances. He believed in his art and regarded his unusual talent as a great gift. The family moved back to Marseillés and Pujol ran bakeries with his family until 1922 when they moved to Toulon and he set up a biscuit factory. When he died in 1945 a medical school offered the family 25,000 francs to be allowed to examine his body, but his children turned the offer down.

Chapter Ten

Sporting Eccentrics

"The word 'genius' isn't applicable in football. A genius is a guy like Norman Einstein"

> Joe Theisman, NFL football
> quarterback and sports analyst

"When the going gets weird, the weird turn pro"
> Hunter S. Thompson (b. 1939)

Sir Atholl Oakeley (1900–1987) was Britain's first professional wrestling baronet. Sir Atholl, known for his distinctive cauliflower ear received in a bout in America when "Bill Bartoch got me in a scissors grip between his knees", was the veteran of 2,000 contests. He was heavyweight wrestling champion of Great Britain from 1930 to 1935 and European champion in 1932, his career described in the 1971 autobiography *Blood on the Mat*. His passion for wrestling began when he read *Lorna Doone* as a boy. The novel itself became something of a lifelong obsession for Sir Atholl. In 1969 he published a book, the little celebrated *Facts on which R. D. Blackmore Based Lorna Doone*, and staged a successful campaign to persuade the Ordnance Survey to alter the map of Exmoor so that Doone Valley was moved from Hoccombe to Lank Combe. He was short for a wrestler at 5ft 9in, but very stout, having built up his body by religiously drinking eleven pints of milk a day for three years. This diet was adopted on the advice of his idol, a giant wrestler called Hackenschmidt. He later confessed to Sir Atholl that the quantity of milk had been a misprint.

The Greek Peregrinus, nicknamed "Proteus", set himself on fire during the Olympic games of AD 165 to prove his faith in reincarnation. He hasn't reappeared at any subsequent Olympic meetings, although he did have a small cult following after his death and his staff was treated as a religious relic.

Sir Charles Aubrey "C.B." Smith was one of the great English cricketing toffs. Smith captained Surrey for two seasons (1887–8) and also captained England on his solitary Test appearance. Later he became a Hollywood actor, and became stereotyped as an English aristocrat in a number of films including *The*

Prisoner of Zenda and *The Life of a Bengal Lancer*. One day Smith was fielding in the slips when he fumbled a catch. He stopped play, requested his butler be brought on to the pitch, and instructed him to fetch his spectacles. Several minutes later, with the other players standing around waiting to resume play, the manservant duly returned with the spectacles. A couple of overs later Smith dropped another easy catch. "Damn fool," he bawled at the butler, "you brought me my reading glasses."

Hugh Cecil Lowther (1857–1944), fifth of Earl of Lonsdale, is forever remembered as the original sponsor of boxing's famous Lonsdale Belt. To his contemporaries however he was known as "the yellow earl" because of the bright yellow livery he designed for servants and his vehicles. He followed the theme through by dressing his gardeners in the same colour – even their wheelbarrows were yellow. As the Earl was also President of the Automobile Association, many believe that the AA's colour scheme may also have been his idea. Apparently he hated his nickname, preferring to be known as "Lordy". The Earl was a fanatical and ruthless huntsman. He was often known to lash out with his whip at other riders – if members of the "lower orders" got in his way he thrashed them too. He once bought a horse for £500, but when it refused to jump he made his groom shoot it.

The Yorkshire CC slow left-arm bowler Bobby Peel (1857–1941) played cricket for England from 1884 to 1896. He was regularly inebriated during matches, often drinking himself into a state tactfully referred to in the cricketing bible Wisden as "unwell" or "gone away". During one county game the Yorkshire captain Lord Hawke was forced to suspend Peel from the side for "running the wrong way" and "bowling at the pavilion in the belief that it was the batsman". Peel was eventually sacked from the Yorkshire team after his performance against Warwickshire at Edgbaston in May 1896. During an unbeaten partnership of 367 with Lord Hawke, Peel relieved himself on the pitch.

The Victorian Thomas Birch, Keeper of Books at the British Museum, was a keen angler. His enthusiasm for the sport was such that he would stand by the river for hours on end disguised as a tree, with his arms held out as branches. The appropriately named Birch believed any movements he made would therefore be interpreted by the fish as "the natural effect of a mild breeze."

For many of the British officers stationed in India during the Mutiny of 1858, butchering the natives was merely a sporting interlude in an otherwise tedious existence. The troops would strap captured mutineers across the muzzle of their loaded cannon and blast them to pieces. It was widely believed in both sides that the Almighty wouldn't be able to reassemble the bits of the body, and so the victim wouldn't have an afterlife. One officer H. H. Stansfeld wrote home, "It is very dull here, now and then a sepoy hung or blown away, a cricket match or two, and a little quail shooting."

Lionel, Lord Tennyson, was the cricketing grandson of the famous poet Alfred and captained Hampshire in the late 1940s. Tennyson played the part of the true English aristocrat to the hilt. Hampshire's wicketkeeper at that time, Walter Livesey, was also Tennyson's manservant, and was always required to pack his master's cricket bag, with instructions from his captain and master to pack enough champagne to celebrate a victory or drown a defeat. When watching from the pavilion, Tennyson liked to keep in touch with his batsmen by telegram. On one occasion, a Hampshire batsman was struggling to hit leather, and was surprised to see a bell boy trotting towards him with a silver salver and a small envelope. Inside was a telegram from the captain, demanding to know whether the recipient knew what his bat was for.

The famous French racing driver Jean Behra wore a plastic right ear after losing one in a racing crash in 1955, and always carried a spare false ear in his pocket just in case.

The seventh Earl of Barrymore was an amateur pugilist, part-time actor and full-time rake, which earned him the nickname "Hellgate". He had two brothers respectively known as "Newgate", thanks to a stay in a debtor's prison, and "Cripplegate" on account of a physical deformity, and a sister known as "Billingsgate", a tribute to her fishwife-like vocabulary. Barrymore was very fond of picnics. He always sent the servants ahead with instructions to bury the food, and the guests were expected to hunt for it. Those guests who refused to join in, or just didn't look hard enough, simply went hungry. One day the

Earl set off in his carriage for a spot of duck hunting with a shotgun in his lap. The road was bumpy, the carriage jolted and the gun went off in his face. He died of his injuries, aged twenty-three, half an hour later.

Jack Mytton, the wealthy nineteenth-century MP and squire of Halston in Shropshire, was one of the great hell-raisers of his era. He was expelled from both Westminster school and Harrow for fighting, then squandered an inheritance of £500,000 on alcohol in fifteen years – he drank at least five bottles of port and five of brandy a day. He often hunted naked, although his wardrobe contained 150 pairs of riding breeches, 700 pairs of boots and 300 shirts. Mytton had a bent for self-destruction and was chiefly famous for his love of dangerous sports. He took so many risks when he was riding that a phrase was coined for any sporting activity that was considered too dangerous – "it would do for Mytton". He "scorned caution and wondered why others did not do likewise." When a friend, visibly shaky as he rode next to him in his gig, confided that he had never been in a crash, Mytton was shocked. "What ho!" he cried. "Never, you say? What a damned slow fellow you must have been all your life!" Then he promptly drove the carriage over the bank and overturned it.

Mytton fought dogs and bears with his bare hands, went duck-hunting in winter wearing only his nightshirt and chased rats across frozen ponds on ice skates. His famous horse Baronet was a one-eyed steed which had been Mytton's charger when he served in the Hussars. He would often, during bad weather, knock on a cottage door and ask the occupants if his horse could dry off in front of the fire. As most of the properties around belonged to him, he was rarely turned away. He once tried to warm up another horse named Sportsman on a chilly day by giving the horse a bottle of port. The horse died soon afterwards. He kept a huge number of pets including 2,000 dogs, 60 cats and a bear called Nell. At one of his dinner parties he suddenly appeared in full dress costume mounted on the bear's back. In the panic that ensued, the bear bit a large chunk out of Mytton's leg.

Mytton died a bloated, paralysed and penniless debtor in the King's Bench prison. After his death at the age of thirty-eight, a friend signed an affidavit to the effect that Mytton had been permanently inebriated for the last twelve years of his life. Within fifteen years he had drunk away his inheritance, gambled away the family estate and lost his parliamentary seat, held by the Mytton family for generations. His death was partly attributed to injuries sustained while setting fire to his own nightshirt to try to cure hiccups. Just before the horribly burned Mytton slumped into unconsciousness he said, "Well, the hiccups is gone, by God."

When nature called the Spanish First Division footballer David Billabone during a game between his club Bilbao and Cadiz, he decided he couldn't make it to half-time and discreetly urinated behind a goalpost. Unfortunately he wasn't discreet enough to escape the attention of a 20,000 crowd and a local photographer who splashed a picture of the leaking Spaniard all over Spanish newspapers. Billabone was fined £2,000.

The Indian Prince the Maharaja of Jaipur declared a fifteen-mile exclusion zone around his capital where he alone was allowed to hunt. He had poachers tortured by pushing ground hot chillies into their rectums.

King Edward VII owned a golf bag made from an elephant's penis. It was a birthday present given to him by an Indian Maharaja who had heard of the king's fondness for golf, big game hunting and adultery, but not necessarily in that order.

The great Gloucestershire and England cricketer Dr William Gilbert "W. G." Grace (1848–1915) was famously idiosyncratic in his interpretation of fair play. He once scolded an umpire who had dared to give him out: "They've come here to see me bat, not you umpiring," then calmly replaced the bails and continued his innings. On another occasion he skied a ball towards the boundary where a fielder was positioned to take an easy catch. With the ball still airborne, he quickly declared the innings closed, then demanded that the umpire rule him not out as play had ended before the ball was caught. In one innings Grace hit ninety-three runs, then dumbfounded everyone by suddenly declaring, seven short of his century. He explained later that he had never hit a ninety-three before.

Valentine Brown, Lord Castlereagh, had his elbow shot away during World War I, and spent the rest of his days carrying the damaged arm at a peculiar angle to his bulky body. The injury did not however hinder his dedication to huntin', fishin' and shootin'. Lord Beaverbrook once remarked to him, "If it's a fine day tomorrow, Valentine, I suppose you'll want to kill something." He owned a vast collection of fishing rods, which were made in St James's Street, London. Whenever he called to make a purchase the shop assistant was required to carry armfuls of rods to the kerbside while his lordship made practice casts into the traffic. He once took 400 books with him on a ten-day cruise. He was an erratic but keen golfer. At an auction he bought a job lot of 147 golf clubs. Whenever he found himself in a bunker, he dropped to his knees and prayed. Once he found himself with a particularly difficult lie, and was seen on his knees in the sand for a full three minutes. He rose, then added before playing his shot, ". . . but don't send Jesus, this is no job for a boy."

Johnny Cochrane, team manager of Sunderland Football Club from 1928 to 1939, was famous for his relaxed style of management, especially during prematch preparations. When his team were about to face Arsenal, Cochrane popped his head round his players' dressing room door wearing his bowler hat, in his hand a glass of whisky, smoking his usual cigar. "Who are we playing today, lads?" he enquired. "Arsenal, boss." Cochrane replied, "Oh, we'll piss that lot," then shut the door and left them to it.

George Osbaldeston (1787–1866) was a short, muscular man known for his fine horsemanship, which earned him the nickname "the squire of all England." He also excelled at several other sports, including billiards, boxing, cricket, fishing, rowing and shooting. Osbaldeston inherited a considerable fortune when he was an undergraduate, and dropped out of Oxford to devote his life to leisure pursuits. He could never resist a bet – the more outlandish the wager, the better. He played billiards for fifty hours nonstop without sleeping and won boxing matches despite giving away up to four stone to his opponents. He once felled 100 pheasants with 100 shots, despite being accidentally shot in the eye himself while he was doing it; he merely remarked to the errant marksman, "I said you would hit something eventually."

At the age of forty-four, while suffering from a badly crippled leg from a hunting accident, Osbaldeston accepted a bet of 1,000 guineas that he could ride 200 miles in ten hours. Although his chances of collecting were slim he decided to make the bet more of a challenge by volunteering to do it in nine hours. Fortified by a lunch of partridge washed down with brandy, he completed the 200 mile circuit in eight hours and forty-two minutes, an average speed of twenty-two miles per hour. He immediately jumped on a fresh horse and galloped off to the Rutland Arms at Newmarket, where he declared himself so hungry he "could eat an old woman". He died a few weeks after winning his final bet: unable to walk and confined to a bathchair, he wagered a sovereign that he could sit for twenty-four hours without moving.

––––––––––––

The Indian Maharaja Jay Singh of Alwar was a personal friend of King George V and was the king's guest at Buckingham Palace in 1931. In 1933 the polo-playing Maharaja had a bad game and decided to blame his horse, which had stumbled and thrown him. As an audience of British VIPs watched, the Maharaja poured a can of petrol over the polo pony and set fire to it.

Chapter Eleven

Royal Eccentrics

"A noble nasty course he ran
Superbly filthy and fastidious,
He was the world's first gentleman
And made that appellation hideous"
> Winthrop Mackworth Praed (1802–39)
> on King George IV

"It is the coolest sort of coiffure"
> Princess Caroline of Brunswick-Wolfenbüttel
> (1768–1821) wife of George IV, explaining to
> a Russian Grand Duke why she was wearing
> half a pumpkin on her head

"The bowels are acting fully"
> Queen Victoria (1819–1901) in a surprise
> telegram to her doctor on the latter's honeymoon

"Abroad is awful. I know; I have been"
King George V (1865–1936)

When the sixteen-year-old Farouk became the ruling monarch of Egypt on the death of his father, King Fuad I, in 1936, as occupier of the world's oldest extant throne he also became almost incalculably wealthy. He owned five palaces, two yachts, several aircraft and thousands of acres of valuable farmland. He also owned more than one hundred cars, painted a bright red so that police would know not to stop him when he was speeding, and he shot at the tyres of any car that attempted to overtake him. He was remarkably acquisitive, especially when it came to beautiful women.

Although fantastically wealthy, the immature young king was also a compulsive thief. He pilfered anything that took his fancy, even from friends and fellow rulers. He once stole a jewelled dagger from the visiting Emir of Yemen. When the father of the Shah of Iran died in South Africa and the body passed through Cairo en route to a state burial, Farouk secretly had it stripped of a ceremonial sword and medals. His minions went on scouting missions to homes to which he was invited, to identify objects for him to nick. Farouk was a skilled pickpocket. He once boasted that he had released a criminal from prison specifically to teach him how to steal. Once, British Prime Minister Winston Churchill was seated at Farouk's table when he discovered that his watch, a valuable heirloom passed down from his ancestor, the Duke of Marlborough, was missing. The young kleptomaniac vigorously denied taking the watch, but left the table, returning with it later. He explained to Churchill, none too convincingly, that he had managed to apprehend the real thief. Farouk was also a compulsive and outrageous liar. He even bought trophies commemorating imaginary sporting triumphs.

Inevitably, King Farouk was overthrown by Egyptian army officers led by General Mohammed Naguib and Colonel Qamal Abdel Nasser and sent into exile in 1952. When the new regime decided to auction off the contents of the ex-king's Cairo palace, an inventory of Farouk's possessions revealed not only thousands of expensive watches and rare coins and stamps and jewels, but also a bizarre assortment of bric-a-brac including thousands of matchbox tops, razor-blade packets, gold holders for pop bottles, tons of pornography of every conceivable type, American comic books and seventy-five pairs of binoculars. One journalist noted that it was "the world's biggest and most expensive accumulation of junk".

Anne Boleyn had a diverting habit, first observed during her coronation banquet, of vomiting during meals. She employed a lady-in-waiting whose job it was to hold up a sheet when the Queen looked likely to throw up.

Queen Victoria collected dead flowers taken from the graves of deceased royals. She began her collection with some that grew on her late husband Albert's last resting place and it just sort of took off from there. After his death, Queen Victoria's mourning was so intense and her behaviour so eccentric that some of her ministers thought that her ghoulish cult of Prince Albert was a sign of something more sinister and that she, like her grandfather George III, had lost her mind. The widowed Queen at first contemplated suicide, then spent the best part of forty years wearing black mourning clothes. She once scolded her eldest son, the Prince of Wales, for writing to her on paper which had insufficiently thick black borders. She retained all of Albert's personal equerries and grooms and his rooms were maintained exactly as they were the day he died. Every evening hot water was taken to his chambers and fresh clothes were laid out on his bed. When Victoria commissioned a memorably gruesome portrait of her daughter Alice, depicted as a nun in the presence of a vision of her dear departed father, the Queen's closest adviser and mentor Baron Stockmar became convinced that Victoria had become mentally unhinged. Queen Victoria was also a hypochondriac; she would summon her personal physician up to half a dozen times a day with various imaginary complaints, usually concerning her digestive system.

The Italian born Empress Anna, wife of Ferdinand V, lived in Austria for fifty years without bothering to learn one single word of German. Although the Bourbon Henri V of France never reigned, as his countrymen had decided to become citizens of a republic by one vote in 1875, he never went anywhere without his valet, because he had never learned how to tie his own cravat.

Prince Felix Yusupov was probably the richest and one of the most bizarre nobleman in pre-revolutionary Russia. Yusupov had two serious claims to lasting fame: the first was that he helped to murder the so-called "mad monk" Rasputin, and the second was that he was such a convincing transvestite that he came within an ace of being seduced by King Edward VII. In his teens Yusupov lived a double life, by day an ordinary schoolboy, by night a transvestite. He lived dangerously by flirting with Guards officers, and once barely escaped with his life when four Russian soldiers, taking him for a female prostitute, attempted to gang rape him. Yusupov often visited Paris where he passed convincingly for a woman. On one of his excursions he visited the theatre with his brother Nicholas, and during the first half of the play Yusupov, dressed in an expensive ball gown, caught the eye of a fat, elderly man who was leering at him from an adjacent private box. When the lights went up at the interval he realized that his admirer was the king of England. A few moments later his brother Nicholas was approached in the foyer by one of the king's companions: his majesty would dearly like to know the name of the lovely young lady he was escorting. The Yusupov brothers fled before events took a nasty turn.

Although Louis XV was arguably the most powerful man in Europe his grasp of economics was somewhat flawed. When he heard that the workers were starving, he sympathetically sacked eighty gardeners. He took them back when someone gently explained to him that he had just ensured that they too would starve.

The Russian Empress Anne loved game hunting, but couldn't be bothered with the thrill of a long chase, or for that matter any chase at all; most of the time she couldn't even be bothered to get out her carriage. A special hunting area was prepared in the park at Peterhof which was so thick with imported bears, wild boars, stags and other animals that all she had to do was poke her gun out of her carriage window to be sure of hitting something. Nothing however was left to chance: to ensure that she went home with plenty of trophies, the animals were driven past the muzzle of her gun at point-blank range. Every now and then the Empress would fancy a spot of hunting but was too idle to get out of bed. For these occasions the palace aviary was always fully stocked so that she could have a few flocks to shoot at from her bedroom window.

Anne was also fond of making up new and interesting punishments to fit the crime. When she decided that two overweight noblewomen were guilty of greed, she had them force-fed huge amounts of pastries until they almost choked to death on their own vomit. Few complained about their treatment: the Empress always had their tongues pulled out.

George II suffered dreadfully from piles and an anal fistula but was very vain and notoriously touchy about his ailments, which were supposed to be a secret from everyone. When one of his Lords of the Bedchamber tactlessly enquired after the king's health, George sacked him on the spot.

All the kings of Great Britain's ruling house of Hanover were noted not only for their ugliness but also for their eccentric tastes in wives and mistresses. The attentions of King George I were shared by two middle-aged ladies who, because of their diametrically opposing figures, were known as "the Elephant and the Maypole". Queen Caroline of Ansbach, wife of George

II, chose his mistresses for him, taking care to select only women who were even uglier than she was. George III's wife, Queen Charlotte of Mecklenburg-Strelitz, was so physically repulsive it was suggested at the time that the king's bouts of madness were brought on by the trauma of having sex with her. When she arrived in England to take her throne, Londoners greeted her with cries of "pug-face". When Charlotte requested a translation, she was told that it meant "God Bless Her Majesty". George IV's mistress Maria Fitzherbert is described as having a long pointed nose and a mouth misshapen by badly fitting false teeth. He was revolted by the sight of Caroline of Brunswick, the bride his father had selected for him, the moment he clapped eyes on her. On his wedding day he went through the marriage ceremony "looking like death", and at one point tried to run off but was restrained by his father. William IV, after proposing to but being turned down by eight different women, found a bride at last in Princess Adelaide of Saxe-Coburg-Meiniengen, who was described by a contemporary as "frightful . . . very ugly with a horrid complexion".

Spain's Queen Maria Christina threw lavish fancy dress balls and encouraged her guests to dance and make merry until the early hours, but afterwards always sent them a bill for the food and drink they had consumed.

William, Duke of Gloucester and nephew of King George III, was the original "silly billy". He was both quite stupid and fanatical in matters of etiquette. He never allowed men, even extremely old men, to sit down in his presence. On a visit to

Russia he was dancing in St Petersburg when a buckle on his shoe became unfastened: he stood and waited until an equerry bent down and buckled it up for him. Once, a visitor to his home saw a violin lying around and asked if he played. William replied "only God save his uncle and such little things".

Traditional Spanish royal protocol, the most eccentric of all forms of European court etiquette, was still in use well into the nineteenth century. The Duke of Sutherland once observed Spain's Queen Ena taking a seaside dip at San Sebastian. She was accompanied, as always, by two fully armed and uniformed soldiers. As the Queen walked into the sea they marched alongside her, staring rigidly ahead, until only their heads could be seen above the waves.

Russia's first ever book of etiquette was published by Empress Anne in 1718. She had revolutionary ideas about good manners and was keen to keep up with European standards of good taste. Entitled *The Honest Mirror of Youth*, the slim volume advised discerning Russians how to use a knife and fork, when not to spit on the floor, to refrain from clearing their nasal passages in public by applying a digit to one nostril while blowing down the other, and not to jab their elbows into their seating partners during formal dinners or place their feet in guests' dishes while standing on the dining table.

In fact the Russian royal family discovered western-style court etiquette very late in the day, but once they had taken it on board they developed an exclusively eccentric variant. Czar Alexander II's daughter Marie, as a Grand Duchess of Russia, insisted on a convention which allowed no one to ever turn their back on her. One day while her husband the Duke of Edinburgh was walking the Grand Duchess through the gardens of a country estate, the head gardener was summoned so they could congratulate him on his work. When the audience was over the gardener found there were no nearby exits to ease the necessary backward retreat. Instead of allowing the poor man to make a dignified exit, she stood and watched him walk backwards for several hundred yards until he was completely out of sight.

Another gardening incident had a less amusing outcome. In 1882 Czar Alexander III was out walking in the royal park at Peterhof when he beckoned to one of the workers so he could ask him some questions. The gardener threw down his tools and ran towards him, but when he got within a couple of yards of the Czar he was shot dead by a bodyguard. The royal minder was following orders to shoot to kill anyone who came near without a prior appointment.

Emperor Menelik II of Ethiopia heard about America's exciting new means of executing criminals, the electric chair, and decided to order one. When it arrived the Emperor found there was just one snag: he couldn't get it working because Ethiopia didn't have any electricity. He had it converted into a new throne instead.

King George I introduced himself to his prospective new daughter-in-law Princess Caroline of Ansbach by lifting her skirts to see for himself whether or not his son was marrying a virgin.

In 1866 Queen Victoria's third daughter, the extremely plain Helena, was married to Prince Christian of Schleswig-Holstein. Prince Christian was thirty-five, very fat, balding and a heavy drinker, but he was the best they could do in the circumstances. Christian was also desperately slow on the uptake. When he was summoned to England he misread the situation and presumed he was being lined up as a second husband for Victoria to replace the deceased Albert.

In December 1891 Christian was shooting pheasant with his brother-in-law Albert, the Duke of Connaught, when Albert carelessly blasted him in the face with his shotgun, and Christian had to have an eye removed. He went on to collect a number of glass eyes which he was fond of producing at dinner parties and explaining the history of at length, until he became a renowned "glass-eye bore". His favourite was a blood-shot one which he wore when he had a cold.

The Russian Empress Catherine I was so permanently inebriated that she was once too soused to realize that anything had happened when she survived an assassination attempt. She was reviewing a Guards regiment when a bullet flew past and struck an innocent bystander dead. The pickled Empress moved on without flinching.

King Frederick V, ruler of Denmark from 1746 to 1766, was so vain he had his portrait painted at least seventy times by the same artist, Carl Pilo.

King George III's daughter Elizabeth was married at the age of forty-eight to the immensely fat German widower Frederick, Landgrave of Hesse-Homburg. Frederick, popularly known as "Humbug", cut a bizarre figure and was known chiefly for his huge moustache and offensive body odour. A courtier who met him commented, "An uglier hound with a snout buried in hair I never saw . . . a monster of a man, whose breath and hide is a compound between tobacco and garlick." The Landgrave had to be almost forcibly immersed in hot water several times to make him fit to attend his own wedding. At the ceremony he promised in his impenetrable German accent to "lof her", then threw up as the couple drove away. Bets were taken on whether or not the shock of seeing her daughter enter into such a desperate marriage with the repulsive Humbug would finish off Princess Elizabeth's mother, the dying Queen Charlotte.

King George V was a renowned stickler for the time-consuming but utterly useless framework of royal etiquette. He even used to wear his crown every day while he was signing State papers "to remind himself of the importance of it all".

Queen Elizabeth II's uncle Henry, Duke of Gloucester, was prone to giggling fits or bursting into tears for no apparent reason and known in family circles as "poor Harry". In old age the Duke took refuge in his favourite pastime, watching children's television. He once kept King Olav of Norway waiting for half an hour because he couldn't be torn away from an episode of "Popeye".

When King George IV's wife Princess Caroline of Brunswick-Wolfenbüttel first stepped on English soil in 1795 she went on the charm offensive at her very first official engagement at Greenwich Naval Hospital. Upon being presented to a number of crippled war veterans, she remarked, "Mein Gott . . . have all the English only one arm or one leg?" From their wedding day onwards George and Caroline rarely exchanged a word. It was said that their home was deliberately vast so that they need never meet. When protocol or some other reason required them to share the same room, the prince would surround himself with friends so that he wouldn't have to make small talk with his strange wife. "I had rather see toads and vipers crawling over my victuals," he told friends, "than sit at the same table with her." Caroline meanwhile modelled wax effigies of her husband, stuck needles in them and roasted them in the fire.

Caroline left the country and for the next few years she and her large personal entourage of about 200 hangers-on criss-crossed Europe. The further she travelled, the more outlandish her behaviour became. The British press picked up every new scrap of gossip as she entertained and shocked international society. She once made an extraordinary pilgrimage to the Holy Land and insisted on riding into Jerusalem on an ass. Although Caroline was well beyond her first flush of youth and was almost as wide as she was tall she was convinced she was highly attractive to men and became notorious for her décolletage: the Whig MP Samuel Whitbread wrote her a letter advising that she did not expose quite so much of her bosom when she went to the opera. She also acquired a habit of suddenly shedding her corset and exposing her bare breasts, and commissioned a portrait of herself naked from the waist up. Caroline died of constipation, in spite of being force-fed so much castor oil, according to an eye-witness, that it "would have turned the stomach of a horse".

George VI was a royal anorak. He kept a game book continuously from 1907 to 1952 in which he personally recorded everything he'd shot and the weather conditions.

Archduke Franz Ferdinand, whose assassination at Sarajevo in 1914 began the train of events leading to the outbreak of World War I, was highly unpredictable and given to violent mood swings. His mental state was at the time attributed to his mad grandfather King "Bomba" of Naples, but it was equally likely to have been inherited from his Habsburg antecedents. In accordance with the social demands of the day he hunted wild animals, but his mania for bloodsports was grotesque even by royal standards. Franz Ferdinand's favourite hunting weapon was the machine gun. Animals were deliberately driven into his line of fire so that he could simply mow them down in large numbers. In his relatively brief lifetime he exterminated hundreds of thousands of birds and animals. On one of his trips to Poland he killed so many European bison that he personally brought the species close to extinction. Once when he and the Kaiser were out shooting together sixty boars were driven before the Archduke's gun: he killed fifty-nine outright but flew into a blind rage when the sixtieth wounded boar escaped. The Archduke's hunting lodge at the castle of Konipiste in central Bohemia, home to his massive collection of game trophies, was said to be the most tasteless royal residence in Europe. Thousands upon thousands of animal heads, bodies, teeth and antlers were mounted on walls or stored in display cabinets. Later the lodge became a favoured weekend holiday retreat for the Nazi SS.

Franz Ferdinand married a non-royal Czech girl, Sophie Chotek, and so had to surrender his children's rights to succession. On their fourteenth wedding anniversary, 23 June 1914, ignoring advice to stay away from Bosnia, the Archduke and his wife set off from Konipiste for Sarajevo. Franz Ferdinand was incredibly vain, and insanely fussy about his personal appearance. On important occasions he insisted on being actually sewn into his suits so that he could appear perfectly crease-free. This eccentricity contributed to his death. When he and his wife were gunned down by Serbian terrorists in Sarajevo no one could get his jacket off to stop the bleeding because he was sewn into it. By the time they found some scissors to cut his clothes off, it was too late.

When King George I's mother the Electress Sophia finally lost her teeth she replaced all her missing dentures with little squares of wax.

The German Kaiser Wilhelm II would kill a conversation by proudly producing from his wallet a collection of snapshots, not of his children, but of his deceased Hohenzollern relatives dressed in their funeral attire. "Kaiser Bill" hero-worshipped his illustrious German predecessor Frederick the Great to the point of obsession. He even aped Frederick's famous passion for greyhounds by keeping a pack of court dachshunds which roamed and fouled the palace.

The Austrian Emperor Franz Josef had a nephew, Archduke Otto, who was famous for strolling around Vienna's most exclusive hotels wearing his gloves and his sabre, but otherwise stark naked. One day Otto was out riding with his cousin when they came across a funeral procession, and decided to amuse themselves with an exhibition of show-jumping over the coffin. The incident was subsequently mentioned in the Austrian Parliament by a deputy. A few days later two unidentified army officers went round to the deputy's house and savagely beat him up. The assault had been paid for by Otto's cousin, the Austrian Crown Prince Rudolf.

The Emperor himself did not show any obvious signs of inbreeding by his Habsburg or Wittelsbach antecedents, but he was undeniably odd. Apart from hunting he allowed himself little leisure. He always slept in an iron cot and before he would put on his lederhosen always had a valet wear them first to break them in. The Emperor despised mealtime small talk and had his staff trained to serve and clear away a twelve-course meal in less than an hour. He ate extremely quickly, and because he was always served first and the table was cleared away as soon as he had finished, his guests learned to eat quickly too if they were going to eat at all. There was another incentive not to linger over luncheon as the Hofburg palace dining room was lit by huge silver and crystal chandeliers which had a habit of crashing down on the heads of unsuspecting visitors.

After six years the marriage between the Emperor and his beautiful young Empress Elizabeth effectively ended because she was to spend the rest of her life – thirty-five years in all – roaming around Europe using a variety of assumed names. The Emperor was reduced to communicating with his wife by letter. On one of the few occasions when he got to speak to her face to face, Franz Josef asked her what she would like for a Christmas present. Elizabeth replied that she had her heart set on a fully equipped lunatic asylum. The Empress was a frequent visitor to insane asylums in Vienna, Munich, and Bedlam in London. At one time she also owned a fully equipped circus for her personal entertainment. She spent much of her time sailing through the Greek islands, insisting upon travelling in the most terrible weather, and had herself tied to the mast so she could watch the storms. Her favourite island was Corfu and she considered settling there permanently. She had a neo-Greek palace called the Achilleion built on the highest point of the island, but then just as quickly lost interest, sold the palace and moved on. She retained her good looks to the end, in spite of her anorexia which compelled her to live on a starvation diet of six cups of milk a day, and occasional experiments with a diet of sand.

Moulay Ismael, the Sultan of Morocco from 1672 to 1727, gifted samples of his bowel movements to ladies of the court as a mark of special favour.

King Phillip II of Spain's son and heir Don Carlos was so disappointed with a pair of boots that had been made for him that he had them cut into pieces and forced the cobbler to eat them.

Queen Isabeau, wife of King Charles VI of France, decreed that the waistlines of all her court ladies-in-waiting should not exceed a maximum of thirteen inches, causing a few of them to starve to death in the process.

Kaiser Wilhelm II endured the ultimate in royal mother-in-law from hell experiences. The Dowager Adelaide, wife of the late Duke Frederick of Schleswig-Holstein, had an obsession with personal hygiene. She evolved a system of washing which involved dividing her body into twenty-four washable sections, or "hemispheres". Each section required an individual but complete set of bowl, pitcher, soap dish, soap and towel. This eccentric routine had a ruinous effect on the domestic arrangements of her hosts and the patience of her son-in-law. Even more embarrassing was the predatory old dowager's behaviour with young men. At two state dinners she made sudden assaults upon her male neighbours at table and when she was strategically positioned out of harm's way between her daughter and a lady-in-waiting she became violent and abusive.

The Russian Grand Duke Constantine, grandson of Catherine the Great, often amused himself by kicking hussars to death and firing live rats from cannon. He would have found a soulmate in King Miguel of Portugal who liked to toss live piglets in the air so he could catch them on the point of his sword.

The court of King Richard II was known for sartorial eccentricity – the king himself was known for his fantastic gemstone-covered ballgown and is associated with the greatest fashion mistake of all, the codpiece. Richard was also probably the first man ever to use a pocket handkerchief and – a dead giveaway for effeminacy in the fourteenth century – took a regular bath.

Adolphus, Duke of Cambridge, was the youngest of King George III's seven sons. The Duke was a highly strung and confused man; the Duke of Wellington described him as "as mad as Bedlam", which was more bad news for the British royal family gene pool as his immensely fat daughter, the Duchess of Teck, was Queen Mary's mother. He was an odd-looking character with a peculiar little beard, known as a Newport Fringe. He had a habit of talking in an excitable, unfathomable high-pitched babble and often startled churchgoers by shouting out loud at inappropriate times during sermons. Adolphus was on the face of it an unlikely family man, as for most of his life he showed no interest in women at all and went around wearing a blond wig. When the prospects opened up by the death in childbirth of Princess Charlotte, heir to the throne, dangled before him, he proposed within a week of his niece's funeral to a woman he didn't know, Princess Augusta of Hesse-Cassel, a severe-looking, beetle-browed woman who appeared more of a man than he would ever be. His German wife also had a very limited grasp of English and an even thicker accent than his. This made conversation with either of them strained, and it was possible for visitors to the Cambridge household to come away without having understood a single word that either of their hosts had said.

Louis XIV had a habit of granting audiences to people while he was sitting on his close-stool: some visitors, including the English ambassador Lord Portland, even regarded it as a special honour to be received by the Sun King in this manner. Louis in fact announced his betrothal to his second wife Mme de Maintenon whilst in the middle of a crap.

The Grand Duchess Catherine of Oldenburg was the sister of Alexander I, Emperor of Russia during the Napoleonic wars. When she discovered that the Prince Regent had become estranged from his wife Princess Caroline of Brunswick, she invited herself to London, determined to take advantage of the situation, but threw a temper tantrum when she saw the small unimportant-looking vessel sent by the British Navy to fetch her. She got her way and was rewarded with the impressive frigate *Jason*. Unfortunately it was hate at first sight. The Duchess was an immensely fat Slavonic woman, prone to epileptic fits. She was also a widow at twenty-six and spent her entire visit dressed in mourning clothes. When the prince threw a lavish party for her at his home and ordered carefully chosen music to accompany the meal, she announced that she couldn't bear any form of music because it made her vomit. She also found the prince to be pretty revolting, "a man visibly used up by dissipation and rather disgusting" and even "obscene" with "a brazen way of looking where eyes should not go". The Duchess did however receive a wedding proposal from the prince's more desperate younger brother the Duke of Clarence (the future William IV) but turned him down on the grounds that he was an imbecile.

When Persia's ruling monarch Reza Shah had an overnight stay in a remote village, all of the dogs within a one-mile radius were put down in case they barked and disturbed his sleep.

Czar Ferdinand I of Bulgaria was the newly independent state's first monarch and one of the most flamboyant royal characters of the twentieth century. He was related on his father's side to Britain's ruling royals, the house of Saxe-Coburg-Gotha, and was also second cousin to Queen Victoria. Six foot tall and heavily bearded, Ferdinand wore women's jewellery, powdered his face and slept in a pink nightgown trimmed with Valenciennes lace. Although he married twice to keep up appearances (and produced an heir, Prince Boris) he spent his days chasing butterflies or seducing his male chauffeurs.

The fact that the Czar was homosexual was made brutally apparent to his second wife Princess Eleonore von Reuss-Köstritz on their wedding night. When her new husband discovered that they had been assigned a double room, he flew into a furious rage and had it immediately swapped for two singles. Czar Ferdinand, who had jug ears and a huge nose, was cripplingly self-conscious about his appearance. His defence mechanism was to make elaborate jokes about his ears and his nose; he even kept pet elephants in his palace grounds so that he could repeat his line about how their features reminded him so much of himself.

The French Empress Eugenie, wife of Napoleon III, attempted

suicide by breaking the heads off phosphorus matches and drinking them dissolved in milk.

King George III kept his daughters hidden from the world for as long as he could in what became known as the "Windsor Nunnery". Some married very late in life, the lucky ones not at all. The first daughter to marry was the unfortunate Charlotte, the Princess Royal. When she first met her husband, Frederick I, King of Württemburg, she almost fainted. He was forty-three years old and so fat that when he sat down to play cards a convex segment had to be cut out of the table to make room for his gut. Napoleon said that God had created him only to demonstrate how far the human skin could be stretched without bursting. Another black mark against King Frederick was that he was widely suspected of having murdered his first wife, Augusta. The massive fiancé arrived to claim the Princess Royal's hand in marriage in a wedding costume made of silk and shot with silver and gold, looking much like a heavily embroidered Zeppelin. Charlotte's entire family including George III wept throughout the ceremony. The marriage was childless: his wife spent her days in preoccupation with her pet kangaroos, while Frederick drank himself to death.

The Württemburgs were a singularly unattractive family. Frederick's gluttonous younger brother, Prince Alexander, whose face was memorably disfigured by a huge tumour in the middle of his forehead, was even more gross than his brother. He was married to the beautiful Antoinette of Saxe-Coburg, whose nephew Albert would become the consort of another British princess. In the early morning after her wedding night Antoinette was awakened by strange grunting noises to find her new husband under the bedclothes gnawing on a huge leg of ham.

Romania's queen consort Elizabeth of Wied nearly became queen of England, as Queen Victoria had once earmarked her as the ideal wife for her son, the Prince of Wales. Bertie however had already set his sights on Alexandra of Denmark and his preference for the attractive young Danish princess prevailed. If Queen Victoria had done her homework she would have found plenty of evidence of mental instability in Elizabeth of Wied's family. However, so as not to waste a good "find", Elizabeth found herself at the top of the shortlist of suitable brides for Bertie's younger brother Alfred, the Duke of Edinburgh. The young Duke was packed off to Germany to meet his intended. The meeting ended prematurely with Alfred beating an embarrassed and rapid retreat back to England. The couple had barely been introduced to each other when the Princess Elizabeth, upon learning that Alfred played the violin, insisted that he perform for her and her mother right there and then, in the woods outside the castle. As soon as the impromptu woodland concert was over the reluctant violinist fled.

Elizabeth was eventually married to King Carol I of Romania and decided to dedicate her life to the arts. Unfortunately the arts weren't quite ready for Queen Elizabeth. With a boundless enthusiasm the Queen applied her inconsiderable talents to poetry. Composing under the pen name of Carmen Sylva, she established herself a reputation as a Romanian William McGonagall. Anyone unfortunate enough to pass by her rooms was likely to be dragged in and treated to a preview of her latest poem. Over the years Elizabeth somehow acquired a cult lesbian following and surrounded herself with a posse of young females posing as art lovers. While the Queen lay around the palace with her long white hair and long flowing robes reciting poetry, working on immense paintings, playing the piano, or eating her favourite ham sandwiches, her entourage would lie at her feet looking suitably impressed. Elizabeth visited Queen Victoria at Balmoral and the assembled British royal family sat through one of Elizabeth's infamous recitals – a Greek play, written by Elizabeth herself, in German. Queen Victoria's diary entry noted, "Many of course could not understand, but all were interested."

Elizabeth never missed an opportunity to inflict her art on her people, or to get herself noticed. When she wasn't reciting poetry to her adoring female disciples she would stand at all hours of the day and night on the terrace of her house overlooking the entrance to Constanze harbour, calling out poetic blessings to departing ships on a megaphone. She would often fling open a window of the palace and pose semi-naked, dressed only in her flimsy nightgown, while a crowd gathered below. When her nephew the Crown Prince Ferdinand was struck down with typhoid fever in May 1897, she passed news of his condition to the larger than usual gathering below her window by miming medical bulletins to them as though it was a game of charades. Her habit of hanging around on her balcony in her nightie finally caught up with her in 1916 when she caught pneumonia and died.

When Peter the Great's son Alexis went to Dresden in 1712 to marry a German princess, the Elector of Hanover Ernst August noted with distaste in a letter to his wife that the Czarevitch shat in his bedroom and wiped his backside with the curtains.

Queen Victoria's favourite Uncle Leopold, King of the Belgians, is often referred to by historians as "the midwife of the British monarchy", not because he ran around in a pinafore shouting "push" but because it was he who engineered the meeting between the young Queen and his nephew Prince Albert. Leopold was a little man who wore a feather boa and three-inch heels – his androgynous appearance, however, belying the fact that he was a compulsive womanizer. He was also reputed to be one of the most boring men in Europe. He trapped people in his home and delivered endless sermons, mostly on current affairs. Although an infamous penny-pincher (according to one mistress Karoline Bauer the king went to bed with two little clamps between his back teeth to prevent wear on the enamel while he slept) he always made generous provision for his bastards: illegitimate daughters were taken care of by arranged marriages, and sons received diplomatic postings or army commissions.

In his youth Leopold was regarded as both handsome and virile, but he became prematurely aged. His physical decline accelerated at an alarming rate and he took on a disconcertingly cadaverous appearance, but he refused to grow old gracefully. He painted his sunken cheeks with rouge, pencilled in his eyebrows and hid his bald head under a jet black wig. He spent his last couple of years in agony with a bladder stone. The pain was so severe that he had to sleep upright wedged between two horsehair mattresses, yet to the bitter end he continued to surround himself with his small harem of mistresses.

Kaiser Wilhelm II had a withered arm and a chip on his shoulder, the result of a bungled breech-birth. He spent a lifetime trying to compensate for his physical disability and his

feelings of personal inadequacy. He endured horrific orthopae-
dic cures during his boyhood, including electric shock treatment. At the age of four he was strapped into a contraption
made from leather belts and steel bolts in an attempt to realign
his spine. His childhood experiences left a permanent mark on
his personality. In later years he let it be known that he always
slept with a cocked, loaded pistol in a bedside drawer, just to
show how tough he was. He always made a point of sitting on a
hard chair even if there was a soft one available. He deliberately
wore the stones on his many diamond and sapphire rings facing
inwards so that they hurt people when they shook his hand.
When he handed out photographs of himself to his friends, he
always took care not to show the stunted little arm which
barely reached his left jacket pocket. He wore so many medals
that his chest was described as "a declaration of war".

King Christian VII of Denmark was one day visited by an
ambassador from Naples, who made a profound bow to his
host. Christian responded by bowing even lower. The ambassador was obliged to bow again, this time his head almost
touching the ground; as he did so, King Christian quickly
placed his hands on the ambassador's shoulders and leap-
frogged him.

The Swedish King Eric XI was obsessed with the idea of
claiming the hand in marriage of England's "Virgin Queen"
Elizabeth I. He bombarded her with love letters in Latin and
dispatched his half-brother John to her court to press his suit.
According to a courtier, John "scattered silver like a shower of

falling stars in the London streets, and told the crowds that whereas he scattered silver, his brother would scatter gold". Elizabeth kept the Swede at arm's length for years but no amount of refusals could deter lovelorn Eric from his wooing. He heard some gossip about the Queen's relationship with her favourite, Robert Dudley, and challenged him to a duel. Fortunately, the Swedish ambassador in London managed to convince Eric that Dudley, as a mere courtier, was an unworthy rival. In 1560 Eric tried to visit Elizabeth personally to seduce her. Unfortunately it was a bad day for sailing and his fleet was scattered. Eric's attempts to marry Mary Queen of Scots were similarly fruitless, after which he lowered his sights and married a Swedish commoner and had her crowned Queen Karin in 1568.

Even more than most monarchs, King Edward VII was hypersensitive about matters of precedence. He once became visibly upset when someone suggested to him that an English duke should take precedence over an Indian prince and he threw the crowned heads of Europe into a royal panic at Queen Victoria's funeral when he correctly insisted that King Kalukua of the Cannibal Islands (now Hawaii) took precedence over his brother-in-law, the Crown Prince of Germany. When the Germans complained, Edward snapped back, "Either the brute is a king, or else he is an ordinary black nigger. And if he is not a king, why is he here?"

When the Orient Express carried Czar Ferdinand of Bulgaria and the Archduke Franz Ferdinand of Austria to London for King Edward's funeral, they had a blazing row over who should have a carriage nearer to the front. The Austrian Archduke appeared to have won by having his private carriage placed immediately behind the engine. Czar Ferdinand retaliated by refusing to allow the Archduke to pass through his carriage to get to the dining car. The Archduke waited until the train reached a station, then ran down the platform to the dining carriage. When he finished eating he waited until the train stopped at the next station then ran back.

The senior member of the house of Savoy, King Victor Emmanuel I, spent most of the Napoleonic wars in hiding. When the wars were over, after a seventeen-year absence, he was restored to his throne. Upon his return King Victor Emmanuel cheerfully promised his subjects that he would carry on exactly where he had left off. This was a man to be taken at his word. The king, as though emerging from a lengthy coma, went about his business exactly as though it was still 1798, the year of his flight into exile. The clock was turned back in the whole administration. Jobs were given back to people who had retired years ago and men who were now in their forties were made to resume their positions as page boys. In 1821 a military uprising forced the king to abdicate in favour of his manic-depressive brother Charles Felix. The new king shut himself away for ten years waiting for his death, brightening up only briefly to advise his successor Charles Albert, "Hate Austria."

The most underemployed person in the history of the French court was the beautiful, pipe-smoking Madame de Grancey, official court mistress of Philippe Duke of Orleans. As younger brother of King Louis XIV, the Duke was the second most important man in the most powerful country in Europe. He was also quite openly homosexual, but obliged by rigid Versailles etiquette to keep a mistress. The Duke of Orleans was a bloated little man with a mouthful of rotten teeth and a penchant for women's perfume. He married twice and conceived eleven legitimate children, seven of whom were stillborn or died in infancy, but never made any secret of the fact that he considered the business of begetting his brood a revolting chore which he'd rather forgo. Apart from the no-fuss but necessary business of procreation he couldn't bear to be touched in bed by either of his two wives, both of whom were relegated to edge of the mattress. Philippe was an effeminate but extremely brave soldier, confusing the enemy by turning up at the battle painted, powdered and covered in ribbons and diamonds. He refused to wear protective headgear in case it ruined the lie of his wig and was more concerned about the effect of the dust of the battle and the sun on his complexion than he was about enemy fire. King Louis XIV turned a blind eye to most of his brother's more outrageous activities, including his predilection for turning up at court functions wearing expensive ball gowns.

In 1670 Philippe was married to the Bavarian Princess Elizabeth Charlotte, known to her contemporaries as "Liselotte". Little of her past was known to the French court, other than that she had once shot her governess in the backside with an arquebus. Liselotte was eighteen inches taller than her new husband, very fat, red-faced and partial to beer and sausages: it was recorded that she had the figure of a Swiss Guard. When the tiny Philippe first saw his Teutonic blonde bride-to-be he whispered to a friend, "How on earth am I to sleep with that?" Although the only interest that Philippe shared with his wife was a taste in jewellery, the odd couple somehow managed to produce three children. Philippe's friends were amazed. He confided to them that he too had doubted his ability to cope. It had only been made possible, he revealed, by rubbing his penis with a holy medal for luck.

Although Catherine the Great was one of history's biggest nymphomaniacs, her husband spent his entire honeymoon and most of the rest of his married life playing with his toy soldiers under the bedsheets.

When George VI became king by default after the abdication of his brother Edward VIII it was rumoured that he had a complete nervous breakdown, and it was so widely doubted that he would even turn up for his own coronation that London bookmakers took odds against it. At times he appeared to be completely out of touch with reality. In 1939 he astonished his Prime Minister by twice offering to write to Hitler "as one ex-serviceman to another" in an attempt to avert war, and on 20 April of that year he sent congratulations to the Führer on the occasion of his fiftieth birthday. In September 1940 Buckingham Palace was bombed. Although large chunks of London had already been blitzed by German bombers, the king took this bomb very personally. He claimed it had been deliberately dropped on his house by a distant Spanish cousin, the fifth Duke of Galliera. This duke, claimed the king, was involved in a German plot to restore his brother to the throne. Only a close relative of the family, he explained, could have known exactly where to aim. It had not occurred to him that German intelligence may have been clever enough to acquire a map of central London.

George VI was a compulsive shot, a hobby he indulged at

Balmoral and Sandringham almost every day of the week. When Britain declared war on Germany one of the king's chief concerns was that the international crisis might interfere with the Balmoral grouse season. In 1924 the future Queen Mother went on a four-month big game shooting holiday in Africa. With her 0.275 Rigby rifle she killed a rhinoceros, a buffalo, a waterbuck, an oryx, a Gant's gazelle, an antelope, a Kenyan hartebeest, a steinbuck, a water-hog and a jackal. In Uganda her husband shot an elephant whose tusks weighed 90 lbs each. "It was very lucky," he noted afterwards, "as there are not any very big ones left."

George VI inherited his father's ignorance of art. He once saw the paintings of John Piper, who was known mainly for his storm scenes, and stammered, "Pity you had such bloody awful weather."

Queen Henrietta, wife of the Belgian King Leopold II, kept a pet llama which she taught to spit in the face of anyone who stroked it.

Ferdinand VI, king of Spain, was severely paranoid and lived in constant dread of assassination, and like his father Philip V he was also addicted to sex. His wife Queen Barbara meanwhile lived in constant fear of being left a penniless widow. Her confidence that she would outlive her husband was however misplaced. In 1757 she took to her bed in terrible pain and became covered in boils, and after a horrible and lingering eleven-month illness she died. It was discovered that her private apartment was literally crammed to the ceiling with

Spanish currency which she had stashed away to see her through a comfortable widowhood.

Queen Victoria was highly sensitive about her grandfather "mad" King George III and both she and Prince Albert lived in perpetual dread that hereditary insanity would strike their own children. When they had their eldest son's bumps felt by a leading "expert" in phrenology it appeared to confirm their worst fears. Sir George Combe examined the prince's cranium and gravely pronounced that the poor boy had inherited the shape of his brain from George III "and all that this implied". King Edward VII was not however insane, although what modern psychoanalysis would have made of his lifelong hobby of recording the weight of everyone who visited Sandringham is another question.

The Medicis of Tuscany were a dysfunctional family even by royal standards. Grand Duke Cosimo III de Medici was a severely melancholic man who, it was said, never laughed in his life. His wife on the other hand, Marguérite Louise of Orléans, was beautiful, fun-loving and known for her great wit. The Grand Duke was also not overly fond of any sort of physical contact, and feared that sexual activity would undermine his health. The Electress Sophia of Hanover noted: "He sleeps with his wife but once a week, and then under supervision of a doctor." Eventually the Duchess could no longer bear to be touched by her prematurely grave husband and was temporarily exiled from court for refusing to join in the weekly romp. She did however become pregnant three times despite several deliberate attempts to induce miscarriages. When she became pregnant with her third child, Gian Gastone, the Duchess tried to starve herself to death. Four years after the child's birth she went abroad, never to return.

Like father, like son, Gian Gastone was a very serious lad and allergic to women. Grand Duke Cosimo arranged for his son to marry Anna Maria of Saxe-Lauenburg, an ugly but extremely wealthy widow whose sole interests were hunting and horses. Gian Gastone reacted to married life badly. He hated his new home in Bohemia, was sickened by the smell of horses, and terrified by the possibility of intercourse with his physically repulsive wife, who in turn considered her husband an effeminate weakling, but nevertheless tried to lose some weight to improve her chances of conception. Gian Gastone fell into a deep depression, sustained by his alcoholism and temporarily alleviated by homosexual affairs with footmen, although from time to time, upon the insistence of his father, he returned to his wife to beget a Medici heir.

In 1713 his elder brother, Ferdinand, died insane as a result of syphilis and when their father died ten years later Gian Gastone succeeded him as Grand Duke of Tuscany, a prematurely aged, drunken sodomite. Giuliano Dami acted as pimp for the Grand Duke's orgies, seeking out young men and boys known as the "ruspanti" because they were paid a fee from one to five ruspi for their services. During this period Gian Gastone entertained around 370 ruspanti. The Grand Duke would invite the chosen youth to his bedchamber, examine his teeth, ply him with drink and feel his private parts to see if they were well shaped. In 1730 he sprained his ankle and took to his bed more or less permanently for the last seven years of his life.

The general behaviour of King George IV was so strange that many people who were personally acquainted with him, including a few doctors and several close friends, believed that he, like his late father, was mad. The Duke of Wellington was convinced that George IV was mentally deranged and made comments to that effect several times. When George complained of gout in his foot, his younger brother the Duke of Cumberland sarcastically observed that the seat of his illness was higher than the foot and that "a blister on the head might be more efficacious than a poultice on the ankle". After the birth of his daughter Charlotte, George had a nervous breakdown and made a will leaving everything he had to "Maria Fitzherbert who is my wife in the eyes of God and who is and ever will be such in mine". As soon as he recovered he had the will put aside and forgot all about it.

He would fake a terminal illness over the most trivial ailment and intermittently threatened suicide. When he was given news of the victory at Waterloo in 1815 he became hysterical and had to be tranquillized with a large quantity of brandy. Although he had never set foot abroad throughout the war with Napoleon and spent most of it cowering in his Brighton Pavilion, years later he would embarrass his ministers by claiming he had fought at Waterloo. He would also describe how he had helped to win the Battle of Salamanca by leading a charge of dragoons disguised as General Bock. Another favourite anecdote was how he had ridden the horse Fleur-de-Lis in the Goodwood Cup. George's acquaintances couldn't help noticing at that time that he was so obese that he was incapable of mounting a horse at all without being lifted into the saddle by a complicated mechanism involving cranks, winches, platforms and rollers.

Emperor Wilhelm I and his wife the Empress Augusta were Germany's oddest royal couple. The Empress, sometimes known as the "Dragon of the Rhine", was highly strung and said to be the most argumentative woman in Europe. She became more unpredictable as she grew older, occasionally making passes at her ladies-in-waiting and often disappearing for months on end. The Emperor and Empress shared a lifelong mutual loathing and it was said that barely a single day of their marriage, which lasted nearly sixty years, passed without a terrible row. On their days off they simply refused to speak to each other and conducted their arguments via a third party. If Augusta addressed the Emperor, even though he was directly in front of her, he would ignore her and ask some nearby aide to repeat what she'd said. Wilhelm did not even bother to tell his wife when he became Emperor and she received the news from one of her footmen.

In 1885 the Empress Augusta lost the use of her legs and was confined to a wheelchair. Once envied for her perfect cheekbones and porcelain skin, she was reluctant to acknowledge that the passage of time had long since relieved her of her best assets. In old age she took to wearing vast quantities of cosmetics and acquired a huge personal wig collection. The aged Augusta lived on, immobilized by infirmity and the weight of her make-up, occasionally giving out signs that she was still alive by trembling with the palsy. In 1887 the invalid Empress was wheeled out to break the ice at her husband's ninetieth birthday, looking "like someone dug up from the dead . . . something of a skeleton and something of a witch". The only visible parts of her body, her hands, head and shoulders, were thickly encrusted in white enamel.

Soon afterwards the Empress became seriously ill, and Wilhelm was visibly upset. A puzzled visitor asked one of the Emperor's aides why this should be so: after all, the constant enmity between the two was common knowledge. "Wait till you have been married for fifty years and have quarrelled with your wife every day," explained the aide, "and then, when you are faced with the prospect of this habit's coming to an end, you will be unhappy too." The Empress finally expired from influenza in 1890 aged seventy-eight, outliving her husband by nine months.

King Charles III of Spain, worried about the family history of madness, gave express instructions to the royal tutors that none of his children should be taught anything in case it put too great a strain on their minds and tipped them over the edge. This regime guaranteed that his two eldest sons grew up to be ill-educated delinquents who between them ruled most of southern Europe, the elder as king of Spain, the younger as king of Naples and the Two Sicilies. The latter son, Ferdinand, was very tall with a jutting jawline, and was known as "Nasone" because of his huge nose. This feature was unfortunately exaggerated by his unusually small head. His entire body was also covered in herpes, a sign, his doctors assured him, of the most excellent health. On the morning after his wedding night, when Ferdinand was asked how he liked his bride, he replied, "She sleeps like the dead and sweats like a pig."

King Ferdinand spent his days leap-frogging, fondling the ladies of the court, and shrieking obscenities at the top of his unusually high-pitched voice. When the Emperor Joseph II of Austria attended a court ball at the Palazzo Reale in 1769 he wrote a letter home describing an incident he encountered in the palace. The king and queen, accompanied by two chamberlains, were making a dignified approach to an ante-chamber where they were awaited by several officials, when Ferdinand suddenly began to gallop around the room, kicking out at his courtiers. When the king wanted to play the whole court was expected to join in. Soon the entire throng, including elderly men and quite senior ministers, were galloping through the corridors of the Neapolitan court. The French ambassador, who unhappily found himself in Ferdinand's path, received a punch in the face and his nose collided with a wall. Ferdinand also insisted on having a crowd around to keep him amused while he laboured on the toilet. The Emperor Joseph related, "We made conversation for more than an hour, and I believe we would still be there had a terrible stench not convinced us that all was over." Joseph however declined an offer to view the fruits of Ferdinand's labours.

The French King Louis XVIII at the age of fifteen was married to Maria Giuseppina of Savoy, daughter of the king of Sardinia. She was very short and ugly, and so smelly that the bridegroom's grandfather King Louis XV had to beg her parents to persuade her to wash her neck and clean her teeth. Her favourite hobby was catching thrushes in nets, and having them made into soup. However, as Louis XVIII was homosexual, impotent and preoccupied with the consumption of food to the exclusion of almost everything else, their bedrooms occupied separate floors.

Frederick the Great's marriage to Elizabeth Christine of Brünswick-Beyern was one of the oddest royal relationships. No one, not even his wife or his personal valet, was ever allowed to see him naked. His marriage to Elizabeth was never consummated and they went their separate ways immediately after the wedding ceremony. One morning Frederick dashed off a note to his wife. It read: "Madam, a rush of business has prevented me from writing until now: this letter is to take my leave of you, wishing you health and contentment during the troubled times ahead." She didn't see her husband again for another seven years. When she eventually greeted him at the palace gates on his return his first words to her were "Madam has grown fatter".

Frederick the Great's sister Wilhelmina left a diary of daily life in the Prussian court, including details of a visit by her three times married great aunt, the Duchess of Saxe-Meiningen, a huge woman over sixty years old who continually patted her large, flat and shrivelled breasts with her hands to attract attention to them. According to Wilhelmina's memoirs Frederick was afflicted with such a dire dose of venereal disease that his doctors had to perform corrective surgery on him. This operation, performed entirely without anaesthetic, was so badly botched that he was rendered permanently incapable of having normal sexual relations. This story was confirmed by the Swiss doctor who examined the Prussian king's body after he died. It would also explain why he spent the rest of his life avoiding women. It was rumoured in his later years that he was romantically attached to his pack of Italian whippet bitches.

In time Frederick became more eccentric and miserly. He drank up to forty cups of coffee a day for several weeks in an experiment to see if it was possible to exist without sleep. It took his stomach three years to recover. His palace became a slum as his pampered greyhounds soiled everything and tore his furnishings to ribbons. The most heroic figure in German history died filthy and neglected, dressed in rags, the shirt on his back so rotten that his valet had to dress him in one of his own for the burial.

The fifteenth-century German Emperor Wenceslas, a violent and unstable drunk, had his cook roasted on a spit when his normally exemplary meals fell below standard. On another occasion Wenceslas was out hunting when he came across a passing monk and shot him dead: the Emperor simply commented that in his opinion monks had better things to do than wander about in woods.

King Eric XIV of Sweden was highly paranoid, convinced that all of Sweden's noblemen were plotting against him. He took to stalking the palace with his sword drawn, ready to use it against anyone he could pick an argument with. He saw subversion everywhere – even a sudden movement or a cough could result in bloody death. He even suspected servants who were smartly turned out of intending to seduce the court ladies, and had them put to death. Hundreds of Swedish noblemen were sentenced to death on trumped-up charges of treason – he even stabbed to death his former tutor for allegedly talking about him behind his back. With Sweden's prisons packed with noblemen awaiting execution and the country degenerating into chaos, Eric was finally proved right when his two younger brothers John and Karl joined forces to have him arrested and subsequently assassinated by poisoning.

King Henry Christophe of Haiti, who once insisted upon drawing attention to his country's chief export by having himself anointed with chocolate syrup, ordered his entire personal bodyguard to prove their loyalty to him by marching over the edge of a 200-foot cliff to certain death. Those who disobeyed were tortured and executed. King Henry decided to tighten security by having himself a new castle built at the top of a high mountain, fortified by twenty cannon. One by one the men required to drag the huge guns up the side of the mountain dropped with exhaustion, and so the king had them executed on the spot: in total the exercise cost the lives of about 20,000 men. When the king's subjects finally rebelled against him in 1820 he cheated a lynch mob by shooting his own brains out.

Czar Paul I passed a law which forbade his subjects to wear round hats, top boots, straight pants or shoes with laces – modern dress which had become associated in the Czar's mind with the French revolution and progressive political ideology. To enforce this regulation a couple of hundred armed troops were sent on to the streets of St Petersburg with orders to randomly attack anyone who didn't conform to the Czar's dress restriction. People were stripped of clothing where they stood in the streets: shoes, hats, breeches and waistcoats were ripped to shreds or confiscated.

Queen Elizabeth II's great-grandmother Princess Mary Adelaide of Teck was born in 1833, the daughter of George III's seventh son Adolphus Duke of Cambridge, and was known to everyone in the royal family as Fat Mary, as she was extremely short and weighed about eighteen stone. Her favourite hobbies were eating and dancing, the two often combining with often dangerous results, as she cavorted on a crowded dance floor squashing any unfortunate prince who got in her way. Fortunately Mary was quite oblivious of the stares and comments about her weight that followed her everywhere she went. When she and Queen Victoria met in 1866, Mary required two chairs. "Mary is looking older," Victoria noted in her diary, "but not thinner."

Although even the homeliest of royal princesses could usually find themselves a husband if they tried hard enough, Fat Mary's matrimonial prospects were hampered by the attitude of her absurdly hard to please parents, who went about rejecting possible suitors as though their daughter was a great beauty. The British Foreign Minister Lord Clarendon wondered whether any foreign prince in his right mind would be up to "so vast an undertaking". By the time Fat Mary had reached her early thirties and almost resigned herself to spinsterhood a husband was miraculously found in Franz, a prince of Teck. Franz's prospects in the royal marriage stakes were blighted on two counts. First, he was tainted by morganatic blood, and second, Franz's family was also relatively poor. These problems however combined to make him perfect marriage-fodder as far as Mary was concerned, whose parents' search for a son-in-law had by now taken on an air of grim desperation. When a union was suggested to Franz he eagerly agreed, much to the astonishment of everyone, especially those who knew about his taste for slim blondes. It was, he thought, an end to his financial problems. He didn't find out until it was too late that Fat Mary was also broke.

Franz had plenty of time for bitter reflection on his marriage. After several years of living in his wife's shadow his behaviour became increasingly erratic and his blood pressure soared higher. One morning in 1884 he woke up completely paralyzed down one side of his body and unable to speak. His wife diagnosed slight sunstroke and skipped off to a light five-course breakfast. Only after a great deal of persuasion by her doctors did she come round to accepting that her husband had suffered a stroke. From that day on Franz's mental health deteriorated, and although his wife's cholesterol count ensured that he actually outlived her, he spent the rest of his days in a straitjacket.

Many Victorian couples abstained from marital relations on Sundays because sex on the Sabbath was considered improper. Although Queen Victoria valued a healthy sex life, her consort Prince Albert was not a keen collaborator on any day of the week. He always went to bed wearing a little all-in-one woollen sleeping suit, and once said of heterosexual intercourse, "That particular species of vice disgusts me." Ironically, Albert gave his name to a form of body piercing, fashionable among Victorian gentlemen, whereby an erection could be restrained by a device made of little hoops.

King Louis XIV's son and heir Louis, the Grand Dauphin, inherited eccentricity from both sides of the family, Bourbon and Habsburg. His grandfather king Philip IV of Spain, for example, developed a taste for human breast milk well into old age. The Grand Dauphin was particularly known for his unusual taste in women. In the royal tradition a bride was selected for him by his father, in this case a Bavarian princess, Marie Anne Victoire. Although Marie Anne was a good royal match, having all the right blood-lines, the king of France, recalling perhaps the shock of his own engagement to a dwarf, attempted to spare his son any similarly nasty surprises. He sent his ambassador Croissy to Germany to get a sneak preview of the prospective daughter-in-law. Croissy filed his report; the princess didn't have any obvious enormous physical deformities, he noted, apart from brown stains on her forehead, sallow skin, red hands, rotten teeth and a very large, fat nose.

The king decided he needed a second opinion and dispatched a portrait artist to Munich with instructions that he was to paint a truthful, warts-and-all likeness of Marie Anne. When the portrait reached Versailles the French royal family gathered to pass judgment on it. After some debate Marie Anne was given the thumbs up. The painting however was also accompanied by a note from Croissy which stated that in his opinion the likeness was outrageously flattering. Croissy drew attention in particular to the artist's creative interpretation of the Bavarian princess's nose. Although negotiations were now at an advanced stage, the king of France was prepared to abort the engagement there and then. His son however would hear none of it; he considered ugly women erotic, the uglier the better. The more he heard about Princess Marie Anne, the more excited he became. When Marie Anne was summoned to Versailles it became obvious that Croissy had not exaggerated, especially about her nose. The Grand Dauphin however was more than satisfied with his bride. King Louis let it be known that his new daughter-in-law was to be admired and her nose was never mentioned again. Marie Anne and the Grand Dauphin were married and had three children.

When Marie Anne died, barely thirty years old, he took up with her ugliest lady-in-waiting Mademoiselle de Choin, a huge woman well known for her large mouth, her pendulous breasts, but especially for her huge nose.

The Austrian Empress Maria Theresa was an extraordinary woman of great vision and energy. She also had some uncompromising views about marital infidelity and established a commission to track down and punish adulterers and prostitutes. The Empress took the duties of royalty, especially the business of breeding, very seriously. She was working on her State boxes when she went into labour with Marie Antoinette, the fifteenth of her sixteen children. According to legend, the Empress took the opportunity to call for her dentist and had a bad tooth pulled because she wouldn't notice the extra pain. She gave birth, then continued her paperwork.

The transvestite King Henri III was the most bizarre of a very long line of very odd French sovereigns. The "King of Sodom", who ruled France from 1574 to 1589, appeared at official ceremonies in full drag and was regularly followed by an entourage of rent boys, known as his "mignons". The king had long, flowing locks but lost it all when he was quite young because he kept dying his hair with untreated chemicals. Later he went around wearing a velvet cap which had bunches of hair sewn inside the rim.

Chapter Twelve

Eccentric Builders

"If a man does not keep pace with his companions, perhaps it is because he hears a different drummer. Let him step to the music which he hears, however measured or far away"

Henry David Thoreau (1817–62)

"Every time Willie feels bad he goes out and buys something"

Phoebe Apperson Hearst, mother of William Randolph Hearst (1863–1951), justifying her son's Californian estate San Simeon

The wealthy eccentric Edward James (1907–84) was believed by many to be the illegitimate son of King Edward VIII, which would have made him great-uncle to Queen Elizabeth II. James was a tall, thin man who in later life sported a long white beard and always walked with two walking sticks, partly to compensate for the fact that he never cut his toenails. He spent much of his life composing outstandingly poor poetry and helping to bankroll the Surrealist art movement by handing out huge sums of money to the likes of René Magritte and Salvador Dali. In 1945 James purchased several thousand acres of Mexican jungle at Xilitla, and spent his afternoons strolling around naked or smoking marijuana or ingesting psychedelic mushrooms. Taking controlled substances as his main architectural influences, he built a fantastic palace in the middle of the jungle – simply, he explained, so that "when archaeologists come and see this in two or three thousand years' time they won't know what to make of it".

James kept many exotic pets, including a much prized brace of boa constrictors. One evening he was staying at the Majestic Hotel in Mexico City with his snakes, when a live mouse escaped from his suite. A lady guest encountered the mouse and screamed that the hotel was infested with rodents. A maid reassured her, "No, señora, they are not the hotel's mice. They are food for the gentleman's snakes in the room next door."

The world-famous Eddystone lighthouse, standing proud about Fourteen miles south of Plymouth Hoe on the notorious Eddystone reef, was the lifework of the remarkable Henry Winstanley. The Eddystone had always been a dangerous rock for shipping entering the Channel and for centuries there had been suggestions for lighting it in some way. Winstanley built the first wooden lighthouse on the rocks in 1698. Remarkably he was neither a builder nor a seaman, but an artist and engraver who made a lot of his money designing playing cards. He didn't even live near the sea, as he was born at Saffron Walden in Essex and lived at Littlebury in the same county. He was chiefly interested in mechanics and had a workshop at Littlebury where he invented many strange devices. His home was a local curiosity. It was filled with tricks and unusual effects to amuse the many visitors who paid a shilling each to pass through the turnstile that Winstanley had placed at the front gate. He was a practical joker; as visitors went into the main passage of the house and trod upon a certain board of the floor, a door at the end of the passage flew open and out sprang a skeleton. If they entered his summer-house and sat down in front of the duckpond, the seat would suddenly swing round and they found themselves sitting over the centre of the pond. As a draughtsman he made a lot of money producing engravings of the stately homes of England, and a pack of ornate playing cards of his design achieved considerable popularity and nationwide distribution. The most famous of his odd creations other than the Eddystone light-house was a spectacular and novel entertainment centre near Hyde Park which was called "Winstanley's Waterworkes". For more than thirty years people from all over England paid anything up to half a crown to view a dazzling display of fountains and other aquatic effects.

The wealth he acquired over the years of success as a showman was invested in many areas, one of which was the purchase of five ships. When Winstanley lost a couple of them on the Eddystone reef, he decided to do something about it. He began work on the first Eddystone lighthouse on 14 July 1696. That first summer was spent in making twelve holes in the rock and fastening twelve great irons. Fearful of being attacked by French pirates, he asked for the protection of the Royal Navy, and on the days when work was being carried out on the rock a frigate was detailed to act as guardship. One foggy night in 1697 as Winstanley and his men slept on the rock, the guardship missed her position and anchored off Fowey. While she was away a small French sloop sent a boat with thirty armed men, who landed on the Eddystone rock, overpowered Winstanley and his men, and forced them into the boat. The Frenchmen stripped the men naked and turned them adrift; Winstanley was taken to France in chains. His fate would have certainly been sealed if it were not for a chance remark by one of the King's courtiers. When Louis XIV heard about the circumstances of Winstanley's capture he ordered his immediate release. The Englishman's surprise turned to astonishment when he found himself ushered into the presence of the Sun King. Louis apologized for the trouble he had caused and said that he hoped the incident had not unduly delayed work on the lighthouse, for, although he might be at war with England, he was not at war with humanity. Winstanley took the opportunity to explain the principles of his lighthouse design to the king and after an audience of about an hour he departed for England in style and laden with gifts. According to another version, Winstanley was simply used as a bargaining chip for the return of a number of French prisoners of war.

Winstanley's first lighthouse was a strange structure completely unlike the designs we are familiar with today and included several bizarre features and embellishments. It was decorated with vanes and wooden candlesticks and the outside was painted with unusual designs. The building was intended not merely as a lighthouse to warn mariners, but also as a fortress to resist siege. On the top was a moveable platform or chute which could be turned round in any direction, from which stones could be showered upon an enemy attacking the building.

After only a year of exposure to sea and storm, Winstanley realized that his lighthouse not strong enough and extensively modified it. The new structure was even more idiosyncratic than the previous one but Winstanley was delighted with his creation. Some people doubted the new lighthouse would survive a storm but Winstanley laughed at his critics. "I only wish," he said, "that I may be in the lighthouse in circumstances that will test its strength to the utmost." It was not long before his wish was granted. With a remarkable sense of timing, on 26 November 1703 he set off in bad weather from Plymouth for the Eddystone rock, having decided to stay there for the night. It was the night of the greatest storm in recorded history. When daylight dawned on the morning of 27 November and people looked out towards the rock, there were no signs of a lighthouse. The Eddystone lighthouse had been totally destroyed and Winstanley killed as he slept in it. Yet, although the storm inflicted enormous damage and loss of life upon southern England generally and especially upon Essex, the lighthouse designer's home was strangely undisturbed.

In 1996 the city fathers in Vilnius, Lithuania, erected a monument to Frank Zappa. They explained that although the town had no obvious connection to the American rock star, they were confident he would have visited Vilnius had he not died two years earlier.

The legendary American spendthrift William Randolph Hearst, whose life inspired the film *Citizen Kane*, enjoyed an incomparably extravagant lifestyle as heir to a mining fortune and founder of a US publishing empire. During little "Billie Buster's" youth, his father prospected throughout the West, from Mexico to Alaska, becoming a partner in three of the largest mining discoveries in American history.

In 1880, George Hearst accepted a small daily newspaper, the *San Francisco Examiner*, as payment for a gambling debt. The elder Hearst, by now a US senator from California, had little interest in the newspaper business but young Will, a Harvard student at the time, wrote his father a now-famous letter requesting that he be permitted to take over the *Examiner*: "I am convinced that I could run a newspaper successfully. Now, if you should make over to me the *Examiner* – with enough money to carry out my schemes – I'll tell you what I would do!" In time Hearst's twenty-odd newspaper titles alone were to earn him about $12 million a year, apart from the millions earned from his various magazines, film companies and radio stations. His ability to spend however more than kept pace with his income. The auto magnate Henry Ford, staggered by Hearst's expenditure on paintings, asked, "Have you any money?" Hearst replied, "I never have any money, Mr Ford. I always spend any money that I am about to receive before I get it."

Of all his purchases, which included several castles around the world, none could rival his fantastic Californian estate San Simeon, also known as "Hearst Castle" and fictionalized by Orson Welles as Xanadu. Built about 200 miles south of San Franciso, San Simeon was a monument to extravagance. The fabulous estate had fifty miles of ocean frontage and 250,000 acres of grounds. He had his interior designers scour the world for rare paintings, suits of armour, statues, tapestries and other art treasures – about 20,000 items. He purchased entire European villas, palaces and monasteries and had them dismantled and shipped to California to furnish his bizarre seaside estate.

His $400,000 indoor saltwater swimming pool took three and a half years to complete. The grounds were stocked with wild animals and an army of gardeners worked around the clock to create a vast floral extravaganza. Once his gardeners worked through the night so that Hearst's guests could wake on Easter Sunday to see thousands of Easter lilies blooming. Many of the items remained in storage in vast New York warehouses, never to be seen in his lifetime.

Hearst was a racist, using his chain of newspapers to whip up racial tensions at every opportunity. He especially hated Mexicans. Hearst papers portrayed Mexicans as lazy, degenerate and violent, as marijuana smokers and job stealers. The real motive behind this prejudice may well have been that Hearst had lost 800,000 acres of prime timberland to the rebel Pancho Villa. Hearst was one of the chief architects of the infamous Marijuana Tax Act of 1937, the first law that effectively outlawed marijuana in the US. Desperate to protect his vast paper empire, which included millions of acres of timber, from the growing threat of hemp production, Hearst used his newspapers, magazines and film reels to mould public opinion against the lazy and crazed Mexican marijuana smoker.

Irishman Johnny Roche was the son of a carpenter and blacksmith from Walltown, near Mallow, County Cork, who had emigrated to America to make his fortune but returned empty-handed. Back in County Cork he tried running a mill and when that failed, he turned his hand to making tombstones. Roche could also draw teeth, mend clocks, produce sculpture, play the bagpipes and the violin, dance, whistle and sing. His best friend, a retired dragoon called Nixon, was so impressed by his talents that he asked Roche to design his tombstone. Roche subsequently erected a flagpole over the grave of his deceased friend, with the legend "Here lies Nixon".

Although he was very poor, Roche had a secret passion. He had always dreamed of owning a castle of his own, so he simply set about building one with nothing more than his bare hands, a spade, a shovel and an old cart. From 1867 to 1870 he slaved, gathering stones from the river by hand, digging furiously and drawing lime in his cart pulled by an ancient donkey. As "Castle Curious" rose people came from miles around to watch the building take shape. When it was finished it comprised an oval tower forty-five feet high and seventeen feet in length, topped by two oval turrets at right angles to the main building. At the base of the tower a slab of granite was engraved with the lettering "John Roche, 1870–". One of the turrets carried a flag with a dying angel and the walls were ornamented with gargoyles. When the strange castle with its labyrinth of tiny rooms was complete, Roche confounded the locals, all of whom were convinced that he was mad, by moving in and living there for the rest of his life. Roche discouraged visitors and was able to pull up a drawbridge whenever he felt inclined. Whenever his privacy was threatened he would lean out of a tower window and rain abuse at passers-by.

The American billionaire Lord Astor was highly paranoid and had a dread fear of assassination. Deep beneath his London home, the largest private residence on the Victoria Embankment, he constructed a vast steel-lined vault packed with bags of gold. The gold, he explained to guests, would help him slip away to France as soon as the English revolution came. Lord

Astor spent his last days at Hever Castle, former home of Anne Boleyn, locked inside his strong room. He died in 1919.

The fifth Duke of Portland, William Cavendish-Bentinck-Scott, was considered one of the English aristocracy's strangest ever products. According to legend, the Duke was spurned in love by the Covent Garden singer Adelaide Kemble and took rejection badly. He retired to his bedroom more or less permanently, his only means of communication via a letterbox in the bedroom door, through which was posted daily a whole roast fowl. When he did venture out his staff were instructed to ignore him "as they would a tree". He only ever travelled at night, and was always preceded by a woman holding a lantern, who had strict instructions to keep precisely fifty paces in front of him and never to turn round on pain of dismissal. He wore his trousers tied above the ankle by pieces of string, and buried himself under a vast coat and umbrella, and a two foot tall hat perched on top of his long brown wig. In time the Duke became a manic subterranean builder. He loathed meeting people and never invited anyone to his home, but beneath his country estate at Welbeck Abbey he built an astonishing ballroom, said to be the biggest room in Europe, without supporting pillars and lit by 1,000 gas jets; a 250-foot library; a vast glass-roofed conservatory and a snooker room big enough to take a dozen snooker tables.

The Duke was said to be one of the greatest judges of horses in England. Although he hardly ever rode, his stables housed around 100 horses and one of the buildings above ground formed a vast windowless riding school, believed to be the second largest in the world. There were about fifteen miles of tunnels running underneath his home, linking the subterannean rooms with the Abbey and with each other. One of the tunnels, a mile and a quarter long, led directly to the local railway station at Workshop, allowing him to travel unseen when he ventured out to catch a train to London. The tunnel was wide enough to take two carriages and was lit by hundreds of gas jets.

The door of every room at Welbeck Abbey was fitted with two letter boxes, one for ingoing notes and one for outgoing correspondence. His valet was the only servant allowed near him. When the Duke became ill, a doctor was required to stand outside his bedroom while the servant took his master's pulse and reported his condition. The Duke's passion for privacy led to wild rumours. Many people believed that he had become afflicted by a disfiguring skin disease, others were certain that he had gone raving mad. One of the few people who met the Duke in his lifetime however reported that the master of Welbeck Abbey was painfully shy, though "extremely handsome, kind and clever". When the Duke died in 1879, Welbeck Abbey had fallen into a terrible state of neglect. When his cousin arrived with his family to take up his inheritance, he found the grounds overgrown and strewn with rubble. When the front door was forced open, the new Duke of Portland was astonished to discover that the main hall had no floor.

Sarah Winchester, widow of the American gun manufacturer Oliver Winchester, was obsessed with the notion that the ghosts of people killed by her husband's famous rifles would return to haunt her. Accordingly she built a huge mansion, big enough to house an army of "friendly" spirits to defend her against the malicious variety. The building in San Jose, California was extended continuously over a period of thirty-eight years, because Mrs Winchester believed that she would be safe so long as she continued to build. At the time of her death in 1922 the mansion was eight storeys high and had 158 rooms.

Emperor Qin Shi Huangdi unified China under the Chin dynasty in the third century BC via a combination of prolific wall-building to keep out his external enemies and removing the tongues, hands, feet and genitalia of his enemies within. To ensure that no unfavourable comparisons were made between his and earlier regimes, he ordered the mass burning of all of China's history books and decapitated the region's top 160 academics. The Emperor's favourite punishment, however, was sawing his victims in half at the waist. Qin took his paranoia with him to his grave. His giant mausoleum was guarded by 8,000 lifesize terracotta soldiers to ward off the ghosts of the thousands of people he had wronged in his lifetime.

William Beckford (1760–1844) became heir to the biggest fortune in England when at the age of ten his father left him £1 million and an annual income of £100,000. His childhood and early teens were spent in extraordinary ease and opulence; he was given music lessons by Mozart, had completed the Grand Tour before his twentieth birthday and never travelled anywhere without his own bed. Wherever William Beckford stayed he even supplied his own wallpaper – his rooms had to be repapered with his choice of design before he would occupy them. On one occasion he took with him to Portugal a flock of sheep, not to keep him supplied with English lamb, but so that the view from his window could remind him of home. Beckford loved to amuse himself by ordering a vast formal dinner for a dozen guests, then when the table was fully laid and the footmen in position behind the chairs he would sit down alone, taste one dish, then retire to bed. Beckford's social life was ruined by scandal in 1784 when he was caught in the act of sodomizing a boy eight years his junior, the Hon. William Courtenay, son of the eighth Earl of Devon. As buggery was a capital crime in England, Beckford sat out the crisis in exile abroad. He eventually returned home but was ostracized by society and his reputation was never quite fully restored.

Beckford then discovered his true vocation as a builder. He withdrew to his vast estate near Hindon, Wiltshire, and began work on a serious of grandiose building projects. His first folly wasn't particularly ambitious – a romantic ruin and a mock abbey on the grounds of his estate – but soon he and his architect James Wyatt began work on Fonthill Abbey, a huge, fantastic Gothic creation. The crowning glory of this extravagant structure was a huge central tower. Unfortunately Beckford's impatience to have the tower completed, plus his system of plying his workers with alcohol to make them work faster, ensured that a few corners had been cut. In 1797 a gale brought the Abbey tower crashing to the ground, so he replaced it with a 276-foot version, making it one of the tallest buildings in England and considered one of the wonders of the age. By 1800 it was sufficiently complete for him to entertain Lord Nelson and Lady Hamilton in his new building.

Beckford seldom ventured outside the estate, which was surrounded by a wall seven miles long and twelve feet high and topped by spiked railings. He spent most his time surrounded by his pet dogs, a posse of homosexual servants, and Viscount

Fartlebury, an Italian dwarf who allegedly lived on a diet of mushrooms. In 1825 the new Fonthill Abbey tower also collapsed. According to legend Beckford, who had long since fallen on hard times and retired to Bath, watched it fall as he sat in his garden thirty miles away.

In the eighteenth century hermits became so fashionable that no English country seat was complete without a resident hermit living within the grounds. Charles Hamilton, whose estate was at Pains Hall near Cobham, Surrey, had a purpose-built retreat installed on a steep mound near his estate, then advertised in the press for a hermit. The advertisement stated that the hermit was required to live in the hermitage for a minimum of seven years and "should be provided with a Bible, optical glasses, a mat for his feet, a hassock for his pillow, an hourglass for his timepiece, water for his beverage and food from the house. He must wear a camlet robe, and never in any circumstances must he cut his hair, beard or nails, stray beyond the limits of Mr Hamilton's grounds, or exchange one word with the servant." The agreement went on to say that if the hermit could live without breaking any of these conditions for seven years he was entitled to the sum of £700. Mr Hamilton's advertisement attracted just one applicant, who lasted in his retreat for exactly three weeks.

A Lancashire nobleman had more luck when he advertised for a hermit. He offered an annual income of £50 for life for anyone who could live for seven years underground without any human contact, and without cutting his hair, beard, toenails or fingernails. The newspaper advertisement was answered immediately by a happy hermit who went on to complete four years of unseen underground employment.

In 1810 an advertisement in the *Courier* read, "A young man who wishes to retire from the world and live as a hermit is willing to engage with any nobleman or gentleman who may be desirous of one. Any letter directed to S. Laurence (post paid) to be left at Mr Otton's, No. 6 Coleman Lane, Plymouth, mentioning what gratuity will be given, and all other particulars, will be duly attended."

The Wittelsbachs of Bavaria were Europe's most eccentric royal family, enjoying an unbroken rule spanning more than seven hundred years from 1140 to 1914, and blood ties with almost every other royal family in Europe, including Sweden, Holland, Luxembourg, Belgium, Spain, France, Austria, Prussia and Portugal. Although the Wittelsbach "Mad" King Ludwig II is probably the best known and most prolific builder of architectural follies, the creative building urge occurred in several members of the family. Many of Munich's most historically important buildings owe their existence to the generosity of King Ludwig I, grandfather of Ludwig II. The elder Ludwig, although renowned for his personal stinginess, spent public millions on fantastic new building projects in his desire to beautify Munich. He was a stone deaf, shabby, parsimonious little man, generally considered by his subjects to be a harmless lunatic. He was often seen wandering the streets of Munich late at night with his inimitable zig-zagging walk, wearing tatty threadbare clothes and carrying a battered umbrella, which was considered a great novelty at the time. Another of Ludwig's eccentricities was his lifelong hobby of composing outstandingly bad poetry. His muse compelled him to put every experience he ever had, no matter how trivial or mundane, down in rhyme. Once when the king was badly gored by a bull in Italy, he sat down and recorded the event in rhyming couplets. The string of actresses he bedded throughout his reign were all to discover in time that the only gifts that the tight-fisted old king was likely to lavish on them were reams of terrible poetry. He commissioned a series of thirty-six portraits of beautiful women and used them to decorate the walls of his palace at Nymphenburg. The subjects of his Schönheits Gallerie were not famous or aristocratic, they were simply subjects of his lust, irrespective of class, from countesses to laundrywomen, from actresses to chambermaids, even women he had passed on the street. After years of marital infidelity the odd old king suddenly achieved international notoriety by falling for an Irish dancer young enough to be his granddaughter. Ludwig was sixty-one when he met 28-year-old Lola Montez, a dazzling raven-haired femme fatale with a string of famous lovers behind her, including Franz Liszt. It was said that Lola introduced herself to the old king one day by ripping open her bodice and revealing her breasts. Ms Montez was acknowledged as one of the most beautiful women in Europe; her elderly lover on the other hand had few teeth, less hair, a disproportionately large head and a large cyst in the middle of his forehead. Ludwig pledged his undying love to Lola in long poems, but fatally started to seek her opinion on important matters of state. The press called her "the apocalyptic whore" and King Ludwig was subsequently forced by pressure from the mob and his ministers to banish her from the country. Soon afterwards Ludwig was driven to declare his abdication in favour of his son Maximilian. Ludwig never met Lola again, but continued to harass her with his love poems by mail.

His son King Maximilian II and his daughter-in-law Queen Marie were first cousins – a disingenuous arrangement as there were already many known cases of mental instability on both sides of the family. Maximilian was another prolific builder who brought many prominent scientists and artists to Munich. He also suffered from severe headaches, flogged his children and kept them so hungry that they sometimes had to beg food from the servants. His sister Princess Alexandra however was considered even more eccentric than he, thanks to her sincere and unwaverable conviction that she had accidentally swallowed a grand piano made of glass. Another of her idiosyncrasies was her desire to wear white at all times. This was perhaps just as well, as poor aunt Alexandra was to spend a large part of her confused life in a straitjacket.

King Ludwig's second son Otto was another compulsive builder who also enjoyed a brief and eventful career as the first king of Greece. He took up the throne at the age of seventeen and quickly bankrupted the national treasury by turning Athens into a building site. For the best part of thirty years he attempted to rule the locals by pointing Bavarian fixed bayonets in their direction, until in 1862 he and his wife Queen Amelia were finally forced to flee back to Bavaria. The Wittelsbach reign in Greece did leave one enduring legacy, although it was not, as they might have hoped, architectural. One of Otto's Bavarian entourage was a brewer named Fuchs: the Greeks changed the name of his product to Fix and have been drinking to his name ever since.

The tiny Latvian Edward Leedskalnin (1887–1951) was twenty-six when he was engaged to marry the strapping teenager Agnes Scuffs, a girl ten years his junior to whom he was always to refer as "Sweet Sixteen". On the day before the wedding however Agnes quietly informed her suitor that she did not want to marry him because he was too old and too poor. Jilted on the eve of his wedding, the devastated Leedskalnin embarked on a journey that would culminate in one of America's most bizarre landmarks. He left Latvia and wandered Europe for several years, eventually making his way to Canada and then down into California and Texas. Although Leedskalnin was tiny – only 4 ft 8 in tall and weighing 7 stone – he worked in the lumber camps and was involved in at least one cattle drive in Texas.

In 1919 he developed tuberculosis and went to Florida because he had heard that the climate would be good for his chest. He spent the next thirty years in solitary construction in a remote part of the state. Always working alone, he fashioned coral rock into a fantastic series of sculptures, including a dozen rocking chairs, a map of Florida, astronomical instruments, various planets, a twenty-five foot tall obelisk and, as sad monuments to his unrequited love, two single beds and two children's cradles. Over a period of twenty years, he sculpted and carved over 1,100 tons of coral rock. In 1940, after the carvings were in place, he built himself a coral castle. Coral weighs approximately 125 lbs per cubic foot and each section of wall was 8 feet tall, 4 feet wide, 3 feet thick, and weighed approximately 13,000 lbs. His feats baffled engineers and scientists who have compared his secret method of construction of Stonehenge and the Great Pyramids. When asked how he was able to move the blocks of coral, he would say only that he understood the laws of weight and leverage.

Leedskalnin also published a number of eccentric books expounding his controversial views on a variety of subjects including plants and plant growth, electricity and magnetism. One of his most interesting works was *A Book For Every Home*, in which Leedskalnin, a lifelong bachelor, offered his practical advice on various aspects of family life including marriage and parenting. He advised parents not to feed their daughters too much in case they became "too large", and not to allow their children to smile because it encouraged wrinkles. He recommended that girls should ideally be virgins before they married, but advised the bride's mother to copulate with her prospective son-in-law so he could practise sex.

Leedskalnin lived exclusively on a diet of sardines and crackers, and apparently starved to death in 1951. In December of that year he became ill, put a sign on his door saying "Going to the Hospital", and took a bus to Jackson Memorial Hospital in Miami. Three days later he died in his sleep, aged sixty-four. In 1953 a box of his effects was found and examined. It contained a set of instructions which led to the discovery of thirty-five $100 bills – his life savings.

The Turkish Sultan Abdul Hamid II was known by various names, including the Red Sultan, because of the amount of blood he had shed, the Ogre of Yilditz Kiosk, after his fortress bolt-hole overlooking the city of Constantinople, or simply Abdul the Damned. As his two predecessors had been deposed, Abdul Hamid came to the throne a very nervous man and cultivated a surreal obsession for his personal safety. Although he surrounded himself with a personal bodyguard of several thousand tall Albanians, he considered that security at his palaces was far too lax, and set about erecting a new impregnable palace from scratch. To create this new hiding place he had two Christian cemeteries cleared on a hillside at Yilditz and secured the services of a dozen architects. Each was detailed to build just one twelfth of the palace, working in complete ignorance of the work in progress of the other eleven. In effect the Sultan built himself a royal prison. Every wall was mirrored so that he could see the people around him from any angle. Every door was lined with steel. Most of the rooms were

connected by secret underground passages, but only Abdul
Hamid knew where each one led. He owned a thousand
permanently loaded revolvers, strategically hidden around
the palace, including two which hung at each side of his
bath. Some rooms were booby-trapped. At the flick of a
switch, cupboards facing the entrance of the room would
fly open and trip mechanically controlled guns. Part two of
the plan was to build a fake town to go with the palace,
including dozens of fake coffee shops, each of which was
manned by the Sultan's spies. In all the fortress town of
Yilditz was filled with about 20,000 secret agents, who had
orders to spy on the Sultan's bodyguards and on each other.
The only spies that the Sultan truly trusted were the hundreds
of caged parrots which were hung on street corners, trained to
squawk if they sighted a stranger.

Abdul Hamid's biggest phobia, one he shared with his mad
uncle Abdul Aziz, was fear of poisoning. He would refuse water
unless it had been drawn from a secret spring and brought to
him in a sealed container. The business of drinking milk was
similarly tricky: his was the only dairy herd in the world with a
twenty-four-hour bodyguard. The Sultan's kitchens were like
bank vaults. All of his food was prepared behind iron bars and
bolted doors. Each dish was then divided into three portions:
the first was tasted by the Chief Chamberlain, "Guardian of
the Sultan's Health and Life"; the second was given to a cat or a
dog. If both parties lived, the third portion would then be
delivered on a sealed tray. As Abdul Hamid was a fussy eater
anyway the food was usually left uneaten and most of the time
he lived on vitamin pills. He was a chain smoker, and even his
cigarettes had to be tested first. The tobacco was bought
cheaply and randomly in case the Sultan's supply of finest
Turkish tobacco had been got at, and the cigarettes were then
hand-rolled by his most trusted eunuch, who would then be

required to take the first drag. But what if someone tried to poison his clothes? Accordingly, every garment that Abdul Hamid wore had to be first "warmed" by a eunuch before he would go near it.

The Sultan always carried with him a pearl-handled revolver. He was a nervy, jumpy little man, and a crack shot to boot. This was a lethal combination. No one dared put their hands in their pockets in his presence because to do so would be an invitation to the Sultan to take a pot shot. A gardener made a sudden bowing movement and Abdul Hamid blew his brains out. When one of his own daughters gave him a playful shove from behind, he whipped out his gun, spun round, and shot the girl dead before realizing who she was. On his increasingly rare excursions outside his fortress town of Yilditz he always wore a shirt of chainmail and crouched inside his specially built armoured carriage with one of his young sons on his knee as a "human shield". Eventually he retreated almost permanently into the company of his concubines, but even in the harem he found opportunities for paranoia. He had a lifesized wax effigy of himself placed behind a gauze curtain to make it look as though he was always watching them.

A genuine attempted coup convinced Abdul that his fears were justified and that he'd been far too relaxed about the threat of assassination. When the British ambassador Henry Layard arrived at the palace for a pre-arranged audience with the Sultan he found him cowering in a corner behind a wall of bodyguards, shaking visibly beneath his steel-lined fez. Whenever news reached him of assassination attempts elsewhere in Europe he took it personally. He banned all mention of them in the press, with absurd consequences. When the king and queen of Serbia were butchered then tossed out of a bedroom window in 1903, the Turkish press reported that they had both died of indigestion. The murder of the Austrian Empress Elizabeth was mysteriously conveyed to the Turkish public with a statement that she had simply expired in Geneva: no further explanation was offered.

Chapter Thirteen

Hermits, Misers & Misanthropes

"That so few now dare to be eccentric marks the chief danger of our time"

John Stuart Mill (1806–73)

"I want to be unobtrusive"

Howard Hughes (1905–76)

Eighteenth-century London was renowned for dirt and squalor, but one shop was so outrageously filthy that it came to be known throughout the country as the Dirty Warehouse of Leadenhall Street. The premises were owned by the similarly slovenly Nathaniel Bentley, or Dirty Dick as he was generally known. The Dirty Warehouse had a distinguished history and had once been an impressive Bentley family residence until Nathaniel decided to turn it into a commercial venture.

Bentley had in his youth been considered a beau. He had spent some time in Paris, where he enjoyed the social circuit, attending salons and once visiting the French court. Some said that his sudden change in habits was rooted in a disappointment in love. He kept a locked room in the house, and the story went that he had closed it up after preparing a reception for his bride-to-be, who had tragically died suddenly en route to her wedding. He wore patched and ancient clothes he mended himself, he never combed his hair and it was said that he never washed. When a customer chided him for his lack of cleanliness, he replied sadly, "It is of no use, sir; if I wash my hands today they will be dirty again tomorrow." Even when he became notoriously filthy, he still occasionally went to the theatre and other public places in blue and silver finery. "Although involved in dirt," noted one contemporary writer, "his manners bespeak the man of breeding."

Inside the shop, however, he stood with his feet in a box of straw to save on heating. Although quite wealthy he refused to pay for a servant, and as meat was expensive he avoided eating it, living mostly on rotten vegetables scrounged from the local market. The hardware sold by Bentley lay scattered in bales amid decades of dust. Spiderwebs covered the ceiling, and half the windowpanes were missing, hidden by shutters made from tea trays and box lids nailed into place to discourage thieves. Bentley's "Dirty Dick" persona may also however have been part of a smart commercial move. When neighbours offered to pay to have the shopfront repainted, he refused, claiming it was so well known as the Dirty Warehouse that cleaning it would ruin him. It is preserved today by a popular London pub, Dirty Dick's.

The miserly French millionaire Samuel Tapan hanged himself in 1934, leaving behind $1.5 million in cash plus dozens of vineyards and several castles. Tapan had become depressed after losing a mere $50,000 in a speculative business venture. On his last day he went to the village shop and even haggled over the price of the piece of rope he bought to hang himself with.

Thomas Cooke was born near Windsor around 1726, the son of an itinerant fiddler who played at fairs and alehouses. He began work as soon as he was old enough and began to show the first signs of a lifelong obsession with saving money. While his fellow workers pooled together a small part of their weekly earnings to buy food, Cooke limited himself every day to a halfpenny loaf of bread and an apple, washed down with water from a brook. The savings allowed Cooke to hire himself a tutor, and he soon acquired a job with the Board of Excise, where his duties included inspecting factories, including a large paper mill near London. When the owner of the mill died and the business passed to the widow, Cooke discovered a number of serious tax irregularities. Instead of reporting the offences, Cooke gave the widow a choice: she could marry him and make him master of her business, or she could let him report the irregularities and risk losing everything. The poor widow chose the former.

Once married, Cooke became a wealthy man, intent on

hanging on to his fortune by never spending any of it. Cooke's chief economy measure was never to waste any of his own money on meals. He did this by always arranging to be at the home of customers and friends at mealtimes. When asked to stay he at first feigned reluctance, but always gave way to slight persuasion. During the meal he would drop hints about his wealth, thank his generous hosts for their kind hospitality, then carefully write down the names of their children. Many parents, imagining that their children were in Cooke's will, went out of their way to cultivate his friendship. Thus the devious and greedy mill owner became not only a regular dinner guest at dozens of homes but also received many parcels of food; he kept the worst for his household and sold the rest.

When he ran out of acquaintances to exploit, Cooke targeted complete strangers for his meals. He would often pretend to have a fit in the street in front of a selected house. The occupants, concerned by the plight of this apparently respectable businessman, would invariably offer him hospitality and soon they would find themselves on Cooke's list of mealtime destinations. Cooke meanwhile denied his poor wife any luxuries beyond a small ration of table beer, and treated her so badly that her death was said to be of a broken heart. When Cooke died in his eighties the long-suffering families that had fed him and hoped to inherit his wealth were to be disappointed. His will left the bulk of his estate, valued at more than £127,000, to charity.

The penny-pinching Wall Street financier Russell Sage, born a poor country boy in New York State in 1816, quickly learned the meaning of hard work and took lessons in thrift from his father, who advised, "Any man can earn a dollar, but it takes a wise man to save it." Later in life he was fond of recalling that he saved the first dollar he ever earned and that he was never a penny short or a minute late in paying a debt. Sage's first job away from the family farm at the age of twelve earned him four dollars a week in a grocery store run by his older brother in Troy, New York. He invested his first savings in night school, where he learned bookkeeping, but by the age of fifteen he had already saved enough to buy two vacant lots across from the store. He also dabbled in horse trading, putting his profits into more land and a cargo boat that he used to ship horses to New York. Sage soon had his own store, and then branched out into the expanding railroad business. By the age of twenty-two he was worth $25,000 in cash, and within ten years he was a leading local and national politician. After two terms in Congress however he decided his real future lay in business as "politics did not pay".

Sage arrived on Wall Street at the start of the Civil War and quickly earned himself a reputation for his cautious but shrewd investment style. He invested in railroads and transatlantic cables and won handsome returns, ending up as director of more than twenty railroad and steamship companies. He could reputedly get hold of more capital faster than any other financier of his day, and he claimed to have more cash on hand than any bank. In 1884 he suffered his sole major loss on Wall Street of more than four million dollars, according to the New York Times, "without a murmur". Sage's massive fortune, however, did little to change the thrifty habits of his youth. His homes were filled with derelict furniture he had owned for years. He dressed in cheap suits and always took a small pre-prepared lunch to work rather than pay restaurant prices. He rode on public transport rather than buy an expensive car and even then was so reluctant to produce the ten-cent fare that he would cadge a ride if he could.

Although famed for his meanness, Sage's immense wealth often made him a target for people seeking financial help. In 1891 a man confronted Sage in his office with a note demanding $1,200,000. When Sage waved him away, the man detonated a stick of dynamite, blowing himself to pieces. Although the blast killed Sage's typist and injured five other clerks and colleagues, the 74-year-old survived with a few cuts and bruises, plus a lawsuit from visiting Wall Street financier William R. Laidlaw, who was also injured by the blast. Laidlaw was later to claim that the millionaire had used him as a human shield. The courts initially found in Laidlaw's favour, but a New York court of appeal found Sage to be blameless.

After the dynamite incident, Sage vowed never again to give to charity and became even more stingy. He even complained when he saw a newspaper photograph of his wife feeding peanuts to squirrels. Surely, he told her, old breadcrumbs would do? Sage became obsessed with the idea that when he died his body would be kidnapped and used for ransom, so he spent $22,000 on a six-ton copper envelope, which was placed inside a mahogany coffin enclosed in an outer sarcophagus of case-hardened steel and rigged with electrical alarms. After his lifetime of meanness, upon Sage's death his wife Margaret decided it was time to put his money to work to help the less fortunate.

Howard Hughes, inventor, aviator, businessman, film producer and latterly smelly old recluse, once discovered that his room had been bugged and immediately ordered twenty identical brand new Chevrolet cars. His aides, puzzled by the spending spree, politely enquired what their boss planned to do with them. Hughes replied that he would use a different car every day. "No one will be able to bug twenty cars and no one will know which I am going to use."

When visitors drove out to the Nevada desert to meet Hughes they were required to stand in a chalk square drawn on the paving outside his mansion. There they were "inspected" before they were allowed through the door. Eventually even his doctor was only allowed to examine him from the other side of the room. Apart from his pathological fear of germs which obliged him to spend the last years of his life clad in Kleenex tissues, Hughes also suffered from chronic constipation and once spent twenty-eight hours on the toilet. He had an obsession about his own urine, which he had sealed in glass jars, numbered, dated and catalogued by his aides. Over a period of ten years Hughes only twice submitted himself to a barber and manicurist. On both occasions he insisted that the barber "scrub up" like a surgeon. His long, razor-like nails were trimmed back and polished, all except one; he insisted on leaving his left thumbnail half an inch long and squared off the end. He explained, "That's my screwdriver. Don't trim my screwdriver short." It was probably worth the effort: Hughes paid $1,000 per trim.

Hughes often lived on tins of chicken soup for weeks at a time. He ate it so slowly that the tin he was eating from would have to be reheated several times before he finished it. For days on end he would live exclusively on one flavour of ice cream until every ice cream supplier in the district had run out of it. For the last fifteen years of his life he lived almost exclusively on ice cream. Even when he ate relatively "normally" he would stick to the same meal every day – steak, salad and peas. He inspected every pea carefully and all peas over a certain size would be pushed to the side of the plate. Hughes would spend an entire three months on film-watching marathons, eating nothing but candy bars and nuts washed down with glasses of milk. He once watched the film *Ice Station Zebra* 150 times consecutively, with the sound turned up to maximum volume.

Haroldson Lafayette Hunt, the legendary Texas oilman, was once said to be the richest man in America. He was also a bigamist – in fact technically he was a trigamist, as his fifteen children came from three simultaneous marriages. He apparently saw it as his duty to spread what he called his "genius gene".

Hunt was originally a professional cardplayer who won his first oil well in a poker game in 1921, a well that was to earn him one million dollars a week by the late 1940s. Although he was the owner of an ever-expanding international empire worth several billion dollars by the time he died in 1974 at the age of eighty-five, he was not a man of expensive tastes. He spent most evenings in a rocking chair on the front porch listening to country music. He drove around town in an old Dodge, wore cheap suits and owned a single pair of much-mended shoes. Hunt always carried his lunch – carrots, apricots and other health foods – to work in a brown paper bag. He constantly reminded his children, although themselves fantastically wealthy, that a 100-watt light bulb consumed electricity at the rate of four cents an hour. He borrowed cash from his employees, sponged sandwiches from his secretary, and invariably forgot to repay in kind.

Although Hunt was notoriously parsimonious and never once gave to charity, he was keen to bankroll right-wing political campaigns against anything he saw as a threat to the American way of life, including unions. He also wrote a novel, *Alpaca*, in which he envisioned a society where citizens received voting power in proportion to the taxes they paid.

This system, unsurprisingly, would have made Hunt one of the most powerful men in America.

The recluse Jane Lewson, who reached the age of 116, is the most likely of several candidates said to have been the inspiration for the reclusive Miss Havisham in Charles Dickens's *Great Expectations*. "Lady" Lewson, as she was dubbed by the few people she kept contact with, lived in Clerkenwell and became eccentric after the death of her husband when she was just twenty-six years old. She occupied only one room of her large house and to the end of her days continued to wear clothes that were fashionable at the time of her wedding. "Lady" Lewson rarely washed, apparently for fear of catching a cold. She smeared her cheeks with pig fat, adding a touch of rouge to each cheek. Her room was never cleaned and accumulated decades of dirt and cobwebs until the windows were so thick with grime that they didn't allow the light in. She died in 1816.

James Lucas, "the mad hermit of Hertfordshire", turned his family mansion into a fortress and lived for most of his life in the kitchen in conditions of terrible neglect and squalor. He became unbalanced after the death of his mother, to whom he had been utterly devoted. He personally embalmed her body and placed it in a glass coffin in the drawing room, refusing to allow the undertaker to take her away. For over four months he sat by the coffin, barricaded inside the house, until eventually his brother had the police break in and remove the corpse. When they had gone Lucas replaced the barricades and armed himself to the teeth with shotguns and knives. He cleared nearly all of the furniture from the kitchen and slept on a pile of warm cinders from the fire. He wore only a horse rug and never washed or cut his hair, until over a period of several years a layer of black dirt encased his entire body. There were many visitors to "Squire James" in his squalid retreat. He was mostly tolerant of the people who came to peer at him. He kept a supply of sweets and pennies for small girls and tots of gin for visiting gentry who had to converse with him through the bars of his kitchen cell. Charles Dickens once visited him, an unhappy encounter which ended up with Lucas threatening the author with a shotgun. Dickens later wrote "Tom Tiddler's Ground" in which one of the characters was based on Lucas – "a slothful, unsavoury, nasty reversal of the laws of human nature". In his later years he removed from the kitchen to his mother's bedroom. In 1874 police broke into his home for a second time and found him dying from a stroke.

The Welsh Rev. Morgan Jones – "Jones the misogynist" to his flock – was an incredibly miserly vicar often mistaken for a beggar on the streets of his own parish. It was said that he had been betrayed by a woman when he was a young man, and thereafter hated all females, although when he became very old he had to rely on a woman – a distant relative – to look after him. Throughout his forty-three years as vicar of Blewbury he wore the same overcoat, the same hat and the same shirt, which judging by the state of them were already the worse for wear when he arrived to take up his position in 1781. Originally his coat had been a traditional clerical frock coat with long tails, but later he adapted it by turning it inside out. As the lining began to rot away he cut off the tails and used them as patches and when the buttons fell off he replaced them with string. He darned so many holes in his coat that eventually there was little left of the original material. His hat was similarly battered by years of use. At one point he replaced the brim with one he found on a scarecrow. His shirt was washed about once every three months, after which he went around shirtless until it was dry again. He cooked bacon every Sunday and made it last for a whole week, supplemented with bread and cups of tea, but mostly he scrounged meals from his parishioners. To light his home he used leftover candle stubs from his church and he heated it with twigs from the churchyard. Most of the time however he saved on fuel and lighting bills by inviting himself into other houses in his panish. He would stay there until it was dark then go home to his own bed. When he died intestate his parishioners were staggered to learn that he had left £18,000. Ironically, the woman-hating cleric left the lot to his female relative.

The miserly American Henrietta "Hetty" Howland Green, the "Witch of Wall Street", was born in New Bedford, Massachusetts, into great wealth. Her father and grandfather, Gideon Howland, were millionaire owners of a large whaling fleet. Regardless of their wealth the family lived frugal lives. By the age of six Hetty could read the daily financial papers to her father and grandfather and was familiar with the nineteenth-century world of finance and investment, and at the age of eight she opened her own savings account. When Hetty became twenty-one years old she inherited $7.5 million, an inheritance that her natural financial talent and incredible meanness enabled her to multiply many times over. By the turn of the century her annual income was an estimated $7 million. Although the total extent of her wealth was never revealed, she was known to have kept a balance of nearly $31.5 million in one bank alone.

Hetty Green had a foul temper and smelled worse as she rarely wasted money on soap. She always wore an extremely old very long black dress which had turned green with dirt and underneath she wore old newspapers when her petticoats wore out. When her long skirt had accumulated enough of the dirt it swept through she went to Wheeler's Laundry where she instructed them to "wash only the bottom". She waited in her petticoats until her skirt was ready for her. Children ran away from her whenever she walked down the street because she looked like a witch. She carried with her a tatty handbag which was always full of broken biscuits, purchased in bulk from a grocery store at the south end of Atkinson Street, because they were cheaper. In New York she often ate in "Pie Alley" where the main meal of the day cost just fifteen cents. She was too mean to ever buy a meal in a restaurant. She generally worked through her lunch at her desk and every day ate a bowl of dry oatmeal she heated up herself on the office radiators. She said the oatmeal gave her the strength to fight "the wolves of Wall Street". When her son broke his leg she refused to pay a doctor and sent him to a charity hospital, posing as a beggar. The son lost the leg as a result of her meanness. She is said to have once spent hours searching for a two-cent stamp she had lost.

Hetty Green became paranoid about her wealth, obsessed with the idea that she would be kidnapped. She went to bizarre lengths to make life difficult for her would be abductors. She took lengthy detours, doubled back on her tracks and hid in doorways. She also convinced herself that her father and her aunt had both been poisoned. On her seventy-eighth birthday the millionairess informed a newspaper reporter that her good health and long life were possible because of her habit of chewing baked onions. She died after a stroke aged eighty in 1916 leaving behind an incalculable fortune, variously estimated between $100 and

$200 million. In the October 1998 edition of *American Heritage*, she was ranked #36 of the 40 richest Americans in history. She is the only woman on the list.

Daniel Dancer of Harrow Weald near London was one of the great miserly recluses of eighteenth-century England and said to have displayed "one of the most remarkable instances of the insatiable thirst for gold in the history of human nature." He inherited a large and profitable farm, but instead of cultivating it he allowed the place to run wild. He decided that the farmhouse was too expensive to maintain, so he moved into a shack on the farm premises and slept on sacking. He washed only in the summer, when he would wait for a sunny day, immerse himself in a pond and lie in the sun until he was dry; in winter he was conspicuous by his body lice. His weekly food bill comprised one piece of beef and fourteen boiled dumplings, cooked on Sundays. He once found a dead sheep which had expired from an unknown disease, and dined on mutton pies for a month.

For a while he shared his home with his sister. When she lay dying he refused to pay for a doctor, observing to a near neighbour, Lady Tempest, "If the old girl's time is come, the nostrums of all the quacks in Christendom cannot save her". Lady Tempest once took pity on him and sent him a dish of trout stewed in claret. As he never wasted money on fire, he heated the dish by sitting on it until he considered it warm enough to eat. When he died in 1794 it was discovered that he had stashed money away all over the farm, including £2,500 in a mound of cow's dung. Lady Tempest inherited every penny, but sadly died three months later.

New York City's all time most obsessive hoarders of junk were the Collyer brothers, Homer and Langley, sons of a wealthy obstetrician. The brothers became reclusive after the death of their mother in 1933. They withdrew from the world into their four-storey Manhattan townhouse where they lived like vermin amongst tons of booby-trapped rubbish. When the elder brother Homer lost his eyesight he refused to seek medical attention and Langley took care of him by feeding him a diet of water and oranges.

Over the years there were many calls to the New York police about strange goings-on at 2078 Fifth Avenue, mostly complaints about the smell emanating from the apartment. In May 1947 however they received a tip-off that there was a dead body on the premises. When police arrived they found the ground floor windows boarded up and they had to force entry by chopping down the front door with an axe. Once inside they found their progress completely blocked by rubbish. After a few minutes, they discovered the body of an old man, sitting in a tattered bathrobe on the littered floor. It was Homer Collyer. Eventually they found a second corpse. The younger brother was found asphyxiated beneath a mountain of old newspapers. He had apparently been crawling through a tunnel in the debris to bring food to his older brother when the tunnel had collapsed, smothering him to death. The older brother, sixty-five years old, blind and paralyzed, had died of starvation. The police spent three weeks removing 120 tons of rubbish including the parts from fourteen pianos, a dismantled Model T Ford, 3,000 books, several thousand newspapers, guns, swords and a seven-foot segment of tree. The Collyers left over $100,000 in their bank account.

In the case of the eighteenth century parliamentarian John Elwes, frugality was in his genes. Elwes was born in 1714 into a family of notorious Southwark misers. His mother died of malnutrition although she had several thousands of pounds in her bank account. As a young man Elwes was a frequent visitor to his rich, miserly uncle Harvey, hoping to secure a favourable result from his uncle's will. Before he reached the house he always changed into rags, fearing that his uncle would think him a spendthrift and disinherit him. He refused to pay for the education of his two sons, on the basis that education would only give them heretical ideas about spending money.

Elwes was a Member of Parliament for ten years but confessed he had absolutely no interest in politics. Whenever he rode to London he carried a couple of hard boiled eggs in his pocket and slept in a ditch rather than spend his money on board and lodging. He wore a wig he found discarded in a hedge, topped by a hat he stole from a scarecrow. He never once made a speech in the House, and sat on whichever side was convenient. He never cleaned his shoes in case the act of polishing wore them out. He rode his carriage on the grass verge to reduce the wear and tear on horseshoes, and made bizarre detours to avoid paying at toll gates. His eating habits were considered particularly repulsive. He ate meat so mouldy, it was said, that the meat moved on the plate, and he once retrieved a long dead moorhen he found being gnawed by a rat, took it home and ate it. The story goes that he was delighted when he once caught a pike which had an undigested fish in its stomach, noting, "This is really killing two birds with one stone." Elwes once broke both legs in an accident, but would only pay his doctor for one splint to halve the bill. He died aged seventy-five in 1789 leaving a semi-derelict mansion and £75,000 – worth about £20 million today.

Sir Thomas Phillipps (1792–1872) lived as a miser so he could devote his life and all of his money to one obsession – bibliomania. He bought a total of 100,000 books and 60,000 manuscripts, which represented a personal collection bigger than all the combined libraries of Cambridge University. Unusually for a bibliomaniac Phillipps was also an obsessive collector of paper. He never threw a scrap away. He hoarded old and worthless household bills, letters and documents and even took home worthless government documents that had been deemed waste paper and were due to be pulped. Phillipps used his wife and three daughters as virtual slave librarians to catalogue his immense collection. They ate and slept amongst the books, living a miserable existence of endless cataloguing. His wife become a hopeless drug addict and died aged thirty-seven. After her death Phillipps set out to find himself a wealthy replacement who would help finance his obsession and continue the cataloguing. He eventually settled for a clergyman's daughter. The new wife found her new life intolerable, especially the rats, and she had a nervous breakdown.

The miser John Overs, who made a fortune from his Thames ferryboat which ran from Southwark to the City, lived so frugally, it was said, that the rats left his house of their own accord. A contemporary noted, "He hath gone in the night to scrape upon the Dunghill, and if he could have found any bones, but especially marrow bones, he would have borne them home in his Cap to have made Pottage with them." He lived on mouldy bread and meat unfit for a dog. His meanness contributed to his premature death. In an attempt to cut down on his bills, Overs pretended to be dead for a day, believing that his house servants would fast until after the funeral and thus reduce his food bill. The plan backfired when they celebrated instead by throwing open the doors to the pantry. When Overs rose from his deathbed to complain they thought he was a ghost and clubbed him to death with an oar.

As the Church considered the bitter old misanthrope un-worthy of a Christian burial, his daughter had to bribe the friars of Bermondsey Abbey to bury him in their grounds while the Abbot was away. When the Abbot returned however he found out about the burial and had the body exhumed. It was then tied to an ass, which was taken outside the Abbey gates and allowed to wander off. The ass carried the body to a place on the Old Kent Road then known as St Thomas à Watering, where the locals buried it. Overs's daughter Mary retired to a nunnery. She eventually used her father's fortune to found the church of St Mary in the City. It was later renamed St Mary Overs in her memory and was bequeathed all the income from her late father's ferry business. The miserly ferryman is featured in one of the church's stained glass windows.

Augustus Van Horne Stuyvesant, Jr was the last descendant of the seventeenth-century Peter Stuyvesant, the last Dutch governor of New Amsterdam, the city that became New York. Augustus was an eighth-generation Stuyvesant, a near-legend-ary family who had become more reclusive with each passing generation. The last Stuyvesant took his family's inherent reclusivity to extremes. His last twenty-five years were spent alone, living behind three locked bronze doors. He had no family or social life and few business affairs. A tall, dapper but terribly shy bachelor – he had a speech impediment that made him sound like a child – his only recreation was a daily one-hour stroll through the streets near his home. After the death of Anne, the younger of his two sisters, in 1958, his sole contact with outsiders was a weekly church service. He even went days at a time without seeing his servants. His English butler, Ernest Vernon, who worked for the old man for thirty-three years without ever taking a vacation, later revealed that he and his employer were "perfect strangers . . . no one ever passed the time of day with Mr Stuyvesant."

Perhaps the most grossly misplaced act of generosity ever was the last will and testament of John Camden Neild, known to posterity as "the Queen's miser". Neild inherited a quarter of a million pounds from his father. Unlike his dad however, a generous man renowned for his philanthropy and his efforts to reform prisons, Neild Junior was only interested in the accumulation of wealth. He owned a splendid house in one of the most fashionable addresses in London at Cheyne Walk, Chelsea, but occupied one room only to save on heating and maintenance bills. For years he slept on bare floorboards although eventually he allowed himself the comfort of an old bed. Whenever he emerged from his house he always wore the same old-fashioned blue swallow-tailed coat and brown trousers. He refused to have his clothes brushed in case it wore them out. Neild also owned properties in Buckinghamshire, Middlesex and Kent, and rather than pay an agent to collect the rents he preferred to do it himself. On his trips he would often cadge a lift on a coal cart or a farm wagon rather pay for a carriage. When he died in 1852 his incredible stinginess had helped him double his inheritance to a sum worth around £20 million by today's reckoning.

When his will was published he gained national notoriety, for he left almost the entire fortune to Queen Victoria, "begging her Majesty's most gracious acceptance of the same, for her sole use and benefit, and her heirs". The Queen, who was already one of the richest women in the world, was delighted. She and her husband Prince Albert quickly banked the money while continuing to harangue the government for a bigger Civil List. Her jealous uncle Leopold I King of the Belgians wrote to congratulate her on her windfall. "Such things," he drooled, "only still happen in England." At least Queen Victoria made a provision for Neild's old housekeeper, who had existed on a pittance and had been left nothing in the will. Victoria spent the bulk of the inheritance purchasing Balmoral Castle.

Henrietta Schaefer, born a poor child of German immigrant parents in Philadelphia, fell in love with and married a wealthy older businessman Walter Garrett. Their life together was idyllic, in spite of a hostile reception from the local community, who considered Henrietta, eighteen years younger than her husband, an unsuitable match for the heir to a formidable fortune. Garrett was so devoted to his wife however that he deliberately severed all his snobbish social and business connections in order to make her life more happy. After twenty-three years, Garrett died in 1895, leaving his grief-stricken widow $6 million better off.

Henrietta, shattered by her loss, withdrew from the world completely. She rarely left their mansion, which she maintained exactly as it was on the day of his burial. As the years passed by she refused to install such modern conveniences as a telephone or even electric lighting. She retained however a number of servants, and although she ventured out of the house only once during the last fifteen years of her life she regularly placed expensive orders with dressmakers and hat shops. She donated extensively to charity, purchased season tickets for the Philadelphia Orchestra which she never used and sent generous presents to friends. She had such a terrible fear of death that she always refused to even discuss making a will. When she died intestate in 1950, at the age of eighty-one, her estate, worth more than $15 million, was disputed by more than 26,000 claimants. After decades of legal wrangling $3 million went to cover legal costs, $4 million went to the US government, and $8 million went to distant relatives.

When firefighters and police were called to the scene of a suspicious fire in Indianapolis in 1977 they found Marjorie Jackson shot dead on her kitchen floor, the apparent victim of a burglary. The mystery deepened however when a search of the house revealed that the burglars had left behind more than five million dollars, stuffed in closets, drawers, suitcases and garbage cans.

Marjorie Jackson, who inherited a fortune on the death of her husband, heir to a grocery chain, had become something of a regular target for villains. After her husband's death, she lived alone on her large estate, where the overgrown garden created the impression that the house was empty and derelict. When local police came to investigate complaints about the condition of the estate, Jackson ordered them off her property. She had in fact been the victim of an earlier burglary in 1969 when she lost more than $800,000, but refused to testify against the thieves on the grounds that "it was God's will".

In 1976 she had discovered that her bank manager had embezzled $700,000 from one of her accounts. Determined not to be robbed again she began slowly siphoning her money away from the bank in the form of hard cash. Over a period of five months she carried $9 million home from the bank in an old suitcase, resolutely ignoring warnings that news of these huge withdrawals was bound to attract burglars. Over a period of five days in May 1977 her house was raided three times. In the second burglary the two intruders shot her, but later returned and set fire to the house in order to conceal the murder. The partially burned house was so full of junk that police could not determine what had been stolen. In addition to the vast amounts of money, they discovered fifty loaves of bread, 150 lbs of coffee, and 200 dozen biscuits.

Chapter Fourteen

Eccentric Exits

"I'd recognize him straight away. He was in a green
Barnardo's plastic bag . . . Dennis was a bloke in a million"
64-year-old widow, Jean Carberry, sifting
through hundreds of tons of rubbish on
the local council tip after accidentally
putting her husband Dennis's ashes
out for the binmen

When Mrs Margaret Thompson died at her home in Boyle
Street, Mayfair, she left instructions that her coffin be packed
with all her handkerchiefs "together with such a quantity of
best Scotch snuff (in which I always had the greatest delight) as

will cover my deceased body". For her funeral she wanted:

> . . . six men to be my bearers, who are known to be the greatest snuff-takers in the parish of St James's, Westminster; instead of mourning, each to wear a snuff-coloured beaver hat which I desire to be bought for that purpose and given to them. Six maidens of my old acquantance to bear my pall, each to wear a proper hood, and to carry a box filled with the best Scotch snuff to take for their refreshment as they go along. Before my corpse, I desire the minister may be invited to walk and to take a certain quantity of the said snuff, not exceeding one lb, to whom also I bequeath five guineas on condition of him so doing. And I also desire my old and faithful servant, Sarah Stuart, to walk before the corpse, to distribute every twenty yards a large handful of Scotch snuff to the ground and upon the crowd who may possibly follow me to the burial place; on which condition I bequeath her twenty pounds. And I also desire that at least two baskets of the said snuff may be distributed at the door of my house in Boyle Street.

Robert Farrell of Boise, Idaho kept the mummified body of his deceased mother in his house for six years until neighbours complained about the smell. Georgia Farrell was found lying on her sofa in March 1993. It was estimated that she had probably died in 1987 at the age of eighty-eight. The death was never reported by her son Robert, who still lived with her. According to a neighbour whenever Robert was asked where his mother was, he would casually reply, "Oh, she's in."

Hannah Beswick of Cheetwood Hall, Lancashire lived with a constant fear of premature burial. When she eventually expired in 1758 aged seventy-seven, she left £25,000 to her doctor with instructions that he regularly inspect her corpse for signs of life. Her body was embalmed and crammed inside a grandfather clock with a velvet curtain tastefully draped across the glass viewing panel. One hundred and ten years after her demise the trustees of her estate agreed that Hannah Beswick's state of health was finally beyond dispute, and she was granted a decent burial.

The body of wealthy recluse Toivo Sistonen lay decomposing in his house in Thunder Bay, Ontario, for four years, partly eaten by his pet cats while someone collected his mail, cut his lawn and shovelled snow from his driveway. When the body was found in 1999 there were also skeletons of several cats in the house.

When the Rev. Langton Freeman died in 1783 at his family estate at Whilton in Northamptonshire his will contained an extraordinary clause containing final instructions for the disposal of his body. For the first four or five days after his death "till my body grow offensive" it should remain in his bed. Then, the bed with his corpse still in it was to be carried into the garden and placed in the summer-house. The body was to be wrapped in a sheet "as near as may be to the description we receive in Holy Scripture of our Saviour's burial." The door and windows of the summer-house were to be permanently locked and bolted, then the building was to be surrounded by evergreen trees, which in turn were to be surrounded by a fence made of oak or iron, painted dark blue. Apparently the instructions were carried out to the letter.

In 1991 Lai Siang Kwang from Singapore was convicted of keeping the cremated remains of 2,000 people in his bungalow. It was Kwang's fourth similar conviction for hoarding funeral urns in his home.

The ground-breaking research of the important sixteenth-century Danish astronomer Tycho Brahe allowed Sir Isaac Newton to come up with the theory of gravity. In the sixteenth century, it was considered an insult to leave a banquet table before the meal was over. Brahe, known to drink excessively, had a bladder condition, but failed to relieve himself before the banquet started. He made matters worse by drinking too much at dinner, and was too polite to ask to be excused. His bladder finally burst, killing him slowly and painfully over the next eleven days.

After Thomas More's head was chopped off, parboiled and stuck on a pole on London Bridge in 1535, his daughter Margaret bribed a bridgekeeper to let her steal it and take it home – a crime for which she was later arrested and briefly imprisoned. The head was buried with her when she died in 1544.

Major Peter Labellière who died on 6 June 1800 described himself as a Christian patriot and Citizen of the World. In his last will and testament he expressed his disaffection with life by leaving instructions that he should be buried head downwards; "As the world was turned topsy turvy, it was fit that he should be so buried that he might be right at last."

Terry Kath, guitarist with the US rock band Chicago, tried to amuse his party guests by pointing what he thought was an empty gun at his head. He pulled the trigger and blew his brains out.

In 1999 a 52-year-old woman in Hong Kong turned the body of her deceased husband over to the authorities. She said that she had held on to the body for a week in the hope that he would revive, but eventually gave in to the smell.

When D. H. Lawrence died, his lover Frieda had his ashes tipped into a concrete mixer and incorporated into her new mantelpiece.

In 1993 an Icelandic funeral parlour found itself under investigation following a complaint by the bereaved family of Henri Labonte. They told local authorities that the deceased had been dressed for his 26 December funeral in a Santa Claus costume and was wearing a fake beard.

In accordance with his last wish, in 1973 a Swedish confectionery salesman from Falkenberg, Roland Ohisson, was buried in a coffin made entirely of chocolate.

The great jazz musician Joe "Poolie" Newman, trumpet player with Count Basie and Lionel Hampton, was a notorious lothario. In 1989 Newman, determined to live up to his reputation, tried to his enhance his flagging sex life with a penile implant. A build-up of pressure however caused his member to explode one evening while he was in a restaurant, causing him to haemorrhage to death.

The Spanish Queen Juana was driven to distraction by her faithless and mostly absent husband. When her beloved Philip died aged twenty-eight she resolved to see more of him in future by having his body embalmed and keeping it by her side at all times, even at mealtimes and in bed.

When the Stevenage grocer Henry Trigg died in 1724 he left curious instructions to keep bodysnatchers away from his corpse. His coffin was placed in the rafters of his barn, where it remained on view for almost 250 years while the premises changed hands, and were used as an inn, and later a bank. When the coffin was finally taken down and opened it was found to be empty: it seems the bodysnatchers, or "resurrection men" as they were known, may have got to him after all.

When Enrico Caruso died in 1921 the great Italian opera singer was laid to rest on show in a glass coffin, allowing his adoring fans to study his corpse. Five years and several new suits later however his widow decided to give him a more dignified interment in a private tomb.

The Tomb of Mausolus was one of the Seven Wonders of the World, completely destroyed by an earthquake. It was built in 353 BC in Turkey by Queen Artemisia on the death of her husband King Mausolus. The original idea was that the king's body was to be placed in the tomb, but there was a last-minute change of plan: the Queen had him cremated, then poured his ashes into a goblet of wine and drank him.

To circumvent a French law which bans the burial of animals in human cemeteries, in 1977 Helene Lavanent and Yvette Soltane booked themselves graves in a pet cemetery so that they could be buried with their dogs.

The Sussex MP John "Mad Jack" Fuller (1752–1834) was a builder of follies. He declined a conventional burial because of his irrational fear of being eaten "by his own relatives". Fuller reasoned thus: "The worms would eat me, the ducks would eat the worms, and my relatives would eat the ducks." In order to avoid this train of events he had a pyramid-shaped mausoleum constructed in which he sits in an armchair wearing a top hat and holding a glass of claret.

A Russian court official Count Karnice Karnicki once witnessed the premature burial of a young Belgian girl. He was so moved by the experience that he vowed to patent a new type of coffin which would ensure that such a terrible mistake never happened again. His "safe" coffin had a long tube which extended six feet above ground. The uppermost part of the tube led to a sealed box, while at the other end a glass ball, attached to a wire spring, was to be placed on the deceased's chest. The coffin was also fitted with an interior electric light bulb. The slightest movement would activate the spring, and the sealed box would fly open and release light and air into the coffin. At the same time a flag would extend outside the coffin, the interior light would switch itself on and a bell would ring for thirty minutes.

The tenth Duke of Hamilton Alexander Douglas outbid the British Museum when he paid £11,000 for a magnificent ancient tomb which had originally been made for an Egyptian princess. Douglas housed it in a fabulous mausoleum at his ancestral home, Hamilton Palace. It wasn't until his death in

1852 that it was discovered that he was too tall to fit inside it: the only way they could get him in was by sawing his feet off.

In 1950 the reclusive philosopher Jeremy Bentham had his first change of underwear in 100 years. Bentham believed that corpses could be put to practical use – i.e. every man, properly embalmed, could be used as his own statue, or "auto-icon" as Bentham called them. The possibilities were endless: portraits of ancestors could be replaced by actual heads, "many generations being deposited on a few shelves or in a modest sized cupboard". When Bentham died he had left instructions that his own body be dissected for the benefit of medical science, then embalmed, dressed in his own clothes and placed in a glass case. His head however had to be replaced by a wax version because his face had adopted a somewhat frightening expression during the embalming process. Bentham's physician Dr Southwood Smith kept the body until his own death in 1850 whereupon it was presented to University College, London.

Bentham's idea was not entirely original. Maori tribesmen often preserved the elaborately tattooed heads of their deceased relatives as "auto-icons" to keep alive the memory of the dead. The heads would be steamed several times in an oven, smoked dry, and their hair carefully combed into a topknot. In 1770 the British explorer Sir Joseph Banks acquired the first specimen Maori head ever seen in Europe, and heads suddenly became fashionable and highly collectable items. The Maoris overcame their early objections to selling off the heads of their loved ones when they found that British museums and private collectors were prepared to pay top money for good quality, highly decorated specimens. As genuine Maori heads became scarce, unscrupulous dealers would supply the untattooed heads of recently deceased slaves: few people could tell the difference between an antique relic and a recently decapitated slave, freshly tattooed *post mortem*. By this time the greedy dealers were only one short step away from depriving living Maoris of their heads. In 1832 the gruesome practice was finally made illegal.

The French composer Jean-Baptiste Lully died of gangrene after accidentally stabbing himself in the foot with his baton.

When the American dancer Isadora Duncan took delivery of a brand new Bugatti racing car in 1927 she naturally wanted to show it off to her friends. She stepped into it for the first time, waved gaily and sped away. As she did so her long red scarf became entangled in the spokes of her rear nearside wheel, snapping her neck and killing her instantly.

Christine Chubbock, the late US TV newsreader, committed suicide by shooting herself live in front of the cameras while she was reading the news. It emerged later that she had scripted her death so as not to disrupt the TV schedule.

The famous duellist Brian Maguire was a descendant of an ancient Fermanagh family and an officer in the East India Company. Maguire was a highly volatile man who would pick a fight for the flimsiest of reasons. He practised his gunmanship by shooting at a lighted candle held by his wife. He threw dirt from his window on to the heads of passers-by just to provoke a challenge. If anyone so much as looked up at him he would spit down and offer a duel. When his son George died aged twelve in 1830 Maguire however proved himself to be a big softie at heart. He was so inconsolable that he decided to craft a permanent and cherished keepsake. He embalmed the boy himself and kept him in a glass case which he carried with him everywhere, until his own death five years later of a heart attack.

After the execution of Sir Walter Raleigh in 1618, his head became the Raleigh family heirloom. His widow Elizabeth kept it for twenty-nine years before passing it on to their son Carew, who looked after it until 1666 when it went with him to his grave.

Arthur Mandelko, a 24-year-old Superman fan, froze to death in his fridge while dressed as his favourite TV superhero. Mandelko had spent about a month in the fridge when his landlord found his frozen corpse. The landlord revealed that his lodger had spent most evenings jumping from one roof to another and had been warned about this activity when neighbours complained about the thumping sounds. Police theorized that Mandelko's planned escape by using his super-heated X-ray vision had somehow gone wrong.

Chapter Fifteen

Unstrung Heroes

"At the peremptory request and desire of a large majority of the citizens . . . I, Joshua A. Norton, declare and proclaim myself Emperor of the United States"
Joshua Abraham Norton (1818–80)

"The streets are safe in Philadelphia. It's only the people who make them unsafe"
Frank Rizzo (1920–1991), ex-police chief and mayor of Philadelphia

"Your experience will be a lesson to all men not to marry ladies in very high positions"
Idi Amin (b.1925), President of Uganda, in a letter to Lord Snowdon after the latter's divorce from Princess Margaret in 1976

Lord Curzon (1859–1925), Viceroy of India at thirty-nine, was widely detested by his contemporaries because of his insufferable superiority complex. He had such an inflated view of himself, someone remarked, that he went everywhere "as if accompanied by elephants". Curzon had a disproportionately large head – so big that it once caused him as a child to overbalance and fall down a flight of stairs – and he was known all his life as "Moonface". At Eton a schoolmate wrote a ditty in his honour:

> My name is George Nathaniel Curzon
> I am a most superior person
> My cheek is pink, my hair is sleek,
> I dine at Blenheim once a week.

Curzon was an obsessive writer of very long letters, which caused the great actor Sir Herbert Tree to remark, "I will not go as far as to say that all people who write letters of more than eight pages are mad, but it is a curious fact that madmen never write letters of less than eight pages."

Brazilian Joseph Moura has been threatened, punched and arrested in pursuit of his hobby of kissing the famous, especially famous TV celebrities, athletes, politicians and visiting dignitaries to his native Rio de Janeiro. His greatest success to date came in 1980 when he kissed the feet of Pope John Paul II. His most public humiliation was when he was thrown off court while attempting to snog Martina Navratilova while she was playing Monica Seles.

The legendary founder of NCR, John Henry Patterson (1844–1922), held down various jobs until 1884 when he bought a major interest in the National Manufacturing Company, a purchase for which he was so badly ridiculed that he tried to buy his way out. When that failed, he renamed it the National Cash Register Company, and by 1921 had turned it round into an international industry leader.

Patterson pioneered the development of company training techniques and was famed for a business training school years ahead of its time. He was also unpredictable and impulsive. While travelling in Bulgaria in 1902 he noticed two things: that the locals ate a lot of paprika, and that they had good teeth. He immediately cabled back home with instructions to order 4,000 lbs of the spice. Patterson took four baths a day and wore underwear made from pool table felt. He always slept with his head hanging off the side of the bed so he could avoid breathing in air he had already exhaled. Patterson issued a flow of memoranda on the recommended width of ties, the proper amount to leave as tips, and the recommended leisure pursuits for the families of company employees. He was particularly fond of equestrianism; it was said that for a manager at NCR riding was a prerequisite of job security. He wanted all household cats and dogs banned from Dayton because they were agents of disease. Above all else, however, he had a genius for firing people.

He fired people who threatened him, he fired people who bored him, he even fired people just for practice. He could fire spectacularly. One NCR executive returned from a business trip and found his desk and chair ablaze on the company lawn. Once when he became dissatisfied with the performance of his cost accounting department, he marched the entire department, with their ledgers under their arms, down to the company boiler room, ordered them to throw the ledgers into the flames, then fired the department en masse. John H. Patterson's dismissals created vacuums to be filled by subordinates who caught the great man's eye for whatever reason. For one junior manager, Edward Deeds, promotion came swiftly when he impressed his chairman by climbing the company chimney and bringing back photographic evidence of loose brickwork. Another, Stanley Alleyn, joined the company as an accounts clerk, but six months later was a director of the company, because according to Patterson he had "the most efficient walk I have seen".

The Chinese communist leader Chairman Mao Tse-tung (1893–1976) never took a bath or brushed his teeth, because he'd heard that tigers never brushed their teeth either. Mao achieved an epic personal hygiene problem which grew steadily worse as the years went by. His only concession was to allow servants to wipe him down with a wet towel. Mao seldom got out of bed before noon, would frequently summon his ministers to meetings in the middle of the night, rarely bothered to get dressed and spent most of his time in bathrobes: he only ever wore his famous Mao uniform when there were cameras around.

The press baron Lord Northcliffe was an unpredictable employer; short-tempered and highly opinionated, with a well known loathing for, amongst other things, Americans and inherited wealth. During the Great War he became convinced that the Germans were plotting to assassinate him. He was convinced that he was the reincarnation of Napoleon Bonaparte. The latter delusion – almost de rigueur for paranoid megalomaniacs – became fact in his own mind when he tried on Napoleon's hat and found that it was a perfect fit. Northcliffe once phoned the editor of one of his newspapers and informed him, "There is a story going around that I am mad. I hope we're covering it." He cabled the editor of the *Daily Mail* complaining that there weren't enough giraffes in the Teddy Tail comic strip, and on another occasion instructed him to publish the entire contents of every menu on board the ocean liner *Aquitania*. He once even cabled George V: "I am turning Roman Catholic." The king cabled back, "I cannot help it." On a trip to Europe Northcliffe became convinced that someone was trying to kill him by poisoning his ice cream, and was subsequently returned to England in a straitjacket. His newspapers asserted that the great man was suffering from "a disordered appendix".

The seventeenth-century Ottoman Sultan Murad IV was an early and passionate supporter of the anti-smoking lobby. He decreed the death penalty for anyone who was caught smoking tobacco and wherever he travelled around Turkey his stopping off points were usually marked by spot executions of smokers. Even on the battlefield nicotine addicts were not safe from the Sultan. He had offending soldiers from his own ranks beheaded, or hanged and quartered, or would sometimes crush their hands and feet and leave them helpless in no man's land.

Emperor Menelik II of Ethiopia believed that he could cure himself by eating pages from the Bible. In 1913 he had a stroke and died while attempting to consume the entire Book of Kings.

Even in a period in Roman history known for culinary experimentation, the third-century Emperor Elagabalus was renowned for his adventurous diet. He dined on heads of parrot, flamingo brains, thrush brains and camel heels, and at one feast astonished his guests by serving up 600 flamingo heads, from which they were expected to scoop out and eat the brains with gold spoons.

Lord Baden-Powell in his book *Rovering For Success* warned Boy Scouts against the dangers of masturbation. "It cheats semen getting its full chance of making up the strong manly man you should otherwise be . . . you are throwing away the seed that has been handed down to you as a trust instead of keeping it and ripening it for bringing a son to you later on."

Joshua Abraham "Emperor" Norton was an Englishman, born to Jewish parents in London in 1815. His family emigrated to America in the 1840s during the California Gold Rush and by 1853 he was worth an estimated $250,000 from the sale of supplies to miners and various land deals. Norton however gambled and lost his fortune in an attempt to corner the San Francisco rice market – he bought and stockpiled all the available supply of rice, thereby artificially inflating the price. His plan failed when several ships laden with rice sailed in, glutting the market and causing prices to plummet. In 1856 he filed for bankruptcy and was reduced to working in a sweat-shop.

After losing all his money the 40-year-old former business-man became a little odd and began to assume the identity of Norton I, Emperor of California. By 1859 he had decided that California was too small for him and he styled himself Emperor of the United States and Protector of Mexico. Norton said he believed that America was drifting towards disaster and needed the firm hand of an autocratic monarch. His elevation was declared one evening in September 1859 when he called on the editor of the *San Francisco Bulletin* and left him a huge and impressive looking document:

> At the peremptory request and desire of a large majority of the citizens of the United States, I, Joshua A. Norton, declare and proclaim myself Emperor of the United States; and in virtue of the authority thereby in me vested, do hereby order and direct the representatives of the different states of the Union to assemble in Musical Hall, of this city, on the first day of February next, then and there to make such alterations in the existing laws of the Union as may ameliorate the evils under which the country is labouring and thereby cause confidence to exist, both at home and abroad, both in our stability and in our integrity.
>
> Signed Norton I, Emperor of the
> United States and Protector of Mexico

Norton suspended the Constitution, dissolved all political parties and printed his own currency in 25 and 50-dollar notes. He also attempted to negotiate loans of several million dollars from the major US banks, but found them oddly resistant to his imperial demands. When the Central Pacific Railroad refused his request for a free meal he retaliated by abolishing them. Norton was held in some affection by the American public who regarded him as a harmless lunatic. He held court in a shabby, fifty cents a day rented room, with faded pictures of Queen Victoria and Empress Eugenie looking down on his sparse camp bed and broken washstand. For more than twenty years the stocky, bearded Emperor patrolled the streets in his second-hand army officer's uniform – a blue tunic with golden epaulettes, a ceremonial sword, a plumed beaver hat and a rosette. In good weather he flourished a walking stick, in rain a brightly decorated Chinese umbrella. He was invariably followed by a couple of mongrel dogs and a posse of small children. People he met on the street bowed and curtsied. He always ate out, often at expensive restaurants, but was hardly ever presented with a bill. He also rode on public transport free of charge and often enjoyed complimentary theatre seats. In 1869, finding his uniform rather threadbare, he issued a new edict:

> Know ye whom it may concern that We, Norton I, Emperor Dei gratia of the United States and Protector of Mexico, have heard serious complaints from our adherents and all that our imperial wardrobe is a national disgrace, and even His Majesty the King of Pain has had his sympathy excited so far as to offer us a suit of clothing, which we have a delicacy in accepting. Therefore we warn those whose duty it is to attend to these affairs that their scalps are in danger if our said need is unheeded.

The King of Pain referred to in the Emperor's edict was a "courtier", a street seller of patent medicines, who wore a scarlet velour robe and a stovepipe hat decorated with ostrich feathers, and kept a black coach drawn by six white horses. The San Francisco City Board of Governors decided to go along with the joke and bought Norton a new uniform. He was so touched by their generosity that he knighted the lot of them. In 1880 Joshua Norton collapsed and died in the street, wearing full uniform, aged sixty-one. Newspaper headlines announced "The King Is Dead" and more than 3,000 people attended his "lying in state".

Willie Coombs, also known as George Washington II, was a small-time phrenologist and a contemporary and rival of Joshua Norton. Coombs spent his days walking through San Francisco, carrying a banner and wearing a tricorne hat over his long powdered hair. He spent his evenings in a bar drinking steam beer and poring over maps and documents, planning his battles. He composed messages to Congress and to other nations, much as Norton did. Coombs took his persona seriously and once spent a winter starving himself until friends convinced him that Valley Forge was over.

Coombs left the city abruptly after a clash with the Emperor. One day he stormed into the police station, claiming that Norton was tearing down his posters. The police simply laughed and informed him that as there was no law against this, he would have to resort to civil action. As George Washington II had no money he went to one of the most popular newspapers of the day, the *Alta California*, and told them his story. When they asked him why Norton would do such a thing, Coombs replied, "Because he is jealous of my reputation with the fair sex." Soon after the *Alta* published an article describing its two resident eccentrics, poking fun at both men. Coombs and Norton were united in outrage and together they stormed into the *Alta* and, declaring their perfect sanity, demanded a retraction. A few days later, the *Alta* printed a new proclamation from Norton directing the Chief of Police to "seize upon the person of Professor Coombs, falsely called Washington No. 2, as a seditious and turbulent fellow, and to have him sent forthwith, for his own good and the public good, to the State Lunatic Asylum for at least thirty days". Coombs quickly returned to his native New York. Mark Twain found him there in 1868, still believing himself to be George Washington's reincarnation and displaying his legs for the enjoyment of the ladies.

James A. Harden-Hickey was one of the greatest nineteenth-century American romantics. Born in San Francisco in 1854 into the family of a wealthy Irish miner he was sent to be educated in Paris, where he was deeply impressed by the glamorous, decadent court of Louis Napoleon III. Upon his father's death he inherited enough money to buy himself out of the army and married a countess. He then embarked on a writing career, producing eleven French novels under the pseudonym Saint Patrick. He also wrote several pamphlets defending Catholicism, for which he earned the title Baron of the Catholic Church, while at the same time editing a satirical magazine calling for the restoration of the French Bourbons. Baron Harden-Hickey effected a spectacular U-turn, however, suddenly divorcing his wife and renouncing Catholicism – although not his new title – and set off to India for two years of religious mysticism.

On the way a storm forced his ship to put into a small uninhabited South Atlantic rock called Trinidad – several hundreds of miles south-east of the much larger Caribbean island of the same name. Harden-Hickey clambered ashore and claimed the barren island in his own name. When he returned home he married the American oil and steel heiress Anna Flagler. He then wrote a bizarre manual entitled *Euthanasia: The Aesthetics of Suicide*, in which he listed the 400 best methods of suicide as proposed "by the greatest thinkers ever produced", including eighty-eight poisons suitable for killing oneself. It is generally believed that he made most of it up. By the time the book was published in 1894, Harden-Hickey had declared his ownership of Trinidad to governments around the world and crowned himself King James I. He opened a chancellery in New York and advertised for settlers. He published a manifesto describing his new military dictatorship, including descriptions of the island's many alleged attractions, for example, "the surrounding sea swarms with fish, which are as yet wholly unsuspicious of the hook".

Unfortunately for Harden-Hickey's fascist/fisherman's Utopia, the British government had already decided that the island would be useful for a cable-laying project and seized it in 1895, thus beginning a lengthy feud with Brazil. Neither Britain nor Brazil however paid any attention to the territorial claims of James Harden-Hickey. When the *New York Times* gave him some sympathetic coverage he awarded its editors the Cross of Trinidad and the promise of a pension. Suddenly, in January 1896 Britain withdrew from the tiny island, leaving the barren rock to Brazil who immediately claimed it for themselves. Harden-Hickey was furious over his loss, especially Britain's role in it, and quietly plotted an invasion of England via Ireland. Inconveniently, his coup required large sums of money. Harden-Hickey desperately tried to raise funds by selling his own ranch in Mexico, then fell into a deep depression. He checked into a hotel room in El Paso and on 9

February 1898 King James I of Trinidad retired to his room and overdosed with morphine.

The Ottoman Sultan Mahomet IV appointed an historian called Abdi to write a running biography of his reign. One evening the Sultan asked Abdi what he had written about him that day Abdi truthfully replied that he hadn't written anything; it had been rather a quiet day and nothing particularly noteworthy had happened. Mahomet casually picked up a hunting spear and ran it through the author. "Now," he told the dying Abdi, "thou has something to write about."

Czar Alexander of Russia, fêted throughout Europe as the great enlightened liberator who conquered Napoleon, became incestuously obsessed with his sister, the Grand Duchess Catherine Pavlovna, a petite woman with "eyes of fire and the figure of a demi-goddess". Alexander and his sister became almost inseparable, and when they were apart he showered her with passionate letters written in French. The affair ended abruptly around the time of Napoleon's retreat from Moscow when the Czar's life took another unexpected turn. He became involved with an obscure religious cult and surrounded himself with shadowy "priests". The Czar's death at the age of forty-seven was shrouded in mystery and myth. Some believed that Alexander faked his death and lived out the rest of his years as a religious mystic.

When Catherine the Great found out that she was suffering from dandruff she had her hairdresser locked in an iron cage for three years to prevent him from telling anyone else about it.

Alexander the Great, who conquered most of the known world, liked to dress as the goddess Artemis while he was riding around in his chariot.

The Shah of Persia Nasir Ud-din became well known to the British public in Victorian times for his visit to Buckingham Palace and his enormous moustaches. He once visited an English prison and when he was shown the gallows asked if he could see someone being hanged. He was politely informed that this would not be possible, as there was no one about to be executed. The Shah simply pointed to his entourage and offered, "Here, take one of my suite."

The Turkish Sultan Abdul Aziz once made a state visit to London where Queen Victoria grudgingly agreed to come out of retirement to greet her Crimean War ally. She invited the Sultan to Windsor, noting later in her diary that if he never came again it would be too soon. The Sultan was dazzled by the trappings of western European wealth and made some bizarre purchases. He ordered dozens of pianos which he intended to strap to the backs of his servants so that he could hear music wherever he walked, but which were never played because no one in the Turkish court knew how. He bought locomotives which never ran because he had no tracks to run them on, and several ironclad ships which never sailed.

Although the Sultan had soaked up a certain amount of western European culture, a return visit to Constantinople by the French Empress Eugenie demonstrated that the Turks still had much to learn about the etiquette of royal receptions. When the French imperial yacht L'Aigle approached the Bosphorus, a salute was fired by thirty Turkish cannon. Unfortunately the gunners had not been told to fire blank rounds at their guests, and the Empress Eugenie had to dive for cover as cannon balls rained down around her yacht. Her visit was made even more memorable by the Sultan's parting gift, a Turkish carpet fashioned from human hair, which made such an impression that it caused one of her ladies-in-waiting to faint.

When Aziz discovered that one of his employees was also named Aziz he passed a law which made it illegal for anyone else to share his second name – an act comparable to banning the surname Smith in England. He also developed a phobia about black ink and had every government document in existence rewritten in red.

The President of Uganda, Idi Amin, or to accord him his full title "Lord Of All The Beasts Of The Earth And Fishes Of The Sea And Conqueror Of The British Empire In Africa In General And Uganda In Particular", was a former heavyweight boxing champion of Uganda. In 1978 he planned a full-scale invasion of neighbouring Tanzania, but first decided to lull Tanzania's President Julius Nyerere into a false sense of security. He sent Nyerere a telegram which read, "I love you so much that if you were a woman I would consider marrying you."

When Amin's plan failed and he found his country being overrun by Tanzanian troops, he suggested that he and Nyerere settle the war between them in the ring with Muhammad Ali as referee.

One of Idi Amin's two favourite hobbies was erecting statues all over Uganda to his two greatest idols, Queen Victoria and Adolf Hitler. The other was crushing the genitals of his victims with his bare hands.

To mark the anniversary of his military coup in 1977, Amin invited the former Prime Minister Edward Heath to fly to Uganda "with his band" to play before him during the celebrations. Amin said he regretted that Mr Heath had been demoted to the obscure rank of bandleader, but noted that he'd heard that Mr Heath was one of the best bandleaders in Britain, and offered to assist the ex-PM with a supply of goats and chickens. By now the British were used to Amin's philanthropic gestures: he once offered to send a shipload of vegetables to England to solve the recession.

Amin once refused to attend the Commonwealth Games unless the Queen sent him a new pair of size 13 boots.

Before he became President of Haiti "Papa Doc" Duvalier spent two years in hiding from the government of the day dressed as a woman. When Papa Doc needed advice on matters of state he mostly got it by sitting in his bathtub wearing a a black top hat while consulting the entrails of a dead goat. He also claimed he could predict the future from late night conversations he had with a severed human head which he kept in a cupboard in the presidential palace. Papa Doc had the Lord's Prayer rewritten for use in Haitian schools:

Our Doc, who art in the National Palace for life, hallowed by Thy name by present and future generations. Thy will be done in Port-au-Prince as it is in the provinces. Give us this day our new Haiti, and forgive not the trespasses of those anti-patriots who daily spit upon our country . . .

When Papa Doc discovered that tourism in his country was down by 70 per cent, he was torn between his need for revenue and his natural mistrust of foreign troublemakers. He decided on a compromise. He launched a publicity drive to tempt the visitors back, then had the corpse of a dissident flown into the capital Port-au-Prince where it was left to rot in public: it was strategically placed by an exit from the airport next to a sign which read "Welcome to Haiti".

Benito Mussolini originally adopted the Roman-style straight-arm greeting as the fascist salute, later copied by Hitler, because of his irrational fear of germs. The Italian dictator thought that shaking hands with people was unclean.

The North Korean leader Kim Il Sung compelled the entire population of his country to wear lapel badges with his face on them and had every road in North Korea built with an extra lane for his sole private use.

The Russian Czar Peter the Great kept the head of one of his favourite former mistresses pickled in alcohol in a bedside jar.

The Czar also tried to pay for his almost perpetual war-making by imposing massive taxes on beards and bee-keeping.

The Ottoman Sultan Ahmed III (1673–1736) had such an obsession with tulips that the period of his reign became known in Turkish history as the Tulip Age. It began as a harmless hobby when Ahmed imported 1,200 different rare bulbs from Mongolia for his gardens. Each April the Sultan held a fantastic tulip fête, always on a moonlit night. Tulips in multi-coloured vases and jugs of coloured water were displayed on miles of shelving in the palace gardens, while turtles carrying candles on their backs wandered around the tulip beds. Guests were forbidden to wear clothes that didn't colour co-ordinate with the Sultan's tulips. Soon Turkey's ruling class, eager as always to imitate the Sultan, were competing with each other in the cultivation of tulips. The wealthiest men in Turkey ruined themselves financially in an effort to throw the best tulip parties. Horticultural tips were guarded as jealously as state secrets. Rare blooms became the currency of the rich and were used to bribe public officials. The Sultan's gardening fetish became such a massive drain on Turkey's economy that he was assassinated in a palace coup.

The Ottoman Empire's last Sultan was Mahomet V, who was allowed to rule nominally by the new Turkish civilian government but played no part in affairs of state and was in effect their prisoner. In 1909 the old Sultan had a royal visitor when the former French Empress Eugenie paid a visit to Constantinople. He watched her carefully as she sipped tea with him, then quickly snatched the cup from her hand the instant she had finished. He explained that his last European royal visitor, Leopold II, King of the Belgians, had pocketed a pipe after he had finished smoking it and he had no intention of being caught out twice.

Ghengis Khan killed his own brother in an argument over a fish.

Plennie Wingo, a 36-year-old former restaurant owner from Abilene, Texas, was, like most other people in the US, in the terrible grip of the Depression in 1931 when he suddenly resolved to do something about his predicament. He would achieve fame and fortune, he informed a few close friends, by walking around the world backwards. His friends were still laughing when Wingo began practising his backward locomotion and found himself falling over a lot. Luckily he spotted a magazine advertisement for sunglasses fitted with small rear-view mirrors, intended for motorcyclists. They were ideal for Wingo's purposes as well and he soon became highly skilled at walking backwards. He was confident that a sponsor, possibly a shoe manufacturer, would find such a trek irresistible. Wingo scoured first Abilene and then Fort Worth for backing, but no one signed up. None the less on 15 April 1931 the sponsorless Wingo put his best foot backward and set off from Fort Worth. He travelled light, carrying nothing but his coffee-wood walking stick and a sign round his neck reading "Around the World Backwards". In his pocket was a letter of introduction from the Fort Worth Chamber of Commerce and a Bible. He scraped together enough money to survive along the way selling postcards bearing his picture to people he met, many of whom invited him in for a meal or a night's rest. Wingo reversed through Dallas to Chicago, then eastward to Washington, DC. He reached Boston then backtracked to New York where he got a job on a freighter bound for Hamburg. Wingo resumed his backward journey in Germany and crossed eastern Europe to Turkey, where government officials refused him an entry visa, thus effectively ending his trip. On his way back to the United States Wingo accepted an offer of a ride to Santa Monica, California. He walked the 1,400 miles from Santa Monica to Fort Worth, striding backwards into town on 2 October 1932 to discover that his wife had divorced him *in absentia*. During his eighteen-month ordeal he had covered 8,000 miles and worn out thirteen pairs of unsponsored shoes.

The world record for walking backwards is now held by Marvin Staples, a Chippewa Indian from Minnesota, who took it up after seeing the Dustin Hoffman film *Little Big Man*, in which an Indian warrior has his life saved by Hoffman, a white man, and is so embarrassed that he vows to live his life in reverse until he can regain his honour in battle. Mr Staples credits walking backwards with a number of health benefits, claiming that he feels "years younger" and no longer suffers from chronic backache or arthritis in his knees.

The seventeenth-century Irish farmer Robert Cook wore nothing but white linen, a sartorial eccentricity so well known that he was famous throughout Ireland as "Linen Cook". It was not only his suits, coats, hats, shirts and underclothes that always had to be white. At his farm in County Waterford he refused to have any black cattle and even his horses were chosen for their colour – white. Cook was extremely health conscious and a vegetarian ahead of his time. He lived a long and healthy life, died in 1726, aged eighty, and was buried in a white linen shroud.

A Christian radio station in Vevay, Indiana was burgled and set ablaze in 1994. Police revealed that their prime suspect was a caller who had become irate when a DJ refused to play "Don't Take the Girl" by Tim McGraw. Twelve months later in Wanganui, New Zealand, a 21-year-old man who said he had a bomb took over the local STAR FM radio station, demanding to hear the song "Rainbow Connection" by Kermit the Frog.

Australian waitress Hannah Finlander was fired from her job in a restaurant in Perth in 1994, after a customer sent back his stew, complaining that there wasn't enough meat in it. She returned the dish with a dead mouse in it.

In 1989 Walter Scott Knieriemen admitted breaking into a woman's home in Wheeling, Vancouver, but was acquitted of burglary charges after a jury found that he acted without illegal intent. A psychiatrist testified that Knieriemen suffered from a sexual dysfunction that compelled him to follow a pair of leather gloves he had recently seen the woman wear.

In Giessen, Germany, Helga Briemer divorced her husband Rolf after six months of sleepless nights. She cited problems caused by his nocturnal cravings for large quantities of crunchy celery.

The American millionaire James Buchanan Brady – Diamond Jim, as he was better known – was an ostentatious bon vivant who followed a simple rule: "If you're going to make money, you have to look like money." Brady built up his fortune by selling railroad equipment and was regarded by many at the end of the nineteenth century as America's greatest salesman. In New York he kept a collection of twelve gold-plated bicycles and on his New Jersey farm his cows were milked into gold buckets. He owned at least 200 tailored suits and was always bejewelled with diamonds, rubies, emeralds and sapphires. His favourite diamond ring and scarfpin, each set with a single stone, together amounted to fifty-eight carats. He gave away an estimated $2 million in baubles to female companions. His long-standing girlfriend was actress and singer Lillian Russet. He gave her a bicycle with handlebars covered with mother of pearl and spokes garnished with rubies and sapphires. His own collection of jewellery was conservatively estimated to be worth $2 million.

His favourite hobby, however, was gluttony. Diamond Jim was a regular at the New York restaurant Charles Rector's, an exclusive establishment on Broadway. The owner described Diamond Jim as his "best twenty-five customers". Although he never drank wine, spirits or coffee, he swigged vast amounts of orange juice. He would down three dozen oysters for a mid-morning snack, followed by luncheon comprising two broiled lobsters, devilled crabs, steak, more oysters, a fruit pie and a large box of chocolates. The usual evening meal began with an appetizer of two or three dozen oysters, six crabs, and a few servings of green turtle soup. The main course comprised two whole ducks, six or seven lobsters, a sirloin steak, two servings of terrapin and a variety of vegetables. He finished with a platter of pastries and often a 2lb box of chocolates. Brady boasted, "Whenever I sit down to a meal I make a point to leave just four inches between my stomach and the edge of the table, and then, when I can feel them rubbing together pretty hard, I know I've had enough." He was particularly fond of chocolate. In Boston, Brady visited a small manufacturer of chocolates and requested several hundred boxes to send as gifts to friends and business associates, but was informed that that amount of chocolate would seriously deplete their stock. He simply took out his chequebook and gave them a $150,000 advance towards the construction of a bigger chocolate factory.

In 1994 three council employees in the town of Cartago, Colombia nailed themselves to wooden crosses with five-inch nails. They were reinforcing their demands for a salary increase and additional perks.

In 1994 in La Paz, Bolivia, Maria Vasquez lost her cool when customer Luis Gomez complained that he had observed her sneezing in his soup as she was serving it. The waitress forced him to eat it at gunpoint.

No one has ever been quite sure whether the eighteenth-century US entrepreneur "Lord" Timothy Dexter was a brilliant businessman or whether he was a madman who survived through sheer luck. Dexter was born into a poor Massachusetts family in 1747 and went to work on a farm at the age of nine. He was apprenticed to a leatherworker in South Carolina at sixteen, received virtually no education and finally escaped from his apprenticeship, illiterate, when he was twenty-two. He settled in Newburyport, Massachusetts and in 1769 married a widow with four children and set up a leather shop. By the time America had won independence from Britain, Dexter had saved several thousand gold dollars, which he used to buy up the almost worthless Continental dollars that had been issued during the war. The investment appeared to be financial suicide until America's first treasury secretary Alexander Hamilton persuaded Congress to back the Continental currency by establishing a national bank. Suddenly, Dexter was a rich man. In the years that followed he added to his fortune by a variety of equally unlikely transactions. He sold cats to the topics, where they were needed to control mice, and sold thousands of bed warming pans to molasses makers in the tropical West Indies. He even sent Virginia coal to Newcastle, England and made an enormous profit because the miners were on strike.

Dexter was socially ambitious. He bought himself one of the biggest houses in Newburyport, where the former leatherworker was sneered at by the snobbish locals. He offered to pave the main street through town on condition the name was changed to Dexter Street, and to erect a large municipal market building to be called Dexter Hall. Both proposals were dismissed. Frustrated by the snub, Dexter took to drinking heavily and began to behave very oddly. He began referring to Elizabeth, his wife, as a ghost and pointedly ignored her. He once took a shot at a passer-by who was looking at his house, for which he spent two months in prison. In 1798 Dexter briefly left Newburyport for Chester, New Hampshire, a less wealthy community only too happy to acquire a rich resident, but returned to Newburyport a year later and bought himself an even bigger mansion. He claimed that while he was away New Hampshire had made him a lord – "the first lord in America". He had accepted this title reluctantly, he explained, only because it had been thrust upon him by the "voice of the people". In keeping with his new-found aristocratic status he hired his own poet laureate, a former local fish salesman, who was paid to compose such verse as:

> Lord Dexter is a man of fame
> Most celebrated is his name
> More precious far than gold that's pure
> Lord Dexter shines forevermore.

Dexter commissioned a local craftsman to carve a series of forty huge wooden figures depicting history's greatest personages. The carvings, completed in just over a year, and placed around the grounds of the mansion, included King Louis XVI, Adam and Eve, Aaron Burr, Benjamin Franklin, the Emperor of China, a piece representing Motherly Love and two statues of Lord Timothy Dexter, one marked with the inscription, "I am the first in the East, the first in the West" and the other with "I am the Greatest Philosopher in the Western World". Dexter published a rambling autobiography outlining his world political plan, *A Pickle for the Knowing Ones, or Plain Truths in a Homespun Dress.* When it was pointed out to him that the text contained not a single punctuation mark, Lord Dexter obliged by adding to the end of subsequent editions of the book a pageful of commas, full stops, question marks and semi-colons.

He stage-managed a rehearsal of his own elaborate funeral, complete with the lowering of an empty coffin into the ground, to see if people would mourn him properly. His long-suffering "ghost" wife did not apparently display sufficient signs of grief, so he beat her. Dexter died for real in 1806 at the age of fifty-nine. The forty statues stood until 1815 when a storm destroyed most of them. A few were sold for a small sum and the remainder, including those of Lord Dexter, were burned.

The Greek philosopher Diogenes demonstrated his contempt for comfort by living in a bathtub.

In Perth, Australia in 1994 street trader Igor Roskny was beaten to death by an irate customer because he put mustard on his tuna sandwich by mistake. The murderer complained that he had clearly requested mayonnaise.

Jemmy Hirst, a tanner from Rawcliffe in Yorkshire, made a large fortune from selling farming produce. He was also a natural showman; he rode a bull named Jupiter and wore a lambskin hat with a nine-foot rim. His carriage was fitted with sails and equipped with a wine cellar and a double bed. Hirst's eccentricity eventually made him so famous that he was invited to meet King George III. To the absolute horror of all his friends Hirst wrote back to the king to explain that he was going to be too busy to visit for the next couple of months or so as he was teaching an otter to fish. In 1824 he created his own

"Bank of Rawcliffe" and began issuing banknotes in denominations of "five half pence". Hirst also collected coffins. When he died aged ninety he left instructions that his own should be carried to his grave by eight old maids marching to the sound of bagpipes and fiddles.

Orville Wright (1871–1948) numbered the eggs that his chickens produced so he could eat them in the precise order they were laid. He also had a morbid fear of public appearances. When President Franklin Roosevelt went to Wright's home town, Dayton, Ohio, to campaign for re-election, Orville was invited to lunch with him. He could hardly refuse the invitation, but later when he found himself in the back of the President's touring car, being driven though cheering crowds, at the first opportunity he hopped out, thanked the President for lunch, then walked home.

Fifty-nine-year old German Jost-Burkhard Anderhub spent several days in prison in Newport, Kentucky before pleading guilty to a federal gun charge. He was so impressed with the service that he later sent the jailer a $200 tip. The accompanying thank you note explained, "The treatment by the officers was absolutely flawless."

As every British schoolboy should know, the Great Fire of London began on a very windy night, 2 September 1666, in a City bakery in Pudding Lane. Even one of the most famous

events in British history however was not about to faze
London's laconic Lord Mayor, Sir Thomas Bloodworth, not
a man to be disturbed in his sleep. When he was awoken in the
early hours of the morning and told about it, he said, "Pish. A
woman might piss it out."

Thomas Rawlinson, the nineteenth-century bibliomaniac,
filled his rooms at Gray's Inn so full of books that he was
forced to sleep in a passage.

The Regency dandy Henry Cope was known as "the green man
of Brighton". A local journalist recorded that he always wore
"green pantaloons, green waistcoat, green frock coat, green
cravat, and though his ears, whiskers, eyebrows and chin were
powdered, his countenance, no doubt from the reflection of his
clothes, was also green. He ate nothing but green fruits and
vegetables, had his rooms painted green, and furnished with
green sofa, green chairs, green table, green bed and green
curtains. His gig, his livery, his portmanteau, his gloves and his
whip were all green. With a green silk handkerchief in his hand,
and a large watch-chain with green seals fastened to the green
buttons of his green waistcoat, he paraded every day on the
Steyne." The local newspaper went on to note: "The Green
Man continues daily to amuse the Steyne promenaders with his
eccentricities." There was however a grave footnote. In 1806
the Green Man jumped out of the window of his lodgings on
Brighton's South Parade, ran across the road and threw himself
off the cliff opposite. He survived the drop, but as the *Journal*
recorded: "Mr Cope, the Green Man, is pronounced out of

danger from his bruises; but his intellects have continued so impaired as to render a strait waistcoat necessary."

One of the less successful inventions lodged at the British Patents Office was a device for flushing out the Loch Ness monster with a series of electric shocks.

George "Beau" Brummell, the most famous Regency dandy of all, was considered highly eccentric because he had a wash before dressing. Ironically, Brummell was the grandson of a humble valet. His family rose in social status thanks to the efforts of Brummell's father William, a government clerk who married a wealthy heiress and eventually became private secretary to the Prime Minister Lord North. Brummell Senior made enough money to send young Beau to Eton and Oxford, where he acquired a taste for high living. Thanks to his friendship with the Prince of Wales, Brummell was given a much-prized army commission in the 10th Light Dragoons. He managed to keep his uniform in prime condition by skilfully avoiding any contact with soldiering. Though he looked good in Hussar uniform, he was not a good officer. Most of all he hated being away from the fashion centres of London and Brighton. The last straw seemed to be when his regiment was ordered to Manchester. "I really could not go!" he told the Prince. "Think, your Royal Highness, Manchester!"

His reputation began after he bought himself out of the army to concentrate on his career as a Regency fashion victim. Brummell was not particularly handsome. His portraits show him with sandy hair and thick pouting lips. When he made his debut in London, it was the fashion for men to be very overdressed and extremely smelly. It was not thought necessary to wash before putting on lace-edged finery. Brummell did exactly the opposite. His clothes were simple and well cut, and it took him two hours to wash. After shaving he would pluck out any offending hair with a pair of silver tweezers. Before dressing he scrubbed his whole body with a stiff brush until he was "red as a lobster". He never wore perfume, preferring to change his shirt three times a day, and sent his linen to be laundered in the country so that it should "smell of new-mown hay". Brummell's laundry bills were the biggest in London. He lived for the art of dressing. He made the cravat his trademark; it created a sensation when he first wore it. One speck of dirt or a crease and the cravat was cast aside and the painstaking ritual of tying it would begin again. The floor of his dressing room was often littered ankle-deep with yards of discarded material. His long-suffering valet explained, "These are our failures." He had three people to make his gloves, one of them specializing in the thumb alone. Brummell was so obsessed with his appearance that he ordered his valet to polish his shoes, including the soles, with champagne froth.

Brummell would not leave his house until he considered he was groomed to perfection. Rather than risk dirtying his shoes, he had his sedan chair carried indoors so he didn't have to step outside to board it. He never raised his hat to a lady in case he failed to replace it at precisely the right angle. At mealtimes he never turned his head to talk for fear of creasing his cravat. One weekend he went to stay at a country house and a friend asked whether he had enjoyed himself. "Don't ask me, my dear fellow," groaned Brummell. "I actually found a cobweb in my night pot." After this Brummell travelled with a folding chamberpot in a mahogany case.

Brummell became such a fashion icon that the Prince of

Wales would call at Brummell's home in Chesterfield Street just to watch him dress. He wielded great influence over the prince, whom he called "Prinny", and over the fashions of his court. Once when Brummell told the prince that he did not like the cut of his coat, Prinny burst into tears. Brummell was immensely popular with women, but his sexuality was an enigma; it is likely that he remained celibate all his life. He hated vegetables, and one relationship ended abruptly: "What could I do?" he complained. "I discovered that Lady Mary actually ate cabbage."

Eighteen years of rubbing shoulders with royalty meant that Brummell could get away with criticizing the Prince of Wales's dress sense, but he pushed his luck too far when he encountered the prince with a friend, Lord Alvanley, and fired off his famous salvo, "Ah, Alvanley, who's your fat friend?" The prince never spoke to Brummell again, and he died, in poverty, in Caen lunatic asylum in 1840, aged sixty-two.

Two Brazilians, Waldir de Souza and Maria de Conceicao, murdered six children in Cantigulo in 1979, including a two-year-old boy. They confessed that the killings were ritual sacrifices to ensure success in their new cement business.

Henry Ford I took to eating weed sandwiches every day when he heard that the American scientist George Washington Grover did the same.

Excesses in the appetite department have been met with astonishment since ancient times. Astydamus the Milesian Olympic athlete was once invited to a banquet for nine people and ate the ration for the entire party. Milo the Crotonian wrestler bore an ox on his shoulders for a furlong, then ate it. The Roman Emperor Claudius Albinus was extraordinary, for he was a vegetarian glutton. He was reported to have eaten for breakfast "as many apples as no man would believe, 500 Greek figs, 10 melons, 20 lbs of grapes, 100 gnat-snappers, and 400 oysters".

The presence of royalty can do strange things to intelligent men. Consider the plight of Sir Peter Scott, probably the world's greatest twentieth-century conservationist. Prince Bernhardt, husband of the Queen of the Netherlands Juliana, shared the Duke of Edinburgh's professed interest in the preservation of wildlife. In 1970 Queen Juliana and her consort arrived at a dinner on behalf of the World Wildlife Fund, the Queen ostentatiously wearing a huge red fox fur stole. Peter Scott, in a desperate attempt to rescue the tricky situation, explained that the Queen had not after all committed a gaffe. "It is only slightly anti-wildlife", he told the press, "because these species are in no danger of extinction."

The de rigueur fashion item for both men and women in the eighteenth century was a set of mouseskin eyebrows stuck on with fish glue.

The most bizarre American mail order con of all time began in 1946 and lasted for a decade. William Johnson, a semi-literate miner from Kentucky, cashed in on a rumour sweeping North America that Adolf Hitler had been smuggled out of Europe after World War II and was alive and well and living in the US. Johnson posed as the Führer, who was now settled in Kentucky with some of his Nazi chiefs of staff and was planning to take over the US. He made a public appeal for cash to help his cause, and right-wing Americans and fascists of German extraction sent him a steady stream of postal orders as he elaborated on his dastardly plans for space ships, "invisible ships" and underground hoards of ammunition. The fact that Johnson often signed as his name as "the Furrier" didn't prevent the American public from sending him tens of thousand of dollars.

Kevin Record, twenty-eight, was convicted in 1994 for killing his father with a chainsaw in Brattleboro, Vermont. Upon sentencing, when asked by the judge if he had any regrets Record replied, "One – that I wasn't able to take the chainsaw to the rest of my family."

Foot fetishists Steven Bain, twenty-seven, and Steven Gawthrop, thirty-one, were sentenced to eighteen months in prison after tricking thousands of people into giving up socks, claiming they were collecting for a charity. Police found the floor of the men's Liverpool apartment eighteen inches deep in socks. Another 2,000 pairs were found wrapped in sandwich bags, each labelled with the donor's name.

In 1984 a set of bones belonging to a missing nineteen-year-old, Carlos Sanchez, were discovered beneath a Buenos Aires building which was used by devil worshippers. The occupants explained that they had phoned an order for pizzas, but after an interminable delay had decided to eat the delivery boy instead.

A handkerchief dropped at a holdup scene led a Wells Fargo detective to discover the identity of "Black Bart", an eccentric bandit who had been terrorizing his stagecoach line for two years. Black Bart turned out to be a shy and retiring bank clerk named Charles E. Bolton, a man not believed by anyone who knew him to be given to violence in any form. Bolton picked exclusively on the Wells Fargo company and as a calling card he often left terrible poems. Sample:

> I've laboured long and hard for bread
> For honour and for riches
> But on my corns too long you've trod,
> You fine-haired sons of bitches.

Upon his release from San Quentin in 1888, the warden asked Bolton if he had given up his life of crime. "Yes," said Bolton, "I have." "Are you going to write any more poetry?" asked the warden. Bolton replied, "I told you I wasn't going to commit any more crimes."

In Xiantao, China in 1992 a teacher was imprisoned for two years for punishing children who had failed to do their homework by forcing them to eat cow dung.

In 1994 in New Jersey a man was arrested for shooting his computer. He complained that he had not committed an offence, and did not see why he should not be able to shoot his computer in the privacy of his own home. Local police said they would have had a more tolerant view of the incident, except that he fired illegal hollow-nose bullets from an unregistered weapon.

In 1994 Kostas Tsenkides, twenty-four, was arrested for hijacking an Olympic Airlines jet, threatening to blow the plane up unless it made a forced landing. In his defence, Tsenkides said that he had inhaled a crucifix shortly after take-off and had simply panicked when it became lodged in his throat.

In Toronto in 1993 Michael Wrightman, thirty, admitted beating David Marlatt to death, after an argument got out of hand over which of them had the longer criminal record.

In 1994 Thai businessman Chan Ka Sek walked into a Bangkok karaoke bar with his two bodyguards and spent the next three hours at the microphone, treating fellow customers to "Candle in the Wind" four times. When an irate customer complained that Sek was hogging the microphone, one of the bodyguards shot him dead. Sek confessed, "We were carried away by the beauty of my voice."

In 1998 Vickie Lemon was leaving Kohl's Food Store when she was assaulted in the supermarket car park by a man with a pocket knife who sliced off part of her nose. He said he became angry when he observed her going through the express check-out lane with more than the maximum ten items.

In January 1995 an Egyptian threw his wife from the window of their second floor Cairo flat because his dinner wasn't ready.

Brenda Hunter, of Zion, Illinois, shot her brother in 1994 because she disliked the type of cheese he was putting on their chilli dinner.

Heinrich Gembach of Munich choked his wife to death in 1995 by force-feeding her wheat cereal. He told police that this was what she had given him for breakfast every morning for the last ten years.

In 1994 Peter Weiller, a German filmgoer, was beaten to death by ushers in a Bonn cinema because he had brought his own popcorn.

Noël Carriou murdered both of his wives because they were poor cooks. He was sentenced to eight years in jail in 1978 after killing his second wife for cooking him an overdone roast. Seventeen years earlier he broke his first wife's neck after she served him an undercooked meal. In passing sentence the judge sympathized with the 54-year-old Frenchman: good cooking, he agreed, was an important part of married life.

In March 1983 the Danish hair-fetishist Luigi Longhi was jailed for life after he was found guilty of kidnapping, then murdering, a West German girl hitch-hiker. Longhi admitted that before strangling her he had washed her hair four times.

On 10 December 1898 the Empress Elizabeth, wife of Austria's Emperor Franz Josef, was assassinated on a quayside in Geneva by a 26-year-old Italian builder's labourer, Luigi Lenchini, who stabbed her through the heart. Lenchini later explained that he had nothing whatsoever against the Empress: he had really wanted to kill King Umberto of Italy, but couldn't afford the extra fifty lire he needed to travel to Rome.

Halfway through divorce proceedings, Xu Cheng-shun, an actor with a Beijing opera troupe in Shanghai, surprised his estranged wife by leaping at her in the courtroom and biting off her nose. He explained that this action had been a noble attempt to save his marriage, because if she was disfigured nobody else would want her.

In 1992 Richard Dickinson from Hobart, Tasmania was allowed prison leave, accompanied by two wardens, to attend a concert by his idol, Bob Dylan. Dickinson was in the fifth year of a life sentence after kicking his mother to death to the tune of Dylan's song "One More Cup of Coffee for the Road". She apparently told him to turn down the music.

Edgar Cayce (1877–1945) was an American Nostradamus known as "the sleeping prophet" because of his habit of going into a trance to predict the future or heal the sick. His followers, the Association for Research and Enlightenment, keep the great man's memory alive from their base at his former home in Virginia. Although Cayce's track record on the predictions front was generally so erratic that he was obliged to keep up his day job selling photographic supplies, he had one notable success just before the 1929 Wall Street Crash when he advised a client against investing in the stock market because he saw "a downward movement of long duration". Cayce is also credited with predicting World Wars I & II, the independence of India, the creation of the state of Israel and the assassination of President Kennedy. He also foresaw the fall of communism in China, the disappearance of California into the sea in 1969, and that Christ would return after World War III in 1999. In the year 2000, Cayce predicted, the earth's axis will shift and mankind will be destroyed by flooding and earthquakes.

In 1996, Philip Johnson, thirty-two, was hospitalized after shooting himself in the left shoulder with his .22-calibre rifle "to see how it felt". Twelve months later an ambulance crew was again called to Johnson's home, where he was bleeding from another left-shoulder gunshot. According to the local newspaper, Johnson said the earlier shooting felt so good he had to do it again.

Fifty-seven-year-old Monique Bazile lost her job in Irvington, New Jersey for conduct deemed inappropriate in a high school teacher. While attempting to subdue a class of rowdy thirteen-year-olds, she began "shaking and chanting" while waving a crucifix at them, threw powder on them and told them that their souls were going to hell. She also added that she would be around later to burn their houses down.

In 1896, riding a wave of American interest in the exciting new technology offered by X-ray equipment, enterprising X-Ray machine salesman Herbert Hawks set himself up in a busy shopping precinct and focused rays on his head so that passers-by could see his jawbone on a screen. He stopped doing it after a few days when he lost his hair, eyebrows and eyelashes, his eyesight deteriorated, his gums bled, his fingernails stopped growing and the skin peeled off his chest.

At Harvard College, Boston in 1939, student Lothrop Withington Junior swallowed a live goldfish to win a ten-dollar bet, thus sparking a nationwide craze. Throughout the spring of 1939 the US goldfish population nosedived as students all over the country vied to outdo each other in the consumption of finny comestibles. An unofficial record for goldfish swallowing was established – forty-three in one sitting – although the teenager who accomplished this was kicked out of his school for "conduct unbecoming a student".

Every day for eighteen years the elusive and probably late Lord Lucan ate grilled lamb cutlets for lunch.

The CIA has to date spent millions of US taxpayers' dollars on a series of experiments, including training cats to carry bombs, employing otters to plant underwater explosives, and research into whether or not plants can be used to spy on people.

Exhibits at the first Great Exhibition in Hyde Park included an "alarm bed" which catapulted the sleeper bodily across the room at a chosen hour, and a physician's walking stick whose handle doubled as an enema.

In 1959 Bertha Dlugi of Milwaukee became the first and only person to realize the major commercial possibilities of the bird nappy, allowed pet birds to fly freely around the house without depositing droppings.

This impressive invention was alas too late for King George V, who was renowned for his cheerful tolerance of his pet parrot, which roamed and soiled the royal residence at will. Whenever the parrot deposited faeces on the dinner table, the king would simply slide a mustard pot over the mess.

It was once common for German farmers to stack piles of excrement – animal and human – in front of their farms and dwellings. The size of his pile was the farmer's way of showing off to his neighbours that he had loads of livestock and could afford a huge family.

In the 1960s the American Society for Indecency to Naked Animals (sic) claimed a membership of 50,000 people who were dedicated to forcing animals to wear clothes for the sake of decency. The society's president Clifford Prout asserted that his pressure group was so strong that within a few years it would be normal to see dogs and cats wearing trousers. In 1963 they picketed the White House in an attempt to make Jackie Kennedy clothe her horse. Mr Prout explained that the Society's misleading name was due to an unfortunate grammatical error which could not now be changed for financial reasons.

In Trumbull County Jail, Ohio, a 33-year-old inmate Lisa Layne was separated from other inmates in 1994. The *Youngstown Vindicator* reported that this had become necessary because of her habit of removing her clothes and smearing faeces over her body. She said she did this for religious reasons.

Connecticut housewife Norma Jean Bryant lives with an avalanche of household garbage comprising everything she has ever owned. Her collection is so vast that it is now housed in a vast disused opera house. As she likes to be surrounded by her belongings at all times, she never goes out without a supermarket trolley, specially fitted with headlights, filled with a few of her treasures. Ms Bryant is also a committed Anglophile. Every summer, during the Wimbledon lawn tennis championships, she throws a garden party, serving strawberries and ice cream, dressed as a member of the British royal family.

Sixty-eight-year-old Wilmetta Billington of Illinois used to be North America's most obsessive collector of household waste, until 1996 when she was smothered to death after stumbling and falling into her rubbish. The room was so full of trash that it took twenty minutes to recover her body from the debris.

In 1995 artists in Lviv, Ukraine formed the International Masoch Fund to honour the centenary of the death of the city's most famous son, Leopold von Sacher-Masoch, who gave his name to masochism – pleasure from being abused. They were however unsuccessful in their attempts to persuade the United Nations to name 1995 "the year of Masoch".

In 1993 Californian high school biology teacher David Hanley was ordered to cease his practice of eating live, newborn mice in front of his classes to demonstrate that food is a cultural choice.

In 1995 Rob Watkins, thirty-five, of Odessa, Ontario claimed to have eaten 10,000 Kraft macaroni and cheese dinners over his lifetime, including many days when he ate Kraft macaroni and cheese for breakfast, lunch and supper, adding, "I don't consider it an addiction."

Malicious phone caller Martin Schuss was arrested in New York City in 1993 after making dozens of calls to the LaGuardia Airport control tower. He accused air traffic controllers of having a vendetta against him and deliberately routing planes over his home.

In Washington, DC Anoki P. Sultan sued Roman Catholic Archbishop James Hickey, claiming that the Church was responsible for the devil's having taking over his body in 1983. Sultan blamed the devil for putting him out of work, making him drop out of college, and his needing mental-health treatment, smoking cigarettes, speaking in tongues, and engaging in homosexual acts. He claimed either $100 million in damages or an exorcism. The suit was dismissed.

One of the early American folk heroes John Chapman (1768–1847), born in Springfield, Massachusetts, was widely known as "Johnny Appleseed", thanks to his obsession with apples. Chapman spent his entire life travelling throughout North America planting countless thousands of apple trees over an area of about 100,000 square miles. He was described as "wiry with long, dark hair and a scanty beard that was never shaved, and keen black eyes that sparkled with a peculiar brightness". He dressed in old coffee sacks with holes cut for his arms and legs, and always travelled barefoot except in extreme cold. Chapman was revered by everyone, including native Indians who believed he was guided by holy spirits.

In Stuttgart, Germany, Wilhelm Schulz demanded a divorce when his 37-year-old wife Anna insisted that her male psychoanalyst shared their marital bed. She said that it was so he could interpret anything Wilhelm said in his sleep.

The anti-royalist John Bigg was a wealthy scholar and private secretary to one of the judges who passed sentence on King Charles I during the English Civil War. When the monarchy was restored under Charles II, Bigg withdrew from the world in protest. For the next thirty years he lived in complete isolation as the Hermit of Dinton, and spent his time sewing thousands of scraps of leather on to his clothing.

John Thrift was probably the most inappropriate person ever to have held the position of London's chief executioner. Thrift was an eighteenth-century convicted murderer, pardoned on condition that he did the government's dirty work as an axeman. He was desperately unsuited to the job: he was highly strung, hopeless with the axe, and liable to burst into tears at the most inopportune moments – just before he removed a head, for example. His most serious limitation however was that he couldn't stand the sight of blood. When he was called upon to execute the Jacobite rebel Lord Balmerino at the Tower of London in 1745, he fainted, then lay on the ground sobbing while onlookers tried to persuade him to get on with it. When Thrift finally took up his axe, he took five blows to sever Lord Balmerino's head. Thrift never quite got the hang of it, although he somehow managed to blunder and hack his way through a seventeen-year career. He was widely hated by the public for his clumsiness, and when he died in 1752 a jeering mob pelted his coffin and his pall-bearers with stones and the rotting bodies of dead cats.

In 1914 Natalie Stolp from Philadelphia patented a device to discourage men from rubbing their thighs up against ladies in crowded trains. Her spring-loaded undergarment responded to unwanted male pressure by releasing a metal spike into the offender's thigh.

The founder of the Ford Motor Company Henry Ford always washed his hair in water containing rusty razor blades because he believed that rusty water was a hair restorer.

A 22-year-old Dutchman went on the rampage causing £30,000 damage to a barbershop in Hengelo in 1993, apparently upset because the barber had enthusiastically misinterpreted his request for "a slight trim".

The US Society for Prevention of Cruelty to Mushrooms has 300 members dedicated to the protection of poisonous and edible mushrooms from abuse. President Brad Brown says that the remit of the society also extends to protecting vegetables, "and any other neglected or mistreated forms of life, regardless of age, race, sex, religion or other stereotypical attributes".

The Gloucester branch of Depressives Anonymous banned several people in 1991 because they weren't depressing enough. Group chairman John Hooper explained why cheerful people had been excluded. "We did not foresee that the group itself would develop its own severe personality problem. Those with sensitive tender feelings have been put off by more robust members who have not always been depressives."

In 1997 a Danish taxi driver Jorgan Gilberg took a booking from an elderly man for a 7,600-mile round trip from Copenhagen to the Vatican – total cost £2,500. When they arrived in Rome the passenger asked the driver to wait while he nipped into the Vatican to collect the fare from the Pope, who apparently owed him £4,400. The passenger later conceded that he may have been misled by voices in his head.

Dale Elder, twenty-two, walked into a police station in Columbus, Ohio with a length of wire protruding from his forehead and informed the desk officer, "I think I need an X-ray. I want to make sure I have a brain." Elder then pulled another three inches of wire from the bleeding hole in his head before police handcuffed him. He was removed to a local hospital, where doctors removed the rest of the wire. Elder had apparently drilled the hole in his head and slid the wire inside in an elaborate attempt to evade a court appearance on a drink-drive charge.

A German, Ernst Horst, spoke an average three and a half words a day to his wife, Suzanne. At their divorce hearing she agreed that they never rowed because he hardly ever spoke. She kept a diary of his utterances, of which the longest ever recorded was, "This coffee tastes like dishwater." When she asked for a divorce, he replied, "I agree."

Francine Wickerman of North Dakota spent thirty years in a bomb shelter, convinced by her jealous husband the world had been destroyed by nuclear war.

During his divorce hearing in Cologne in 1995 a Frenchman was found to have concealed within his trousers a Japanese ceremonial sword with a three-foot blade. He told the court he was planning to use it to make sandwiches if there was a long delay before his case came up.

Retired schoolteacher Mildred Sherrer was 1998 winner of America's Most Boring Hobby contest. She collects caps from vinegar bottles and has over 2,000 identical caps from the same brand of vinegar.

Nineteen-year-old Lisa Collins tried to commit suicide by jumping off the Tacoma Narrows Bridge in Tacoma on 23 June 1983. Instead of achieving fame as the span's fiftieth suicide, however, she became the first to survive the plunge.

Charles Vance Millar, a Canadian lawyer, died a bachelor in 1926. Millar left the bulk of his estate to whichever Toronto woman gave birth to the largest number of children in the ten years after his death. Four women tied, with nine children each.

When the wealthy Englishman Henry Budd died in 1862 he left an estate to each of his two sons on the condition that they did not wear moustaches. Moustachioed Walt Disney hated beards so much that he would not allow bearded men to work for him. Margaret Thatcher wouldn't allow bearded men into her cabinet.

The identity of the mysterious "old leather man" was never known to the people who regularly saw him trudging along the rural roads of nineteenth-century Connecticut and New York. Always clad in the same home-made leather outfit, for thirty years he doggedly followed a circuit of some 365 miles and 34 days. The northernmost point on his journey was Harwinton, Connecticut. From there he regularly headed south-east through Burlington, Forestville, Southington, and several other towns. He traversed a corner of Middletown and then followed the Connecticut River to its mouth at Saybrook. Then he turned west through Westbrook and several other communities to Guilford. He skirted the city of New Haven and again reached the coast in Milford. He travelled down the coast through Stratford, northern Bridgeport, Fairfield, and Westport, then headed north to Wilton and west into New York. He completed his circuit in Harwinton.

The laconic mystery man became something of a celebrity. Farmers and villagers along his route joked that people set their clocks by him. He made regular stops at houses of his choosing, and when he knocked on the kitchen door, he made it clear with a gesture or a grunt that he wanted nothing but a meal and perhaps a bit of tobacco. He divulged nothing about himself, not even his name. Even after years of stopping at one house, the Leather Man's conversation was limited to the statement, "Piece to eat." What few words he uttered were in broken English. From the first sighting of the Leather Man the late 1850s, he always wore a voluminous patchwork coat and trousers made of leather scraps held together by thongs; a visored cap; and wooden-soled boots. A large leather bag was slung from his shoulder. People were afraid of him at first and parents occasionally used him as a bogeyman to keep rowdy children in line. Eager for some shred of information about him, villagers sometimes invited him to join them at an inn, hoping that alcohol might loosen his tongue. He occasionally accepted these invitations but after a couple of beers he would take leave of his disappointed audience in silence. Since people had no real information about him he was the subject of endless speculation. One popular theory held that he was doing penance for some terrible crime, like the Christian hermits of old. The Leather Man made the news in December 1888, when he ran away from a Hartford, Connecticut hospital where he had been taken for examination of a cancerous lip.

Afterwards a local newspaper asserted that the Leather Man's name was Jules Bourglay and that he was French. The story went that he had emigrated to the United States after a heartbreak in Lyons. Bourglay apparently fell in love with a French girl, the daughter of a wealthy leather merchant. The father did not consider Bourglay a suitable match, but agreed to give him a chance to prove himself in the family business. Bourglay quickly learned the leather business and the merchant put him in charge of his company's investments. Bourglay's luck ran out when he invested heavily in leather just before the market crashed. The angry merchant forbade the marriage. The heartbroken Bourglay wandered the streets of Lyons until eventually the French authorities confined him to a monastery, from where he eventually escaped and made his way to the United States. Once in the US, Bourglay again took up his habit of wandering. This story, however, and the various versions of it that began to circulate, may have been romantic fiction. When he died of cancer in March 1889 his collection of belongings was examined, but no clues to his true identity were found.

Chapter Sixteen

Wizards of Odd

"What dreadful work cutting grass is, with scissors. 90 feet by 12, say. Hard on the back, very."
Oliver Heaviside (1850–1925)

"Thank God for eccentrics. Take Gunner Octavian Neat. He would suddenly appear naked in a barrack room and say, "Does anybody know a good tailor?' "
– Spike Milligan, (1919–)

The British scientist Bertie Blount, known to his friends as "the Colonel", spent the Second World War working for the government's undercover "dirty tricks" department, the special operations executive (SOE). Blount was required to invent ingenious methods of assassination, including one to kill Hitler using anthrax, and known as Operation Foxley. The devilish plan was hatched in December 1944. Blount pondered ways of hiding the lethal agent: he suggested the assassin could wear glasses or false teeth, or perhaps should have a ."physical peculiarity such as wearing a truss or a false limb". He also advised, "Guns and hypodermic syringes disguised as fountain pens are usually not a bit convincing and are likely to lead to the death of the operator before he has had any opportunity of making his attack". Blount was also president of the International Institute of Refrigeration. However, he spent many years without a refrigerator, until it was pointed out to him that this was probably why his milk turned sour.

In October 1999 three men were put on trial in Texas, accused of conspiring to assassinate US President Bill Clinton with a cactus. The three men – members of a group fighting for an independent Texas – planned to infect the cactus thorns with the AIDS virus and shoot the spikes at the president using a modified cigarette-lighter.

The third week in October is National Deep Scalp Itch Prevention Week in the United States. There was, however, a conflict of interests on Thursday 23 October; it clashed with National Drainage and Seepage Law Day.

The irascible seventeenth century Puritan William Prynne was one of the few authors to have his ears cut off twice. The argumentative Prynne's lobes were partly removed in 1630 when he wrote a pamphlet denouncing the theatre as immoral, unaware that the Queen was quite keen on amateur dramatics. He lost the remainder in 1634 after he wrote something quite rude about the Bishop of Norwich.

The ancient Russell family, Dukes of Bedford, produced one prime minister in Lord John Russell, one great philosopher in Bertrand Russell and a host of oddballs. The 3rd Duke of Bedford, said to be weak in the head, was easy prey for every gambler in London. He became a laughing stock after losing almost a quarter of a million pounds in one evening – at the time a record gambling debt. Mostly, however, the Bedfords were miserly misanthropes. The Duchess of Bedford, wife of the fourth Duke, once gave a grand ball at Woburn Abbey, which was famously cold and damp because the Russells would not heat it properly. On this occasion it was even more inhospitable, thanks to the strange eighteenth-century custom of washing down the walls before a party. Three of the guests, Lord Thorn, George Selwyn and Horace Walpole found themselves so freezing cold that they sought refuge in a small room that had a fire in the grate. The Duchess followed them and made no comment; a few minutes later however, a workman appeared and removed the door from its hinges.

The incredibly wealthy seventh Duke grew more miserable as his vast income increased. It was said that he rose at five a.m. every morning, so that he could spend the day worrying about his inheritance. In spite of his colossal fortune, the Duke was notoriously parsimonious, caring only for "the pleasure of accumulation". Disraeli once remarked to Queen Victoria that the Duke "never retired to rest satisfied unless he could trace that he had saved that day at least a five pound note". Lord William Russell, brother to the seventh Duke commented, "Good God, how the Duke freezes me . . . I think if all the hearts of the Russells were put together they would not yet make one good heart". Prime minister Lord John Russell, brother to the seventh Duke, was renowned for his chilling, unfriendly and often offensive manner: Queen Victoria made a point of avoiding him whenever possible.

The eighth Duke was miserable and reclusive; Lord Grey found the twenty-five-year-old to be "the most impenetrable person I have ever met with . . . more silent even than (prime minister) Russell . . . it is impossible to get a word out of him." The Duke and his wife led separate lives, but frequently quarrelled by letter. In time he became terrified of any kind of social interaction and only ever left his home with the windows on his carriage tightly shuttered. The ninth Duke, also a man of few words, was a morose hypochondriac. He and his wife were known as "the Icebergs". This Duke shot himself in a fit of depression during a bout of pneumonia.

The eleventh Duke, who had also inherited the congenital family coldness, hardly spoke more than a few words throughout his entire life. As his wife the Duchess was stone deaf, however, she probably wouldn't have replied anyway. The Duke had a staff of over 200, including fifty footmen with powdered wigs, and eight chauffeurs, most of whom he never saw. His workmen and gardeners would station themselves at strategic intervals on the family estate so that they could signal each other to hide at the Duke's approach to spare his lordship the unpleasant sight of a workman. Although the Duke and Duchess had only one son and heir, the child was never, ever invited to breakfast with his parents. Instead, he would stand in a corner, while his parents ate in silence, until the Duke dismissed him with the words, "Tavistock, you may leave now" (The Marquess of Tavistock being the title traditionally carried by the eldest son.) The Duke in fact went for twenty years without speaking to his son at all. When the Duchess died, his grandson, in a rare display of family affection, visited the bereaved Duke to express his condolences. The old man stiffly observed that the grandson did not have an appointment and, after a five-minute audience, the young visitor set off to catch the first train back to London.

The twelfth and possibly the most peculiar of all the Bedford dukes, Hastings Russell, was known as "Spinach". A solitary man and deeply mistrustful of human nature, he was known for his controversial and unpopular views. He was a pacifist during the first World War, giving the rest of the Russell clan, never the most communicative of families at the best of times, an excuse to sever all contact with him. He was known for his outrageous speeches in the House of Lords. His views were considered so offensive that resolutions were passed that "the Duke of Bedford be no longer heard". His pacifism earned him a national reputation as a heretic and a crank, especially his sincerely held conviction that Hitler would behave himself if only he was shown a little love and understanding. Living with the twelfth Duke was a daily trial for the Duchess, who was not allowed to buy new clothes because fashion was "unworldly". The Duke was also a hypochondriac. The family home, Woburn Abbey, was permanently drenched in antiseptic germ-killing sprays. His obsessive fear of germs led him to change his underwear three times a day and to carry with him at all times a bottle of TCP lozenges, which he would suck furiously if anyone coughed or sneezed. In 1953, in a fit of depression, he walked off into the woods and shot himself dead with his 12-bore.

In October 1999 a Hong Kong woman was stung by a conman when she paid him £10,000 for some pills. Apparently the woman, who thought that the millennium bug was a stomach ailment, was hoping to sell them at a huge profit.

The American Henry Partch, a young composer in the 1920s, suddenly ditched a promising career when he discovered that he was offended by the "even temperament" which had been imposed on Western music by classical musicians centuries earlier. Partch decided to break free of the harsh ground rules laid down by the likes of Bach and Beethoven and completely reinvent music. He began by burning all his sheet music in an old wood stove. By the late 1960s Partch had assembled a large orchestra of new instruments all tuned in "just intonation", employing a scale of forty-three notes to the octave, as opposed to the usual twelve. His instruments included the Spoils of War, made from old artillery shells and several guns, the Mazda Marimba, a xylophone-like instrument with hollow lightbulbs for keys, a huge bamboo contrivance called the Quadrangularis Reversum, and the incredibly low-pitched Marimba Eroica. Other Partch instruments included the Crychord, the Zymo-xyl, the Harmonic Cannon, the Chromelodion and the Mbira Bass Dyad. Copies of his instruments, which have remained silent since the day of Partch's death in 1974, are to be found in the Smithsonian Institution.

Robin Macnaghten was headmaster from 1974 to 1988 of Sherborne, the top West Country public school. He once opened a new sports hall by reading a few Latin verses he had composed, then diving off the swimming pool springboard to a fanfare of trumpets. His weak eyesight gave rise to a number of stories. One of the most widely circulated was how he once misidentified a coat hanging on a peg at the end of the classroom. "Sit down!" he yelled at the coat, which failed to do as instructed. "Right," said Macnaghten, "take 250 lines".

General George Custer was an unstable egomaniac who progressed from being the most useless student in his class at West Point to become one of the US Army's most incompetent generals. Custer was a cowardly commander who, by massacring 103 Cheyenne, earned the nickname "squaw-killer". Every one of Custer's 211 men were scalped at Little Big Horn – save Custer himself. Perhaps fearing the worst, he had already had his famous golden locks shorn off in favour of a close crew-cut.

The Duke of Wellington, victor of Waterloo, prime minister of Great Britain and field marshal of the army, was legendary in many ways. He was also incredibly testy, irascible, curmudgeonly and taciturn. He was nothing if not blunt. When a lady enquired whether the great man had been surprised to discover he had won the Battle of Waterloo, he replied icily, "not half so much surprised as I am right now, ma'am". Wellington could swear with the best of troopers, yet he would not tolerate foul language in his presence, even from the Prince Regent: "Damn me", he complained, "if I am not ashamed to walk into a room with him". He was scornful even of the elite troops of his army, the cavalry: "The only thing they can be relied on to do", he commented, "is to gallop too far and too fast". Wellington despised even his victorious troops at Waterloo, calling them "the scum of the earth . . . they have enlisted for drink, that is the simple truth". Wellington had little time for music, especially anything remotely contemporary. In Vienna he sat through a performance of Beethoven's "The Battle of Vienna". When asked by a Russian diplomat whether the music resembled the real battle, the Duke replied, "By God, no. If it had been, I should have run away myself."

An American group called Michigan Lawsuit Abuse Watch has an award for the most eccentric warning labels on consumer goods. Recent winners include a baby stroller that warned: "Remove your child before folding"; a laser printer cartridge that warned: "Do not eat toner"; a fire-lighter that urged: "Do not use near fire"; and a prescription for sleeping pills that bore the message: "This drug may cause drowsiness".

Shopkeeper Rob Christopher, in spite of changing his name by deed-poll to Free Rob Cannabis, was found guilty of cultivating cannabis plants in a floral display outside his shop in Glastonbury, Somerset. Mr Cannabis claimed that somebody else had planted the cannabis seeds and he had only watered them. The floral display later won first prize in the Glastonbury in Bloom competition.

The eighteenth-century Earls of Abercorn were notoriously pompous. The eighth Earl (1712–89), a lifelong bachelor, was so laid back that it was said he completed the obligatory grand tour of Europe without ever touching the back of his carriage seat. He once received the Queen as a house guest. Afterwards, the King took him aside and said that he was afraid that his wife's visit had given him a great deal of trouble. Abercorn replied, "a great deal indeed". The Earl did not welcome unexpected visitors and refused to receive anyone who dared call upon him without a formal invitation. The Earl was at his Scottish estate one day when an innocent local historian called upon him to pay his respects. The visitor found the Earl in his gardens and commented on how well his Lordship's shrubs had grown. Abercorn snapped, "They have nothing else to do," then turned his back and walked away.

His successor, the ninth Earl, was even more pompous and was said to have such an overbearingly aristocratic manner that even the King was afraid to speak to him. Most of his contemporaries thought him quite ridiculous however and named him "il magnifico". Lady Holland noted, "his pride is beyond belief . . . he is a little cracked". He wore his ceremonial Blue Ribbon of the Knights of the Garter at all times, even when he went hunting. He allowed himself no contact with people of lesser status. His servants were expected to wear white kid gloves when they changed his bed linen and his footmen were expected to dip their hands in a bowl of rose water before handing him a dish. Between 1803 and 1816 four of the Earl's children died of consumption. When his youngest daughter died he was grief stricken, but was too proud to admit that a member of his family had died of a disease associated with poverty and the working classes. He persuaded his doctor to write a letter to *The Times* announcing that the death had been caused by something else. The ninth Earl was also extremely vain. In old age, he broke both his legs, when his carriage overturned. The crippled Abercorn fretted that his elegance might be compromised and sought reassurance from his physician. The doctor replied that at his advanced age, these things were bound to happen. The doctor was paid his fee and told that his services were no longer required: apparently no one had ever dared tell the Earl before that he was no longer in his first flush of youth.

In 1999 a seventy-seven-year-old Irishman was fined £130 for attempting to smuggle two potatoes into New Zealand. He explained that he was planning to grow them, as he could not obtain a floury potato there.

In 1986 an entire jury pool of 86 people, assembled for a criminal trial in Centerville, Tennessee, had to be dismissed because too many members of the jury were related to each other.

A Canadian woman who grabbed the testicles of elderly men before stealing their wallets was finally apprehended in October 1999. Michelle Lawes, aged thirty-five, had attacked more than a dozen men between the ages of sixty and eighty-three. She would ask them for a light or for a cigarette, then grab them between the legs while she searched for their wallets. A Toronto police spokesman explained, "It was basically a type of distraction."

Christina Foyle, former managing director of Foyle's, the famous London book-shop, founded a monthly literary luncheon, the first of which was held in 1930. Over the years the guests of honour included such luminaries as Edith Sitwell, Roger Moore, J. B. Priestley and George Bernard Shaw – the latter attracted about 2,000 people to his luncheon. Afterwards Shaw wrote to Foyle to say that if he ever came to one of her events again she was to remember that he was a vegetarian. When she did invite him again, enclosing a proposed menu featuring cheese and celery, Shaw wrote back to decline: he simply could not bear the thought of 2,000 people simultaneously eating celery.

Christina Foyle once recalled that the worst luncheon she ever held was that for Sir Walter Gilbey, head of the gin firm. "He spoke for one and a half hours . . . the man in front of my father fell asleep, so he hit the chap with the toastmaster's gavel. The man said, 'Hit me again, I can still hear him.' "

The singer Frankie Vaughan will forever be associated with his signature tune, "Give Me the Moonlight", his matinee-idol looks, his rakishly tilted straw boater and his twirling cane – a relic of an act that became ever more flamboyant over a period of forty years until he died aged seventy-one. He was also famous for turning down Marilyn Monroe, to the disbelief of millions, and for his uncompromising views about his fellow entertainers. Two of his favourite targets were Elvis Presley, whom he found "ridiculous . . . he just can't sing – a spell in the army might make a man of him", and The Beatles, who were "an evil influence".

The American guitarist Charlie Feathers (1932–98) was rock n' roll's great conspiracy theorist. Although almost unknown in the UK, Feathers was a legend in his own mind. He claimed credit for many things, including the early Elvis sound of the Sun Records, giving Buddy Holly his trademark hiccough, persuading Carl Perkins to sing "Blue Suede Shoes" and for teaching Jerry Lee Lewis how to play the piano. Feathers, who blamed poor management for his own low profile, was largely ignored until the 1970s when a UK rockabilly revival created a cult demand for his records. In 1977 Feathers came to Britain for a concert at the Rainbow in London. He was only used to playing in small Memphis bars and was so disturbed when he saw the size of the theatre that he refused to rehearse and threatened to return home.

William Cobbett (1763–1835), soldier, crusading journalist and radical politician, was known for his almost limitless invective and highly eccentric opinions. He first made his mark as a very angry young pamphleteer. Horrified by the American and French revolutions, Cobbett launched a scathing personal attack upon England's greatest radical: "How Thomas Paine gets a living now, or what brothel he inhabits I know not . . . like Judas he will be remembered by posterity; man will learn to express all that is base, malignant, treacherous, unnatural and blasphemous by the single monosyllable – Paine". In one of many U-turns that came to mark Cobbett's career he was to become a passionate supporter of Paine's ideas. Cobbett later tried to make amends for his embarrassing attack by removing Paine's remains from the unhallowed ground where they lay in America, with the idea of erecting some sort of fitting memorial in England. It was a bizarre episode. Cobbert had Paine dug up and shipped back to England, but then completely forgot about his plan and left the bones lying for years in an old suitcase. When Cobbett died the remains became completely lost.

Cobbett was indiscriminate in the targets for his abuse. He would start off on a discussion about political reform, then suddenly launch into a violent diatribe against writers of the classics and literary giants alike – no sacred cow was safe from Cobbett's invective. Horace was "a bore, servile, self degraded wretch". Virgil likewise was "a crawling and disgusting parasite, a base scoundrel and pandar to unnatural passion". Milton's *Paradise Lost* was "such barbarous trash, so outrageously offensive to reason and to common sense that one is naturally led to wonder how it can have been tolerated by a people amongst whom astronomy, navigation and chemistry are understood". Nor was he keen on Dr Johnson. Cobbett had some other odd notions. He even worked up a head of steam against the cup of tea – a bland and evil beverage that would weaken England's moral fibre: "the gossip of the tea table is no bad preparatory school for the brothel", and the humble potato: "the most despicable of all plants that polluted the table of the farm worker".

In the name of performance art, Californian Zhang Huan took off his clothes, smeared himself with puréed hot dog and flour, then allowed himself to be sniffed by eight dogs at San Francisco's Asian art museum. Zhang said that his aim was to "explore the physical and psychological effects of human violence in modern society". The exploration ceased when one of the dogs bit him on the bottom. Meanwhile, sixty-eight-year-old Bruce Baker of Lingfield, Surrey, spends his days sitting on a hill playing "Jingle Bells" on his xylophone. Nothing to do with art this time – Bruce just wants to make sure that he is among the first to greet visiting aliens.

In 1998, residents of a new town in Canada narrowly voted against renaming their community Mars, opting instead for the more down-to-earth South Bruce Peninsula. A disappointed local official told news reporters, "It's a pity . . . I was looking forward to becoming the first mayor of Mars."

In 1999, a Canadian court dismissed thirty-four-year-old sales manager Rene Joly's claim that a bank, the defence minister and several drug-store chains planned to kill him because he was a Martian. The judge rejected the claim on the basis that Joly, as a Martian, had no status before the courts.

Lord Birkenhead, appointed Lord Chancellor in 1919, was a regular visitor to the National Liberal Club, which he used exclusively to avail himself of the men's toilet. One day he was stopped by an irritated member who complained: "I do wish you wouldn't use this club as a urinal." The chancellor replied, "Oh I see. It's a club as well, is it?"

The words Oliver, Reed and hellraiser were regular companions right up to the day of the actor's death in March 1999.

The prodigious imbiber spent much of his later life being thrown out of pubs and hotels after marathons of bibulous excess, which he called "tests of strength". In 1974 Reed played the part of Athos in *The Three Musketeers*. During filming in Spain, police were summoned to Reed's hotel to arrest him for dancing naked in a giant goldfish tank. Later that year Reed invited thirty-six rugby players to a party at his home, and between Saturday night and Sunday lunchtime they consumed sixty gallons of beer, thirty-two bottles of whisky, seventeen bottles of gin, four crates of wine and one bottle of Babycham. The party concluded with Reed leading the players on a nude dawn run through the Surrey countryside. His notoriety increased in 1985 when he married twenty-one-year-old Josephine Burge after a five-year courtship. At his stag party, which lasted two days, Reed allegedly drank 136 pints of beer. In 1986 Reed dug up nine acres of his back garden after forgetting where he had buried his wife's jewellery when drunk.

Brigham Young (1801–77) was the second leader of the Mormon Church and Governor of Utah. It was he who directed the move to the valley of the Great Salt Lake in 1846. Young married at least twenty-seven and possibly fifty-six times, and fathered at least fifty-seven children. He consumed vast quantities of dairy foods in the belief that cow's milk promoted virility; as many of Young's wives were thirty or forty years younger than him, few in Utah were prepared to argue the point. When his twenty-seventh wife was in the process of divorcing him she recalled how the seventy-two-year-old Mormon leader became angry when he was refused sex. Young always maintained, however, that he was not promiscuous because he only ever slept with one woman at a time. Twelve years after his death, the Mormon Church officially renounced polygamy.

The fifth Duke of Sutherland (1888–1963) was one of the greatest threats to British wildlife of the twentieth century. His greatest joy in life was to kill wild animals. He felled his first stag when he was ten years old and killed more than a thousand more over a lifetime of idle slaughter. At his vast estate at Lilleshall in Shropshire he would shoot anything from 800 to 1,000 pheasants in a single day. He especially liked to shoot elephants, which he thought "exciting". One day a man in his shooting party, Montague Guest, fell dead. The Duke paused awhile before reloading, then observed, "Personally, I can imagine no pleasanter way to die".

The early nineteenth century Duke of Montagu, although not particularly noted as a philanthropist, was given to spontaneous bouts of generosity. He once met a tramp in the Mall and insisted that the man dine with him the following Sunday. During their brief conversation the Duke was able to find out that the tramp had a family who were living in poverty in Yorkshire. When the man arrived for his appointment, again dressed in rags, he was ushered into the great Montagu dining room and told that there were some people the Duke wanted him to meet. The doors were thrown open to reveal, to the tramp's astonishment, his wife and children, brought down from Yorkshire by the Duke. They were in for another surprise – the Duke called in his lawyer and right there and then settled an annuity of £200 on the family.

In 1999, a US court ordered hotelier Clifford Shattuck to stay away from his guests because he was too rude. Shattuck, of the Lighthouse Motel, Lincolnville, Maine, was also fined $9,400. The judge heard that sixty-six-year-old Shattuck was abusive to guests who wanted to see rooms before they registered.

Australian footballer Garry Hocking, captain of the Geelong Cats, changed his name to "Whiskas" in a unique sponsorship deal. He adopted the name of the catfood brand by deed poll in exchange for a deal worth up to £85,000 in 1999. "I'm probably going to cop a bit of flak for this," explained Whiskas, "but I see it as a great thing for the club and Whiskas". In France, meanwhile, a couple were prosecuted for causing unnecessary suffering to their son by naming him Zebedee, after the character in *The Magic Roundabout*.

The Soviet leader Josef Stalin was a boot fetishist. He was never seen without his high, heavy black riding-boots, even on the most inappropriate occasions and in the most uncomfortable conditions. He once had one of his bodyguards sent to the salt mines for not wearing boots. It turned out that the bodyguard had taken to wearing slippers so as not to wake Stalin when he was sleeping. Stalin accused him of planning to assassinate him. A guest once asked Stalin why he never took his boots off even

on a stiflingly hot day. The Russian leader replied, "Because
you can kick someone in the head with them so hard he'll never
find all his teeth".

Brigadier Wilfred Ponsonby (1905–99), an escapee from German prisoner-of-war camps on three occasions, was also a fine
horseman, a champion boxer, amateur magician and creator of
two of the most challenging stage acts of the 1920s – "Otto the
Mechanical Duck", and his celebrated razor-swallowing performance. Ponsonby was raised by eccentrics; his father, an
officer in the Royal Engineers, became increasingly odd during
his military career. He believed that there was nothing in the
Bible to say that a man should not have more than one wife.
However, when he attempted to put his theory into practice,
his first wife quickly divorced him.

The Dukes of St Albans were descended from one of Charles II's
bastards, born to Nell Gwynn. According to legend, the former
orange-seller suspended little son Charles by his heels over a river
and threatened to drop him unless his father gave the boy a title.
The twelfth Duke, Osborne de Vere Beauclerk, known as
"Obby", would often say, "Bury me where I drop", although
no one took him at his word when he died in 1964 aged eighty-
nine. Unlike several members of his noble family he was not
certifiably insane; in fact, some believed that his general zaniness
was carefully cultivated for effect. Obby insisted on appearing at
the Queen's coronation in 1953 with a live falcon, a reminder to
everyone that he carried the title Hereditary Grand Falconer (to
this day it entitles the owner to cheap venison from Richmond

royal park). When permission was denied he sulked and refused to go at all. In the church near his home he was known for slumbering through the sermons with a silk handkerchief over his face, waking occasionally to interrupt the vicar with shouts of "Rubbish". He once visited Lord Dunraven, arriving at the doorstep with only a brown paper bag containing his pyjamas and a toothbrush, and was known to ask the hall porter at his club to wind his wristwatch for him. He once sat alone, in a hotel restaurant, refusing to budge after the fire alarm went off. When the waiters pleaded with him to move, he replied, "Nonsense! Bring me some more toast".

A Californian surgeon was convicted of second-degree murder after amputating a seventy-nine-year-old man's healthy leg below the knee. The patient died when the operation went wrong. The surgeon's lawyers said that there was one mitigating factor: the victim was an apotemnophiliac, i.e., someone who gained sexual gratification from the removal of limbs. Their client was only doing him a favour.

The artist Henri de Toulouse-Lautrec, son of an eccentric French count, broke both his thigh bones as a youngster and grew up deformed and dwarflike. His father gave him the benefit of a unique education which involved hunting stags by day and visiting prostitutes by night. By the age of twenty he was familiar with every brothel in the red-light district of Montmartre. When Lautrec became famous as an artist women would queue up to meet him, curious to know if he really lived up to his nickname "Tea-pot". Lautrec's paintings show that he was obsessed with women's noses. According to one theory this was because he was so short that when he looked up at a woman, it was the first thing in his line of vision. He died, syphilitic, at the age of thirty-six.

The third Duke of Rutland, the Marquess of Granby, was a much respected soldier. Apart from the Duke of Wellington, he has more public houses and inns named after him than any other person in history. Rutland's son, the fourth Duke, was famous, however, for spectacular over-indulgence. He began each day with a breakfast of six or seven turkey eggs, then spent the rest of the day washing them down with port. His bizarre appetite resulted in an early death – at the age of thirty-three – from liver disease.

Blackmailer Alexandru Nemeth, who demanded money from a German branch of Nestlé, was apprehended after ordering the company to place diamonds in pouches hung around the necks of homing pigeons. When the police knocked at his front door after simply following one of the pigeons to the blackmailer's Frankfurt home, Nemeth said he thought his scam was bullet-proof, but now accepted that this was not the case. Meanwhile another German blackmailer demanded £3.5 m from the car giant Mercedes. If they did not pay up, he threatened to throw bricks and manhole covers at Mercedes cars. In the event one car was reported hit by a paving slab.

A woman was arrested and fined £1,800 in Perth, Australia, after attempting to smuggle seven parakeet eggs, worth up to £1,200 each, through customs, in her bra. Officials said they were alerted by the unusual shape of forty-nine-year-old Christine Rabczynski's bust.

Victor Hugo was a sexual athlete, renowned for his prodigious libido and reckless promiscuity. Hugo required only four hours' sleep a night. His ideal day was to have a prostitute before breakfast, an actress either side of lunch, his regular mistress in the afternoon and another mistress in the evening. Hugo seduced a twenty-two-year-old when he was seventy and was still sexually active when he died at the age of eighty-three. He did most of his writing, however, standing up.

The venal 4th Duke of Queensberry (1724–1810) – "old Q" or "degenerate Douglas" to his friends – was a tiny man, reviled at Windsor Castle for getting permanently drunk throughout the Regency crisis on George III's champagne while the old king lay terminally ill. He was also one of the greatest lechers of his age. The libidinous old Duke lived in Piccadilly, London. On most days he could be seen sitting outside on a little chair on his first-floor balcony, a strategic position from whence he could ogle every woman who passed by. Although he had lost the sight in one eye, was deaf in one ear, had lost most of his teeth and was severely arthritic – "a wrinkled, palsied Don Juan" in the words of Thackeray – Old Q retained a libido of Jaggeresque proportions. He was not fussy about the multitude of women he propositioned. He pursued women of every size and shape "and with so much ardour at fourscore as he had done at twenty". The old roué went to great lengths to revive his flagging sex drive. He kept a doctor in full-time attendance – the doctor was paid handsomely so long as the Duke remained alive, but understood he would not receive a penny if his patient died. He bathed only in milk. His death, it was said, was hastened by eating too much fruit.

In 1999 magistrates in Swafham, Norfolk, jailed a man who had threatened to murder his social worker. The man was apparently livid over delays in arranging a course in anger management.

In the annals of useless scientific research, the name of the American Seabury Doane Brewer stands alone. Brewer did not limit his research to just one field of science, or even to science. The subjects he explored included Psychology, Government, Life, Evolution, Education, Astronomy, The Laws-of-Nature, Balls of Lightning, Shadow Bands Caused by the Sun's Eclipses, Northern Lights, Radio, Mathematics, Miscellaneous, "Nothing" and "Myself". His treatise entitled *124 Discoveries Made between 1892 and 1930 by Seabury Doane Brewer, of Lake George, New York, and Montclair, New Jersey* was published when he was seventy years old and still hard at work. It contained a number of revelations, including "temperature, with its variations, is one of the most wonderful things and is always present everywhere," and "physicians should be compelled to destroy all unfit specimens of humanity immediately upon their birth". Much of his "scientific" research could be

confused with the ramblings of a self-opinionated old man
man, for example:

1. That our thoughts have been, are being, and will be,
thought by other thinkers.

28. That there is no such thing as Platonic love between
normal males and females.

30. That umbilical cords should be allowed to wither away
naturally. Man alone interferes with the impregnation,
interferes with the embryo and interferes with birth. How
unfair to the child. Watch the animals, birds and insects;
watch all things in their various processes of being born.

39. That the inexorable economic law of supply and
demand is a fake – as well as many another economic
laws.

52. That phonetic spelling should not be allowed.

69. That twin stars do not exist. That what is seen is the
result of optical reflection.

70. That Saturn's ring does not exist. That what is seen is
the result of optical reflection.

In 1929 Brewer corresponded with Einstein, with whom he was
less than impressed, under his nom-de-plume, "Mrs Mary Bryant", enclosing one dollar "for an authentic translation of his
latest article". In his letter Brewer pointed out that as long ago as
in the 1880s, "I had discovered that all things (even gravitation,
magnetism, electricity, chemistry, and even Life itself) are so
interwoven, intermingled, and mixed up together, that it is
almost impossible to tell where one thing leaves off and an other
thing begins." Einstein kept the dollar but did not reply.

The Contemporary History Conference in Braunau-am-Inn, Austria, birthplace of Hitler, held a conference to discuss the plight of people with problem names. Among the guests were Adolf Hitler, retired bus driver, and Heinrich Himmler, brick-layer. The lesser known Herr Hitler complained that frequent jokes at his expense had contributed to the break-up of his marriage and caused many work-related problems. Once, when required to drive a coachload of Jewish tourists, he had to have his name changed for the day to Adrian Heller.

In 1999, a motorcyclist caught speeding at 115mph near Poole, Dorset, told magistrates he had just washed his bike and was trying to dry it.

Twenty-one-year old Olga Karpov was arrested in Moscow after hurling herself eight times under the cars of good-looking drivers, because "I thought that one of the men might ask me out to make up for it". Olga never did get to date the drivers however, as she was far too busy being taken to hospital.

Lawyer Ambrose Appelbe (1903–99) served many famous cli-ents, ranging from the actress Ingrid Bergman to the mass murderer John Christie. He was also a famous founder of eccentric causes. At fifteen he joined the British army just in time to serve in the last few weeks of the First World War. The brief wartime experience made him a pacifist. In later years, if there was a war film on TV he would leave the room. After the war Appelbe travelled to England earning money as a concertina-player before he became a solicitor. Before going to the gallows in 1953 John Christie bequeathed his reading glasses to the poor-sighted lawyer. Appelbe was happy to wear the killer's half-moons on the end of his nose for the rest of his courtroom career.

In 1935 Appelbe embarked upon his most ambitious lost cause when, together with George Bernard Shaw and H. G. Wells, he founded the Smell Society, an organization which sought to eliminate foul odours. They hoped to refresh the nostrils of London commuters with sheets of paper impregnated with seaside smells. The society also created new words to describe the smell of such things as roast turkey, mimosa and tar. The Smell Society once held an "aromatic dinner" at the Grosvenor House hotel in a room squirted with lemon scent. Appelbe was also a co-founder of the Anatomical Donors Association, but was posthumously frustrated in his attempts to leave his own body to medical research. Unfortunately science had no use for a ninety-six-year-old stiffy.

A Burger King assistant foiled an armed robbery in Michigan by explaining that he could not open the cash register without taking an order for food. "Okay, give me some onion rings," said the robber. The assistant replied, "Sorry, they're off", and the robber fled empty-handed. Meanwhile an armed robber ran into a bank in Dresden, only to discover that it had changed ownership a few days previously and that he was now in a lingerie store. "In that case," he snapped, pointing to a rack of frilly underwear, "give me all of those".

The Scottish philosopher Dr Adam Smith (1723–90) was a pioneer in the science of economics. Smith became professor of logic at Glasgow and took up the chair of moral philosophy the following year. In 1776 he moved to London, where he published a seminal 900-page essay: *An Inquiry into the Nature and Causes of the Wealth of Nations*. Smith's work identified basic market laws and shattered economic theories that had reigned unchallenged for 200 years. He was held in awe by academic society and corresponded with Johnson, Voltaire, Franklin and Burke. When Smith was received by King George III's ministers, they all rose to their feet. Smith was astonished. "We all stand, Mr Smith," William Pitt explained, "because we are all your scholars". Smith was, however, the archetypal absent-minded professor (he once accidentally brewed a slice of bread and butter and declared it "a very bad cup of tea") with few social skills and some alarming habits. As his chaotic lifestyle made him unmarriageable, Smith always lived with his mother. Among his many idiosyncrasies were his peculiar voice and his inimitable "worm-like" gait. He was often seen wandering the streets of Edinburgh, half dressed and talking to himself in a distinctive high-pitched babble. He once walked straight into a tanning pit while still talking.

The Australian Rodney Ansell was the real-life inspiration for the film *Crocodile Dundee*. He first became a local hero in 1977 after being swept out to sea and landing on a small island with nothing but wallabies to eat for two months. He was eventually saved by the timely visit of an aboriginal tribe to the island. Ansell was also known for his immense courage and lightning reactions when out pig-sticking. Much of the humour in *Crocodile Dundee* was inspired by Ansell's book tour in Sydney, when he insisted on sleeping in his sleeping bag in the five-star Sebel Townhouse and was completely mystified by the bidet in his room. Sadly, Ansell never reaped the financial benefits of being the original "Croc" and became bitter, unable to come to terms with the fact that actor Paul Hogan was living a Hollywood lifestyle while he languished in obscurity.

The name Alan Turing (1912–1954) ranks alongside that of Charles Babbage as one of the major figures in the development of the modern computer. Turing's expertise in mathematical logic was put to its best use during the Second World War. In 1938 a Polish engineer called Robert Lewinski turned up at the British Embassy in Warsaw, claiming that he had inside information about a secret factory in Germany where the Nazis were manufacturing code-signalling machines. The "Enigma" machines were to be used by the German high command to send coded orders to forces in the field. Although the machines were very simple to operate, the encoding system was so incredibly complex that the Germans were confident that their communications system was uncrackable. Lewinski, however, had committed the details of the machine to memory. He was smuggled out of Poland to Paris, where he supervised the construction of a clone Enigma. Soon, the Allies knew exactly how an Enigma machine was constructed and how it worked. The complexity of the code-scrambling device, however, was such that breaking the code appeared to be a near-impossible task.

Alan Turing, a fellow of King's College, Cambridge was twenty-seven at the time. He had established himself as the most brilliant young mathematician in the country with a paper entitled *On Computable Numbers* which to the few who even vaguely understood it was recognised as a sensational, epoch-making document. When war broke out in 1939 Turing was seconded to British intelligence duties at Bletchley Park, outside London. He was to take charge of a code-breaking team, a top secret project under the strictest military surveillance. Turing and his team set about the exhausting task of sifting through hundreds of thousands of scrambled Enigma messages, searching for recurring combinations of letters or any other clues which might be amenable to decipherment.

Eventually, Turing's team broke the code. Within days the position of every German U-boat in the Atlantic was pinpointed. and before long, almost all German communications were an open book. Allied convoy losses dropped so dramatically that the Germans immediately became suspicious, but they were so convinced that the Enigma code was unbreakable that they continued to use it.

For the brilliant code-cracking team at Bletchley, Turing was the greatest enigma of all. He was a loner, a stammerer and in the best tradition of absent-minded professors was very neglectful of his personal hygiene. He was also extremely boyish, looking at least ten years younger than his age, taking on the appearance of a very scruffy schoolboy. His hair was so dishevelled it looked as though he had been sleeping rough, his fingernails were filthy and his trousers were held up with his old school tie. He gave up shaving on a regular basis because he once cut himself with his razor and the sight of blood made him faint. His voice was a curious high-pitched stutter, occasionally punctuated by a nervous laugh, said to resemble the grating bray of a donkey. Whenever he was lost in thought on an intense mental exercise he would suddenly emit high-pitched squeaks and squawks. Turing was socially inept: he tended to ignore people whose intellect he considered inferior, which in his case included just about everyone, especially the military staff he was required to work with on the Enigma operation. Turing was also openly gay at a time when homosexuality was still illegal, and he had a disconcerting habit of making flip offhand remarks in front of his colleagues about his sexual preferences. He was also a fitness fanatic. Several times a week he would set off on punishing cross-country runs through the local fields. Bemused locals would see him grasp a handful of grass and chew it as he ran. This was Turing's way of making up for vitamin deficiency in his wartime diet – before rationing he had always eaten an apple in bed before going to sleep.

At the outbreak of war Turing had converted his life savings into silver bars and secretly buried them in the woods near Bletchley and committed the location to memory. After the war, however, he found that he couldn't remember where he had buried them. He never recovered his silver bars, in spite of conducting several thorough treasure hunts and even inventing his own metal detector.

In the 1950s Turing went to live in Wilmslow, a suburb on the outskirts of Manchester, where he occasionally amused himself by cruising for rent boys. When one of his pick-ups, a teenager named Alan Murray, stole some items from Turing's home, including a shirt, a couple of pairs of shoes and some silver fish knives, Turing reported the theft. The local police were quick to sniff out the homosexual sub-plot. In 1952 Turing was arrested on a charge of gross indecency. Although the trial was not widely reported in the newspapers, apart from a piece in the *News of the World* under the banner headline ACCUSED HAD POWERFUL BRAIN, the man who had played such a major role in winning the war was humiliated by his public disgrace. He pleaded guilty and was put on probation on condition that he underwent a course of hormone treatment to "cure" him of his problem. The drug treatment had terrible side-effects on his physique and rendered him impotent. Turing confided to a friend on a visit to Cambridge, "I'm growing breasts!"

On the evening of June 1954 Turing went to bed and ate his customary bedtime apple, this time generously laced with cyanide.

A Singapore court sentenced a forty-three-year-old truck driver to twenty-five weeks in prison for stealing smelly footwear. Shoe-fetishist Zainal Mohamed Esa would sniff the footwear until the smell wore off then donate them to the Salvation Army.

The eighth Duke of Devonshire (1833–1908), known for most of his adult life as "Harty-tarty", was a cabinet minister, having three times turned down the chance to serve as prime minister during Queen Victoria's reign. He was considered one of the most staggeringly boring men of his era, a fact he was only too ready to acknowledge. His interminable monotone speeches were delivered without a trace of humour – a contemporary noted that his public speaking was "the finest example of pile-driving the world has ever known". The Duke was once caught yawning in the middle of a speech in the House of Lords; he immediately apologized, explaining that what he had to say was "so damned dull". He fell asleep everywhere – at dinner, on the stairs, in cabinet meetings. He once fell asleep in the House of Lords, woke up with a start, looked at the clock and exclaimed, "Good heavens! What a bore . . . I shan't be in bed for another seven hours!" He once told of an experience he had at Westminster: "On one occasion I had a horrid nightmare. I dreamed I was making a speech in the House of Lords and I found I was actually doing so."

The Welsh poet Charles Horace Jones was probably the only poet to have been thrown bodily out of the Royal National Eisteddfod. Jones, a self-styled south Wales street-corner poet, stood beside a lamppost in the high street at Merthyr Tydfil, Glamorgan, every day for forty-five years, with only an hour's break for lunch. Jones the poet always carried a knuckle-duster in his pocket as protection against the Welsh people whom his poems attacked with increasing savagery. During his career he was beaten up in the street, attacked in a cafe, knocked unconscious and once set on fire. When asked why he stood next to the lamppost he said it was because it left one less side from which he could be attacked.

An Atlanta pharmacist John Pemberton first stumbled across the original recipe for Coca-Cola in 1886. At the time he was working on a series of failed patent medicines and hair restorers, including Triplex Liver Pills, Indian Queen Hair Dye and Globe of Flower Cough Syrup. Pemberton found his new "soda" when he combined sugar, coca leaves, kola nuts and several flavourings. He then advertised it as the perfect lift for a "turbulent, inventive, noisy, neurotic new America". In fact, Pemberton was well qualified on the subject of neurosis, as he was more than a little odd himself. One of his contemporaries noted, "We did not know at the time what was the mater with him, but it developed that he was a drug fiend". Pemberton was a morphine addict. His attempts to wean himself off morphine had led him to dabble with cocaine and his experiments convinced Pemberton that coca was a healthy substitute for opium. He wrote, "It supplies the place of that drug, and the patient who will use it as a means of a cure may deliver himself from the pernicious habit without inconvenience or pain". Pemberton first hailed Coca-Cola as a "great blessing to the unfortunate who are addicted to the morphine or opium habit or the excessive use of alcoholic stimulants". In the beginning, not only did every bottle of Coca-Cola contain the equivalent of a small line of cocaine, the cocaine content was also intensified by the kola nut's caffeine. By the end of the century, however, cocaine had begun to acquire a negative press. At first the Coca-Cola Company was horrified at the idea, but in 1902 they were forced into quietly removing cocaine from their product.

Carpenter David Metcalf practised his imitation of a female turkey for an hour every day to win the $5,000 first prize in the 1999 Grand National Turkey Calling championship, held in Charlotte, North Carolina. The fifteen contestants, all wild turkey hunters, make a living by attracting male turkeys with their imitations of hens. Metcalf said afterwards, "This is as good as it gets". In November 1998 turkey farmer Ollie Baker refused to kill his 1,200 birds because they were hiding his pet turkey, Trudy. Baker, of Chichester, West Sussex, had hand-reared Trudy before she escaped and joined the flock, which was ripe for seasonal slaughter. "I spend four hours a day searching for Trudy," Baker told local news reporters. "I call her name, but they just stare back at me."

In 1999 white witches campaigned against plans to erect a mobile phone mast near an ancient landmark in East Sussex. In a ceremony next to the Long Man of Wilmington the high priestess of British white witches led a chant of "Vodafone begone".

Charles Burgess Fry had several nicknames including "Charles III", "Almighty" and "Lord Oxford", but to friends and fans alike he was mostly "CB". He was arguably the greatest all-rounder in British sporting history and undoubtedly one of the most extraordinary men ever to step on to a sports field. Fry was an astonishing athlete. He gained twelve Blues at Oxford, including athletics, cricket and soccer and later represented his country in all three; only an injury deprived him of a Blue in rugby. His life was packed with colourful and dramatic incident. At Wadham College, Oxford, his friends were Hillaire Belloc, Max Beerbohm, the future Lord Chancellor, F.E. Smith and a future foreign secretary, John Simon. He met prime ministers from William Gladstone to Winston Churchill and hobnobbed with Hitler, Cecil Rhodes, C. Aubrey Smith and Basil Rathbone. He watched the *Titanic* depart from Southampton and lived long enough to appear on *This Is Your Life*. He once knocked out Joseph Wells, the Kent cricketer and father of H.G., who was umpiring a match when Fry drove the ball and hit him on the head. In athletics he excelled in the hundred yards and the long jump. On the Iffley Road track at Oxford University he equalled the world-record long jump of 23 ft $6\frac{1}{3}$ in (7 m 18 cm) – a record that remained intact for well over twenty years. According to legend he arrived for the jump long after the contest had started, formally dressed, and after a hefty lunch, a whisky and a cigar. He was also a talented boxer, an excellent golfer, swimmer, sculler, tennis player and javelin thrower. He missed out on gold at the Olympics of 1896 because he didn't know they were taking place. He was still hurdling in his mid-fifties. After he had celebrated his seventieth birthday, Fry told his friend Denzil Batchelor that he had done most things but was now looking for a new world to conquer and proposed to interest himself in racing, "attach himself to a stable and then set up on his own". Batchelor asked the maestro: "What as, Charles? Trainer, jockey or horse?"

It is for cricket that Fry is best remembered. He played for Oxford, Surrey, Sussex and Hampshire until he was fifty. In a remarkable first-class career spanning thirty years, Fry scored ninety-four centuries. He played twenty-six Tests for England and with Don Bradman holds the record of six consecutive centuries in first-class cricket. He opened the England batting with W.G. Grace in 1899. "Look here Charlie Fry," Grace warned him as they set out for the middle, "I'm not a sprinter like you". As captain of England he was never on the losing side. There are at least two epigrams on the game of cricket which are credited to Fry: "Batting is a dance with a stick in your hand", and, when taunted with being a batsman with only one stroke, "Yes, but I could make the ball go to ten different parts of the field".

In 1901, at the pinnacle of fame as a batsman, Fry was capped for England against Ireland at Association football. The very next season he played fullback for Southampton in the F.A. Cup final. His defensive partnership with W.J. Oakley was legendary, although later he was fond of grossly exaggerating his career in top flight soccer. Fry's near-perfect sporting physique earned him the accolade "most handsome man in England" and he even had a brief career as a nude model. He was, however, a notorious snob, an anti-semite and highly racist. Although his achievements were many, he didn't mind lying to enhance them or simply making them up. He could also be incredibly boring and liked to talk incessantly. His friends noted that he was capable of speaking at length on almost any subject, no matter how obscure, and without much encouragement; he once treated his cricketing colleagues to an impromptu half-hour lecture on iambics.

In 1934 Fry was invited to Germany by Adolf Hitler to explore the possibility of building links between the British Boy Scouts and the Nazi Youth Movement. Fry kept the interpreter, Ribbentrop, busy for an hour and a quarter. Neville Cardus noted later that it was a pity Fry didn't speak German, because had he done so, war could have been averted as "Hitler might have died of a fit trying to get a word in". The starry-eyed sportsman returned home with fulsome praise for the Führer. Later when Fry heard about the "Night of the Long Knives" when Hitler had many of his Nazi colleagues locked up or murdered, he found it difficult to believe that such acts could have been committed by "such a nice man". Thanks to his Nazi connections, Fry never made the honours list and was passed over for the presidency of the MCC. The cricketing establishment later made amends, however, by moving a statuette of him from the basement to the Long Room, causing Fry to quip: "I spent 20 years in the cellar and now I am on the shelf."

After his flirtation with fascism he returned to more liberal politics and following retirement from cricket there followed careers in journalism, diplomacy and politics. Fry stood three times for parliament unsuccessfully as a Liberal candidate.

After the first World War he had acted as India's delegate to the League of Nations. It was during this ambassadorial stint that there occurred the most bizarre episode in Fry's remarkable life. The new state of Albania, after nearly 400 years of Ottoman rule, had creatively chosen a Protestant German prince, William of Wied, as their new ruler. He found himself presiding over a country which was 70% Moslem and had half a dozen political factions, each claiming to be the legitimate Albanian government. The new king spent just six months trying to bluff his way through the situation, then gave up and caught the next train back to Germany. After years of political confusion through the First World War the country was finally guaranteed independence. Albania looked around for a new king, a search that became increasingly more eccentric. The ideal candidate, the Albanian government concluded, would be "an English country gentleman with an income of £10,000 a year". In due course a three-man Albanian delegation, including a bearded bishop who ironically bore an uncanny resemblance to W.G. Grace, offered the vacant throne of Albania to Fry, who was at the time working in Geneva. Fry was keen to accept, as he later put it, "on the nail", but reluctantly declined. He met the first requirement – he was English and undeniably a gentleman – however, he did not quite have the required funds. The Albanians turned their attentions to another English gentleman; Lord Inchcape. He received an extraordinary letter inviting him to accept "The kingship of Albania", with the footnote, "in case you turn it down entirely perhaps you would feel called upon to suggest the name of some wealthy Englishman or American with administrative power who would care to take up the cudgels on Albania's behalf". Inchcape's response was not as the Albanians had hoped. After telling his butler he had no idea where Albania was, his reply was to the point: "I duly received your letter of the 29th . . . it is a great compliment to be offered the Crown of Albania but it is not in my line. Yours sincerely, Inchcape." C.B. Fry reflected years later, upon hearing that Mussolini had Albania, that the Italian invasion would never have happened had he been king. He would have introduced the Albanians to cricket, he reasoned, and then "nobody would have dared to invade Albania with county cricket going on. The British Navy would have been absolutely obliged to step in and prevent it".

C.B. Fry's fiercesome wife Beatrice, ten years his senior, was the subject of a torrid Victorian sex scandal before he met her. She was seduced at fifteen by a wealthy banker, bore him two illegitimate children and probably had a third after marrying Fry.

For the best part of forty years Fry and his wife ran a "training ship" for boys called the Mercury – a sort of floating boarding school to educate boys in a "classical sense of values". Beatrice Fry was a sadist; she encouraged the boys to box until they bled and staged "punishment fights" between small boys and much bigger boys. She also inspected their pyjama trousers daily for evidence of self-abuse.

Fry's dress sense was highly eccentric. His clothes often inspired incredulity and amusement. On tour with the England cricket team, Neville Cardus observed that Fry's wardrobe was a constant source of wonderment, a confusing variety of "clothes of strange dyes, patterns and purposes". One of Fry's outfits made him look like "a deep sea monster" and on another occasion he arrived for a match as if dressed for a South Polar expedition. One costume, featuring a topee and leather shorts, led Cardus to suggest that Fry "was about to trace the source of the Amazon". Fry was also prone to bouts of spectacularly odd behaviour. In Australia, he waved from the door of his train carriage to cricket fans, dressed as a Chinese mandarin. Sometimes he would dress up as an Indian rajah. As a cricket journalist he regularly appeared wearing a naval uniform with his obligatory eye glass and pipe and watched his cricket from the grandstand through a telescope. A fellow cricket writer noted that Fry looked like "something between a retired admiral and an unusually athletic Oxford don".

Fry was a lifelong believer in the supernatural. Although one of his greatest friends was with the legendary cricketer Ranjitsinhji, he developed a morbid fear of Indians. He came to believe on a tour of India that a native prince had cast a spell on him to unhinge his mind. He became increasingly paranoid and maintained that Indians were trying to steal his personal papers. Back in England he continued to believe that he was being persecuted by Indian thieves and he took to clutching his papers tightly to his person wherever he went. Although the glamorous and much-envied sportsman conveyed an aura of effortless superiority, he suffered from at least two nervous breakdowns and was in fact mentally ill for long periods of his life. The last of his breakdowns lasted six years and he was treated by electro-convulsive therapy for about a decade. He was seen in dance halls waltzing with invisible partners, or mounting his horse backwards, or casting a fishing rod out of his bedroom window. Once, in while staying in Brighton, he suddenly shed his clothes one morning and trotted around the beach stark naked. Fry finished his days in night clubs with girls young enough to be his great-grandchildren. His biographer John Arlott recalled how Fry took a young girl to a nightclub when he was seventy-eight. She confided to Arlott later, "Do you know, he didn't have a piss for five hours!"

A man hid in a cave in Ohio for two days in 1999 to avoid a meteor. Sheriff's deputies found Lloyd Albright with his tent, a huge supply of dried food and sixteen guns. "He very sincerely thought that a meteor was going to hit the Atlantic and cause a tidal wave 200 ft high," explained a police spokesman. Albright worked as a computer programmer at the Kennedy Space Centre.

The British diplomat Sir David Muirhead (1918–99) was known for his whimsical turn of phrase. When he was once asked whether the occupants of a car that had crashed off the Salazar Bridge in Lisbon were safe, the ambassador replied: "They are very wet, and a little dead."

The Ukrainian-born impresario Lord Lew Grade (1906–98) was one of the most extravagant characters in British showbiz, famous for his nine-inch cigars, his Phantom VI Rolls Royces and his multi-million-dollar transatlantic telephone deals. Grade's idea of a perfect day was to get up at six a.m with an idea for a new TV series, sell it to an American backer by noon and inform his business partners of the deal over lunch. He was also known for his epic flops; his full-length feature film *Raise the Titanic* lost so much money that Grade joked. "It would have been cheaper to lower the Atlantic." Like Sam Goldwyn, Lew Grade was the source of many anecdotes, the majority of them apocryphal. A true one concerned the time he was watching a comedy act at the Metropolitan Theatre, London. He was mightily impressed and rushed backstage to greet the comedian. "I'm Lew Grade. Your act was amazing. How much are they paying you?" "£25 a week, Mr Grade," replied the comic. "Ridiculous. Absurd. Outrageous. I could get you £200. Who's your agent?" "You are, Mr Grade."

The fourth Duke of Marlborough (1739–1817) was cripplingly self-conscious, so shy that he once went for three years at a stretch without uttering a single word. He was jolted out of his silence at the beginning of the fourth year by the imminent arrival of the Frenchwoman Madame de Staël; when informed of her visit he said simply, "I'm off". Marlborough, like many of his contemporaries, employed a running footmen – a servant dressed in full livery and employed to run alongside his Lordship's coach. A good running footmen could average about seven miles per hour – and more, it was said, if they were fed white wine and eggs. It was the practice for noblemen to amuse themselves by betting on races between footmen and horse-drawn coaches. One of the last races ever recorded of this kind was staged between the fourth Duke's footman and the Duke himself, riding in a carriage and four, from Windsor to London. The Duke won by a narrow margin, the footman died from his efforts.

John Ruskin, English author and critic, married his cousin Effie Gray in 1848, but on his wedding night found the sight of his bride's pubic hair so shocking he vowed never to sleep with her again. Ruskin later relented and promised to sleep with her once more when she was twenty-five – she had just turned twenty at the time. On her twenty-fifth birthday Ruskin extended the deadline. The long suffering Mrs Ruskin, however, met the artist Millais, who led her to discover a few things, including the fact that an unconsummated marriage was grounds for divorce.

Queen Victoria's extraordinarily sinister uncle Ernest, Duke of Cumberland, was one of the most hated men of his day. It was said that if the people of Britain had to choose in a popularity contest between Napoleon and the Duke, Napoleon would win. Unlike most of Queen Victoria's Hanoverian relatives who tended to be squat, portly avuncular types, Cumberland was tall and lean, his face disfigured by a sabre scar. He was involved in two of the most sensational royal scandals of the day. Incredibly, Cumberland was widely suspected of having incestuously raped and impregnated his younger sister Sophia. In August 1800 the unmarried twenty-two-year-old Princess Sophia "secretly" gave birth to a baby at Weybridge. Everyone in the British royal family family knew about the pregnancy except King George III, who was informed that she was bloated with dropsy, but at Weybridge had taken a mysterious cure comprising a roast beef diet. The King thought it was "an odd business" but accepted the explanation. King George was not at that time yet considered "mad" but he did have eleven other children to keep tabs on, and by this time his vision was also seriously impaired. The royal rape story originated with the court diarist Charles Greville, a man normally considered by historians to be a reliable source. The palace, without formally acknowledging the existence of the child, leaked an approved version in which the real father of the child was the Princess's secret lover, an equerry named General Thomas Garth. The old equerry, however, was an unconvincing scapegoat; he was ugly, dwarfish, his face badly disfigured by a large purple birthmark and thirty-three years older than the Princess. General Garth retained his high-ranking job in the royal household and was still there when he died at the age of eighty-five: his continued service, it was noted, was an odd way to treat an alleged adulterer. Several members of the royal family were privately convinced that Cumberland was the child's real father, including Queen Charlotte, who banned her sons from going anywhere near their sisters' apartments.

Cumberland was at the centre of a scandal again in 1810. In the early hours of 31 May, shortly after the Duke returned home to his apartments at St James's Palace, his servants were disturbed by noises from Cumberland's chambers. His page Neale rushed to the Duke's quarters to find him standing in the middle of the room, covered in blood, and with a sword at his feet. The Duke claimed he had been attacked, and although he had himself been seriously wounded had managed to force the assailant to flee. Two hours later, Cumberland instructed Neale to fetch his Corsican valet Joseph Sellis from his room. The tiny Sellis was discovered propped upright in his blood-soaked bed, his throat cut from ear to ear. The wound was so deep that his head was almost completely severed from his neck. At the other end of the room, much too far away for Sellis to have dropped it, lay a razor. At the formal inquiry into Sellis's death, Cumberland claimed that the valet had attempted to murder him in his sleep. According to the Duke, he had fought off his assailant, who had fled and decided to take his own life rather than submit to arrest. Although no motive was ever offered for the alleged murder attempt by Sellis on his master, this was the improbable version of events accepted at the inquest and a verdict of suicide was brought against Sellis. The verdict caused a sensation. Most people believed that Cumberland had butchered his valet to prevent a blackmail attempt: he had slit his manservant's throat with a razor while he was asleep, cut himself with his sword to make it look as though he had been in a struggle, then returned to his own room. One popular theory for the motive was that Sellis was black-mailing Cumberland because the Duke had made a homosexual pass at him. Another was that Cumberland had been caught in bed with the butler's wife. The most fancied rumour was that Cumberland had raped Sellis's daughter, who committed suicide when she found she was pregnant. After the trial Cumberland was openly booed on the streets of London and on one of his rare public excursions he was dragged from his horse and lynched but was lucky to escape with his life. When King William IV died and Victoria became Queen, Cumberland was offered the vacant throne of Hanover, and asked the Duke of Wellington for advice as to when he should go. "Go now," replied Wellington, "before you are pelted out".

Lord Denning (1899–1999) became in his lifetime a national institution, reigning as Master of the Rolls for twenty years from 1962 until he was eighty-three years old. His tenure in office inspired a colleague to remark that Denning possessed "every Christian virtue except resignation". His style was unique; he once opened a judgment with the words, "It happened on April 19, 1964. It was bluebell time in Kent," and on another occasion, "In summertime, village cricket is a delight to everyone . . .". Denning first became a household name in 1963, when prime minister Harold Macmillan asked him to undertake the inquiry into the security risks arising from the Profumo scandal. The Denning Report became an instant best-seller, with chapter headings such as: "Christine tells her story"; "The Slashing and the Shooting"; and "The Man in the Mask". Among the sensational revelations in the report was one that on Denning's suggestion a cabinet minister had allowed his genitals to be inspected by a Harley Street specialist to clear himself of the charge of being "the headless man" in an obscene photo.

A forty-five-year-old man from Huddersfield, jailed for a year after he admitted having sex with a Staffordshire bull terrier named Badger by the roadside in Bradford, claimed he had been seduced. He told magistrates: "I can't help it if it took a liking to me. He pulled my trousers down."

A Brazilian police superintendent, who believed that the total solar eclipse of 1999 heralded the end of the world, set three prisoners free and then got drunk with them. He sobered up when he found out he had been sacked.

Barmaid Beverley Nina Avery of Los Angeles, California, had been through sixteen divorces by 1957, by which time she was forty-eight years old. Fourteen husbands were involved, only five of whom broke her nose.

The "Mad Monk" Grigory Rasputin (his surname is Russian for "debauchee") was neither mad nor a monk, although he was once a member of an obscure Christian sect which believed in worship through sex and encouraged orgies of bloody self-mutilation followed by mass copulation. Rasputin's close relationship with the Russian Empress Alexandra, following his apparent success at treating her son's haemophilia, made him famous in St Petersburg, especially with wealthy hostesses, who apparently found him sexually irresistible in spite of his crude manners and shocking personal hygiene. He often went for months without washing even his hands or face, offering the excuse that water sapped his libido. Rasputin's body odour was so bad that women literally bathed themselves in perfume before sleeping with him to try to overpower it. Nevertheless, he was able to persuade them that by submitting their bodies to him in a spare bedroom he called his "Holy of Holies" they could purge themselves of sin. In 1911 he was accused of the attempted rape of a nun. However, on this occasion he was saved by the personal intervention of the Empress.

Although he came under increasing scrutiny by the police and press following a series of reported sex attacks, his consolidated hold over the Romanov family meant that he was effectively immune from prosecution. In a notorious incident in April 1915 Rasputin became drunk in a Moscow bar and boasted that he was the Czarina's lover. When he was challenged by the police to prove his identity, he dropped his pants and waved his penis at them. The Czarina's failure to have Rasputin locked up immediately was seen by many as conclusive proof that she and Rasputin were lovers – in truth Rasputin owed his freedom to the fact that the Czar's family saw him as the only hope to cure their son's illness – the nature of which was completely unknown outside the palace and even to the majority of palace insiders.

Rasputin survived several murder attempts by embittered husbands and fathers. Two of his eventual assassins were members of the Russian royal family. The assassination itself, grown in legend over the years, did not go quite to plan. Using his wife as bait, one of the royal co-conspirators, Prince Yusupov, lured Rasputin to his home, correctly gambling that he would find the prospect of sleeping with a member of the Imperial family irresistible. The popular version, greatly enhanced by Prince Yusupov himself as the years went by, is that while Rasputin waited for the arrival of the Princess Irena he ate enough poisoned cakes and wine to kill half a dozen men, but because of his mystic powers was largely unaffected. A minor army medic, Dr Lazovert, had been given the task of lacing the cakes and wine with potassium cyanide. Lazovert, however, confessed on his deathbed that he had lost his nerve and had not in fact administered any poison at all. This was how Rasputin was able to carry on gorging himself with food and drink while his terrified assassins sat around waiting for him to drop dead. Eventually they all lost their nerve and shot him once in the back. He lay motionless for a while, apparently dead, but then dragged himself to his feet and ran out of the house into the courtyard. Two more bullets and a kick to the head finished him off, after which they dumped the corpse in the river. After Rasputin was variously poisoned, shot, drowned, castrated and shot again, his penis was hacked off and preserved in a small velvet-lined polished oak box. When it was opened and the contents examined sixty years later it was said to contain something resembling "a blackened overripe banana, about a foot long."

Turkish surgeons removed twenty-seven screws, twenty nails, a screwdriver, six magnets and several pieces of wire from the stomach of twenty-year-old Cem Demeza after he complained of stomachache. The handyman from Ankara noted later: "These things haven't given me tummy ache before. It must have been the screwdriver."

King Solomon, ruler of Israel for forty years (973–933BC) was famous for his wisdom. He also had a way with women, judging by his alleged 700 wives and countless mistresses. According to the *Song of Solomon* in the Old Testament, his chat-up technique included the lines, "Thy hair is as a flock of goats" and, "Thy teeth are like a flock of sheep that are even shorn".

The statesman Viscount Castlereagh (1769–1822) as foreign secretary to the British prime minister Lord Liverpool was at the heart of the coalition against Napoleon. In 1822 in the middle of delicate diplomatic negotiations following the Napoleonic Wars, Castlereagh suddenly and mysteriously slit his own throat with a penknife, apparently fearing homosexual blackmail. A few days earlier Castlereagh had confronted King George IV, wildly confessed to buggery and showed the King some blackmail letters which, he said, meant he must flee the country immediately. It was a puzzling confession to make, given that Castlereagh was not gay. He had, however, become obsessed about the scandal involving the Bishop of Clogher who had recently been arrested for homosexual activities with a guardsman. The statesman had approached several people close to him, including the Duke of Wellington, claiming that he had been receiving anonymous blackmail threats ever since his visit to a gay brothel three years earlier. These accused him of "a crime not to be mentioned". According to an account published some thirty years later, Castlereagh had been tricked into entering the brothel by a "woman" who turned out to be a man. After the suicide friends and colleagues rallied round to deny any deviant activity on Castlereagh's part and it was asserted that the strain of overwork had driven him insane.

In 1809 MPs had been shocked to discover that cabinet colleagues Castlereagh and George Canning had fought an early morning duel on Putney Common after a long-running feud. Canning, who had never fired a pistol before, missed and was hit in the leg by Castlereagh. Canning later became prime minister, but Castlereagh was so unpopular by the time of his death that his funeral cortege was booed by onlookers.

The Portuguese saint Wilgefortis was famed for being able to get rid of unwanted husbands – her fee was a peck of oats. Apparently she grew a beard to discourage her suitors.

A drunk tried to flee in a seven mph milk float when police raided a party in Leicester. Three officers walked briskly behind the float to catch up with twenty-three-year-old Matthew North, who was apparently already serving a ban for drink-driving in a steamroller.

Unlike his younger brother Modest, Russia's most celebrated composer Piotr Ilyich Tchaikovsky went to extraordinary lengths to hide the fact that he was gay. He became engaged to a French opera singer Desirée Artot, who left him for a Spanish baritone when it became very apparent to her that all was not as it should be. Nevertheless Tchaikovsky believed that he could overcome his sexuality by sheer willpower. In May 1877 he suddenly proposed to a female admirer named Antonina Milyukova, a twenty-eight-year-old who had bombarded Tchaikovsky with letters threatening to kill herself if she had to live without him. Unfortunately, the composer found his bride-to-be not only physically repulsive but also quite ignorant of his music. As the July wedding drew nearer, however, he was close to breakdown, worried about his "Z", as he always referred to his homosexuality in his diaries and private letters to his brother. Immediately after the service he ran off and two months later attempted suicide by throwing himself into the icy Moscow River, hoping to catch a fatal bout of pneumonia, but could only manage a nasty cold.

Tchaikovsky, funded by the patronage of another female admirer, this time a wealthy widow, elected to spend as much time as possible abroad rather than with his wife Antonina, who remained blissfully and probably insanely ignorant of her husband's sexual proclivity. He later became infatuated by his thirteen-year-old nephew Bob Davydov and dedicated his last and greatest symphony to the boy.

Nine days after conducting the first performance of the *Pathétique* in St Petersburg in 1893, Tchaikovsky was dead. The cause of death offered by the composer's family was that he had contracted cholera by drinking a glass of unboiled water during a cholera epidemic, but most of Tchaikovsky's biographers believe that this version of events was false. Various suicide theories have it that the composer became depressed because of his unrequited love for his nephew, or that he had been exposed in a homosexual affair with a member of the Russian Imperial family, or that a "court of honour" from an old school had threatened to expose him. The explanation favoured by his recent biographers was that Tchaikovsky had contracted cholera from a male prostitute in St Petersburg and had invented the glass of unboiled water story to protect his reputation. His widowed wife Antonina was committed to a lunatic asylum where she spent the last twenty years of her life.

In 1999, an Egyptian lawyer lost his libel claim against US President Bill Clinton. Mohammed Baddy demanded $5 million in compensation for the mental anguish caused when the president named his dog Buddy. Mr Baddy said he had been teased mercilessly by his Cairo neighbours ever since.

An Austrian civil servant went on sick leave for two years because he was allergic to the telephone. His doctors said he found the ringing of the phone "psychologically disturbing".

The irrepressible Augustus II, the seventeenth-century King of Poland and Elector of Saxony, must be the most adulterous royal personage of all time. He was known as Augustus "the Strong" for his exceptional physical size and strength, his gluttony, his drinking prowess and his lechery, but most of all for his astonishing virility. Over a period of half a century he fathered 365 bastards, plus one legitimate heir. Augustus II presided over an enormous warren of concubines, some of whom enjoyed official status, and others he preferred to keep quiet about, especially his incestuous relationship with his daughter, the Countess Orzelska. The most unusual of all his many affairs was with the former mistress of the British ambassador to Saxony – the only woman whom the king failed to impregnate in half a century of indiscriminate sexual congress. Although Augustus the Strong's libido was one of the great marvels of the age it didn't go down well with his new Polish subjects, who were outraged by his private life, nor with his wife Eberdine, daughter of a German Margrave, who was so embarrassed by his flagrant infidelities that she refused to set foot in Poland throughout her husband's reign. Augustus recognized he had a slight problem in the end: as he lay on his deathbed in 1733 he conceded, "My whole life has been an unceasing sin – God have mercy on me".

Hotel staff in Schwerin, Germany, called police after a guest tried to settle his bill by offering them a 5 ft iguana. Police later discovered two more iguanas at a nearby hotel. The guest, a thirty-six-year-old man, was sent for psychiatric treatment.

The seventh-century Pope Gregory I was obsessed with sexual practice. He considered himself a great authority on sexual behaviour and wrote several books on the subject, including a treatise on spontaneous ejaculation. The Pope spent his whole life deliberating on homosexuality, bestiality and "unnatural" intercourse within marriage. He arrived at a number of unusual conclusions, including his belief that incest was quite "natural" provided it led to procreation.

A banned driver was apprehended after being stopped by police in Darlington, Co. Durham, despite giving a false name. Police were able to spot the man's real name tattooed on his hand. Meanwhile police in Fort Smith, Arkansas, had little difficulty apprehending a suspect following a hold-up at a store. James Newsome held up the store while wearing a hard hat marked with the words "James Newsome".

Proverbial as the narrator of ridiculously exaggerated exploits, Baron Karl Friedrich Hieronymous von Münchhausen was a man so strange that he had a mental illness named after him. Born in 1720 in Bodenwerder, Germany, Münchhausen was a professional soldier, serving initially as a page to Prince Anton Ulrich von Braunschweig and later as a cornet, lieutenant and cavalry captain with a Russian regiment in two Turkish wars. After the death of his first wife Münchhausen married a seventeen-year-old noblewoman. This marriage, an unhappy one, constantly drove him into debt.

Münchhausen was known during his lifetime as a raconteur of anecdotes about war, hunting and travel adventures and was in the habit of embellishing his stories. The first published collection of Münchhausen stories appeared anonymously in 1781–3 in a German magazine. In 1785 a jewel thief from Hanover named Rudolf Erich Raspe published a book in England which claimed to be based on the baron's life and times, entitled *Baron Münchhausen's Narrative of his Marvellous Travels and Campaigns in Russia*. The book was a great success and a second edition was translated into German in 1786 by the writer Gottfried August Bürger, who added eight of his own stories to it. The second version became the prototype for the Münchhausen fantasy tales. In 1788 Bürger added another five tales to an enlarged second edition. In subsequent years there were several adaptations of the Münchhausen stories in different forms. The real von Münchhausen meanwhile did not complain about these books, enjoying his enhanced reputation as "the Baron of lies", even when they included such tall stories as the time the baron tethered his horse to a "small twig" in a snowstorm, and discovered when the snow melted that the twig was actually a church steeple. For reasons obscure, Münchhausen's syndrome has come to be specifically attributed to individuals who wander round the country presenting themselves at different hospitals with different but spurious physical complaints.

In 1996 Reuters News Agency reported the fate of a thirty-year-old drunken Polish farmer, whose drinking companions set out to prove who of them was the most macho. First, they stripped off and beat each other over the head with icicles. Then one took a chainsaw and cut off his foot. "That's nothing," said the farmer, who then took the chainsaw and cut off his head. One of the friends said later, "It's funny – he wore women's underwear when he was younger . . . but he died a man".

An Eccentric Bibliography

The Romance of Leprosy - E. Mackerchar, 1949

Why Bring That Up? A Guide to Seasickness - J. F. Montague, 1936

Penetrating Wagner's Ring - John L. Di Gaetanao, 1978

Scouts in Bondage - Geoffrey Prout, 1930

Jews At A Glance - Mac Davis, 1956

Constipation and Our Civilization - J. C. Thomson, 1943

A Pictorial Book of Tongue Coating - Anon., 1981

A Government Committee of Enquiry on the Light Metal Artificial Leg - Captain Henry Hulme Chisholm Baird, 1923

Daddy Was An Undertaker - McDill, McGown and Gassman, 1952

A Short Account of the Origin, Progress and Present State of the New Rupture Society - Anon., 1816

Teach Yourself Alcoholism - Meier Glatt, 1975

Amputation Stumps: Their Care and After-treatment - Sir Godfrey Martin Huggins, 1918

How to Cook Husbands - Elizabeth Strong Worthington, 1899

A Study of Masturbation and its Reputed Sequelae - J. F. W. Meagher, 1924

Sex After Death - B. J. Ferrell and D. E. Frey, 1983.

Bibliography

Acton, H. – *The Bourbons of Naples* – Methuen (1956)
Anger, Kenneth – *Hollywood Babylon* – Arrow Books (1986)
Aronson, T. – *The Coburgs of Belgium* – Cassell (1969)
Ashdown, Dulcie – *Royal Weddings* – Robert Hale (1981)
Avery, Gillian – *Gillian Avery's Book of the Strange and Odd* – Penguin (1975)
Barber, N. – *Lords of the Golden Horn* – Macmillan (1973)
Barnes, Alison – *Essex Eccentrics* – Boydell Press (1975)
Bauer, L. – *Leopold the Unloved* – Cassell (1934)
Bennet, Daphne – *King Without a Crown* – Heinemann (1977)
Bernstein, Mark – *Grand Eccentrics* – Orange Frazer Press (1996)
Blunt, W. – *The Dream King* – Hamish Hamilton (1970)
Bradford, Sarah – *George VI* – Weidenfeld & Nicolson (1989)
Buchell, Peter – *Great Eccentrics* – George Allen & Unwin (1984)
Burgess, G. – *The Curious World of Frank Buckland* – Baker (1967)
Carlton, Charles – *Royal Childhoods* – Routledge & Kegan Paul (1986)
Caufield, Catherine – *The Emperor of the United States and Other Magnificent Eccentrics* – St Martin's Press (1981)
Cawthorne, Nigel – *Sex Lives of the Great Dictators* – Prion (1993)
Cawthorne, Nigel – *Sex Lives of the Hollywood Idols* – Prion (1997)

Cawthorne, Nigel – *Sex Lives of the Hollywood Screen Goddesses* – Prion (1997)

Channon, H. – *The Ludwigs of Bavaria* – (1934)

Chapman-Huston, D. – *Bavarian Fantasy* – John Murray (1955)

Constant, S. – *Foxy Ferdinand, Czar of Bulgaria* – Sidgwick & Jackson (1979)

Coughlan, R. – *Elizabeth & Catherine* – Macdonald & Jane's (1975)

Cullen, T. – *The Empress Brown* – Bodley Head (1969)

Crankshaw, E. – *The Habsburgs* – Weidenfeld & Nicolson (1971)

Davies, N. – *Europe, A History* – Oxford University Press (1996)

Davies, W. – *Punch and the Monarchy* – Hutchinson (1977)

Duff, D. – *Alexandra Princess & Queen* – Collins (1980)

Edwards, Anne – *Matriarch: Queen Mary & the House of Windsor* – Hodder & Stoughton (1984)

Friedman, D. – *Inheritance* – Sidgwick & Jackson (1993)

Gainham, Sarah – *The Habsburg Twilight* – Weidenfeld & Nicolson (1979)

Gillen, Mollie – *Royal Duke* – Sidgwick & Jackson (1976)

Gooch, G. P. – *Louis XV* – Longmans (1966)

Gordon, Richard – *Alarming History of Sex* – Sinclair-Stevenson (1996)

Green, V. – *The Madness of Kings* – Alan Sutton (1993)

Hall, P. – *Royal Fortune* – Bloomsbury (1992)

Haslip, Joan – *Madame du Barry* – Weidenfeld & Nicolson (1991)

Haslip, Joan – *Marie Antoinette* – Weidenfeld & Nicolson (1987)

Hatton, R. – *George I* – Thames & Hudson (1978)

Hedley, O. – *Queen Charlotte* – John Murray (1975)

Hibbert, C. – *George IV Regent and King* – Penguin (1973)

Holme, Thea – *Caroline* – Hamish Hamilton (1979)

Howarth, T. E. B. – *Citizen-King: the life of Louis Philippe* – Eyre & Spottiswoode (1961)

Hubatsch, W. – *Frederick the Great* – Thames & Hudson (1973)

Hunter, R. and Macalpine, Ida – *George III and The Mad Business* – Penguin (1969)

James, R. – *Albert: Prince Consort* – Hamish Hamilton (1983)

Jay, Ricky – *Learned Pigs and Fireproof Women* – Farrar, Straus & Giroux (1986)

Jones, S. – *The Language of the Genes* – Flamingo (1993)

Judd, D. – *Prince Philip: A Biography* – Michael Joseph (1980)

Katz, R. – *The Fall of the House of Savoy* – George Allen & Unwin (1972)

Lewis, W. H. – *The Scandalous Regent: a life of Philippe duc d'Orleans* – Deutsch (1961)

Lincoln, W. B. – *The Romanovs* – Weidenfeld & Nicolson (1981)

Listowel, Judith – *A Habsburg Tragedy* – Ascent (1978)

Longford, Elizabeth – *The Oxford Book of Royal Anecdotes* – Oxford University Press (1989)

Louda, J. and Maclagan, M. – *Heraldry of the Royal Families of Europe* – Orbis (1981)

Love, Andrea – *Sex Lives of the Rich and Famous* – Carlton Books (1997)

Lynch, J. – *Bourbon Spain 1700–1808* – Blackwell (1989)

McIntosh, C. – *The Swan King* – Allen Lane (1982)

Marek, G. R. – *The Eagles Die* – Hart-Davis, MacGibbon (1975)

Mitford, Nancy – *Frederick the Great* – Hamish Hamilton (1970)

Mitford, Nancy – *The Sun King* – Hamish Hamilton (1966)

Nicholas, Margaret – *The World's Greatest Cranks and Crackpots* – Hamlyn (1982)

Noel, G. – *Ena: Spain's English Queen* – Constable (1984)

Norton, Lucy – *The Sun King and his Loves* – Hamish Hamilton (1983)

Oakley, S. – *The Story of Denmark* – Faber & Faber (1972)

Palling, Bruce – *Book of Modern Scandal: From Byron to the Present Day* – Orion (1996)

Parker, J. – *King of Fools* – Macdonald & Co. (1988)

Petrie, C. – *King Charles III of Spain* – Constable (1971)

Pickover, Clifford A. – *Strange Brains and Genius: The Secret Lives of Eccentric Scientists and Madmen* – Plenum Trade (1998)

de Polnay, P. – *A Queen Of Spain: Isabel II* – Hollis & Carter (1962)

Porter, R. – *English Society in the Eighteenth Century* – Penguin (1982)

Reddaway, W. F. – *Cambridge History of Poland* – Cambridge University Press (1950)

Rice, Tamara Talbot – *Elizabeth Empress of Russia* – Weidenfeld & Nicolson (1970)

Roby, K. – *The King, the Press and the People* – Barrie & Jenkins (1975)

Rose, K. – *King George V* – Weidenfeld & Nicolson (1983)

Seward, D. – *Naples: A Traveller's Companion* – Constable (1984)

Sitwell, Edith – *English Eccentrics* – Penguin (1971)

Smith, D. M. – *Italy and its Monarchy* – Yale University Press (1989)

Somerset, Anne – *The Life and Times of William IV* – Weidenfeld & Nicolson (1980)

Somerville-Large, P. – *Irish Eccentrics* – Hamish Hamilton (1975)

Stevenson, R. S. – *Famous Illnesses in History* – Eyre & Spottiswoode (1962)

Sutherland, J. – *The Oxford Book of Literary Anecdotes* – Clarendon Press (1975)

Thomas, H. – *Madrid: A Traveller's Companion* – Constable (1988)

Timpson, J. – *Timpson's English Eccentrics* – Jarrold (1991)

Trench, C. – *George II* – Penguin (1973)

Troyat, H. – *Alexander of Russia* – New English Library (1982)

Warwick, C. – *George and Marina* – Weidenfeld & Nicolson (1988)

Whittle, T. – *The Last Kaiser* – Heinemann (1977)

Williams, G. – *The Age of Agony* – Constable (1975)

Wilson, A. N. – *The Rise and Fall of the House of Windsor* – Sinclair-Stevenson (1993)

Wilton, I. – *C. B. Fry: An English Hero* – (1999)

Winter, G. and Cochran, Wendy – *Secrets of the Royals* – Robson (1990)

Woolf, S. – *A History of Italy 1700–1860* – Methuen (1979)